Building Better Interfaces with Microsoft® Foundation Classes

Keith Bugg

Wiley Computer Publishing

John Wiley & Sons, Inc.

NEW YORK · CHICHESTER · WEINHEIM · BRISBANE · SINGAPORE · TORONTO

Publisher: Robert Ipsen
Editor: Cary Sullivan
Assistant Editor: Kathryn Malm
Managing Editor: Micheline Frederick
Electronic Products, Associate Editor: Mike Sosa
Text Design & Composition: Benchmark Productions, Inc.

This publication is designed to provide accurate and authoritative information in regard to the subject matter covered. It is sold with the understanding that the publisher is not engaged in professional services. If professional advice or other expert assistance is required, the services of a competent professional person should be sought.

Library of Congress Cataloging-in-Publication Data:

Bugg, Keith E. (Keith Edward), 1952–
    Building better interfaces with Microsoft foundation classes / Keith Bugg.
        p. cm.
    "Wiley computer publishing."
    Includes index.
    ISBN 0-471-33181-3
    1. User interfaces (Computer systems) 2. Microsoft foundation class library. I. Title.
QA76.9.U83B84 1999
005.4'28--dc21   99-11440
                                                                 CIP

Printed in the United States of America.

10 9 8 7 6 5 4 3 2 1

CONTENTS

INTRODUCTION

T his book is all about building better interfaces for your Windows-based applications, using MFC and Visual C++ as the development platform. The user interface is the first thing the user sees—it provides the conduit that allows the user to touch your application. This is most generally accomplished through the use of controls; these comprise the major portion of this book. A good deal of this material is devoted to creating owner-drawn controls that allow you to provide an icon or image to visually cue the user as to the underlying functionality.

But there's more here than just controls. You'll learn how to implement many of the common dialogs, like the somewhat challenging Find-Replace dialog box. If your applications do a lot of text processing, gadgets like these can come in handy.

Overview of the Book and Technology

The overall goal of this book is to help you to get past the learning curve for working with the esoteric features of owner-drawn controls and the common dialogs. I've included sample code for just about all the topics covered, as I feel this is the best way for a developer to learn: by example. You'll also find plenty of additional material covering unique ways to enhance the user interface. Examples of this genre include context menus, adding a Tip of the Day popup window when your application starts, and lots more.

Although the technology for Windows development changes rapidly and is in a constant state of flux, some things never go out of style. For example, the user's PC is sure to have disk drives of various types—floppy, hard, and CD-ROM. You'll find plenty of code here that shows how to visually represent these items using icons. Not only can you use these in your own applications, but you'll see how to maximize your efforts with nice little touches like tool tips, animation sequences, and more.

How This Book Is Organized

This book is organized in a sequential manner. It proceeds from the basic building blocks of the user interface to the more complex. Chapters 1 through 13 deal mainly with the controls, while Chapters 14 through 17 look at the common dialog boxes.

The remaining chapters deal with special features like splitter windows and help files. The following is a list of the chapters, along with a brief description of the content:

Chapter 1: Controls and the User Interface. This chapter introduces the heart of the user interface, the controls. Topics discussed include established industry standards for controls (for example, orientation and placement, state representation), how controls function as input/output devices, and more.

Chapter 2: The Buttons. Chapter 2 deals with the basic element of any user interface, the command button. The chapter looks at how to properly organize buttons, how to represent them as bitmapped images, their styles and properties. Attention is paid to additional topics such as tabbing order and keyboard accelerators.

Chapter 3: Edit Boxes. Chapter 3 covers the next control used most often, the edit box. In addition to styles and properties, you'll see how to implement edit boxes to accept formatted input, and how to subclass them.

Chapter 4: Listboxes and Checklist Boxes. More complicated controls are exposed in Chapter 4, the listbox and the checklist box. Topics covered include how to implement them as owner-drawn, using bitmaps to represent directories, and more. The checklist box, which is a list box containing several checkbox controls, allows the user to specify multiple options. A discussion as to when and where these should be used accompanies this topic.

Chapter 5: Status Bars. Although you probably haven't given it much thought, an application's status bar can be used to enhance the user interface. This chapter demonstrates how to add and configure a status bar with multiple panes, and how to spice it up by adding a bitmap such as a company logo. You'll also see how it can be used to provide help messages similar to tool tips.

Chapter 6: The Combo Box. Chapter 6 looks at combo boxes, with the emphasis on implementing the owner-drawn feature. Besides taking a good hard look at the class methods (which provide methods for searching the combo box, adding and deleting strings, etc.), the sample program illustrates techniques for interrogating the user's platform to determine its disk configuration.

Chapter 7: Toolbars. In Chapter 7 you'll learn all about toolbars. Not only does this chapter look at their styles, properties, and class methods, you'll also learn how to customize them by adding other controls, like combo boxes. Features such as these can greatly extend the power and flexibility of your interface.

Chapter 8: The New Common Controls. As I mentioned earlier, Windows and related technologies are in a constant state of flux. Microsoft recently released new controls via the common controls DLL, comctl32.dll. This chapter takes a look at these, and provides plenty of sample code to help you get a leg up on your development efforts. Most noteworthy is the new date-time picker control, which really takes a lot of the work out of any application that needs to manipulate dates.

Chapter 9: Multimedia Enhancements. Chapter 9 shows you how to enhance the user interface with the prudent use of multimedia. You'll see how to use the multimedia control to play video clips and/or sound, plus learn how to create animated sequences using a free tool from Microsoft, VidEdit.

Chapter 10: The Spin Control. Chapter 10 takes a look at the spin control, or spinner. This control is often used with another control called a buddy control; this is usually an edit box. You'll learn how to detect if the user is spinning up or down, and how to translate that into action.

Chapter 11: Progress and Slider Controls. Chapter 11 looks at two separate controls, the progress gauge and the slide control. The first control is used to indicate the progress of some operation, and the second is used to adjust some setting (for example, how much red to add to a color selection). The slider control, also called a track bar, is similar to a sliding volume control on a stereo. The sample program combines both into one—a slide control is used to adjust the speed of a progress gauge.

Chapter 12: The Tree Control. This chapter is devoted to the TreeView control, used to represent information in a hierarchical fashion. It looks at the various properties of the control as well as the class methods available for your use. In addition, you'll learn how to include bitmaps in the tree to represent data. The sample program demonstrates how to detect and respond to mouse clicks on the different nodes of the tree.

Chapter 13: The RTF Edit Control. In Chapter 13, you'll learn all about using the Rich Text Format edit control, the big brother to the edit box. Topics discussed include the system structures used by the control, class methods and messages, and so forth. The sample program includes a toolbar with paragraph formatting buttons that format the text in the control.

Chapter 14: The Common Color Dialog. In Chapter 14 we begin our look at the common dialogs. These are provided by MFC and obviate the need to reinvent the wheel. In this chapter, I present the common color dialog box, its structures, properties, and class methods. This dialog can be used in a wide range of applications, such as selecting the color of a brush, pen, font, and so forth. There is also a discussion of the CommDlgExtendedError() method; this is used with all the common dialogs to respond to errors.

Chapter 15: The Common File Dialog. In this chapter, I give you a look at the common file dialog class, CFileDialog. This class gives you an easy way to prompt the user for a file to open, or to save. Again, there is a structure that you can manipulate to filter files, specify extensions, and so forth. Regardless of the type of application you create, this material is sure to come in handy.

Chapter 16: The Find-Replace Dialog. Chapter 16 provides an in-depth look at one of the more esoteric classes rarely covered in other books, the Find-Replace common dialog box. The sample program shows you how to implement this class and how to customize the dialog for any special needs you may have.

Chapter 17: CFontDialog and CPrintDialog. Chapter 17 continues the theme of exploring the text-related common dialogs by examining the common dialogs for selecting font/font properties and the print dialog. The sample program, which is almost a fully functional editor in its own right, lets you open a text file and then change the font, font color, and so forth. Then, by using the print dialog box, you can print the file.

Chapter 18: Tabbed Dialog Boxes. Chapter 18 covers the tab control, used to create tabbed dialog boxes or property sheets. Topics covered include the control's class methods and messages. The sample code demonstrates how to make these owner-drawn, allowing you to add bitmaps to the tabs to convey more information to the user visually.

Chapter 19: Class CFormView. In this chapter you'll see how to implement a CFormView-based application that allows you to place controls directly in your application's view instead of using a dialog box. Topics discussed include the steps to take to create a CFormView object, the class members, and special considerations if the view contains slide controls or spin controls. You'll also find a discussion of drawing techniques to ensure your controls are properly painted.

Chapter 20: Component Gallery and Special Operations. Chapter 20 is more or less a catch-all repository for all those little things that don't fall into any particular category, but go a long way toward enhancing the user interface. Topics covered include Context menus, a Tip of the Day feature, Adding a CDialogBar object to the application, and adding Internet browsing capability to your application.

Chapter 21: Splitter Windows. This chapter discusses splitter windows. The sample program is pretty sophisticated—it creates a splitter window of two panes, with one pane split into two additional panes. The single (that is, nonsplit) pane contains a TreeView control that acts like a menu for the other pane—you can configure the panes to contain a ListView control and/or an edit box control. The listview is used to list all the files in the current directory, so you'll learn more than just splitter windows in this chapter.

Chapter 22: Adding Help to the Interface. Chapter 22 takes a look at adding help to your application. The chapter is divided into two major parts: help files based on RTF-files, and help based on HTML files. Customization of both flavors are discussed, with plenty of sample code for each.

Who Should Read This Book

This book was written with the intermediate programmer in mind; that is, someone who is well-grounded in Visual C++ and MFC but wants to take his or her interface development to the next level. Because of the heavy reliance on using the owner-drawn property of controls, the reader should be comfortable with using Class Wizard and App Studio. Developers with these skills may wish to use this book as a reference, skipping chapters that are not of immediate interest. Beginning programmers are encouraged to read the book from start to end, as it does follow a logical progression.

Tools You Will Need

To build the projects found in the book, you'll need to have Visual C++ version 5 or better installed on your computer. To build the ancillary multimedia projects, you'll need to download and install Microsoft's free utility, VidEdit. Links are provided on the companion Web site for this purpose. You'll also need WinZip to unzip the project files.

The Web Site

The companion Web site is located at www.wiley.com/compbooks/bugg. It contains all the sample code from the book, as well as Visual C++ projects and zip files, plus links to the VidEdit and HTML Help toolkits.

Summary

Hopefully, this book will pique your interest in building better interfaces to your Windows applications with Visual C++/MFC. A few words of caution: Keep your applications consistent, and don't overdo it by making everything owner-drawn. Consistency allows the user to learn your application more quickly, and moderation in using graphics prevents the user from being distracted by all the bells and whistles you've added. This is more or less an art, not a science. I hope you find this book useful in learning the difference.

K eith Bugg is a software engineer specializing in Windows development using Visual C++. He has worked with Visual C++ since version 1 and has developed a wide range of applications for a variety of clients. He is the author of several books on Windows and related technology in addition to numerous articles that have appeared in *Doctor Dobb's Journal*, *The Visual C++ Developer*, and *The C/C++ Users Journal*. He can be contacted through his Web page at wwwdev.qsystems.net/kbugg/kbugg.htm. To view this Web site using Netscape Navigator, the Java option must be enabled.

CHAPTER 1

Controls and the User Interface

This chapter provides some refresher material on controls and the user interface. We cover the basics of the user interface, the roles that controls play, owner-drawn controls and techniques, and dialog-based applications. Let's begin with a review of exactly what controls do, why they're important, and their significance to the developer from the standpoint of building a better user interface. This will lay the foundation for a solid understanding of the most commonly used controls, and will better prepare you to interact with specific controls in your own applications. Controls have a philosophical dimension that transcends their purely mechanical properties. Examples of this phenomenon include cultural interpretations of color, symbols, and so forth. For example, in most Western cultures, red means "stop" or "danger," while in the East, red is associated with "happiness" and "good fortune." Also, it's critical to be sure your application doesn't change the host machine's configuration—avoid hard coding values whenever possible. Hard coding means to insert a value, such as that for a color, as defined by the programmer. In contrast, such values can be obtained by querying the user's system and selecting the value based on these findings.

The art of creating a better user interface begins with an understanding of these issues. For example, there are some situations in which the user must select an option from a narrow range of choices. By using a listbox instead of an edit box, you force the user to *select* data, not *supply* it. This simple act can greatly reduce the need for redundant error checking in your Windows programs.

First and foremost, controls are the mechanisms by which the user touches your application. With the proper techniques, controls greatly extend the power of your application.

The User Interface

The user interface is one of the most critical aspects of the software development cycle. Your application may have the world's slickest sort routine, but the user will never see this—all users care about is how easy the application is to use, and whether it does what they want it to do. So the first stop on the road to building a better user interface is understanding the purpose of the application. For example, if the application you're writing involves a lot of text processing, including formatting, you may use the RTF edit control in your application. In other words, form follows function. By really understanding the nature of the application, you'll be better equipped to select the right control(s) to use for the job, plus be able to incorporate operational features that exceed the user's expectations.

In addition to understanding the purpose of the application, there are other factors to consider. Stop and think for a moment of a software package you've used that you felt had a good interface. What features or components caused you to take notice? The following list of these additional factors comes to mind:

- An easy-to-use install/uninstall utility
- Prolific help features, both spontaneous and on demand
- Clear, concise forgiving error messages and traps
- Smooth operation—no crashes (for example, a bug-free application)

As part of your design phase, user interface planning needs to clearly define the system requirements for your software product. You'll see an example of this later in Chapter 6, "Combo Boxes," which deals with combo boxes. A combo box is a control that combines an edit box with a listbox. The combo box is populated with a list of all disk drives on the host machine. At first glance, you may think there are only three: a floppy drive, hard drive, and CD-ROM drive. But that's omitting a network drive and a RAM disk drive—your user interface must work properly across a wide range of configurations. The simple rule here is to "plan for the worst and hope for the best." The point is that you only get one chance to make a first impression. Your user interface, and the features it supports, will be the milestone by which your overall product is judged. Having said all that, I'll now give you an introduction to the most fundamental component of the user interface, the controls.

Role of Controls

The controls you use in your Windows applications fall within one (or more) of the following categories:

- A data entry device
- A data output device
- A feedback device

Obviously, controls have a major impact on software as input/output devices. They are what the user experiences when using your application. The controls you select influence the way in which the user perceives and uses your application. Examples include spin controls, sliders, progress gauges, and animation sequences. Let's examine each of these roles in greater detail.

Data Input

The most common perception for the use of a control is as a data entry device. Clicking a check box, pushing a button, or entering text into an edit box are all classic examples of ascertaining the user's intentions. While I advocate the use of controls for this purpose, you should look for opportunities to apply the best control for the task. For example, suppose you're writing a communications package, and you need the user to select a port. Since there are only four choices (COM1–COM4), a group of mutually exclusive radio-buttons would be preferable over, say, using an edit box. With either control, data is entered. However, since the edit box would require considerably more error checking and validating (as opposed to simply testing a group of four radiobuttons), its use would be ill-advised. Or, if screen real estate is at a premium in your application, you might use a spin control slaved to an edit box to get the user's input. A spin control is simply two arrows arranged either horizontally or vertically. Clicking the arrow changes some value, up or down. A control is said to be slaved if its value changes when the spin control is clicked. The point is, there is more than one way, sometimes, to get this input. As you learn more about the controls and their features, you'll be better able to select the right control or combination of controls to create the best interface possible.

Data Output

Controls can also be used to report information back to the user; edit boxes that have been defined as READONLY are excellent choices for this category. Examples of data output controls include:

- Returning the number of records found
- Populating data fields, as in a personnel database application
- Displaying available choices, as in a list of fonts

Controls as data output devices are input devices in reverse. For example, just as you can use an edit box to receive input from the user, so you can use it to display output to the user. You can use these as safety valves to allow the user to preview some incoming traffic, for example, and give him or her a chance to skip a potentially time-consuming step (like downloading a huge file at 9600k!).

Feedback

Controls can also be used to provide continuous feedback to the user. This is a subtle variant of the role of controls as a data output device. For example, suppose you're writing a client-server application and the user requests a subset of the personnel records, which reside on the server. If the query produces say, 100 records found, your application should display a progress gauge that is updated as each record is fetched. This gives the user visual feedback—he or she can see the program processing information. This is very reassuring to the user, especially if you have changed the cursor to an hourglass and disabled other controls until the record transfer completes. The animation control, discussed in Chapter 9, "Multimedia Enhancements," is often useful when used with controls in a feedback mode, because it provides some sort of motion that lets the user know the program is still working and has not locked up somehow. Inserting WM_TIMER messages at strategic locations on the screen is another way to calm the user's anxieties—a popup message box that allows the user to cancel a selection can give your application a big boost.

Special Controls

There are some controls whose functions fall outside of the strictly data in, data out variety. These are special controls and include spinners, sliders, and OCXs.

The use of special controls should be minimized in order to maintain compatibility with other Windows programs, and to obviate the need to ship additional controls with your application. While the suite of controls that ship with Visual C++ will usually be enough, you shouldn't hesitate to consider OCX controls for special situations. A good example is with database applications. You may wish to use a grid control to display/edit records. As always, get the right tool for the job.

Controls, Dialog Boxes, and Standards

When it comes to working with controls and dialog boxes, certain standards and guidelines ensure that your applications are Windows compatible. The Windows standard is similar to the IBM Common User Access (CUA) definition, published by IBM in 1989. Although many new controls have been added, the basic concept of Windows hasn't really changed all that much. Examples include the arrangement of controls, establishment of a default command button, keyboard access, and control properties and behavior. In this section, I'll breeze over these with a somewhat succinct overview of the basics. Bear in mind that only a few controls can be covered, as there are no established standards for the use of most controls. While some of this material is more of a review than ground-breaking news, it is important for ensuring the standardization of your application. For example, have you ever forgotten to add the ellipsis (...) to a menu item that started a dialog box, as recommended by the *Microsoft Application Design Guide*? This section should help you overcome these trivial, but sometimes noticeable, anomalies. This discussion is limited only to those controls for which standards have evolved. Let's start with the buttons.

Command Buttons

Command buttons should always be placed along the bottom of the dialog box or along the left side. As much as possible, this scheme should be used consistently across all your dialog boxes. Also, keep the OK and Cancel buttons in the same location from box to box; where possible, define the same key to be the default. If a dialog box can corrupt data (for example, delete a file, and so on), the Cancel button should be the default, in case the user hits the Enter key by mistake. If a command button is disabled, the text should be shown dimmed (that is, grayed out). This is easily done using the MFC CWnd member function EnableWindow() as you'll see later in the book. Remember, controls are really nothing more than child windows, so it should come as no surprise that class CWnd plays a prominent role in manipulating controls.

Radiobuttons and Checkboxes

Radiobuttons and checkboxes are used to specify mutually exclusive choices and multiple options, respectively. For example, you might use a group of radiobuttons when prompting the user to select a video resolution. Since the video can only be in one mode at any given time (for example, CGA, VGA), a radiobutton is perfect for this situation. On the other hand, suppose you are prompting the user to designate a target device for a file. The user could send the file to the screen, to the printer, or to a network device, all at the same time. Checkboxes allow these kinds of multiple choices. When the user is presented with many options that can be turned on/off as with a checkbox, consider using a checklist box. This control makes it easier to manage a whole list of checkboxes, which can be owner-drawn to enhance the visual appeal of your application.

Regardless of whether you're using radiobuttons or checkboxes, related controls such as these should be designated by a group label (for example, *Baud Rate, Destination*). These you can add in App Studio by using the frame control, or simply by adding a static text label. For both radiobuttons and checkboxes, the associated text should be dimmed when an option is unavailable.

Listboxes

Listboxes are another way to present multiple choices to the user. An item that is not available should usually be removed from the list. If it is necessary, however, to inform the user that the choice exists, even though it is unavailable, the item should be dimmed. An example of this can be found in selecting fonts and font sizes—certain font sizes may not be available for a given font, but the user should still be advised that such a font size exists. Or, if your application is of a medical nature, a listbox could hold all the lab tests that are available—the pregnancy test would be disabled when the patient is male.

You'll find an example of disabling a listbox item later in this book in Chapter 4, "Listboxes and Checklist Boxes." Remember to give your listboxes a static text label— don't force the user to open the box just to figure out the meaning of the content. Like most controls, listboxes can be owner-drawn, which means you can insert small graphical images next to the text in the listbox. Owner-drawn controls form a major focus of this book—it's one of the easiest ways to turn out a first-class user interface.

Tree Control

The Microsoft Foundation Classes include a control for representing data in a hierarchical fashion. This control also supports graphical symbols in addition to text labels. As with disabling a listbox string, you can use a special icon to visually cue the user that something is disabled or not available. This control also allows the user to edit the text labels, making it a unique data input device.

The strong point of the tree control, in relation to building better user interfaces, is not only its hierarchy properties, but also the fact that it can be expanded and collapsed. Again, very helpful if you have a really crowded screen.

Using Dialog Boxes

Dialog boxes are where controls are most commonly found. In fact, as you examine the sample programs on the companion Web site for this book, you'll find that nearly all the controls are demonstrated from inside dialog boxes.

There are a few common-sense rules to follow for using dialog boxes. First, you should disable any background menu options and command buttons, and reenable them after the dialog box is closed. This helps to focus the user's attention on the dialog box itself, and provides a visual cue that the user must respond to the dialog box (since all the other controls/options have been disabled). You can easily create a member function just for this purpose, as in this example:

```
void CMyClass::DoMenu(UINT nStyle)
{
    CMenu *pMenu = AfxGetApp()->m_pMainWnd->GetMenu();
    int nItems = (int)pMenu->GetMenuItemCount();
    for( int i=0; i < nItems; i++ )
    {
        pMenu->EnableMenuItem( i, MF_BYPOSITION | nStyle );
    }
    CWnd::DrawMenuBar();

}         // end DoMenu()
```

This method works for the main menu. In the event you need to disable a menu attached to a dialog box (not recommended, but sometimes necessary), replace the line

```
CMenu *pMenu = AfxGetApp()->m_pMainWnd->GetMenu();
```

with the following:

```
CMenu *pMenu = CDialog::GetMenu();
```

Regardless, you can now make the following call to disable the menu:

```
DoMenu(MF_GRAYED);
```

Then, to enable the menu:

```
DoMenu(MF_ENABLED);
```

Another suggestion for the use of dialog boxes involves adding a Help button. Since a dialog box, by virtue of its OK and/or Cancel button(s) is a stopping point, the user may be uncertain as to what to do next (that is, should I answer OK, or should I click

Cancel?). A Help button provides the user with a certain comfort level—it also gives him or her a more detailed explanation as to what to do next, and the consequences of those actions. You should always include bubble help whenever possible and include context help with the dialog box itself. Context help is specific help related to the control that has the focus. I'll cover these topics in much greater detail in Chapter 21, "Splitter Windows," but for now, just be aware that you need to consider these design elements when creating your dialog boxes.

One last point to make with dialog boxes involves the tabbing order. The focus is moved from control to control in a dialog box by pressing the Tab key. The order in which the controls appear in the resource file (.RC) determines the tabbing order. Often controls are added "as needed," which can sometimes have the deleterious effect of producing an illogical tabbing order (for example, the focus moves from the OK button to an edit box, then to the Cancel button and back to a listbox). To correct this situation, simply open the dialog box and use the Tab Order menu option under Layout in App Studio to reorder the controls. This is also where you can make sure your controls are properly aligned and evenly spaced.

Owner-Drawn Controls and Techniques

One of the easiest ways to build a better user interface is to avail yourself of owner-drawn controls. Because so much of this book demonstrates this property, I'll provide a quick overview of this topic now and save the details for the chapters covering individual controls.

When using owner-drawn controls, the burden of drawing the control shifts from the underlying MFC framework to you. You must override the WM_DRAWITEM message for the class, determine which control is being drawn (you'll probably have more than one in the dialog), then determine its state (up, down, disabled, and so on) and display it accordingly. The OnDrawItem() method is very important—here is its prototype:

```
OnDrawItem(int nIDCtl, LPDRAWITEMSTRUCT lpDrawItemStruct)
```

The first parameter is the ID of the control—you can test this in the handler to see which control to draw—you draw, say, an owner-drawn combo box differently than an owner-drawn checklist box, so you absolutely have to trap the WM_PAINT message for the control being drawn. For the most part, you'll be drawing small bitmaps such as those representing different disk drives, a company logo, and so forth.

In some cases, you'll also display text with the image. In this book, the coding examples use a splicing technique when mixing text with graphics. The bounding rectangle for the item in question (for example, a listbox entry) is treated much like a film strip in photography (thus the reference to *splicing*). This rectangle is cut, an image is inserted, and the text is spliced or glued on to the end of the image just inserted. The CDC method TextOut() is used for this purpose.

Another trick to use in the OnDrawItem() method when drawing text is to query the user's installation and use his or her default colors for highlighting text. You can call

GetSysColor(int nIndex) for this, passing it the ID of the color for the display element you're after. For example:

```
DWORD dwVal = GetSysColor(COLOR_HIGHLIGHTTEXT);
```

This returns the value of the color to use when text is to be displayed as highlighted. This technique is vastly superior to simply setting it yourself—you might forget to set it back and hence change the user's configuration when other applications are run, causing much confusion ("Why are my text colors suddenly yellow and not blue?").

The second parameter to OnDrawItem() is a pointer to a DRAWITEMSTRUCT structure. This structure's members hold all sorts of good information. Because you're going to be seeing (and using) it frequently, here is a quick overview of the structure, beginning with the prototype.

```
typedef struct tagDRAWITEMSTRUCT
{
    UINT CtlType;       // the control type: combobox, button, etc
    UINT CtlID;         // resource.h ID of the control
    UINT itemID;        // index of item if list or combo box
    UINT itemAction;    // drawing action required
    UINT itemState;     // item's state: checked, disabled, etc
    HWND hwndItem;      // control's window handle
    HDC hDC;            // device context to use for drawing
    RECT rcItem;        // bounding rectangle
    DWORD itemData;     // extra 32 bits for list & combo box items
}DRAWITEMSTRUCT;
```

Although you could probably guess the meaning of each member just from the name, I've added some comments just in case. When we get into looking at specific controls, you'll see how this structure comes in very handy. This brings up another good point: Many of the controls (and common dialogs) use system structures like this that can be manipulated, or exploited, by the developer. This is a classic example of the efficiency of object-oriented programming—you're allowed to "see" certain data values associated with an object.

Another technique you'll see is the use of the CImageList object for managing the bitmaps used in owner-drawn controls. This class is only available under Windows 95/98 and NT v3.51 and later. This class behaves just like a roll of 35mm film—each image comes one right after the other, and they're all the same size. By using this class, you have access to a zero-based index into the roll of images or icons. The class contains a rich set of methods for manipulating the image list. Lists can be created and destroyed, images can be added and replaced, and so forth. You'll find some sample code for the class later in the book.

Dialog-Based Applications

For the benefit of those of you who haven't experimented with the Visual C++ App-Wizard, I'd like to close things out with a quick look at using dialog-based applications. This is one of the options you can specify in the very first step of creating a new project. Figure 1.1 shows part of that screen. Note the three options: SDI, MDI, and Dialog.

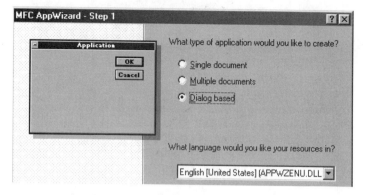

Figure 1.1   Specifying the Dialog option in AppWizard.

Dialog-based applications should be considered when the required functionality of the application is limited, and the I/O is fairly simple. A classic example is the Calculator program that ships with Windows—it does basic math and there aren't many keys. If you have an application that falls within this genre, then that just might be the best user interface of all. I have included an ad hoc sample program on this book's Web site you may wish to build. The project is a sunrise/sunset calculator that also demonstrates using spin controls, edit boxes, and owner-drawn buttons.

Summary

In this chapter, you've become acquainted with the fundamental role of controls, plus reviewed general design standards for using them. Hopefully, this has given you food for thought and will help you design and implement better user interfaces. As you'll see in the upcoming chapters, the mechanics of manipulating controls really aren't that difficult. The truly hard part is in the design—thinking through how your application will function, who will be using it, and so forth. It's easy to introduce bugs into your application simply by picking the wrong control. For example, by using checkboxes where you should have used radiobuttons—you could inadvertently allow the user to make ambiguous or conflicting choices. Careful attention to these issues on the front end can save you lots of time and work on the back end.

You've also been exposed to the fundamental mechanics for enhancing the user interface with owner-drawn controls that support graphics. Keep these in mind as you review the brief code listings you'll find in the remainder of the book. You'll start to see owner-drawn controls beginning with Chapter 2, "The Buttons."

The Buttons

In relation to the user interface, buttons function a lot like menu options—you click them and something happens. This chapter gives you an in-depth look at the three kinds of buttons: the radiobutton, checkbox, and the command button. You'll see plenty of examples that can be applied to virtually every type of user interface you'll ever write. The buttons are important because they can allow you to divide the functional requirements of your application into groups. These groups are not only arranged visibly in the window, but give you much control over the program's behavior. Examples of such groupings include picking a baud rate for a communications port (for example, a group of radiobuttons such that the user can only select one option), and assigning properties using a checkbox. In the first example, only one item in the group can be selected, but in the second, multiple selections are possible. This concept is easily seen in the Properties dialog when you select an item in App Studio—you can give the item different properties simultaneously.

A Windows program uses command buttons more frequently than any other control. Command buttons are most often used to start/terminate an action, solicit Help, or cancel an operation. In fact, when you create a dialog box in App Studio, it automatically creates the OK and Cancel command buttons.

As you will see in this chapter, the MFC code necessary to manipulate the properties of a button is not difficult. The more difficult task is in the proper design of the dialog box, especially as it relates to using buttons. Because this is such a very important component of successful software engineering, I'd like to begin with a discussion of the design standards for command buttons. This discussion will include not only a look at the CButton class but also its cousin, the bitmapped button of class CBitmapButton. Along the way we'll peek in on keyboard functions just to complete the circle.

Design Standards for Command Buttons

Command buttons are rectilinear shapes that use either a text label or a graphical icon to represent the action the button performs. A toolbar is a common example of the use of a graphical icon. If you're using Visual C++ or any of the other Windows-based development tools for MFC, you've already seen these.

Text labels are the most common way to describe the function of a button, especially when that function or meaning cannot be easily conveyed by an icon of some sort. Graphical buttons are ideal for dialog boxes that have a lot of screen clutter, because they tend to be smaller in size than buttons with text labels. These buttons can be depicted as two-dimensional or three-dimensional shapes. Three-dimensional buttons used to set a property (for example, bold, italic) are shown in the depressed state when the property is in effect. When a button's associated action or property is not available, the button label is shown as dimmed.

Command Button Orientation

In all but the rarest of cases, all command buttons are aligned horizontally along the bottom of the dialog box, or vertically along the right side of the dialog box. Figures 2.1a and 2.1b illustrate this design standard using the same dialog box as a model.

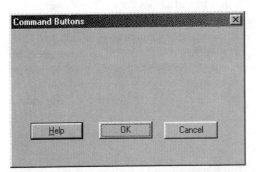

Figure 2.1a

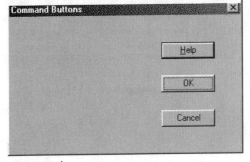

Figure 2.1b

Figure 2.1 Correct button alignment.

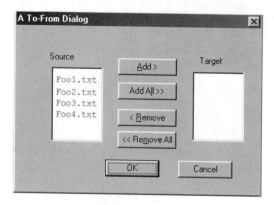

Figure 2.2   Exception to standard alignment.

An acceptable exception to this design guideline is the familiar To-From dialog box, as shown in Figure 2.2. In this configuration, entries made in one listbox are transferred to another. Here it makes sense to place the command buttons between the listboxes. This allows the user to more clearly see the connection between the buttons and the listboxes.

Labeling

All command buttons have labels that are terse descriptions of the action or property it represents. If clicking a command button invokes a dialog box, be sure to include ellipses (...) in the button label, as seen on the Options... button in Figure 2.3. This cues the user that clicking the button will open another dialog box.

The Default Pushbutton

A pushbutton button automatically receives the focus when the dialog box is opened, and is shown with a thick, black border. Windows allows only one command button in a dialog box to be declared as the default pushbutton. The action represented by this button is executed if the user presses Enter without selecting another control in the

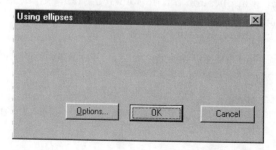

Figure 2.3   Visual cues and button labels.

box. It is good design practice to designate one command button as the default; this is usually the OK button. For those cases in which the user can make an irreversible or damaging change such as deleting a file or closing a communication connection, the Cancel button is designated as the default.

The default pushbutton is identified in the resource file by the label DEFPUSHBUTTON, as in this example:

```
DEFPUSHBUTTON    "OK",IDOK,126,11,50,14
```

To determine if a button is the default pushbutton, query it using the CButton member function GetButtonStyle(). This function is prototyped as

```
UINT GetButtonStyle() const;
```

and returns only the properties identified with the BS_ prefix. The following is an example that uses this function to query the button and determine its type, or style (for example, a pushbutton). It assumes a button has been given the identifier IDOK in App Studio.

```
CWnd* pCtrl; // declare a pointer to the button
pCtrl= CWnd::GetDlgItem(IDOK); // get pointer to button
if(pCtrl->GetButtonStyle() == BS_DEFPUSHBUTTON)
    AfxMessageBox("The IDOK button is the default.",MB_OK);
```

The converse of the GetButtonStyle() function is SetButtonStyle(), which lets you change the style or appearance of a button. This practice is discouraged in order to avoid confusing the user.

The Tabbing Order

Although the mouse is generally used to interact with an application, the ability to use the keyboard with your application is essential. In fact, in order to have your software certified by Microsoft as being "Windows compatible," it must include keyboard access.

The tabbing, or visit, order is the sequence in which dialog box controls gain the input focus as the tab key is pressed. This is an important design consideration. You must always designate a default pushbutton to guarantee that a control gets the focus when the dialog box is opened. The default button is recognizable by the dark gray box around the text. This allows the user to quickly see which key is the default, should the user press the Enter key. If your application can do something dangerous, like delete files, you wouldn't want the OK button to be the default. If you accidentally press Enter, the OK button would assume you want to delete the files!

The tabbing order is directly related to the order in which the controls are defined in your .RC file. Consider the following dialog box:

```
IDD_MYDIALOG DIALOG DISCARDABLE  0, 0, 185, 92
STYLE DS_MODALFRAME | WS_POPUP | WS_VISIBLE | WS_CAPTION | WS_SYSMENU
CAPTION "Tabbing Order Example"
FONT 8, "MS Sans Serif"
BEGIN
```

```
DEFPUSHBUTTON    "&OK",IDOK,126,11,50,14
PUSHBUTTON       "&Cancel",IDCANCEL,126,58,50,14
COMBOBOX         IDC_COMBO1,7,11,101,30,CBS_DROPDOWN | CBS_SORT |
                 WS_VSCROLL | WS_TABSTOP
END
```

In this example, the focus is on the OK button when the dialog box opens. Pressing the tab key would move to the Cancel button; pressing it again would move the focus to the combo box.

When building complex dialog boxes, the developer is usually thinking about what controls are needed, and not the tabbing order. When the box is tested, the order is almost always not what is desired. It is very easy to change the tabbing order—just use the Layout...Tabbing Order option in App Studio to change the order of the controls. When this menu option is selected, a small number appears next to each control, indicating the control's current position in the tabbing order. Simply start clicking on controls in the order you want to establish a new tabbing order. Remember to skip static text labels.

Keyboard Accelerators

Keyboard accelerators are keystroke combinations used to jump directly to a button, or other control. For command buttons designed in App Studio, simply prefix an ampersand (&) to the letter that is to be designated as the accelerator. The framework will underline the designated character; pressing the ALT key in conjunction with this character will select (but not activate) the button. In the tabbing order example, the O button is the accelerator for the OK button, and the C is the accelerator for the Cancel button.

Advantages of Keyboard Accelerators

There are several implicit advantages to using keyboard accelerators. First, it provides a quick and uniform way to navigate your application. Second, if you use an accelerator with a button that corresponds to a menu option, you eliminate the need to duplicate the programming logic.

For Multiple Document Interface (MDI) type applications, accelerators become even more important. Windows sends a WM_COMMAND message (as opposed to a WM_CHAR or WM_KEYDOWN, etc.) to the window procedure when accelerators are used. This means the programming code for responding to accelerators in the main window is not repeated for every window procedure. This is because child windows do not receive the WM_COMMAND message. Hence, if an accelerator is designed to move between windows, you only have to write the code to handle it in one place.

While keyboard accelerators are an excellent addition to dialog box controls, care must be taken that you do not assign the same key to more than one control. No warnings or error messages are generated, and the framework uses the first accelerator encountered as the target. The best cure in this case is prevention—check your work closely as you design your dialog boxes, and test them thoroughly.

TIP

A general guideline for keyboard access is to use the F1 function key to invoke help. Avoid using the F4, F5, and F6 keys as these are often reserved for special functions in MDI programs.

The CButton Class

All your buttons begin their incarnation as a member of class CButton, which is derived from class CWnd. Although this class includes radiobuttons and checkboxes, the current discussion will focus only on command buttons.

If you cut your programming teeth on the SDK, you know that all controls are considered by Windows to be nothing more than child windows. As such, you can easily exchange messages with them. Whether your buttons are of the simple, garden variety, or the more elegant bitmapped type, all interactions with them are basically the same.

Command buttons may be used by themselves or in groups. They may have captions, or appear without text. The appearance of most buttons changes when clicked; unless you are using some variation of owner-drawn buttons, the framework takes care of these display properties for you. In either case, you create a button using App Studio, or by calling the class constructor from your code, using the new() function. If you create it in App Studio, the class destructor is called automatically when the dialog box is closed. If you create it, it is up to you to explicitly destroy it at the appropriate time by calling the delete() function.

Properties and Styles

All dialog box controls, including command buttons, have properties and styles. Because these will pop up again in the later chapters on radiobuttons and checkboxes, the following is a summary of the various button styles that such controls can assume. Button styles are defined in windows.h, and are recognized by their BS_ prefix (for example, BS_CHECKBOX, BS_3STATE, etc.).

BS_PUSHBUTTON. This style creates a push (command) button. Such buttons send a WM_COMMAND message to the parent window when the user selects the button.

BS_RADIOBUTTON. This creates a radiobutton, which is a small circle that has a label displayed to its right (unless this style is modified using the BS_LEFTTEXT style). Radiobuttons are generally used in groups of similar but mutually exclusive choices, such as selecting a port, baud rate, and so on.

BS_AUTORADIOBUTTON. This style is the same as BS_RADIOBUTTON, with one slight twist: When the button is selected, it highlights itself and clears all the other radiobuttons in the same group.

BS_3STATE. This style creates a checkbox that can be grayed *and* checked. Thus, it can have three states: checked, unchecked, and grayed. This last state is generally used to indicate that the option represented by the checkbox is unavailable. Check the box marked "Tri-State" in App Studio to assign this style.

BS_AUTO3STATE. This style is the same as BS_3STATE, except the *state* of the box changes whenever the user selects it. The box cycles through checked, grayed, and normal (ungrayed, unchecked).

BS_CHECKBOX. This style creates a checkbox, which is a small square that has a label displayed on the right (unless modified by the BS_LEFTTEXT style).

BS_AUTOCHECKBOX. This is the same as BS_CHECKBOX, except the box is marked with an X when the user selects the option, and is removed the next time the box is selected.

BS_DEFPUSHBUTTON. This style creates a command button that has a thick, black border. This identifies the default option if the Enter key is pressed. Only one button can have this style.

BS_GROUPBOX. This style draws a rectangle in which you can group related buttons. A label is displayed in the rectangle's upper-left corner. Groups are used to classify related options, such as baud rates for a communications port, selecting a printer port, and so on.

BS_LEFTTEXT. You can use this style with both radiobuttons and checkboxes. Normally, these controls display their labels on the right side of the control. By ORing this style with the control, you cause the text of the label to be displayed on the left side of the control.

BS_OWNERDRAW. This style creates an owner-drawn button; this style *cannot* be combined with any other button style. The parent window receives a WM_MEASUREITEM message when the button is created, and a WM_DRAWITEM when the button needs to be redrawn. If you select this style, be sure to trap both these messages in Class Wizard.

No matter what type of button you add to your interface in App Studio, you use the same Properties dialog to assign functional attributes to the button. For example, there are times when you'll want to put the text on the left side of a checkbox instead of on the right, which is the default. Now let's look at an easy way to enhance the user interface: bitmapping the buttons.

The CBitmapButton Class

A very easy way to add a touch of elegance to your command buttons is to draw them with bitmaps instead of simple text descriptors. Not only is this a simple procedure, but there is very little penalty to be paid in terms of resource consumption—the bitmaps are loaded when needed, and discarded when the dialog box is closed. Using a bitmap as the face of a command button can change the perception of your application. Furthermore, if you want a quick and easy way to display a graphic such as a company logo, you can create a bitmapped button without a message handler. You can also incorporate properties such as 3-D lettering, color, and shading. In this section, I'll walk through the steps for adding a bitmap to the face of a command button.

At the heart of this technique is the class Cbitmapbutton. Objects of this class consist of up to four bitmaps, corresponding to each of the possible states a button can possess.

- Up
- Down
- Focused
- Disabled

Only the bitmap for the Up state is required; the rest are at the discretion of the developer. For simple OK and Cancel buttons that immediately close a dialog box when clicked, this is all that is necessary. More complex dialog boxes require some or all of the other states. For example, if your application requires the user to make a selection from a combo or listbox before an action can be completed, you will want to show the OK button as disabled until such a selection is made. Naturally, the Cancel button should always be available.

When you create the bitmap for the button, pay close attention to the border of your image, because this is used to provide visual feedback to the user regarding the state of the button. As an example, the button that currently has the focus is generally identical to the one for the Up state, except it has a thicker border. Likewise, a disabled button is identical to the Up bitmap, except it appears dimmed or grayed out. The bottom line is this: It's up to you to know all the possible states your button(s) can have, and provide bitmaps for each state.

Implementing Bitmapped Buttons

Now let's see how it's done. There are six main steps to follow in order to use a bitmapped button in a dialog box.

1. Draw the necessary bitmaps.
2. Create the dialog box template, positioning the buttons where desired.
3. Declare a resource ID and button caption.
4. Insert the bitmap references into your .RC file.
5. Add a CBitmapButton member object to the dialog's class.
6. Load the bitmaps in the dialog box's OnInitDialog() routine.

For this discussion, App Studio is used as the drawing tool for the bitmaps in order to make it easier to discuss the associated properties, resource ID, and so on. When drawing the bitmap(s) for your buttons, strive to keep them as 16×16 pixels, or 16×32. However, they can be any size, and all are treated as the same size as the bitmap for the Up state. Depending upon how your dialog box is laid out, you may have to adjust the position of your buttons in the dialog box after testing. The snap-grid feature of App Studio is useful for this purpose.

While in App Studio, assign the button a unique ID (for example, ID_CANCEL, etc.) and the BS_OWNERDRAW style. You also *must* assign a caption to the button, even though it will be covered by the bitmap. This is very important, because this caption is related to the name of the bitmap that becomes the face of the button. The framework looks for the letters U, D, F, and X appended to the caption of the button, which signify up, down, focus, and disabled, respectively. Let's say you give the button the caption CANCEL. In your resource file (.RC), you must have a bitmap with the ID CANCEL**U** for the Up state bitmap, a CANCEL**D** for the Down state, a CANCEL**F** for the focus bitmap, and a CANCEL**X** for the disabled bitmap. Thus, your .RC file might contain the following declarations for a Cancel button having these four states:

```
CANCELUBITMAP   DISCARDABLE     "RES\\CANCELU.BMP"
CANCELDBITMAP   DISCARDABLE     "RES\\CANCELD.BMP"
CANCELFBITMAP   DISCARDABLE     "RES\\CANCELF.BMP"
CANCELXBITMAP   DISCARDABLE     "RES\\CANCELX.BMP"
```

Let's look at a specific example. Suppose you want to create a dialog box for a class called CNewProj, which has two bitmapped buttons, OK and Cancel. In App Studio, you assigned the IDs IDOK and IDCANCEL, and the captions OK and CANCEL. You create two bitmaps, OKU.BMP and CANCELU.BMP. The file newproj.rc should be modified to include the following two lines:

```
OKUBITMAP   DISCARDABLE     "RES\\OKU.BMP"
CANCELUBITMAP   DISCARDABLE     "RES\\CANCELU.BMP"
```

The modifications to the file newproj.h are shown here in bold typeface.

```
// CNewProj dialog
class CNewProj : public CDialog
{
protected:
// array of buttons constructed with no attached bitmap images

// Construction
public:
CNewProj(CWnd* pParent = NULL);// standard constructor
// Dialog Data
//{{AFX_DATA(CNewProj)
enum { IDD = IDD_DIALOG1 };
CBitmapButton btn_cancel;  // define the Cancel button
CBitmapButton btn_ok;// define the Ok button
//}}AFX_DATA

// Implementation
 .
 .
 .
```

The last thing to do is change the OnInitDialog() routine for CNewProj. It would look like this:

```
BOOL CNewProj::OnInitDialog()
{
CDialog::OnInitDialog();
btn_cancel.AutoLoad(IDCANCEL, this);
```

```
btn_ok.AutoLoad(IDOK, this);
.
. (additional statements would go here)
.
}
```

That's all there is to it. When the dialog box is activated, the buttons will have the bitmaps attached. Notice that you do not have to explicitly load each bitmap for each of the four states—this is handled for you automatically by the framework. You must, however, make sure these bitmaps are part of your resource file if you plan to show the button(s) in different states. I've found it easiest to create the bitmap for the button in its normal (up) state, then insert or import the bitmap into my project from the Visual C++ Workbench menu. You can right-click them in the resource window to bring up their Properties dialog, and rename them accordingly. Then, it's a simple matter of editing the bitmaps to conform to the other three states.

Using Member Variables

There is one caveat with using CBitmapButton objects: You cannot add member variables in Class Wizard. For example, suppose you need to disable the Cancel button. Normally, you just create a CButton-class member variable by clicking Add variables... in Class Wizard, and assign it a variable called, for example, m_OK. Then, to disable the button, you simply write:

```
m_OK.EnableWindow(TRUE);
```

With bitmapped buttons, you have to get a CWnd-class pointer to the control, and then call EnableWindow(). The following snippet of code, which assumes you've assigned the string IDOK to the button in App Studio, illustrates how to accomplish the same thing.

```
CWnd* pOK_btn;// declare a pointer to the OK button
pOK_btn= CWnd::GetDlgItem(IDOK);// get pointer to OK button
pOK_btn->EnableWindow(FALSE);// disable the OK button
```

To create CBitmapButton member variables, use Class Wizard to create member variables for the buttons. These will default to CButton. Then, edit the associated header file, and simply replace the CButton definition with CBitmapButton. There's an example in the Example1 project on the companion Web site.

Enabling and Disabling Buttons

A necessary feature of command buttons is the ability to selectively disable them, and to reenable, them at will. For example, if an option is unavailable until some other action is first taken, then the button should be displayed as disabled. Upon successful completion of the prerequisite action, the button's state is changed to enabled. The MFC library provides a single member function in class CWnd for this purpose.

Remember that all controls are treated as *child windows*, so it is only natural for the function to be a member of this class. The function is EnableWindow(), which is prototyped as follows:

```
BOOL CWnd::EnableWindow(BOOL bEnable)
```

where bEnable is set to TRUE to enable the window, and FALSE to disable it. The return value is also a Boolean value—it indicates the state of the control before the call to EnableWindow(). This is zero if the control was previously enabled, or if an error was encountered.

There are several ways to use this function. The simplest method is to create a member variable in Class Wizard (of type Control), and use the standard C++ dot notation. For example, suppose you have a button identified as ID_OPTIONS with the caption Options.... You assign this a member variable in Class Wizard called m_Options. To disable this button, you would use the following statement:

```
m_Options.EnableWindow(FALSE);// disable the Options...button
```

Another way to accomplish this is to use the member function GetDlgItem(). This function is prototyped as

```
CWnd* GetDlgItem( int nID ) const;
```

where nID is the identifier of the control assigned in App Studio (in my Options... example, this is ID_OPTIONS). The code to disable this button using this technique is as follows:

```
CWnd* pCtrl;// declare a pointer to the button
pCtrl= CWnd::GetDlgItem(ID_OPTIONS);// get pointer to button
pCtrl->EnableWindow(FALSE);// disable the button
```

As you can see, there's not much to disabling and enabling buttons. As usual, the burden is on you, the developer, to know when and where to use it in your application. Use the return value from EnableWindow() to ascertain the state of a button to help you manage these properties.

Changing a Button's Text

Although it is rarely necessary, you may need to change the caption of a command button from time to time. One possible example of changing a button's caption at runtime is in a client/server or a data communications application. A button could be initially labeled Connect, but if the data link to the host was lost, you might want to change the caption to Reconnect or something similar.

CWnd has two member functions to help you with this chore: GetWindowText() and SetWindowText(). The prototypes for GetWindowText() are

```
int GetWindowText( LPSTR lpszStringBuf, int nMaxCount ) const;
```

and

```
void GetWindowText( CString& rString ) const;
```

The prototype for SetWindowText() is

```
void SetWindowText( LPCSTR lpszString );
```

These member functions are used in the same manner described for enabling and disabling buttons; that is, use a member variable or pointer to the control. Here's an example using the Options... button discussed previously:

```
CString rCaption;// variable to hold button caption
m_Options.GetWindowText(rCaption);// get button caption into rCaption
m_Options.SetWindowText("Choices...");  // change the button's caption
.
```

That's it for changing the button's text, and pretty much wraps up the basics. Now we'll take it up a notch and add some more enhancements by adding some user help to the buttons. Although the subject of help will be covered in Chapter 22, "Adding Help to the Interface," you might as well take this peek while it's fresh in your mind.

Connecting Help

It is very easy to connect a command button to a topic in a Windows Help file. In general, you should always include a button labeled Help with your dialog boxes. When the user clicks the button, a topic in an associated Help file is displayed. The MFC library contains a simple API call for this purpose, WinHelp(). This function is prototyped as follows:

```
virtual void WinHelp(DWORD dwData,UINT nCmd);
```

The parameters dwData and nCmd are interrelated. The parameter nCmd specifies the type of help requested; dwData is dependent upon this value. For example, if dwData is set to HELP_CONTENTS and nCmd is 0L, the associated Help file is opened to the table of contents. Table 2.1 enumerates the various values and their meanings.

Of the entries listed in Table 2.1, the HELP_CONTEXT is the most prevalent, and, generally speaking, is the form you will use to connect a Help topic to a command button. Each topic in a Help file is identified by a unique context ID number that has been defined in the [MAP] section of the Help file's project (extension .HPJ) file. For example, consider the following hypothetical message handler for responding to a BN_CLICKED message.

```
void CSomeClass::OnClkHelp()
{
// TODO: Add your command handler code here
//
theApp.WinHelp (IDD_MY_TOPIC,HELP_CONTEXT);
}
```

In this example, the topic associated with the context identifier IDD_MY_TOPIC is displayed when the Help button is clicked.

Radiobuttons

In many dialog boxes, it is often necessary to ask the user to select one option from a category of several, or to define certain preset conditions. For example, in the case of

Table 2.1   The WinHelp() Parameters

DWDATA	NCMD	MEANING
HELP_CONTEXT	Topic ID no.	Displays topic associated with nCmd.
HELP_CONTENTS	0L	Opens Help file to table of contents.
HELP_SETCONTENTS	Topic ID no.	Changes the table of contents to a new topic.
HELP_CONTEXTPOPUP	Topic ID no.	Displays topic in a popup window.
HELP_KEY	Pointer to string	Displays keyword topic or Search dialog box.
HELP_PARTIALKEY	Pointer to string	Displays keyword topic or Search dialog box.
HELP_MULTIKEY	Pointer To a MULTIKEYHELP structure	Displays the Help topic identified by a keyword in an alternate keyword table.
HELP_COMMAND	Pointer to a string	Executes a Help macro.
HELP_SETWINPOS	Pointer To a HELPWININFO structure	Changes size and position of primary Help window.
HELP_FORCEFILE	0L	Ensures WinHelp opens correct Help file.
HELP_HELPONHELP	0L	Displays the contents of the specified Using Help file.
HELP_QUIT	0L	Closes the Help file.

configuring a serial port's baud rate, a user may be presented with a list of available rates (for example, 1200, 2400, 4800, 9600) and asked to pick one and only one. Or, a user might be asked to set a file's attributes by selecting read-only, hidden, and so on. For these types of programming chores, radiobuttons are ideal.

NOTE

Closely related to both types of controls is the concept of a *group*—this establishes a relationship between similar controls. In this section, I'll give you a closer look at how groups are used, and when. An important note: Since both the radiobutton and checkbox controls are members of CButton, I will present one section for both radiobutton and checkbox operations, and indicate any peculiarities between the two. This will obviate the need for a "Radiobutton Operations" section and a "Checkbox Operations" section, since these two controls are so closely related.

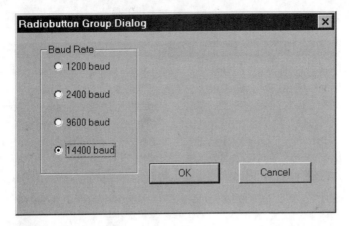

Figure 2.4 A radiobutton group.

A radiobutton is a small, circular control with descriptive text usually used in a group such that only one control can be checked. A radiobutton is considered checked if the circle has a heavy dot in the center. Figure 2.4 shows a typical arrangement of radiobuttons. Radiobuttons that are part of a group do not function as "toggles"; that is, clicking a checked radiobutton does not uncheck it. To uncheck a radiobutton, you must click another button in the group, or press the spacebar. For this reason, you should not use radiobuttons to define binary state properties—use a checkbox instead.

Properties and Styles

When you create a dialog box with radiobuttons, you can assign eight properties to the button:

ID. Every resource must have a unique identifier. This is a string that identifies the control; it appears in the dialog box definition in the .RC file, and in resource.h. While App Studio will always assign an ID for you by default, it is a good idea to replace it with something more descriptive. For example, in Figure 2.4, the radiobuttons should be assigned IDs such as IDC_BAUD1200, IDC_BAUD2400, and so on. This makes editing the resource files a lot easier, because you can more readily identify what a control is from the ID.

Caption. The Caption property reflects the text to be associated with the radiobutton. App Studio assigns a caption, but you will need to override this default. The caption you provide should be descriptive of the action represented by the button. Using the example found in Figure 2.4, the caption for IDC_BAUD1200 is 1200, for IDC_BAUD2400 it is 2400, and so on. You can assign keyboard accelerators to the radiobutton by placing an ampersand (&) in the caption in front of the letter to be used as the accelerator. Unless you can assign a unique accelerator to each radiobutton in the group, you're better off using an accelerator for the first radiobutton only. Using the accelerator moves the input focus to the button *and* checks it. Once in the group, the user is free to move around using the arrow keys. You'll see some code later in this chapter that shows how to navigate a group of radiobuttons.

Visible. This property, which defaults to TRUE (checked automatically in App Studio), indicates if the button is to be visible when the dialog box is displayed. While your controls usually will be visible, there are times when you will want to keep them invisible. One example is the protection of proprietary data—you may wish to keep a control related to, say, salary information, invisible until an authorized password is entered. This lets one dialog box service both privileged and unprivileged users. Also, you can avail yourself of the Sort property when using listboxes, and keep string data sorted invisibly. The visible property of *any* control should be exploited when it comes to building a better user interface.

Group. This style is generally reserved only for a collection of radiobutton objects. As soon as one of the buttons acquires the focus, you can use the arrow keys to navigate from button to button. Usually, you will want to designate the first radiobutton in a related collection as having this style (WS_GROUP). Using Figure 2.4 as an example, only radiobutton IDC_BAUD1200 would be assigned this style; all the other baud buttons *must not* have this style. However, the next control in the tabbing order *should* be assigned the group style in order for the dialog manager to recognize where one group ends and another starts.

Auto. When a radiobutton is defined with the Auto property, it means the button is checked automatically, and all the other radiobuttons in the group are unchecked. By default, the checkbox for this property is checked (TRUE) whenever a radiobutton is created in App Studio.

Disabled. The disabled property makes a radiobutton nonselectable, and dims the caption. This is a property that can be set dynamically, depending upon the nature of the application. Again, with Figure 2.4 as an example, suppose your application is installed on a machine that does not support a baud rate of 14400 baud. Your Init-Dialog() routine should detect this and disable this radiobutton.

Tab Stop. This property indicates if the radiobutton is in the tabbing order. By default, the tabstop property, which is a Boolean value, is set to TRUE. This means the user can set the focus to the control by using the TAB key. Only the first radiobutton in a group should have this property set.

Left Text. By default, a radiobutton's caption appears on the right side of the button. Setting this property to TRUE causes the text to be displayed on the left side of the control.

In App Studio, the ID and the Caption are entered using edit boxes; checkboxes are used to select or assign the other properties.

Radiobutton States

Radiobuttons, taken by themselves, are either on or off (checked or unchecked). But there are additional properties to consider: Does the button have the focus? Is it highlighted? The MFC class library provides member functions for reading and writing the state of a radiobutton. To read a button's state, use the GetState() function of class CButton, which is prototyped as follows:

```
UINT ret_val= GetState( ) const;
```

To ascertain the state of the button, you'll need to test the return value against a bit mask using a Boolean AND; the pertinent values are 3, 4, and 8. The meaning of each bit mask, for radiobuttons *only*, is as follows:

0x0003 & ret_val If TRUE, the button is checked. If FALSE, it is unchecked.

0x0004 & ret_val If TRUE, the button is highlighted. If FALSE, it is not.

0x0008 & ret_val If TRUE, the button has the focus. If FALSE, it does not.

That covers the button states, and how to tweak them. Sooner or later, you'll run into a programming situation where you'll need to be able to read and write these properties, so keep your eyes open. The most challenging part is managing the states. As the user makes selections that cause other options to become disabled/enabled, this becomes critical in managing your interface.

Radiobuttons and the Keyboard

While radiobuttons are usually manipulated with the mouse, certain keystrokes have unique meaning when a radiobutton has the focus (or acquires the focus). For starters, the TAB key can be used to move to a radiobutton group. Once in the group, you can use the arrow keys to move between the buttons in the group. Likewise, if you have defined keyboard accelerators for the buttons, these can be used to set the focus. Once a button has the focus, it can be toggled using the spacebar.

Checkboxes

A checkbox is a control in class CButton that appears as a square box with a label; the label generally appears to the right of the checkbox. Figure 2.5 shows a typical dialog box with checkboxes.

The label can be made to appear to the left of the box by assigning the BS_LEFTTEXT style. Checkboxes are used in an application to allow the user to select one or more options.

Checkboxes are similar to radiobuttons in that you use them to set some sort of Boolean condition—something is on (checked) or off (unchecked). But where radiobuttons are

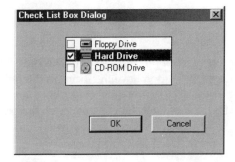

Figure 2.5   Checkboxes in a dialog box.

mutually exclusive in a group, checkboxes are not. In other words, only one radiobutton can be on in a group, but several or all checkboxes can be on in a group. Clicking an empty checkbox causes an X to appear inside the box, indicating the option is on. Clicking it again clears the X, indicating the option is off. As the designer, you'll need to select which control type to use based on the nature of your application. The mutual exclusion principle will likely influence which control to use.

Properties and Styles

To no surprise, checkboxes have properties and styles like any other control. In App Studio, there are seven styles you can select for a checkbox. So to help you get it right, here is a quick rundown on the styles that you can select in App Studio.

Visible. When this checkbox has an X (the default in App Studio), then the checkbox will be visible in the dialog box or CFormView object. Clearing this box will cause the control to have the style NOT WS_VISIBLE.

Disabled. The disabled property makes a checkbox nonselectable, and dims the caption; the checkbox portion is not dimmed. Once a checkbox that is part of a group is disabled, you can't set focus to it using the arrow keys. This means the first member of a checkbox group should never be disabled if you want the user to reach the group via the keyboard.

Group. This style, which is also a Boolean value and off by default in App Studio, assigns the WS_GROUP style to the checkbox. As previously discussed, this style indicates the checkbox is part of a group of related controls.

Tab Stop. This property indicates if the checkbox is in the tabbing order. By default, the tabstop property, which is a Boolean value, is set to TRUE. This means the user can set the focus to the control by using the TAB key. Only the first checkbox in a group should have this property set.

Auto. The Auto style, which is the default selection in App Studio, assigns the BS_AUTOCHECKBOX style to the edit box. This style is responsible for displaying an X in the box when selected, and removing it the next time it is selected.

Left Text. This option assigns the BS_LEFTTEXT style to the checkbox. Checkboxes with this style display the text of their labels on the left side of the box instead of the right (default).

Tri-State. This option assigns the BS_3STATE style to the checkbox, which creates a checkbox that can be grayed *and* checked. Thus, it can have three states: checked, unchecked, and grayed. If this style is not ORed with something else, you cannot set the X in the box by clicking it with the mouse or pressing the spacebar.

Unlike most other controls, checkboxes cannot be ORed together as much as the other controls in MFC. For example, the following style declaration for a check box is invalid.

```
BS_OWNERDRAW | BS_AUTORADIOBUTTON
```

This example shows a style contradiction—the box can't be both owner-drawn and automatically drawn simultaneously (the BS_OWNERDRAW style can't be used with any other style). The class styles for buttons (BS_ prefix) and static controls (SS_ prefix) are mutually exclusive. Button and static styles are defined in windows.h as a numbered sequence (for example, 1,2,3,4...) instead of setting individual bits (for example, 1,2,4,8,...). Some quick bit-math shows that ORing the sequential styles together can yield a style with properties totally different from what you expected.

Radiobutton and Checkbox Operations

As promised at the beginning of this chapter, I'll limit our discussion of the operations you can perform on radiobuttons and checkboxes to just this one section, pointing out any differences as necessary. The scope of the basic operations is pretty simple—determining a button/box's state, style, and so on. For reasons of simplicity, we'll refer to both these controls as *buttons* in the upcoming sections, because they are both members of class CButton. Although these member functions can be used with any object of class CButton (that is, command buttons), our focus is restricted to radiobuttons and checkboxes.

Retrieving a Button's Style

Class CButton has a member function that returns the window *style* of the object. The function is prototyped as

```
UINT GetButtonStyle() const;
```

This function returns a value that is a reflection of all the BS_ style values assigned to the button.

Retrieving the Check State

The CButton member function GetCheck() retrieves the check state of a radiobutton or checkbox. This value does not contain any information about the control's highlight or focus state. Another function, GetState(), is used for that purpose. The prototype for GetCheck() is

```
int GetCheck() const;
```

This function only works with controls that are not owner-drawn. The return values are

0 Button/box unchecked; invalid style.

1 Button/box checked.

2 Indeterminate (only with styles BS_3STATE or BS_AUTO3STATE).

The last return value, 2, is used when the control was created with the tri-state option enabled. Now, here's a quick snippet of code to illustrate the function's usage. It assumes a member variable, m_BtnCtrl, was assigned in Class Wizard to a checkbox created with the BS_AUTOCHECKBOX style.

```
int nRetVal= 0;
nRetVal = m_BtnCtrl.GetCheck();
if(!nRetVal)
AfxMessageBox("The check box is unchecked",MB_OK);
```

```
    else
        AfxMessageBox("The check box is checked",MB_OK);
```

Actually, this is only one weapon in your programming arsenal. Determining if a button is checked only tells you one thing: It's checked! Sometimes you need to know more about the button, particularly its state.

Retrieving the State

The GetCheck() function only tells us if a radiobutton is "on," or a checkbox has the X. The CButton member function GetState() returns not only the check state, but the highlight and focus states as well. This function is prototyped as

```
    UINT GetState() const;
```

The return value is basically a bit mask; the various bit settings reflect the various states. The following is a summary of these return values.

0x0003 The check state; 0 = unchecked, 1= checked.

0x0004 The highlight state; nonzero value= highlighted.

0x0008 The focus state; nonzero value= has focus.

Here's an example, based on the earlier example for GetCheck().

```
    UINT nRetVal= 0;
    nRetVal = m_BtnCtrl.GetState();
    if(nRetVal & 0x0008)
        AfxMessageBox("The check box has the input focus.",MB_OK);
```

Setting the Check State

Class CButton provides a member function that sets/resets a radiobutton's and checkbox's *check* (not highlight) state. The function is prototyped as

```
    void SetCheck (int nCheck);
```

where the parameter nCheck indicates the new check state. This can be one of three values.

0 Set the button/box to unchecked.

1 Set the button/box to checked.

2 Set the state to indeterminate. This can only be used with controls that have the BS_3STATE or BS_AUTO3STATE style.

Setting the Highlight State

A separate member function is used to set a control's *highlight* state. The highlight state is not related to the interior portion of the control (for example, the bullet in a radiobutton, or the X in a checkbox). Instead, the highlight state refers to the darkening of the text and the box/button. The member function, SetState(), is prototyped as follows:

```
void SetState(BOOL bHighlight);
```

where bHighlight is the new highlight state: Zero (FALSE) removes the highlighting, any other value sets it.

Retrieving a Button's Style

You can interrogate a button to determine its style; that is, whether it is a radiobutton or a checkbox. The member function available for this purpose is

```
UINT GetButtonStyle() const;
```

The return value represents the ORed values of the control's BS_ styles; for example, BS_CHECKBOX, BS_LEFTTEXT, BS_RADIOBUTTON, and so forth. A complete list of these styles may be found in the MFC Library Reference and/or Help file(s).

Setting a Button's Style

You can change a button's style using SetButtonStyle(). This member function is proto-typed as

```
void SetButtonStyle(UINT newStyle, BOOL bRedraw);
```

where newStyle is the button style(s) that the button is to assume. The second parameter, bRedraw, indicates whether or not the button is to be redrawn after the style is set. By default, this value is TRUE.

This is a dangerous function, and should be used with the utmost caution. Your application should virtually never change a radiobutton into a checkbox, or vice versa (although this is possible using this function). Generally, the main use of SetButton-Style() is to selectively make a control a tri-state instead of a binary object.

Programming Tips for Button Groups

Now that you've had a glimpse at the resources available to manipulate radiobuttons and checkboxes, let's see how you can combine them to manage a typical application. For this example, I'll use a group of radiobuttons that are used to set the baud rate of a serial port. Because the port can only have one speed, and it has to have a default (in case the user fails to specify the desired baud rate), this makes for a classic example. In a nutshell, we want to show the user a group of radiobuttons, each corresponding to a particular baud rate. One and only one of these will *always* be set. An illustration of a fictitious dialog box for managing the baud rate radiobuttons appears in Figure 2.4.

The first thing you'll want to do when setting up a group like this is assign each radiobutton a member variable in Class Wizard. This makes referencing the control(s) a breeze; we've assigned control-type variables (as opposed to value-type variables) called m_1200, m_2400, and so forth, each representing a selectable baud rate. There is a bug in App Studio that prevents you from assigning member variables to radiobuttons; the option Add Variables remains grayed out *unless* the radiobutton is made part of a group. To work around this problem, follow these steps:

1. Make the button(s) part of a group in App Studio.
2. In Class Wizard, assign the member variable(s).
3. Return to App Studio, remove the button(s) from the group.

The next thing you need to do is initialize the radiobuttons. This generally happens in your OnInitDialog() function, and is not as straight-forward as simply selecting one as the default. For example, you may have to check the application's .INI file for a default setting. Or, suppose the .INI file specifies a default setting of 2400 baud, but the user changes this to, say, 9600. The next time the dialog box is displayed, you want the button for 9600 baud to be enabled, not the 2400, meaning you want to ignore the settings found in the .INI file. We're not going to go that deep into the woods—each application is different, and you should just be aware that these sort of things can, and do, occur. Now for some code—here is how you would initialize the radiobutton group for the dialog box shown in Figure 2.4 on page 24.

```
BOOL CMyComm::OnInitDialog()
{
    CDialog::OnInitDialog();

    // TODO: Add extra initialization here
    m_1200.SetCheck(0);// turn OFF 1200 baud
    m_2400.SetCheck(0);// turn OFF 2400 baud
    m_4800.SetCheck(0);// turn OFF 4800 baud
    m_9600.SetCheck(1);// turn ON 9600 baud

}// end OnInitDialog() for class CMyComm
```

This is the most simplistic approach—simply turn off all the buttons you don't want, and turn on the one you do want. To get the setting from an .INI file, and to remember changes made by the user, use a *static* Boolean variable to determine if this is the first time OnInitDialog() was called. In this example, the OnInitDialog() assumes the variable bFirst was defined at the top of file mycomm.cpp, and is initially TRUE. This variable should be used in conjunction with another global variable to save the control ID of the user's last selection (that is, whenever the user selects another radiobutton).

```
BOOL CMyComm::OnInitDialog()
{
    CDialog::OnInitDialog();

    // TODO: Add extra initialization here
    if(bFirst)// first time dialog box shown...
    {
        m_1200.SetCheck(0);// turn OFF 1200 baud
        m_2400.SetCheck(0);// turn OFF 2400 baud
        m_4800.SetCheck(0);// turn OFF 4800 baud
        m_9600.SetCheck(1);// turn ON 9600 baud
        bFirst= FALSE;// set flag
    }
    else
    {
// insert code to set "saved" configuration
    }

}// end OnInitDialog() for class CMyComm
```

This gets the ball rolling. The next message to trap is a mouse click—here you turn off the previous radiobutton and turn on the one clicked. You must write a message handler for each radiobutton in the group, with each one doing basically the same thing: turning off the other buttons and turning on the one clicked. For example,

```
void CMyComm::OnClickedBaud1200()
{
    // TODO: Add your control notification handler code here
    m_2400.SetCheck(0);// turn OFF 2400 baud
    m_4800.SetCheck(0);// turn OFF 4800 baud
    m_9600.SetCheck(0);// turn OFF 9600 baud
    m_1200.SetCheck(1);// turn ON 1200 baud
}
```

That's all there is to managing a group of radiobuttons. You can probably find a more elegant way to accomplish the same thing. For example, you might make sure that each radiobutton's ID is contiguous in your resource.h file, and set up a loop using these values as the index.

Summary

In this chapter, you've been exposed to the basic building block of a dialog box (or CFormView-class object): the buttons. You've seen how these can be embellished with bitmaps to make the user interface even more graphical. As always, it is incumbent upon the developer to ensure that the placement and usage of command buttons adhere to established standards, and that they are used in a consistent manner. The radiobuttons and checkboxes are specialized weapons in your development arsenal. The buttons are best suited for tasks where one and only one option can be selected from a group; the boxes are best for multiple-selection cases, when more than one choice from a group can be made. In either case, the assignment of member variables to the controls makes working with the control(s) a lot easier. This will turn up again, as in Chapter 3, "Edit Boxes."

CHAPTER 3

Edit Boxes

This chapter examines one of the most widely used controls in the Windows repertoire, the edit box. Edit boxes, while generally used as data input devices, can also be used as a data output, or feedback, control. The MFC classes that we'll concentrate on are CEdit and CWnd because these are the only classes used for text input/output/feedback. But first, let's quickly review some of the styles you can assign to edit boxes, as these greatly influence the behavior of your application.

Edit Box Styles

You can assign various styles, or properties, to your edit boxes. These are assigned in App Studio, using the Properties dialog box, as shown in Figure 3.1.

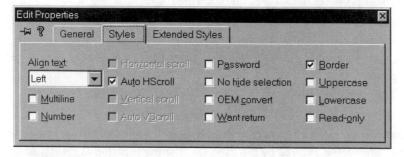

Figure 3.1　The Properties dialog in App Studio.

The following is a brief overview of the different styles, and how they influence your application.

Multiline. This style allows the edit box to have more than one line; it is useful when large amounts of text data are required to be entered.

Number. Use this style to force the edit box to accept only numbers 0–9. This style does not accept decimal points or signs.

Auto Hscroll. This style allows the edit box to automatically be scrolled in the horizontal direction when the user enters more characters than what may be displayed in the edit box window.

Password. This style treats the edit box as a password entry—as characters are typed, they are replaced with an asterisk. You may wish to consider making any password-type edit boxes invisible if the user doesn't have access to what's on the other side of the password wall. For example, if your application is used by users with different access levels (which you would ascertain when they first log in), making the password edit box (and its text label) invisible prevents them from attacking the security system, because they don't know the password box is there. You can easily hide a control once you have a member variable that points to it, such as

m_MyPassWordBox.EnableWindow(FALSE); // double safety!

m_MyPassWordBox.ShowWindow(FALSE); // hide the edit box

No Hide Sel. This property changes the way text is shown when the edit box loses and regains the focus. When set to TRUE, selected text is shown as being selected at all times, even when the edit box loses the focus.

OEM Convert. This property causes text in the edit box to be converted from the Windows character set to the OEM (Original Equipment Manufacturer) character set, and then back to the Windows set. This ensures correct character conversion when calling AnsiToOem() to convert a string to OEM characters. It should be used for any edit boxes that contain, or will contain, filenames.

Want Return. This style lets you type a carriage return inside an edit box. Normally, a carriage return will close a dialog box.

Border. This property draws the edit box with a border.

Uppercase. This style causes all the text entered in the edit box to be displayed in uppercase.

Lowercase. This style causes all the text entered in the edit box to be displayed in lowercase.

NOTE

Be careful when using a single case (that is, uppercase or lowercase) when you must test the string value entered by the user. The C string functions strcmp() and strncmp(), which are generally used to compare two strings, are case-sensitive. Instead, use the functions stricmp() or strcmpi(), which first convert the strings to lowercase before testing for equality.

Edit Box Operations

This section covers some of the edit box operations commonly used in Windows applications. In the examples that follow, a member variable is assumed to have been assigned in Class Wizard to the edit box: This is referred to as m_EditBox.

Retrieving Edit Box Text

To retrieve text from an edit box, use the CWnd member function GetWindowText(). This function is prototyped as follows:

```
void GetWindowText( CString& rString) const;
```

The following is an example of retrieving the text from an edit box. The text is first fetched into a CString object, and then copied into a character array.

```
CString csStr;  // CString object to hold text
char buffer[64];      // assume edit box limited to < 64 characters
memset(buffer,0,sizeof(buffer));// init. string to all NULLs
m_EditBox.GetWindowText(csStr);// get edit box text
char *p= csStr.GetBuffer(64);// convert from CString...
strcpy(buffer,p);// ...into character array
csStr.ReleaseBuffer();// every GetBuffer() needs a ReleaseBuffer()
```

That's all there is to it. Now let's look at going in the opposite direction.

Setting Edit Box Text

To insert text into the edit box, follow this example:

```
CString csStr;// need a CString object
csStr = This is a test;// init. CString object
m_EditBox.SetWindowText(csStr);// insert text into edit box
```

The edit box pointed to by m_EditBox will now contain the text "This is a test".

Disabling an Edit Box

Sometimes you want to temporarily disable an edit box; for example, to force the user to enter data in a proscribed order. Another CWnd member function, which you've seen before, comes to the rescue.

```
m_EditBox.EnableWindow(FALSE);// edit box now disabled
```

Any text in the edit box appears dimmed, and the edit box is unable to receive the focus. To enable the edit box, replace the parameter FALSE with TRUE.

Highlighting Characters

You can selectively highlight a character or range of characters in a control by using the SetSel() method.

```
void SetSel( int nStartChar, int nEndChar, BOOL bNoScroll = FALSE );
```

This is useful when you want to show the user a particular character or string of characters that don't match your input specifications. The first parameter is the index of the character in the string where highlighting is to begin, and the second is the ending index. The last parameter controls whether or not to show the text insertion caret (set to FALSE to show). For example, if an edit box with member variable m_E_Edit contains the string "Hello world", and you want to highlight "orl" in world, the call would be

```
m_E_Edit.SetSel(7,9,FALSE);
```

When this code is executed, the letters "orl" will be highlighted using the system color, as defined on the user's machine.

Subclassing an Edit Box

There are times when you need to trap certain keystrokes in a dialog box. Generally, these are the Tab and Enter keys. But because dialog boxes have their own message queues, these keystrokes cannot be intercepted in Class Wizard by overriding the WM_CHAR or WM_KEYDOWN messages. This section demonstrates how you can trap these (and other) keys. The technique used is called *subclassing*.

Beginning C++ programmers often have trouble grasping the concept of subclassing. Metaphorically speaking, think of it as a form of inheritance. Just as a child inherits traits from its parents, so a subclassed control inherits properties from its parent. Each, however, is unique in its own right. The following section presents some sample code that subclasses an edit box. This code is used to trap the Tab key; when this key is pressed, the code displays a message box saying "The Tab key was pressed". You can easily adapt this code to your applications, replacing this message box with real code.

The Basic Steps

To create a subclassed edit box in a dialog box, all you need do is follow these basic steps:

1. Create the edit box in App Studio.
2. Assign a member variable to it of type control (for example, CEdit).
3. In the header file for the dialog box, give the CEdit object a new name.
4. In the same header file, define a class for the renamed edit box object.

Now all you have to do is add message handlers to trap the keys you're interested in. For this purpose, you need to add the Afx message handler.

```
OnGetDlgCode()
```

The following, taken from subedit.h, shows this process in its entirety.

```
class CMyEditBox : public CEdit
{
// Attributes
public:
    CMyEditBox();       // standard constructor
    ~CMyEditBox();      // standard destructor

// Operations
public:

// Implementation

protected:
    afx_msg UINT OnGetDlgCode(); // for trapping keystrokes
    afx_msg void OnKeyDown(UINT nChar, UINT nRepCnt, UINT nFlags);
    // Generated message map functions
    //{{AFX_MSG(CMyEditBox)
    // NOTE - the ClassWizard will add and remove member functions here.
    //}}AFX_MSG
    DECLARE_MESSAGE_MAP()
};


/////////////////////////////////////////////////////////////////////
/////
// CSubEdit dialog

class CSubEdit : public CDialog
{
// Construction
public:
    CSubEdit(CWnd* pParent = NULL); // standard constructor

// Dialog Data
    //{{AFX_DATA(CSubEdit)
    enum { IDD = IDD_SUBCLASS_DLG };
    CMyEditBox   m_MyEdit;   // ***** the subclassed edit box *****
    //}}AFX_DATA

// Implementation
protected:
    virtual void DoDataExchange(CDataExchange* pDX);  // DDX/DDV support
    // Generated message map functions
    //{{AFX_MSG(CSubEdit)
    virtual BOOL OnInitDialog();
    //}}AFX_MSG
    DECLARE_MESSAGE_MAP()
};
```

The bolded line indicates where I've added the class definition for the edit box (CMyEditBox), and added the message handlers for trapping the keystrokes. Now let's look at the actual source code for the message handlers. This can be found at the bottom of file subedit.cpp.

```
//
// ******************************************************************
//
// * * * * * *   B E G I N   C L A S S   CMyEditBox   * * * * * * *
//
// ******************************************************************

CMyEditBox::CMyEditBox()
{
}

CMyEditBox::~CMyEditBox()
{
}

BEGIN_MESSAGE_MAP(CMyEditBox, CEdit)
    ON_WM_GETDLGCODE()
    ON_WM_KEYDOWN()
    //{{AFX_MSG_MAP(CMyEditBox)
    // NOTE - the ClassWizard will add and remove mapping macros here.
    //}}AFX_MSG_MAP
END_MESSAGE_MAP()


UINT CMyEditBox::OnGetDlgCode()
{
    return DLGC_WANTALLKEYS | DLGC_WANTMESSAGE | DLGC_WANTCHARS |
DLGC_WANTTAB;
}

void CMyEditBox::OnKeyDown(UINT nChar, UINT nRepCnt, UINT nFlags)
{
    // check if tab key pressed
    if(nChar == VK_TAB)
    {
        ::MessageBeep(MB_ICONASTERISK);
        AfxMessageBox("You pressed the TAB key!",MB_OK);
        return;
    }
    CEdit::OnKeyDown(nChar, nRepCnt, nFlags);
}
```

In the message handler OnKeyDown(), I test for the virtual key VK_TAB, and display a message box when it is pressed. If the Tab key is not pressed, we still call OnKey-Down() to make sure whatever key is pressed gets put into the edit box.

Subclassing an edit box like this is also an easy way to format input (that is, allow only numbers) and to perform template matching. You can easily modify code such as this to allow only dates, floating-point numbers, integers, or whatever your specific data needs might be.

Formatting Edit Box Input

There's another way you can restrict the user's input into an edit box without subclassing. This involves building a format string, and trapping certain messages in Class Wizard. In this section, I'll give you an example that uses this technique. One of the greatest benefits derived from input formatting is that it augments the user-interface by eliminating data entry errors. You may not be sure that what the user entered is logical, but you can be sure it will be in the proper format.

To allow formatted input for an edit box, add a class method for checking the input. This method uses a format mask, so you can use the same method with any edit box. This class method needs to accept three parameters.

- A pointer to the edit box being formatted
- A string representing the format mask
- A list of acceptable delimiters

The following is the prototype from my sample code.

```
CheckFormat(CEdit *pEdit, CString csFormat, CString csDelimiters)
```

The first parameter you get is assigning a member variable, of type control, to the edit box. The second parameter is the format you've created for the edit box. The last parameter is a list of delimiters. Take care here—don't assign a delimiter that is a reserved C/C++ keyword. For example, when I was developing this code, I used a format mask that contained "??-". The idea was to use the question marks as wildcards, and the dash as a required delimiter. The code failed—I had forgotten that the sequence "??-" is a tri-graph sequence, a part of the ANSI standard. Other special cases to be on the lookout for are \n, \t, and other escape sequences.

The technique described here follows these ground rules:

1. As the user types a character, it is checked against the format mask.
2. If the user uses the mouse to highlight and change a character, the new change is checked.
3. The contents of the edit box are checked any time the user tries to leave the control.

To accomplish these tasks, you need to trap several messages in Class Wizard. The first of these is the EN_UPDATE message, which means the user has pressed a key and the edit box is preparing to update itself. Also, the EN_KILLFOCUS is important, since this signals that the user is exiting the control. All this can be done by trapping the OnCommand message for the dialog box that contains the edit box. This is because controls communicate with their parent window by notification messages. These are nothing more than WM_COMMAND messages in disguise. By placing all the message management code into this one method, maintenance becomes a lot easier.

Numerical Input

Sometimes, simply assigning the Number property to an edit box is not enough—you need to allow the use of the plus and minus signs, and the decimal point. A Number-type edit box rejects these characters. One solution is to write a universal method that works much like the formatted input described previously. The Web site example code includes such a method, in its own class. The class is called CValid; you can easily add the .cpp and .h files to your own projects. The method is called CheckFloatEntry(), and is prototyped as follows:

```
BOOL CValid::CheckFloatEntry(CEdit *pEdit,float fMaxVal,float fMinVal);
```

The first parameter, pEdit, is a pointer to the edit box that you wish to validate. The next two parameters, fMaxVal and fMinVal, are the maximum and minimum allowable values. For example, suppose you have an edit box to which you've assigned the member variable m_MyEditBox. You want to restrict the user to the range of values of −10.50 to +100.75. Your call to CheckFloatEntry () would look like this:

```
CheckFloatEntry (&m_MyEditBox,-10.50,100.75);
```

The Example1 program on the companion Web site has an example of using this routine; the dialog box is shown in Figure 3.2.

Look at the file FmtEdit.cpp. In order to effectively use this, particular care has to be taken with the EN_KILLFOCUS message. The EN_UPDATE is easy—the user is typing and you're checking the keys. But when the user enters a bogus value, he or she gets a message box while inside CheckFloatEntry(). The message box can be closed by clicking its OK button. This generates yet another EN_KILLFOCUS message. So without adding some logic to the EN_KILLFOCUS message handler, you could end up with the same error message appearing twice. Take a look at the following code segment from the kill focus handler.

```
CWnd *pWnd = CWnd::GetFocus();   // Who's got the focus?
if(pWnd->GetParent() != this)    // last button clicked not
```

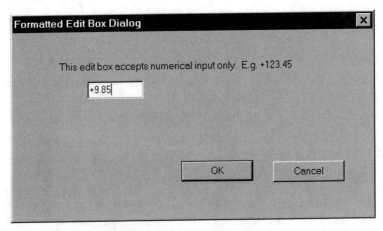

Figure 3.2 The CheckFloatEntry() method dialog box.

```
        return;                        // on this dialog box!
    if( pWnd == &m_Cancel)
        return;   // always allow user to cancel, even with bad input
    //
    CValid cVal; // class that has CheckFloatEntry()
    if(!cVal.CheckFloatEntry(&m_E_NumFmt,12.5,-3.5))
        m_E_NumFmt.SetFocus();     // error, stay in edit box
```

The approach taken here is to see if the control that has the focus belongs to the CFmt-Edit class. To accomplish this, I get the parent of the control that has the focus, and if it's not equal to the this pointer, I know the user has just clicked the OK button in my error message box. Furthermore, if the control in question is the Cancel button, I don't call CheckFloatEntry(), since Cancel will ignore all changes and close the dialog box. But, you will want to trap the OK button on the dialog box in order to do any last-minute error checking (for any other controls you may have).

You may be wondering, "Why not just use the library routine atof() to test the user's input?" The problem with this approach is that atof() will accept, and pronounce as valid, a value such as 12..55. So, it's necessary to examine the string the hard way—looking for duplicate signs and decimal points, and so on, and then validating the input. It's a lot more work, but the user isn't left wondering why 12..55 was accepted.

Let's walk through the CheckFloatEntry() method and explain how it works. Part of the functionality built in to this method is that the user must enter the sign of the number, if any, as the first character. That is, you can't allow an entry such as

    +12.5+9

Here, all the individual characters are valid by themselves, but the sign and decimal point can't be duplicated or appear out of sequence.

```
BOOL CValid::CheckFloatEntry(CEdit *pEdit, float fMaxVal,float fMinVal)
{
    int iDecPt = 0;// number of decimal points found
    int iPlus = 0;// number of plus signs found
    int iMinus= 0;// number of minus signs found
    char str[32];
    memset(str,0,sizeof(str));
    BOOL bErr = FALSE;// assume no errors...
    //
    CString csVal;// what's in the edit box
    pEdit->GetWindowText(csVal);// get text in edit box
    char *p = csVal.GetBuffer(32);
    csVal.ReleaseBuffer();
    strcpy(str,p);
    int len = strlen(str);
    if(!len)
        return TRUE;// nothing there

    char ch = str[len-1];    // last character typed
    if(!( (ch >= '0' && ch <= '9'  ) || ch == '.' || ch == VK_BACK ||
        ch == '+' || ch == '-'   ))
```

```
{
    str[len-1]= 0;
    pEdit->SetSel(0,-1);
    pEdit->ReplaceSel(str);
    AfxMessageBox("Last character entered was invalid.\nIt has been
        removed.",MB_ICONEXCLAMATION | MB_OK);
    return FALSE;
}
//
for(int i=0; i < len; i++)
{
    if(csVal.GetAt(i) == '.')
        ++iDecPt;
    //
    if(csVal.GetAt(i) == '+')
        ++iPlus;
    //
    if(csVal.GetAt(i) == '-')
        ++iMinus;
}
//
if(iDecPt > 1)
{
    AfxMessageBox("Only one decimal point is allowed.\nThe second
      one has been removed.",MB_ICONEXCLAMATION | MB_OK);
    bErr = TRUE;    // set flag
}
//
if(iPlus > 1)
{
    AfxMessageBox("Only one plus sign is allowed.\nThe second
        one has been removed.",MB_ICONEXCLAMATION | MB_OK);
    bErr = TRUE;
}
if((iPlus == 1) && (csVal.GetAt(0) != '+' ))
{
    AfxMessageBox("Plus sign must be the first character.\nThe
        character has been removed.",MB_ICONEXCLAMATION | MB_OK);
    bErr = TRUE;
}
//
if(iMinus > 1)
{
    AfxMessageBox("Only one minus sign is allowed.\nThe second one
        has been removed.",MB_ICONEXCLAMATION | MB_OK);
    bErr = TRUE;
}
if((iMinus == 1) && (csVal.GetAt(0) != '-' ))
{
    AfxMessageBox("Minus sign must be the first character.\nThe
        character has been removed.",MB_ICONEXCLAMATION | MB_OK);
    bErr = TRUE;
```

```
    }
    //
    if(bErr)    // if error, remove last char. typed
    {
        str[len-1]= 0;
        pEdit->SetSel(0,-1);
        pEdit->ReplaceSel(str);
        return FALSE;
    }
    //
    //    last check—is this in range?
    //
    float fCurVal;
    CString csMsg;
    fCurVal = atof(str);
    if(fCurVal < fMinVal)
    {
        csMsg.Format("%s is less than minimum value of %f.  Please
            correct.",csVal,fMinVal);
        AfxMessageBox(csMsg,MB_ICONEXCLAMATION | MB_OK);
        return FALSE; // your method handles this case
    }
    //
    if(fCurVal > fMaxVal)
    {
        csMsg.Format("%s is greater than maximum value of %f.  Please
            correct.",csVal,fMaxVal);
        AfxMessageBox(csMsg,MB_ICONEXCLAMATION | MB_OK);
        return FALSE; // your method handles this case
    }
    return TRUE;
}    // end CheckFloatEntry()
```

This routine begins by checking to see if the last key pressed was an acceptable character; for example, a number, sign, decimal point, or backspace. The number of signs and decimal points are counted, and duplicates are reported. The signs must be the first character typed in order for it to be accepted. Notice also the check at the beginning of the method for the length of the string in the edit box. This method replaces the last invalid character it finds, which generates yet another EN_UPDATE message, which causes the method to be called again. The purpose of this check is to see if we're on the very first character—later I subtract 1 from the variable len to index into the string. Without this test, I'd be trying to use an index of –1 later in the code, which causes it to fail. Also, notice that I don't do anything to the string if it's valid, but fails the minimum/maximum test. You should provide code for that. I don't think it's a good idea to remove a completely valid string from the edit box—you might instead opt to remove the last character typed.

Some final words about this routine: It is possible to circumvent it completely by using the mouse to highlight a character, and then type in something bogus. If you're going to apply this to any of your code, you will need to address this issue. This can be done by trapping the mouse clicks and examining the user's response.

Summary

The edit box is a real workhorse, both in terms of data input and output. While it suffers from some limitations, it is a general-purpose tool well-suited for certain text-processing tasks. As you will see later in this book, the new RTF (Rich Text Format) edit control dramatically alters the development landscape when it comes to text processing. Now let's move on to another set of powerful controls for enhancing the user interface, listboxes and checklist boxes.

CHAPTER 4

Listboxes and Checklist Boxes

T his chapter presents two versatile and slightly related controls, the listbox and the checklist box. Each control belongs to a separate class, CListBox and CCheckListBox, respectively. You'll be exposed to most of the member functions of these classes, plus see how to incorporate them effectively into your designs. In addition, you will learn how to use these controls as owner-drawn. Owner-drawn controls are those for which the programmer is responsible for drawing instead of the framework. These allow you to greatly enhance the user interface by adding graphical elements (like icons) in addition to the text. While these are a lot more complicated than old-fashioned, plain-vanilla controls, they really add a nice touch to an application.

Listboxes

A listbox is a control that displays a list of items, such as a list of names or files. Listboxes can have one or more columns, and allow single or multiple selection modes. The selection modes allow the user to select one or more items from the listbox (although the more common operation is to select just one item). A listbox actually consists of two separate controls, an edit box portion and a listbox portion. The listbox portion is just that, a list of strings. Once the user clicks on a string, it is moved into the edit box portion and is thus selected.

Listboxes respond to both mouse clicks and keyboard entries. When a user clicks a string, or presses the spacebar while on an item in the listbox, the string is selected. This is indicated by highlighting the string in the listbox, and placing it in the edit box portion of the control. An item can also be selected by pressing a key that matches the beginning of a string in the listbox. For example, if a listbox contains the names

```
Jones
Johnson
Martin
```

and you press the letter M or m, the name Martin would be highlighted in the listbox, because this is the first entry that begins with the letter m.

Styles and Properties

The following are styles that you can set in App Studio for a listbox. While most of the meanings are self-evident, you should nevertheless read them carefully, as their usage may affect the behavior of your application when used in conjunction with other properties.

Border

Checking the Border property on the Style dialog box in App Studio draws a boarder around the listbox; this is the default property.

Sort

The Sort property automatically sorts all strings in the listbox. The LBS_SORT style is assigned to the box, which sorts strings when the strings are added via a LB_ADDSTRING message in one of the following two cases:

- The listbox is not owner-drawn.
- The listbox is owner-drawn but has the LBS_HASSTRINGS property.

The LBS_SORT style, when used with owner-drawn listboxes, has some unorthodox behavior. If the Sort property is specified but the Has Strings property is not, the listbox responds to WM_COMPAREITEM messages in order to ascertain where to add the string. Items added using the InsertString() function ignore the sort style.

In some situations, you may want to make a listbox invisible, and use it as an array for string data. As strings are added and deleted from the listbox, you don't have to worry about keeping your array sorted—the listbox does that for you. Because the control is marked as not visible, the user never sees the listbox.

Notify

The LBS_NOTIFY style specifies that notification messages (LBN_SELCHANGE) are to be sent to the parent window when the user makes a selection in the listbox. This style is the default, and should always be set. This style lets you respond to changes made to the listbox selection, mouse clicks, and so on.

Multicolumn

By default, listboxes display their items in a single column. You can change this by checking the Multicolumn checkbox in App Studio. This sets the style LBS_MULTI-COLUMN, which indicates the items will be displayed in more than one column. Use of this style should be restricted to items that are short in length and relatively few in number, such as font sizes. Another example of a multicolumn listbox is the directory window that File Manager displays. This listbox can only be scrolled horizontally.

There are two ways to set the column width for a multicolumn listbox. You can send a listbox a LB_SETCOLUMNWIDTH message and stipulate the width, or you can have the listbox calculate its own width. In this case, the default width is 15 times the average character width for the current font used in the listbox. If the listbox has the owner-drawn style, the column width is set when the listbox is created and in response to a WM_MEASUREITEM message. If the listbox is owner-drawn, it cannot be combined with the Variable flavor of the owner-drawn style, only the fixed. If the LBS_OWNER-DRAWVARIABLE style is used with the LBS_MULTICOLUMN, then the LBS_OWN-ERDRAWVARIABLE style is ignored. Lastly, a multicolumn listbox has special scrolling properties; please refer to the following sections on horizontal and vertical scrolling for information on this behavior.

Vertical Scrolling

Vertical scrollbars are assigned to a listbox in App Studio using the Properties Dialog Box. When the <u>V</u>ert. Scroll box is checked, which assigns the WS_VSCROLL property to the listbox, a vertical scrollbar will be displayed whenever there are more items in the listbox than what can be shown (unless the listbox is multicolumn, as discussed earlier). Even if the WS_VSCROLL style was not assigned, the listbox will still scroll—it just won't display the scrollbars. Clearly, allowing a listbox to scroll without a scrollbar should be avoided so as not to confuse the user.

Horizontal Scrolling

Horizontal scrollbars are assigned to a listbox in App Studio using the Properties Dialog Box. When the <u>H</u>orz. Scroll box is checked, the listbox is assigned the WS_HSCROLL property. Note that the scrollbar is not shown when the listbox is displayed, even if WS_HSCROLL is set. Also, the WS_HSCROLL style causes the vertical scroll style to be set—a single-column listbox can't have a horizontal scrollbar without a matching vertical bar. If the listbox is a multicolumn box and you fail to set this property, the result is a listbox that can only be scrolled horizontally with the keyboard. On the other hand, if the listbox in question is a single-column box and you want to scroll horizontally, you will need to set the *horizontal extent* of the box. Objects created from class CListBox have an extent property, which oversimplified, is the horizontal scrolling *range* of the box. Your applications must set this property for horizontal scrolling. Let's look at an example.

Suppose your listbox is wide enough to display 20 characters at a time, and each character is 8 pixels wide. The listbox can display 160 pixels (20 × 8). Now you add a string to the listbox that is, say, 60 characters long. Because the listbox can only show 20 characters at once, you'll need to scroll 40 characters (6020). Now you need 320 pixels (40 × 8). For the entire 60 characters, you need 480 (60 × 8) pixels; you need to set the horizontal extent of the listbox to this or a greater value. This means you need to watch what your application does when dynamically adding items to such a listbox. When the items going into the listbox are not fixed-length strings, it may be necessary to compare the current extent with the new one, and select the greater of the two values. Class CListBox has two member functions for reading and writing the horizontal extent. These are SetHorizontalExtent() and GetHorizontalExtent(), prototyped as

```
void SetHorizontalExtent(int cxExtent);
int GetHorizontalExtent()const;
```

where cxExtent is the horizontal extent, in pixels. When the listbox is first created, this value is 0. Whenever the extent is 0, a horizontal scrollbar is never displayed. This is why the bar is not seen even though the style WS_HSCROLL was set. In the previous example of a 20-character display box, the extent would have to be set to a value greater than 160 (20 × 8 pixels) in order to show the scrollbar.

No Redraw

By default, a listbox updates it visual qualities whenever changes are made to the box. If you check the No Redraw box in App Studio, the listbox will not redraw itself when you add to or delete strings from the listbox. This is sometimes a desirable effect because it can eliminate flicker during certain listbox operations. Your application can switch this property on and off by sending a WM_SETREDRAW message to the listbox using the CWnd::SendMessage() function with the wParam set accordingly. The prototype is

```
LRESULT SendMessage(UINT message,WPARAM wParam,LPARAM lParam)
```

If wParam is TRUE when a listbox receives the WM_SETREDRAW message, it sets the redraw flag for the box and the background is erased during the redraw. In this case, the flicker cannot be avoided. If it is FALSE, it clears the redraw flag for the listbox. The less drawing your application has to do, the better. The following guidelines are suggested for minimizing the redrawing of listbox objects.

1. Clear the redraw flag for the box by a WM_SETREDRAW message with wParam set to FALSE.

2. Change the listbox—add, delete, insert, and so on.

3. Set the redraw flag using another WM_SETREDRAW message with wParam TRUE.

4. To guarantee a proper visual appearance after the update operation(s), call InvalidateRect() with the fErase parameter set to TRUE.

Here is an example. The following sample code, which assumes a member variable has been assigned to the listbox in Class Wizard, deletes all the items in a listbox, then adds the names of the 50 states, assumed to be stored in lpStates[].

```
m_ListBox.SendMessage(WM_SETREDRAW, FALSE, 0L); // turn off redraw
m_ListBox.ResetContent();// delete all strings
for(int j=0; j < 50; j++)// loop thru all 50 states
m_ListBox.AddString(lpStates[j]);// add strings to list box
m_ListBox.SendMessage(WM_SETREDRAW, TRUE, 0L);// turn on redraw
m_ListBox.InvalidateRect(NULL, TRUE);// repaint background
```

This approach helps make the application more pleasing to use by eliminating the flicker normally associated with redrawing the control.

Use Tabstops

Specifying the Use Tabstops option sets the LBS_USETABSTOPS style, which results in the listbox recognizing and expanding tab characters when drawing strings. By default, this option is not checked in App Studio. Tab positions are set every 32 dialog box units. These units are actually one-fourth of a character's width, in pixels, in the current font. You can change these positions by using a LB_SETTABSTOPS message if necessary.

Want Key Input

The Want Key Input option, which by default is not checked in App Studio, is used whenever your application has some special keyboard processing requirements. It gets a little convoluted, because its behavior depends on a lot of minutia (Is the listbox owner-drawn? Does it have the LBS_HASSTRINGS style?, and so on). When this option is selected, the listbox assumes the LBS_WANTKEYBOARDINPUT style. Now for a shot at an explanation.

When a listbox with this style has the input focus and a key is pressed, the box generates either a WM_VKEYTOITEM or WM_CHARTOITEM message, which you can trap in a Class Wizard message handler. Which message gets sent? It depends on whether the listbox is owner-drawn or not. A regular listbox with the LBS_HASSTRINGS style should trap the WM_VKEYTOITEM message. An owner-drawn listbox must process the WM_CHARTOITEM message. Both messages can be selected in Class Wizard, regardless of the settings made in App Studio. Make sure you trap the right one for your application.

Disable No Scroll

The Disable No Scroll option, also unchecked in App Studio by default, assigns the LBS_DISABLENOSCROLL style to the listbox. This property disables all scrollbar operations when used with the WS_VSCROLL and/or WS_HSCROLL styles. The net effect of this style is that listbox scrollbars remain *visible*, even if the current items fit the listbox. Normally, scrollbars for a listbox are hidden when not needed—this style obviates this behavior. This style is not compatible with Windows version 3.0.

No Integral Height

The No Integral Height listbox style first appeared in Windows version 3.0. It specifies that a listbox's size is identical to that specified by the application when the listbox was created. This style, which is a Boolean data type, is set by default to TRUE when the listbox is added in App Studio. This style lets the listbox be resized by the user without considering the height of the system font.

Selection Modes

In App Studio, there are three styles that affect the mode by which items may be selected from a listbox: single, multiple, and extended. By default, the style is set to single, which allows only one item to be selected at a time. To allow the user to select more than one item, select the Multiple option from the Selection: combo box in App Studio. This assigns the style LBS_MULTIPLESEL to the listbox. Such a listbox is identical to a regular listbox, except the user can select more than one item at a time from the listbox.

The Extended style allows the user to select either one or several contiguous items from the listbox.

Visible

The Visible style, which by default is checked in App Studio, determines if the listbox can be seen in the dialog box.

Using an invisible listbox has its advantages, at least in certain situations. You will see an example of this later in the chapter when I demonstrate owner-drawn listboxes.

Listbox Operations

This section looks at some of the most common operations performed on listboxes, and explores the class member functions used in the operation.

Allocating Memory for Listboxes

The CListBox class provides a member function for allocating memory for a listbox. This is InitStorage(), prototyped as follows:

```
int InitStorage(int nItems, UINT nBytes);
```

The parameter nItems is the number of items to add to the listbox, and nBytes is the amount of memory to allocate for item strings. If the call is successful, the return value is the maximum number of items that the listbox can store before a memory reallocation is needed; otherwise, LB_ERRSPACE, meaning not enough memory, is available. This function should be called before adding a large number of items to a listbox. This function helps to speed up listbox initialization for listboxes with more than 100 items. By allocating memory for the items, subsequent calls to AddString(), InsertString(), or Dir() execute more quickly. If you're not sure how much to allocate, it is best to err on the side of caution, and ask for more than you think you'll need.

NOTE For Windows95, nItems is limited to 16-bit values, meaning a listbox cannot contain more than 32,767 items. Although the number of items is limited, the total size of the items is limited only by the amount of available memory.

Adding a String

You can add a string to a listbox by using the AddString() function, prototyped as

```
int AddString(LPCSTR lpszItem)
```

where lpszItem is the NULL-terminated string to be added. The return value is LB_ERR if an error occurs, or LB_ERRSPACE if you attempt to exceed the listbox's storage space. If the listbox has the LBS_SORT property, the string appears at the proper position in the listbox. If the box is not sorted, the string is appended to the end of the list of items currently in the listbox.

Inserting a String

Strings are inserted into a listbox using InsertString(), prototyped as follows:

```
int InsertString(int nIndex,LPCSTR lpszItem)
```

where nIndex is the index of the position at which the string is inserted. If nIndex is –1, the string is appended to the end of the list. The parameter lpszItem is the string that is to be inserted. If the listbox has the LBS_SORT style, using InsertString() does *not* cause the listbox to be sorted; in other words, it can destroy the sort order if not used properly.

The return value is the index into the listbox in which the string was inserted. It is LB_ERR if an error occurs, or LB_ERRSPACE if there is not enough space to store the new string (that is, exceeding the 64k limit of a listbox).

Finding a String

There are two functions available for finding a string in a listbox, FindString() and FindStringExact().Their prototypes are

```
int FindString(int nIndexStart,LPCSTR lpszItem) const
int FindStringExact(int nIndexStart, LPCSTR lpszItem) const
```

where nIndexStart is the index of the item at which the search is to commence. If the string is not found when the end of the list is reached, then the search continues from the top of the list down to item nIndexStart. Set nIndexStart to –1 to search the entire listbox from the top. In both flavors, the search is independent of case, and the string lpszItem is considered a prefix. The return value is LB_ERR if the string was not found, or the index if a prefix match was found. In other words, if lpszItem is "John" and the listbox contains the names

```
Jones
Johnson
Martin
```

then FindString() would return 1, the index for Johnson, because it matches the string John. This means you must be careful both in how you search, and how you test the return value.

Be advised that FindString() only tells you if a string is in the listbox beginning with the prefix specified in lpszItem. It does not change the listbox selection (the edit box portion of the control)—use SelectString() for this purpose.

If you use FindStringExact() with an owner-drawn listbox that does not have the LBS_HASSTRINGS style, then the function tries to match the double-word value of each listbox item against the value of lpszItem.

Deleting a String

To remove a string from a listbox, use the DeleteString() function, prototyped as follows:

```
int DeleteString( UINT nIndex)
```

where nIndex is the index of the string to be deleted. The return value is the number of strings left in the listbox, or LB_ERR if an error occurs (for example, specifying an invalid index).

Clearing a Listbox

You can completely clear a listbox by using the ResetContent() function, which is prototoyped as

```
void ResetContent()
```

Be careful using both this function and DeleteString(), because once an item is deleted, you'll have to reload it to get it back—this is a lot of work as well as a symptom of a poor design.

The Dir Member

The Dir member function is used to retrieve a list of drives and or directories into a listbox. It is prototyped as follows:

```
int Dir( UINT attr, LPCSTR lpszWildCard)
```

where attr is a combination of file status flags identical to those found in Table 4.1. The second parameter, lpszWildCard, is a string describing a file specification; wildcards such as *.* or *.bak are supported. The return value is a zero-based index into the listbox of the last file added by the Dir() function, or LB_ERR or LB_ERRSPACE if an error occurs.

The Dir() method is quite powerful in that it allows you to quickly populate listboxes with specified files, or disk drives. This is useful when your application's documents have a specific file extension (for example, .prj); you can fill a listbox with only files used by the application.

Table 4.1   The Dir() attr Parameter Values

FLAG	MEANING
0x0000	File is read/write.
0x0001	File is read-only.
0x0002	File is hidden and does not appear in a directory listing.
0x0004	File is a system file.
0x0010	The name specified by lpszWildCard is a directory.
0x0020	File has been archived.
0x4000	Include all the drives that match the name specified by lpszWildCard.
0x8000	Exclusive flag; only files of specified type are listed.

Owner-Drawn Listboxes

Now for the fun stuff, drawing your own listboxes. Owner-drawn listboxes, while they entail more work, add a professional touch to an otherwise mundane user interface. This section walks through the steps to create an owner-drawn listbox that supports bitmaps. The example is a listbox that has the directories of the current device; these will have a folder bitmap to their left, arranged in a hierarchical fashion. The full example appears on the companion Web site in the Example1 project—choose Controls from the main menubar, then Listboxes and Ownerdrawn.... When selected, this displays a dialog box that has a listbox populated with your current path—you will see the directories above and below you, as shown in Figure 4.1.

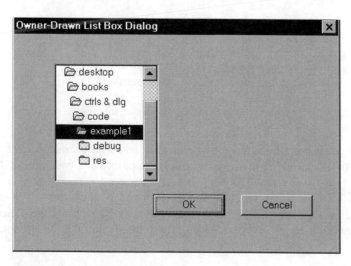

Figure 4.1   An owner-drawn listbox.

The technique for owner-drawn listboxes is basically the same for any other control: Add the control in App Studio, mark it as OWNERDRAWN, and add a message handler in response to a WM_DRAWITEM message. Because this example is a little more involved, let's talk about some of its peculiarities.

First, because bitmaps are used to represent the directory level, these must be identified in resource.h, and installed in the \RES directory. I have three bitmaps: one for the directory above, one for the directory below, and one for the current directory. These MUST be ordered in the resource.h file as follows:

```
#define IDB_FLDCLOSE            10
#define IDB_FLDOPEN             11
#define IDB_FLDSEL              12
```

The names aren't important—you can label your bitmaps anything you like. I've kept them in numerical sequence so they can be loaded into an array using a loop.

Another trick is to add an invisible listbox to the dialog box that contains the owner-drawn listbox. This box gets populated with the raw data returned by the Dir() function. Next, each string is fetched from this invisible box, processed and assigned a bitmap, and moved into the visible, owner-drawn listbox. It's nothing more than a convenient buffer, or working array. The invisible listbox has the SORT property, while the visible box does not. This enables us to show the directory as a hierarchy, with indentation for directories under the current directory.

There are two main workhorses for this example, which may be found in the ownlist.cpp and ownlist.h files. These are InitDirListBox(), which initializes the owner-drawn listbox with the current directory, and OnDrawItem(), which does the actual drawing of the listbox and its contents. Take a look at the following code segments.

```
BOOL COwnList::OnInitDialog()
{
    CDialog::OnInitDialog();
    // TODO: Add extra initialization here
    char szCurDir[_MAX_PATH];// get current directory
    _getcwd(szCurDir, _MAX_PATH);
    InitDirListBox(&m_List, &m_Invisible, szCurDir); // init. list box
    //
    return TRUE; // return TRUE unless you set focus to a control
}
```

When the dialog box is initialized, the application gets the current directory and passes it to InitDirListBox(). By making the current directory a parameter, you can call it from different locations in your code. The next message we need to respond to in Class Wizard is WM_CREATE. This is where I load the bitmaps for the folders. The following code is called by MFC when it's time to create this dialog box. Since the dialog box is now being created, it is necessary to load up the bitmaps that will be used so they will be available for the life of the dialog.

```
int COwnList::OnCreate(LPCREATESTRUCT lpCreateStruct)
{
```

```
    if (CDialog::OnCreate(lpCreateStruct) == -1)
        return -1;


    // TODO: Add your specialized creation code here
    int i;
    for (i=IDB_FOLDERMIN; i<=IDB_FOLDERMAX; i++)
        if((BmpFolders[i-IDB_FOLDERMIN]=LoadBitmap(lpCreateStruct->
hInstance, MAKEINTRESOURCE(i)))==NULL)
                AfxMessageBox("Load of folder bitmaps failed",MB_OK);
    return 0;
}
```

When OnCreate() is called, the bitmaps that will be used in the listbox are loaded. A final reminder: The resource IDs for IDB_FOLDERMIN et al. must be in numerical order in resource.h. The message box in the error trap is minimalist coding and for your benefit as the programmer—your application would naturally have a more elegant error recovery mechanism. Now let's look inside the method that does all the grunt work, except for the actual drawing, InitDirListBox(). You might want to just scan through the code, picking out the major pieces from the comments. I'll give you an explanation of its workings following the listing.

```
void COwnList::InitDirListBox(CListBox* hList,CListBox* hTempList,LPSTR
    pszDir)
{
    UINT    cch, nCount;
    UINT    i, nItem, iIndent;
    LPSTR   psz, pszLast;
    Char    ch;
    Char    szDir[_MAX_DIR];
    BOOL    fFirst=TRUE;
    // ------------------------------------------------------------
    //
    if (NULL==hList || NULL==pszDir)
        return;     // no list box or path!!

    cch=lstrlen(pszDir);    // length of the path string
    // If a path ends in a backslash, remove it
    if (pszDir[cch-1] == '\\')
        pszDir[cch-1]=0;
    //
    //  Clear out all the listboxes.
    //
    m_List.ResetContent();
    m_Invisible.ResetContent();
    //
    // Parse the path, look for a backslash. When one is found,
    // add the path name (in lowercase) between this '\' and the last.
    //
    pszLast=AnsiLower(pszDir);
    //
    //    Save this for changing directories
```

```
//
hList->SetWindowText(pszDir);
//
//    Save the directory & append with "\*.*"
//
wsprintf(szDir, "%s\\*.*", pszDir);

while(1)
{
    psz=_fstrchr(pszLast, '\\');

    if(psz)
    {
    // Store each character as read. If this is the first one,
    // its the root, so we retain the '\'.
        if (fFirst)
            ch=*(++psz);
        else
            ch=*psz;

        *psz=0;
    }
    else
    {
        // If I'm looking at a drive only, append a backslash
        if (pszLast==pszDir && fFirst)
            lstrcat(pszLast, "\\");
    }
    //
    //  Add the drive string--including the last one
    //  where psz is NULL
    //
    nItem=(UINT)(hList->AddString(pszLast));
    //
    //  Figure out how much indentation to use for displaying the
    //  directory structure, and select the appropriate bitmap.
    //  The high word of nItem indicates the bitmap, the low word
    //  has the amount of indentation.

    i= (psz != NULL) ? IDB_FOLDEROPEN : IDB_FOLDEROPENSELECT;
    hList->SetItemData(nItem,MAKELONG(nItem,i));

    if (NULL==psz)
        break;

    // Restore the last character read.
    *psz=ch;
    psz+=(fFirst) ? 0 : 1;

    fFirst=FALSE;
    pszLast=psz;
}  // end while loop thru all the directories
```

```
    //
    //  Get all directories using "Dir()", place in the invisible
    //  list box. Remove the brackets from the directory name,
    //  etc. , and move into the visible list box with the right
    //  amount of indentation.
    //
    iIndent=nItem+1;

    //Get directories using Dir(); szDir is pszDir\*.*
    hTempList->Dir(DDL_DIRECTORY | DDL_EXCLUSIVE,"*.*" );
    nCount = hTempList->GetCount();

    for (i=0; i < nCount; i++)
    {
        cch = hTempList->GetText(i,(LPSTR)szDir);
        //  Skip directories beginning with "." or ".."
        if ('.'==szDir[1])
            continue;

        //  Strip off the ending ']'
        szDir[cch-1]=0;
        //
        // Add the string to the real directory list, which
        // must be UNSORTED!
        //
        nItem = hList->AddString((LPCSTR)(szDir+1));
        hList->SetItemData(nItem,MAKELONG(iIndent, IDB_FOLDERCLOSED));
    }
    //
    //  Now have the list box redraw itself--this will
    //  call OnDrawItem()
    //
    hList->SendMessage(WM_SETREDRAW, TRUE, 0L);
    hList->InvalidateRect(NULL, TRUE);
    //
    //  Checking vertical scrolling range. If there is a vertical
    //  scroll bar, there are more items in the list box than can be
    //  displayed at once. Set the directory "above" the current one
    //  as the first in the list box.
    //
    hList->GetScrollRange(SB_VERT, (LPINT)&i, (LPINT)&nItem);

    if (!(i == 0 && nItem == 0))
        hList->SetTopIndex( max((int)(iIndent-2), 0));

    //  Now make the current directory the current selection
    hList->SetCurSel( iIndent-1);
    return;
}        // end InitDirListBox()
```

This method begins by parsing the string passed in, the current directory path. The root is extracted from this string—the remainder of the string is run through a chopping loop, after first flushing the visible, and invisible, listboxes. This method also illustrates using the SetItemData() method to piggyback data around the listbox entry to the drawing method. In this case, it's the bitmap and the amount of indentation to use for drawing. Many controls give you these 32-bits for free—you can use them to add a nice bit of spit and polish to even the most prosaic application. After the while loop breaks, the SetItemData()method forces a call to OnDrawItem() by invalidating the listbox rectangle. The last thing it does is check if the current directory passed requires a vertical scrollbar. If it does, then the directory above the current directory is scrolled into the top position of the listbox.

I've got one more major chunk of this puzzle to explain, and that is the drawing method, OnDrawItem(). Don't worry, most of the heavy lifting is done. Here's a quick look at the method that does the dirty work—scan it and I'll see you on the other side.

```
void COwnList::OnDrawItem(int nIDCtl, LPDRAWITEMSTRUCT lpDrawItemStruct)
{
    char        szItem[40];      // list box item entry
    int         iType=0;
    int         iIndent=0;       // amount of indentation for entry
    DWORDdw;                     // the free 32-bit ItemData for the entry
    BITMAP      bm;
    HBITMAP     hBmp;            // bitmap for the entry
    COLORREF    crText, crBack;  // foreground/background colors
    //
    if (nIDCtl == IDC_LIST1)     // get item data for owner-drawn list box
        dw= m_List.GetItemData(lpDrawItemStruct->itemID );

    //Get text string for this item (controls have different messages)

    m_List.GetText(lpDrawItemStruct->itemID, (LPSTR)szItem);
    //
    //  is this item in the SELECTED state?
    //
    if ((ODA_DRAWENTIRE | ODA_SELECT) & lpDrawItemStruct->itemAction)
    {
        if (ODS_SELECTED & lpDrawItemStruct->itemState)
        {
            //Select the appropriate text colors
            crText = SetTextColor(lpDrawItemStruct->hDC,
                        GetSysColor(COLOR_HIGHLIGHTTEXT));
            crBack = SetBkColor(lpDrawItemStruct->hDC,
                        GetSysColor(COLOR_HIGHLIGHT));
        }

        /*
         * References to the two bitmap arrays are the only external
         * dependencies of this code.  To keep it simple, I didn't use
         * a CImageList item...
         */
```

```
        //For directories, indentation level is 4 pixels per indent.
        //
        iIndent = 4*(1+LOWORD(lpDrawItemStruct->itemData));
        hBmp = BmpFolders[HIWORD(lpDrawItemStruct->itemData,
                 IDB_FOLDERMIN];
        //
        // get bitmap of list box entry
        //
        GetObject(hBmp, sizeof(bm), &bm);

        /*
         * Paint the text and the rectangle in whatever colors.  If
         * we're drawing drives, iIndent is zero so it's ineffective.
         */
        ExtTextOut(lpDrawItemStruct->hDC,
            lpDrawItemStruct->rcItem.left+bm.bmWidth+4+iIndent,
            lpDrawItemStruct->rcItem.top, ETO_OPAQUE,
            &lpDrawItemStruct->rcItem, szItem,lstrlen(szItem),
            (LPINT)NULL);

        //Go draw the bitmap we want.
        DrawBitmap(lpDrawItemStruct->hDC, lpDrawItemStruct->
            rcItem.left+iIndent, lpDrawItemStruct->rcItem.top,
            hBmp, RGB(0,0,255));
        //Restore original colors if we changed them above.
        if(ODS_SELECTED & lpDrawItemStruct->itemState)
        {
            SetTextColor(lpDrawItemStruct->hDC, crText);
            SetBkColor(lpDrawItemStruct->hDC,    crBack);
        }
    }
    //
    //  Does this item have the FOCUS ?
    //
    if ((ODA_FOCUS & lpDrawItemStruct->itemAction) || (ODS_FOCUS &
lpDrawItemStruct->itemState))
        DrawFocusRect(lpDrawItemStruct->hDC, &lpDrawItemStruct->rcItem);

    return;
}
```

The drawing method begins by getting the 32-bit item data value for the given listbox item. Notice how it also checks the ID of the control. Keep in mind these examples are simple; you can easily have a method that will be required to service several owner-drawn controls. Next, the string for the listbox item is fetched, and the control is checked to determine its state (selected, has focus, and so on). Based on the state, the item is drawn using its bounding rectangle. The colors to use are obtained from the user's installation, so there is no need to hard-code any new values.

This discussion of owner-drawn listboxes has pretty much given you the complete overview of how you'll be using the owner-drawn property of other controls later in this chapter, and in this book. If you haven't read the documentation of the lpDraw-

ItemStruct structure, you should do so at once. Everything you'll need for drawing an item is in there, from coordinates of the rectangle to the handle to the device context. Let's wrap up this look at owner-drawn listboxes by showing you one other trick: How to ghost out a listbox entry.

Disabling a Listbox Entry

Listboxes are a great way to show the user a long list of options; great that is, until you have to show one (or more) of the options as being *present*, but *unavailable*. A classic example is fonts. Suppose you have two listboxes: one has a list of font names, the other has font sizes. However, not all fonts support all sizes. Thus, you would still want the user to know that a font exists, but that the size is unavailable. This could be done by showing the unavailable size as grayed, or dimmed. This section walks you through the steps for disabling a listbox entry using the font name/size model. In the example, you'll see a dialog box with a combo box (which has the font names) and a listbox (which has the font sizes). When the font name Courier is selected, the font size 10 point is grayed out. Figure 4.2 illustrates the dialog box from the sample program from the companion Web site (Example1 program).

Selecting another font name un-dims the 10 point entry in the listbox. Most of the code in this example concerns managing the graying and ungraying, and not the actual graying process itself. The code may be found on the companion Web site, in the files listdemo.cpp and listdemo.h. These files are pretty short, and I strongly suggest taking a closer look at them to better understand what is going on here; that is, some of the variables that appear in the functions are declared global (for example, hBrush, bFlag). In addition, there are member variables (m_FSize) associated with the controls that were created using Class Wizard. To simplify matters even more, this procedure does not draw a listbox selection with the normal blue background, although you can easily add this.

The Basics

The first thing you'll need to do is create the listbox, and assign it the styles LBS_OWN-ERDRAW and LBS_HASSTRINGS. In App Studio, select Fixed when setting the

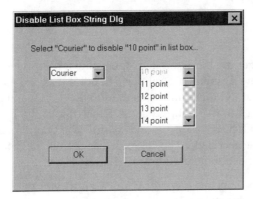

Figure 4.2   Disabling a listbox entry.

Owner Draw style for this example. To keep things simple, I'll show all the listbox entries with the same size, and with the same font.

There are two ways to do the actual graying. One is to use the function GrayString(), and the other is to use SetTextColor(), which uses the color returned by the call to Get-SysColor(), as follows:

```
COLORREF rgbGray;      // return value
rgbGray= GetSysColor(COLOR_GRAYTEXT);   // won't work if rgbGray=0!
```

If rgbGray is 0, you must use GrayString(). A return value of 0 indicates the video device does not support a solid gray color. The function GrayString() will be covered later in this chapter in the discussion for the OnDrawItem() routine.

The first thing we have to do is create a brush to be used as a parameter to GrayString(). According to the documentation, this brush is ignored; nevertheless, it must be created. This is done in response to a WM_ONCREATE message, as follows:

```
int CListDemo::OnCreate(LPCREATESTRUCT lpCreateStruct)
{
    if (CDialog::OnCreate(lpCreateStruct) == -1)
    return -1;

    // TODO: Add your specialized creation code here
    COLORREF rgbGray;
    rgbGray= GetSysColor(COLOR_GRAYTEXT);
    if(rgbGray)
        hBrush= CreateSolidBrush(rgbGray);
    else
        hBrush= CreateSolidBrush(RGB(128,128,128));
    return 0;
}
```

This module includes the code for using GetSysColor(), should you decide to use it in your applications.

Next, fill the listbox with some fictitious point sizes. This is done in OnInitDialog(), which appears next.

```
BOOL CListDemo::OnInitDialog()
{
    CDialog::OnInitDialog();

    // TODO: Add extra initialization here
    //
    CenterWindow();
    //
    //  Populate the list box with a list of fictitious font sizes
    //
    char szFont[16];
    memset(szFont,0,sizeof(szFont));
    for(int i= 10; i < 30; i++)
    {
```

```
        wsprintf(szFont, "%d point",i );
        m_FSize.AddString(szFont);
    }
    //
    //  Whenever initialized, make sure not "Courier" and
    //  not grayed out--set combo box text & bFlag
    //
    m_FName.SetWindowText("Arial");
    bFlag= FALSE;
    return TRUE;  // return TRUE unless you set the focus to a control
}
```

Because this is a sample application, I populated the combo box with the names of the fonts while working in App Studio—you could have done the same here, in OnInit-Dialog().

The listbox items are drawn in the function OnDrawItem(), as follows:

```
void CListDemo::OnDrawItem(int nIDCtl,LPDRAWITEMSTRUCT lpDrawItemStruct)
{
    // TODO: Add your message handler code here and/or call default
    //
    char szItem[16];
    memset(szItem,0,sizeof(szItem));   // a clean string!
    //
    m_FSize.GetText(lpDrawItemStruct->itemID, (LPSTR)szItem);
    //
    //
    if((bFlag) && (strcmp(szItem,"10 point")==0))
    {
        //   Now for my demo:  if user selects the Courier font from
        //   the combo box, gray out the 10 point font size...
        //
        GrayString(lpDrawItemStruct->hDC, hBrush, NULL,(LONG)szItem,
8,0,0,0,0);
    }
    else
    {
        SetTextColor(lpDrawItemStruct->hDC,RGB(0,0,0));  //black
        ExtTextOut(lpDrawItemStruct->hDC, lpDrawItemStruct->
rcItem.left,lpDrawItemStruct->rcItem.top,ETO_OPAQUE,&lpDrawItemStruct->
rcItem, szItem,lstrlen(szItem), (LPINT)NULL);
    }
    //CDialog::OnDrawItem(nIDCtl, lpDrawItemStruct);
}
```

The last line of this method was commented out—it was placed there by Visual C++ as the default (which I have overwritten). The main concern is with the call to GrayString(). I've used the non-MFC version of this function for simplicity's sake. This function grays the text by first writing it to a memory bitmap, graying the bitmap, and then copying the bitmap into the display context using the current font. The text is grayed irrespective of the type or color of brush specified. The function is prototyped as follows:

```
BOOL GrayString(hDC,hBrush, gsprc,lParam,cch,x,y,cx,cy)
```

where hDC is the handle to the device context, hBrush is the handle of the graying brush, and gsprc is the address of a callback function. If this is NULL, Windows uses the TextOut() function instead of GrayString(). Parameter lParam is the string to be grayed, and cch is the number of characters to draw. If cch is –1, and the return value from the callback function is 0, the item is shown, but is not grayed. The next four parameters, x, y, cx, and cy, describe the bounding rectangle of the string: x is the horizontal position, y the vertical, cx is the width, and cy is the height. The return value is TRUE if the function executed successfully or FALSE if one of the following conditions occurs:

- The TextOut() function returned zero.

- The callback function returned zero.

- There was insufficient memory to create the memory bitmap for graying.

The next method responds to selections made in the font name combo box. This doesn't have anything to do with actually drawing the listbox item—we just need to know if the user has selected the font called Courier. If so, the flag bFlag is set to TRUE, and the string 10 point is removed and immediately reinserted back into the font size listbox. This is for the case when the user has previously selected Courier, and now selects another font name—we want the string 10 point to no longer be grayed, and this is a quick-and-dirty way of doing it. Here is the method:

```
void CListDemo::OnSelchangeFontCombo()
{
    // TODO: Add your control notification handler code here
    int fontindex;

    fontindex= m_FName.GetCurSel();// Arial= 0,Courier = 1, see DEMO.RC
    if(fontindex== 1)     // picked Courier
        bFlag= TRUE;
    else
        bFlag= FALSE;
    //
    //    next 2 lines are a quick-n-dirty way to toggle string
    //
    m_FSize.DeleteString(0);
    m_FSize.InsertString(0,"10 point");
}
```

The last step is to release the memory allocated for the brush. This is freed when the dialog box is destroyed, as shown in the following function.

```
void CListDemo::OnDestroy()
{
    CDialog::OnDestroy();
```

```
      // TODO: Add your message handler code here
      DeleteObject(hBrush);
   }
```

While this procedure may have seemed like a lot of work, it really isn't. You need to keep in mind that graying out a listbox item is easy, but you'll need lots of ancillary code to manage the process of graying and ungraying. With a little practice, you'll have the hang of it in no time.

There is a unique common control that combines the properties of a listbox with that of a checkbox, the checklist box. This control allows an application to more efficiently manage a list of options that can be selected or deselected by the user. Figure 4.3 shows a checklist box.

The primary advantage of this control is that it lets you put a lot of checkboxes on the screen without consuming a great deal of the screen's real estate. As with most controls, you can assign it the owner-drawn property and include meaningful bitmaps as visual cues to the user. The sample program demonstrates this aspect of the control.

A checklist box is created by using class CCheckListBox. The first thing you may notice if you're using Visual C++'s App Studio is that CCheckListBox isn't on the tool palette. A checklist box isn't created in the usual fashion. You must first create a class based on CCheckListBox, then call its Create() function. In order to create a checklist box, follow these steps:

1. Create a new class based on CCheckListBox (that is, a new .cpp and .h file).

2. Add the .cpp and .h files to your project.

3. Use the Create() member function of CCheckListBox where you want the checklist box.

The following code is a sample header file that demonstrates just how easy this is to do.

```
// ChkBox.h : header file
class CChkBox : public CCheckListBox
```

Figure 4.3 A checklist box.

```
{
    DECLARE_DYNAMIC(CChkBox)

// Constructors
public:
    CChkBox();
    BOOL Create(DWORD dwStyle,const RECT& rect,CWnd* pParentWnd,UINT
        nID);
    // Implementation
protected:

    // Generated message map functions
    //{{AFX_MSG(CChkBox)
    afx_msg virtual void OnDrawItem(LPDRAWITEMSTRUCT lpDrawItemStruct);
    //}}AFX_MSG
    DECLARE_MESSAGE_MAP()
};
```

This example is based on an owner-drawn checklist box; hence the OnDrawItem()
method in the message map. This is normally unnecessary, but as I mentioned earlier,
this is a slightly more elegant sample than the default implementation. The main point
is that you must use the DECLARE_DYNAMIC macro, and have a constructor as well
as the Create() member function. The .cpp file is almost just as simple.

```
// ChkBox.cpp : implementation file
//
#include "stdafx.h"
#include "ChkBox.h"// the class header file

#ifdef _DEBUG
#define new DEBUG_NEW
#undef THIS_FILE
static char THIS_FILE[] = __FILE__;
#endif

IMPLEMENT_DYNAMIC( CChkBox, CCheckListBox )

/////////////////////////////////////////////////////////////////////
// CChkBox

CChkBox::CChkBox()
{

}
BEGIN_MESSAGE_MAP(CChkBox, CCheckListBox)
    //{{AFX_MSG_MAP(CChkBox)
    ON_WM_DRAWITEM()
    //}}AFX_MSG_MAP
END_MESSAGE_MAP()

BOOL CChkBox::Create(DWORD dwStyle, const RECT& rect, CWnd* pParentWnd,
UINT nID)
```

```
{
    BOOL bVal;
    bVal= CCheckListBox::Create(dwStyle,rect,pParentWnd,nID);
    return bVal;
}


void CChkBox::OnDrawItem( LPDRAWITEMSTRUCT lpDrawItemStruct)
{
    // TODO: Add your message handler code here and/or call default

    CCheckListBox::DrawItem( lpDrawItemStruct);
}
```

You'll probably find it easiest to use Class Wizard to create these files, but any editor will do. No matter how you create them, just remember to add them to your project. The next step is to add the control to a window. Let's assume you'll be adding a checklist box to a dialog box. In the header file for your dialog box, include the header file for the checklist box class you created. In the sample code I used ChkBox.h in the DemoDlg.h file. Next, create a pointer member variable to a CCheckListBox object.

```
private:
    CChkBox * m_chkListBox;// the checklist box object!!
```

The last step is to allocate memory for the checklist box, and call the Create() function. You'll normally do this in the OnInitDialog() method for your dialog box class. Here's the example.

```
CDialog::OnInitDialog();
// TODO: Add extra initialization here
m_chkListBox = new CChkBox;// allocate memory for box

RECT rect;     // size & location of checked list box
this->GetClientRect(&rect);
int iWidth = rect.right-rect.left;
rect.top = 20;
rect.left= (iWidth/2)-75;
rect.right= rect.left+150;
rect.bottom= 150;
//
m_chkListBox->Create(LBS_OWNERDRAWFIXED | WS_CHILD | WS_VSCROLL |
WS_HSCROLL | WS_BORDER | WS_VISIBLE | LBS_HASSTRINGS, rect, this,
IDC_MYCHKLISTBOX);
```

The call to Create() is very important, so let's go over it in more detail. Take a look at the prototype for the method in the header file. This method takes four parameters: the style of the checklist box, a bounding rectangle to size it, a pointer to its parent window, and a resource identifier. You will always want to use the WS_CHILD and WS_VISIBLE styles. The LBS_OWNERDRAWFIXED style is used here because I wanted to make the control owner-drawn and include some graphics. And, because I'll be using text with these graphics, the LBS_HASSTRINGS style is used. The other styles are self-explanatory.

The values of the RECT parameter are purely discretionary—your application may need to do a little bit of number crunching here if your screen real estate is at a premium. Because this checklist box is going into a dialog box, I can simply use the *this* pointer (shown in bold) as the parent. The last parameter, IDC_MYCHKLISTBOX, is defined in the project's resource.h file. If you were to run this code as is, you would see the control in the dialog box without any text inside it. The CCheckListBox class has a member function for just that purpose; it's called AddString(). The sample program is limited to three choices, and initially set to NULL.

```
chkListBox->AddString(_T(""));
```

Although the use of the _T macro may seem superfluous here, it's a good idea to get in the habit of using it with all your strings. The main purpose of adding blank strings is to reserve memory for them, and make them available for drawing. Because this checklist box is owner-drawn, it will be necessary to manually control how the strings appear when the control is drawn. This will become clearer when I show you the OnDrawItem() method, which is next.

Drawing the Checklist Box

If you omit the LBS_OWNERDRAWFIXED style, the code in the previous section could be used to create a default checklist box, complete with the customary checkbox on the left side of the strings. But in keeping with my theme of showing you ways to spice things up, I've added a couple of bitmaps to an image list and "glued" them onto the end of the standard checkbox. These three bitmaps correspond to three disk drives: a floppy drive, a hard drive, and a CD-ROM drive, as shown in Figure 4.3. Now, things get a little more complicated. You have to manage the checkbox, the bitmap, and the string. Furthermore, you have to change the way the string appears when it is selected and/or unselected. The pseudocode for the entire drawing of the checkbox can be expressed as follows: First, check if the list box is being drawn. If so, call the default implementation of CDialog::OnDrawItem()—this draws the checkbox portion for you. These are 20 units wide, so the bounding rectangle for the bitmap will need to be shifted right by 20. Here is the beginning of the OnDrawItem() method:

```
void CDemoDlg::OnDrawItem(int nIDCtl, LPDRAWITEMSTRUCT lpDrawItemStruct)
{
    // TODO: Add your message handler code here and/or call default
    COLORREF crText, crBack;
    CString csLabel;
    //
    if(nIDCtl == IDC_MYCHKLISTBOX)
    {
        //
        CDialog::OnDrawItem(nIDCtl, lpDrawItemStruct);// draw stock item
        CRect rect = lpDrawItemStruct->rcItem;    // get bounding rect.
        CDC* pDC = CDC::FromHandle(lpDrawItemStruct->hDC);   // get a DC
        if (!pDC)
            return;
        int nOldDC = pDC->SaveDC();   // save current DC
```

Up to this point, you can see what's happening. The default OnDrawItem() is called to draw the checkbox, then the given checkbox item's bounding rectangle is saved. The

DrawItemStruct structure has everything needed to make this work. Here's what happens next:

```
if (ODS_SELECTED & lpDrawItemStruct->itemState)
{
    m_ImageList.SetBkColor(GetSysColor(COLOR_HIGHLIGHT));
}
m_ImageList.Draw(pDC,lpDrawItemStruct->itemID, CPoint(rect.left+20,
    rect.top+2), ILD_TRANSPARENT);
```

This checks to see if the item being drawn (one of the three strings/disk drives) is also selected. If it is, the background color of the image list is set to the color the user has specified as the highlight color for his or her Windows installation. This means you don't run the risk of changing the user's setup. Next, the bitmap itself is drawn—note that the rectangle has been adjusted horizontally by 20 units, and vertically by 2. Now I'm ready to "glue" the text onto the end of the bitmap. A switch() statement does this:

```
switch(lpDrawItemStruct->itemID)
{
    case 0:
        csLabel = "Floppy Drive";
        break;
    case 1:
        csLabel = "Hard Drive";
        break;
    case 2:
        csLabel = "CD-ROM Drive";
        break;
}   // end switch
rect.left += 40;
```

Here, the rectangle variable is again adjusted, this time by 40 units (20 for the checkbox, 20 for the bitmap). Because it's time to draw the text, it is necessary once again to check and see if the item is highlighted or selected.

```
if (ODS_SELECTED & lpDrawItemStruct->itemState)
{
    //Select the appropriate text colors
    crText=SetTextColor(lpDrawItemStruct->hDC,
        GetSysColor(COLOR_HIGHLIGHTTEXT));
    crBack=SetBkColor(lpDrawItemStruct->hDC,
        GetSysColor(COLOR_HIGHLIGHT));
}
pDC->DrawText(_T(csLabel), rect, DT_SINGLELINE | DT_BOTTOM | DT_LEFT);
//
//Restore original colors if we changed them above.
//
if(ODS_SELECTED & lpDrawItemStruct->itemState)
{
    SetTextColor(lpDrawItemStruct->hDC, crText);
    SetBkColor( lpDrawItemStruct->hDC, crBack);
}
pDC->RestoreDC(nOldDC);  // restore DC we saved earlier
```

That's it for drawing an owner-drawn checklist box. Because this dialog box allocated memory for the checklist box and the fonts created to show the text, it's necessary to release the memory when the dialog box is destroyed. That method is as follows:

```
void CChkList::OnDestroy()
{
    CDialog::OnDestroy();
    // TODO: Add your message handler code here
    m_SelFont.DeleteObject();
    m_UnselFont.DeleteObject();
    delete m_chkListBox;
}   // end OnDestroy()
```

The checklist box is a very handy way to compress a lot of yes/no options into a small space. Adding the bitmaps and the other owner-drawn features makes the user interface more intuitive and easier to use.

Summary

The listbox and checklist box are versatile controls well-suited for their specialized roles. Each provides a rich set of member functions to allow you to do just about anything you want. As you've seen, you can even use listboxes to sort strings for you by marking them as invisible. Although caution has to be exercised in cases like this (You wouldn't want an invisible control to also be in the tabbing order!), these provide simple shortcuts that can help you to build a better user interface. You'll see some of these techniques again later when we look at the cousin to the listbox, the combo box. In the next chapter, I'll give you a look at another way to enhance the user interface, by using and customizing the status bar.

CHAPTER 5

Status Bars

Another easy way to enhance the user interface is by adding status bars to your application. You've seen these before—the horizontal ribbons at the bottom of a parent window that consist of one or more panes. These can be used to display small, brief
messages to the user about the application or its status. A classic example is to provide
dynamic help to the user about menu options as well as the controls in a dialog box or
window. As the mouse cursor passes over a control, a help message is displayed in the
status bar that describes that control. For example, if the cursor passes over the OK button, the message might be "Click here to close this window," or something similar. An
example of using status bars in this capacity can be found on the companion Web site
under Example1. Status bars can also serve as the lazy man's debugger; you can display the values of variables here while you're developing your application.

There are two kinds of status bars, simple and multiple. A simple status bar has just
one pane, while a multiple status bar has separate windows (up to a maximum of 255)
into which you can insert text and/or graphics. A word of caution about simple status
bars: These do *not* support owner-drawn properties. Finally, an interesting property of
status bars involves the text they display. Text in simple mode is maintained separately
from the text displayed in multiple mode. In other words, you can set the text in a
simple mode status bar and later put it into multiple mode, and not have to reset the
text in any way.

This chapter explores the status bar—the properties you can assign, the class methods
available for your use, and how to use it to provide brief help messages to the user.
This will include a look at some actual working code from the Web site to help you get
your hands dirty.

73

Class CStatusBarCtrl

Beginning with MFC version 4.0, status bars are implemented using class CStatusBarCtrl, which encapsulates a Windows95 status bar control. For backward compatibility, MFC retains the older status bar implementation in class COldStatusBar. The class includes a wide range of styles that you can apply in addition to class methods for manipulating it in a variety of ways. Like the toolbar, the status bar is embedded in the parent frame window and constructed at the same time as the frame window. It is also automatically destroyed. With that in mind, let's take a look at the most important class method, Create(), which is prototyped as follows:

```
BOOL Create(DWORD dwStyle,const RECT& rect, CWnd* pParentWnd,UINT nID );
```

The parameters are all the usual suspects: style, size and position, parent window, and resource ID, respectively. The possible styles are as follows:

CCS_BOTTOM. Places the control at the bottom of the parent window's client area and sets the width to be the same as the parent window's width. Status bars have this style by default. Use this style for most applications.

CCS_NODIVIDER. Prevents the 2-pixel highlight at the top of the status bar from being drawn.

CCS_NOHILITE. Prevents a 1-pixel highlight from being drawn at the top of the status bar.

CCS_NOMOVEY. Causes the status bar to resize and move itself horizontally, but not vertically, in response to a WM_SIZE message. If you use the CCS_NORESIZE style, the CCS_NOMOVEY style does not apply.

CCS_NOPARENTALIGN. Keeps the status bar from automatically moving to the top or bottom of the parent window. Instead, it keeps its position within the parent window despite changes to the size of the parent window. If the CCS_TOP or CCS_BOTTOM style is also used, the height is adjusted to the default, but the position and width remain unchanged.

CCS_NORESIZE. Prevents the status bar from using the default width and height when setting its initial size or a new size. Instead, it uses the width and height specified in the request for creation or sizing.

CCS_TOP. Forces the status bar to position itself at the top of the parent window's client area and sets the width to be the same as the parent window's width. This style is rarely applied and should be used with discretion.

By default, the position of a status bar is along the bottom of the parent window, but you can specify the CCS_TOP style to have it appear at the top of the parent window's client area. You can also specify the SBARS_SIZEGRIP style to include a sizing grip at the right end of the status window. Combining the CCS_TOP and SBARS_SIZEGRIP styles is not recommended, because the resulting sizing grip is not functional even though the system draws it in the status window.

CStatusBarCtrl Class Methods

Besides Create(), there are lots of class methods that go with the status bar. The following is a review of the ones you're likely to use frequently, beginning with SetText(), prototyped as follows:

```
BOOL SetText(LPCTSTR lpszText, int nPane, int nType );
```

The first parameter, lpszText, is a NULL-terminated string to be displayed in the status bar pane represented by the second parameter, nPane. If the nPane parameter is 255, the status bar defaults to a simple type with just one pane. The last parameter, nType, specifies the type of drawing. It can have one of the values shown in Table 5.1.

When nType is SBT_OWNERDRAW, then the lpszText parameter represents 32 bits of data that you can use to specify certain drawing aspects, properties, among others. The return value of this method is nonzero if the call was successful, or zero if it failed.

The sister method to SetText() is GetText().

```
int GetText(LPCTSTR lpszText, int nPane, int* pType ) const;
```

All the parameters are the same as for SetText(), but notice that the last parameter is a pointer to the type. This lets you read the type: SBT_POPOUT, SBT_NOBORDERS, and so forth. The return value is the length, in characters, of the text (ANSI or Unicode).

Another related method is GetTextLength(), prototyped as follows:

```
int GetTextLength( int nPane, int* pType ) const;
```

This returns the length of the text in the specified pane as well as its type (notice the pointer on the last parameter).

The next method is SetParts(), used to divide the status bar up into panes and to set the coordinate of the right edge of each pane.

```
BOOL SetParts( int nParts, int* pWidths );
```

The parameter nParts is the number of panes (or parts) you wish to give the status bar. It must be less than 255; a value of 255 or more causes the bar to have only one pane. The parameter pWidths is the address of an integer array that has the client coordinates of the right edge of the pane. The size of this array must be the same as nParts,

Table 5.1 Values for SetText Drawing Type

VALUE OF NTYPE	MEANING
0	The text is drawn to appear lower than the plane of the status bar, and it has a border.
SBT_NOBORDERS	The text is drawn without borders.
SBT_POPOUT	The text is drawn with a border to appear higher than the plane of the status bar.
SBT_OWNERDRAW	The text is drawn by the parent window.

for obvious reasons. Setting any element in this array to –1 positions the right edge of that pane to the far right of the status bar. Be careful—if you want four panes but set the second element in the array to –1, you'll only get two panes because the –1 chews up all the remaining real estate for the panes. The return value of SetParts() is nonzero if successful; zero otherwise.

Right behind SetParts() is GetParts().

```
int GetParts( int nParts, int* pParts ) const;
```

This method returns the number of panes in the status bar if successful, or zero if the call failed. It also returns the coordinates of the pane specified by nParts into the parameter pParts. If the parameter nParts is greater than the actual number of panes, the array is populated with the coordinates of existing panes only.

To find the status bar's horizontal and vertical border widths, call GetBorders(), which comes in two flavors:

```
BOOL GetBorders( int* pBorders ) const;
BOOL GetBorders( int& nHorz, int& nVert, int& nSpacing ) const;
```

For the first type, parameter pBorders is the address of an integer array of three elements. The first takes the width of the horizontal border, the second the vertical border, and the last takes the width of the border between the panes. For the second variety, nHorz is the address of an integer that takes the width of the horizontal border, and nVert takes the vertical. The last parameter, nSpacing, is the width of the border between the panes. The return value is nonzero on success, zero if it failed. These class methods are most useful when doing complex owner-drawn operations.

Another drawing-related method is SetMinHeight(), which sets the minimum height of the status bar's drawing area.

```
void SetMinHeight(int nMin);
```

where nMin is the minimum height, in pixels, of the status bar.

Closely related is the GetRect() method.

```
BOOL GetRect(int nPane, LPRECT lpRect ) const;
```

This method retrieves the bounding rectangle for a status bar pane. The parameter nPane is the zero-based index of the pane to retrieve. The lpRect parameter is the address of a RECT structure that receives the coordinates of the rectangle. The return value is nonzero if successful, or zero if the call failed.

The last class method is SetSimple(), prototyped as follows:

```
BOOL SetSimple(BOOL bSimple = TRUE);
```

Use this function to specify if a status bar should display simple text or all the panes specified by a previous call to SetParts(). If the parameter bSimple is TRUE, the status bar displays simple text; if FALSE, it displays multiple panes. The return value is nonzero if successful; otherwise, it is zero. If the status bar is being changed from a multipane type to a simple type, the status bar is redrawn immediately.

Status Bar Messages

As you may already know, you can send messages to a status bar instead of calling a member function. This is sometimes necessary, and sometimes simply expedient. The following is a look at these messages, their meaning, and some examples. For the sample code, the variable pStatBar is assumed to be a pointer to the status bar, and hWndStatBar is its handle.

SBT_OWNERDRAW. The status bar is owner-drawn. You must add a message handler for WM_MEASUREITEM and WM_DRAWITEM. The CtlType, itemState, and itemAction members of the DRAWITEMSTRUCT structure are undefined (for status bars).

SBT_NOBORDERS. The text in the status bar is drawn without borders.

```
pStatBar->SendMessage(SB_SETTEXT,1 | SBT_NOBORDERS,
(long)"Text without borders.");
```

SBT_POPOUT. The text appears to be raised. For example,

```
pStatBar->SendMessage(SB_SETTEXT,2 | SBT_POPOUT,
(long)"This text pops out.");
```

HBT_SPRING. The text or bitmap in a simple status bar is allowed to grow (spring) beyond its minimum length if there is enough room on the status bar. A multiple status bar has this property by default; any extra room is spread out among the various sections. Notice that this type begins with the letters HBT, and not SBT. This is because it was originally created for header controls.

SB_GETBORDERS. This message is used to fetch the current width of both the horizontal and vertical borders of a status bar. These values establish both the spacing between the status bar and the outer edge of the parent window, and the interior space between the panes. The wParam parameter is not used and is set to zero. The lParam parameter is the address of an array of integers having three elements. The return value is TRUE if the call was successful, FALSE if not. For example,

```
BOOL bOk;
int iBorders[3];
bOk = pStatBar->SendMessage(SB_GETBORDERS,0,(long)(iBorders));
```

The first element in the array iBorders is the width of the horizontal border, the second is the width of the vertical border, and the last element is the width of the border between the panes of the status bar (for a multiple type status bar).

SB_GETPARTS. This message retrieves the number of panes in a status bar, plus the coordinate of the right side of the bar. The wParam parameter specifies the number of panes to fetch. If this value exceeds the actual number of panes, then the message fetches only the coordinates of the existing panes. The lParam parameter is the address of an array of integers, and the number of elements must be the same as wParam. Each element gets the client coordinate of the right edge of each corresponding pane. If you initialize an element with a –1, then the ridge edge of that pane is extended to the right edge of the status bar. The return value is the number of panes in the status bar if successful, zero if not. For example,

```
int nparts= 0;
int array[3];// wParam MUST be 3; see next line
nparts = pStatBar->SendMessage(SB_GETPARTS,3,(long)array);
```

SB_GETTEXT. This is a very useful message—it retrieves the text from a specified pane of a status bar. The wParam parameter is the number of the pane to fetch, and lParam is the address of a buffer to receive the text. The return value is a DWORD. The low-order word has the string length, the high-order word has the type of operation used to draw the text. The exception to this is if the type is SBT_OWNER-DRAW. In this case, the return value is the 32-bit value associated with the text. For example, suppose you wanted to fetch the text in the second pane.

```
LPSTR szText;

pStatBar->SendMessage(SB_GETTEXT,1,(long)szText);
```

The buffer szText would now contain the string "Text without borders."

SB_GETTEXTLENGTH. This message is used to retrieve the number of characters of the text in a status bar pane. The wParam parameter is an index specifying the pane, and the lParam is not used and is set to 0. The return value is a DWORD. The low-order word has the length of the text, the high-order has the drawing type used. Here's an example:

```
DWORD dwLenType;
dwLenType= pStatBar->SendMessage(SB_GETTEXTLENGTH ,1,0L);
int len = dwLenType & 0x0000ffff;
int type = dwLenType >> 16;
```

After this code executes, len is 21 (the length of "Text without borders."), and type is 256 (the value of SBT_NOBORDERS in commctrl.h).

SB_SETBORDERS. This message sets the widths for both the horizontal and vertical borders of a status bar; that is, they specify the spacing between the panes of a status bar and the outer edge of the window. The wParam parameter is not used and is set to zero. The lParam parameter is the address of an array of integers with three elements. When the message executes, this array will contain the width of the horizontal border in the first element, the width of the vertical border in the second, and the distance between the panes inside the status bar in the third. If you pass in a –1 for any of these, the default width is used. The return value is TRUE if successful, FALSE if not. For example,

```
BOOL bOk;
int iBorders[3];
iBorders[0]= 2;
iBorders[1]= 2;
iBorders[2]= -1;
bOk = pStatBar->SendMessage(SB_SETBORDERS,0,(long)(iBorders));
```

Here, the horizontal and vertical border spacing is set to 2 pixels and the distance between the panes is set to the system default.

SB_SETMINHEIGHT. This sets the minimum height of a status bar, in pixels. Specify the minimum height in the wParam parameter. The lParam parameter is not used and is set to zero. There is no return value.

SB_SETPARTS. This is how you create a multiple-pane status bar. The wParam parameter is set to the number of panes desired, up to a maximum of 255. The lParam parameter is the address of an array of integers that contain the position, in client coordinates, of the right edge of each pane. If an element is initialized to –1, then the right edge for that pane extends to the right edge of the window. This means you will probably never set an interior pane to a –1, since this will overwrite the rest of the panes. But, it is handy to set the last element to a –1. It's like telling the last pane to take up as much room as it can. The return value is TRUE if the call was successful, FALSE if not.

SB_SETTEXT. This message is used to insert text into the status pane, and to define how the text is to be drawn. This message is used for both simple and multiple-pane status bars, with some slight variation. For a multiple-pane bar, the wParam parameter is the index of the pane to use. The drawing type is also set here using a Boolean OR. The lParam is the address of the buffer containing the text to insert into the pane. The return value is TRUE if the text was successfully set, FALSE if not. Here is an example:

```
pStatBar->SendMessage(SB_SETTEXT,2 | SBT_POPOUT,
(long)"This text pops out.");
```

For a simple status bar (only one pane), set wParam to 255.

SB_SIMPLE. This message is somewhat misleading. On the surface, it would appear that SB_SIMPLE is used to define a simple status bar. Actually, you can use it to make both types of status bars. If the wParam parameter is TRUE, the status bar is a simple one. If FALSE, it's a multiple status bar. The lParam parameter is not used in either case, and should be set to zero. The return value is TRUE if the call was successful, FALSE if not.

That wraps up using the status bar messages. Now for the fun part: looking at some real code.

The Sample Program

The sample program, found in Example1 on the companion Web site, demonstrates many of the class methods discussed previously, including the owner-drawn feature. A status bar with four panes is created, and added to a modal dialog box. You'll find the code in the files StatDlg.cpp and StatDlg.h. The output is shown in Figure 5.1.

The dialog box in this figure is used to illustrate how to add a toolbar to a dialog box or window. This portion is covered in Chapter 7, "Toolbars." Here is the code, taken from the CStatDlg::OnInitDialog() message handler. I've expanded on the comments throughout the code to help you understand what is happening.

```
hBmp = ::LoadBitmap(AfxGetInstanceHandle(),
MAKEINTRESOURCE(IDB_BITMAP1));
```

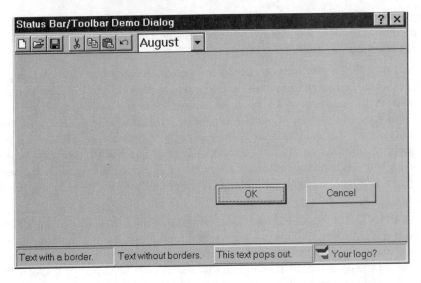

Figure 5.1 The status bar sample program.

Because I'm using a bitmap in one of the panes, this line simply loads the bitmap and makes it available. The next several lines obtain the size of the dialog box so that the status bar can be sized and positioned.

```
//
int nTotWide;// total width of status bar
//
CRect rect;
this->GetWindowRect(&rect);
rect.top = rect.bottom-25;
m_bRvStatOk = m_StatBar.Create(WS_CHILD | WS_BORDER | WS_VISIBLE,
    rect,this,IDC_STATUSBAR);
//
if (m_bRvStatOk == NULL)
{
    AfxMessageBox ("Status Bar not created!", NULL, MB_OK );
}
```

The status bar has now been created (or not). I've added some very weak error trapping here and there, just to remind you that in a real application, you'll need to watch for these possibilities.

```
//
//get size of window, use to configure the status
//bar with four separate parts
//
CRect rWin;
this->GetWindowRect(&rWin);
nTotWide = rWin.right-rWin.left;
//
// Make each part 1/4 of the total width of the window.
```

```
//
m_Widths[0] = nTotWide / 4;
m_Widths[1] = nTotWide / 2;
m_Widths[2] = nTotWide - m_Widths[0];
m_Widths[3] = -1;
//
m_StatBar.SetMinHeight(25);
m_StatBar.SetParts( 4, m_Widths);
```

This section of code sets the size of each pane. The width of the host dialog box is divided into four equal parts, giving each pane one-fourth of the total. Notice that the last pane's width is –1. Recall that this simply means to stretch this pane all the way to the right.

```
//
// now lets put some text, different styles into parts of status bar
//
m_StatBar.SetText("Text with a border.", 0,0);
m_StatBar.SetText("Text without borders.",1,SBT_NOBORDERS);
m_StatBar.SetText("This text pops out.",2,SBT_POPOUT);
//
//make the last part owner-drawn, add a bitmap
//
m_StatBar.SetText(NULL,3, SBT_OWNERDRAW);
```

It's the last pane that requires special attention, since it is owner-drawn. Here is the OnDrawItem() method for this class:

```
void CStatDlg::OnDrawItem(int nIDCtl, LPDRAWITEMSTRUCT lpDrawItemStruct)
{
    //
    // Draw bitmap in status bar
    //
    HDC hdcMem;// device context for memory
    HGDIOBJ hbmOld; // old bitmap area we're over-writing
    BITMAP bm;// bitmap we're using
    //
    // Create a compatible DC in memory
    //
    hdcMem = CreateCompatibleDC(lpDrawItemStruct->hDC);
    // Select the "logo.bmp" bitmap into the DC.
    hbmOld = ::SelectObject(hdcMem, hBmp);
    // Get the size of the bitmap
    ::GetObject(hBmp, sizeof(bm), &bm);
    //
    // Blt the bitmap to the part.
    //
    BitBlt(lpDrawItemStruct->hDC,lpDrawItemStruct->rcItem.left,
        lpDrawItemStruct->rcItem.top, bm.bmWidth, bm.bmHeight,
        hdcMem, 0, 0,SRCCOPY);
    //
    // Add some text & get bounding rectangle, position & display text
    //
    char szText[16];
```

```
RECT rText;   // text rectangle
rText.left = lpDrawItemStruct->rcItem.left+24;
rText.top  = lpDrawItemStruct->rcItem.top;
rText.right = lpDrawItemStruct->rcItem.right-20;
rText.bottom = lpDrawItemStruct->rcItem.bottom;
//
//  add some text after the logo bitmap here
//
memset(szText,0,sizeof(szText));
strcpy(szText,"Your logo?");// text to draw
//
//
SelectObject(lpDrawItemStruct->hDC,GetStockObject(ANSI_VAR_FONT ));
::SetBkColor(lpDrawItemStruct->hDC, 0x00c0c0c0); // set bkg. color
ExtTextOut(lpDrawItemStruct->hDC, lpDrawItemStruct->rcItem.left+24,
    lpDrawItemStruct->rcItem.top+4, ETO_OPAQUE, &rText, szText,
    strlen(szText),NULL );// draw the text in the rectangle rText
//
// End adding text. Reselect the original object into the DC.
//
SelectObject(hdcMem, hbmOld);
// Delete the compatible DC.
DeleteDC(hdcMem);
}    // end OnDrawItem()
```

The only hocus-pocus here is the line

```
::SetBkColor(lpDrawItemStruct->hDC, 0x00c0c0c0); // set bkg. Color
```

The color value, 0x00c0c0c0 is the equivalent of RGB(192,192,192), which is the standard light-gray color used by Visual C++ to draw a dialog box.

This method does its work in an orderly fashion. The memory device context (DC) is created, the icon to draw is loaded, and then it is moved into the DC by the BitBlt() function. Fortunately, the lpDrawItemStruct parameter that gets passed in by MFC provides us with a lot of help. We can easily find the bounding rectangle where the icon and text will be displayed. All that's left to do is get a font, set the background color, and display the text using ExtTextOut(). To finish up, the original DC is restored, and we delete our memory DC.

That's one use for status bars, but they can also be used to give the user some hints about other controls, or even regions of the screen. In other words, they become a forum for help messages.

Status Bars and Help Messages

This section looks at the technique of displaying help messages in the status bar pane. There are two cases here, both of which are implemented in the project Example1, found on the companion Web site. The first details the steps for updating the status bar attached to the main window's frame, and the second demonstration uses a modal dialog box.

Menu Help in the Status Bar

When you build a Windows application with Visual C++, you get menu item help for free. Also known as flyby help, the main frame window's status bar is automatically updated with a help message when the cursor visits a menu item. All you have to do is supply the text for the message in the Pro_mpt edit box using the Properties dialog box. Figure 5.2 shows the Properties dialog box for one of the menu options for the Example1 project found on the companion Web site.

This practice is encouraged—not only does it help the user, but it can help you recall design features while developing the software.

Control Help in the Status Bar

Another way to enhance the user interface is by dynamically updating the frame window's status bar with help messages. In other words, as the user moves the cursor among the controls on a dialog box, a help message appears in the application's main window status bar. This is really a modified version of tool tips, but it does have some unique properties that you may wish to incorporate. The primary unique property is that the user doesn't have to ask for help—the application volunteers it in the hope of stopping the user from going to the help file. This is another disk access, and it slows your program down. Furthermore, it can frustrate the user if he or she is compelled to search the help file often. This breaks the user's concentration, which in turn impedes his or her progress even more. By displaying a brief message about the functionality of a control when the mouse cursor is over it (or when it has the keyboard focus), the user can easily read your explanation of the control in a status bar pane. The source code for the upcoming example can be found in the class files StatHelp.cpp and StatHelp.h in Example1 on the companion Web site. The dialog box for this example is shown in Figure 5.3.

In a nutshell, the basic idea behind this technique is to override the WM_SETCURSOR message in Class Wizard, check if the cursor is over a control (as opposed to the dialog box itself), and if so, update the application's status bar with a message. The only trick comes in creating the help messages—you must add strings to your application's string table giving them the same resource ID as the control. For example, the sample code has an edit box identified as IDC_EDIT1; you'll find a string in the string table

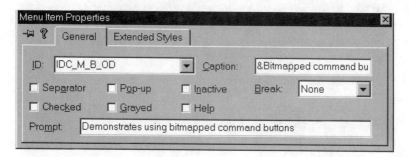

Figure 5.2 Adding flyby help using the Properties dialog.

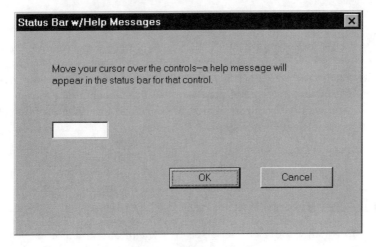

Figure 5.3   Dialog box for control help in the status bar.

with the exact same ID. This lets you create custom messages, and better manage the custodial aspects of developing your application.

The following is taken from StatHelp.cpp.

```
BOOL CStatHelp::OnSetCursor(CWnd* pWnd, UINT nHitTest, UINT message)
{
    // TODO: Add your message handler code here and/or call default
    // if the cursor is not over a child window control, revert
    // to the default status bar text

    if(pWnd == this)      // mouse not over a control
        SetPaneText();
    else                  // mouse over a control, set text
        SetPaneText(pWnd->GetDlgCtrlID());

    return CDialog::OnSetCursor(pWnd, nHitTest, message);
}
```

As you can see, all the work is done in SetPaneText(), which gets passed the resource ID of the control. This is why they need to have the same ID—you can piggyback the message by using the control's ID found by the call to GetDlgCtrlID(). Here is the code for SetPaneText():

```
void CStatHelp::SetPaneText(UINT nID)
{
    if(nID == 0)
        nID = AFX_IDS_IDLEMESSAGE;
    CWnd * pWnd= AfxGetMainWnd()-
>GetDescendantWindow(AFX_IDW_STATUS_BAR);
    if(pWnd)
    {
```

```
        AfxGetMainWnd()->SendMessage(WM_SETMESSAGESTRING, nID);
        pWnd->SendMessage(WM_IDLEUPDATECMDUI);
        pWnd->UpdateWindow();
    }
}   // end SetPaneText()
```

This is where the rubber meets the road. The first thing this method does is check if nID is zero, which means the cursor is not over a control. In this event, the ID of the control is set to AFX_IDS_IDLEMESSAGE. The next thing this does is obtain a pointer to the main window's status bar, and then send the status bar a message that displays the help message (if any). It's short and sweet, with only one caveat: Be sure to include the following headers:

```
#include <afxpriv.h> // for WM_SETMESSAGESTRING and WM_IDLEUPDATECMDUI
#include <afxres.h>  // for AFX_IDW_STATUS_BAR
```

You might want to place these inside your application's CWinApp header file, or in stdafx.h, in order for it to be used by any dialog (my example restricts it to only the CStatHelp class). This technique is very appealing for the simple reason that it gives the user constant feedback. The only drawback is that the user may opt to switch off the status bar from the main menubar, effectively rendering the whole thing an exercise in futility. There are several things you could probably do in this situation if this is a problem (like disabling the ability to hide the status bar!).

Summary

The status bar is a versatile control easily added to any window. The panes can be used to provide not only immediate, dynamic help, but also feedback about the state of the keyboard (for example, NUM LOCK, CAPS) and the application. The owner-drawn property is useful for adding your company logo or other graphic. Now let's look at another control you're sure to use often, the combo box.

Combo Boxes

T his chapter looks at one of the most versatile controls in MFC, the *combo box*. This control shares a lot of the properties and behaviors of its cousin, the listbox. Combo boxes are great additions to applications that require the user to select data, rather than enter data manually. Although this capability limits use to situations where there are few choices from which to select, combo boxes perform very well when they can be used. Like the list-box, the combo box can be owner-drawn, and this chapter includes some code that demonstrates this feature. Let me begin by explaining the combo box, examining the different styles of combo boxes you can create, and the impact of the style on the application.

The Combo Box

The combo box is a combination of two separate controls, the edit box and the listbox. Actually, the class CComboBox supports either an edit box or a static control, but my emphasis will be on the edit box variety, because it is the most widely used and provides more services. The edit box portion can be used as a key or index into the listbox portion because as you type characters in the edit box, the listbox automatically scrolls to any matching entries. For example, if the listbox contains surnames, and you type "Joh," the listbox scrolls to the first hit that begins with these characters. Thus, if the listbox contains names like "Johnson," the edit box portion lets you find these quickly.

The entries in a combo box are selected by using the arrow keys, or clicking with the mouse. When a string is selected, it is displayed using the user's default text highlight color, and appears in the edit box portion of the control. If you use App Studio to add a combo box to a dialog box, be sure you size the drop-down box so that the entries are visible. This can easily be adjusted while you're in App Studio. Also while in App Studio, you can add the data held by the combo box by selecting the combo box and clicking on

87

the Data tab of the Properties dialog box. In the multi-line edit box enter each string followed by CTRL-ENTER. If the data in the combo box will be used elsewhere in your application, then you may wish to keep the data in a file or serialize it. You can use the AddString() method to add strings to a combo box. This and the other class methods are discussed in more detail later in this chapter.

Styles and Properties

There are three styles of combo boxes: simple, drop-down, and drop-down list. Table 6.1 compares these styles.

The following is a more detailed look at the types of combo box styles that you can apply.

CBS_SIMPLE. The listbox is displayed at all times. The current selection in the listbox is displayed in the edit control.

CBS_DROPDOWN. Similar to CBS_SIMPLE, except that the listbox is not displayed unless the user selects an icon next to the edit control.

CBS_DROPDOWNLIST. Similar to CBS_DROPDOWN, except that the edit control is replaced by a static-text item that displays the current selection in the listbox.

CBS_AUTOHSCROLL. This style automatically scrolls the text in the edit control to the right when the user types a character at the end of the line. If this style is not set, only text that fits within the rectangular boundary is allowed.

CBS_HASSTRINGS. An owner-drawn combo box that contains items consisting of strings. The combo box maintains the memory and pointers for the strings so the application can use the GetText() member function to retrieve the text for a particular item.

CBS_OEMCONVERT. Text entered in the combo box edit control is converted from the ANSI character set to the OEM character set and then back to ANSI. This ensures the characters are properly converted when the application calls the AnsiToOem() Windows function to convert an ANSI string in the combo box to OEM characters. This style is most useful for combo boxes that contain filenames, and applies only to combo boxes created with the CBS_SIMPLE or CBS_DROPDOWN styles.

CBS_OWNERDRAWFIXED. The owner of the listbox is responsible for drawing its contents; the items in the listbox are all the same height.

CBS_OWNERDRAWVARIABLE. Similar to CBS_OWNERDRAWFIXED, the owner of the listbox is responsible for drawing its contents, but the items in the listbox can have different heights.

Table 6.1　Combo Box Styles

STYLE	LISTBOX VISIBLE?	STATIC OR EDIT CONTROL?
Simple	Always	Edit
Drop-down	Only when button is clicked	Edit
Drop-down list	Only when button is clicked	Static

CBS_SORT. This style causes all the strings inserted into the combo box to appear sorted.

CBS_DISABLENOSCROLL. The listbox shows a disabled vertical scrollbar when the listbox does not contain enough items to scroll. Without this style, the scrollbar is hidden when the listbox does not contain enough items.

CBS_NOINTEGRALHEIGHT. This style specifies that the size of the combo box is exactly the size specified by the application when it created the combo box. Normally, Windows sizes a combo box so that the combo box does not display partial items.

There are plenty of combo box styles available to suit your needs, many of which bear a striking resemblance to class CListBox.

CComboBox Class Methods

Let's explore the most important or most frequently used class methods for combo boxes.

The first method is Create(). This is prototyped as follows:

```
BOOL Create(DWORD dwStyle,const RECT& rect,CWnd* pParentWnd,UINT nID );
```

The return value is a nonzero value (including negative numbers!) if the call to Create() was successful; otherwise, it is zero. The first parameter, dwStyle, is the style, any meaningful combination presented in the previous section. The second parameter, rect, is the bounding rectangle for the control, its size and position on the parent window. The third parameter, pParentWnd, is the parent window and cannot be NULL. The last parameter is the resource ID assigned to the combo box.

In addition to the combo box styles (which have the prefix CBS_), you can use the window styles, which have the prefix WS_, shown in Table 6.2.

The next method is GetCount(), used to determine the number of items in the combo box.

```
int GetCount() const;
```

Table 6.2 Additional Window Styles Used with Combo

STYLE	WHEN TO USE
WS_CHILD	Always use this style with Create().
WS_VISIBLE	Used to display the combo box—almost always use this style.
WS_DISABLED	Used to disable a combo box—special use only.
WS_VSCROLL	Adds a vertical scrollbar to the listbox portion of the combo box.
WS_HSCROLL	Adds a horizontal scrollbar to the listbox portion of the combo box.
WS_GROUP	Use to group controls.
WS_TABSTOP	Use to place the combo box in the tabbing order.

The return value is the number of items in the combo box, or CB_ERR if an error occurs. CB_ERR is defined as –1, so I suggest you test for CB_ERR explicitly. Also, don't forget that items in the combo box have zero-based indexes. Thus, if you have three strings in a combo box, and you use GetCount() to find the number of strings in order to retrieve the last one, remember to subtract 1 from the returned value. In this example, the return value is 3, so you would use an index of 2 to find the last string. Any reference to an index in this section automatically means zero-based.

One method you'll use frequently is GetCurSel(), prototyped as follows:

```
int GetCurSel( ) const;
```

The return value is the index of the item currently selected in the listbox portion of the combo box. It is CB_ERR if nothing has been selected.

Closely related to GetCurSel() is the SetCurSel() method.

```
int SetCurSel(int nSelect);
```

This method is used to select a string from the listbox portion of the combo box, scroll it into view if necessary, and place it in the edit box portion of the combo box. The return value is the index of the item if the call was successful, or CB_ERR if the call failed. The parameter nSelect is the index of the string to select. You can set this to CB_ERR to clear the edit box and remove the selection state of the listbox item.

Another method for selecting characters in the edit box portion of a combo box is SetEditSel().

```
BOOL SetEditSel(int nStartChar, int nEndChar);
```

The parameter nStartChar specifies the starting position into the string. The parameter nEndChar specifies the ending position. If either of these parameters is set to –1, any previous selection or highlighting is removed. These parameters are also zero-based. For example, if the edit box string contains the word Tennessee, and you set the parameters to 0 and 5, then the letters Tenne would be highlighted. The return value for this member function is nonzero if the call was successful; otherwise, it is zero. A third return value, CB_ERR (–1), is possible if the combo box does not include a listbox or was created with the CBS_DROPDOWNLIST style.

A very important property of combo boxes is that each entry has a 32-bit value associated with it that you can use for any purpose imaginable. A common example is using these bits to reference a bitmap that might get displayed with the combo box item. There are two class methods for this item data, one to read the item and one to write it. These are, respectively:

```
DWORD GetItemData(int nIndex) const;
int SetItemData(int nIndex, DWORD dwItemData);
```

The parameter nIndex is the zero-based index of the combo box item, and dwItemData is the 32-bit value that you supply. The return value is CB_ERR if an error occurs.

The only caveat to using these functions is when dwItemData is a pointer to type void. In this case, you must use the following related methods.

```
void* GetItemDataPtr(int nIndex) const;
int SetItemDataPtr(int nIndex, void* pData);
```

The parameter nIndex remains the same. The parameter pData is the pointer associated with the item. This pointer stays valid for the life of the combo box, even if the item's position inside the combo box changes as a result of an addition or deletion. So while nIndex can change, pData remains reliable. The return value is CB_ERR for all of these methods if an error occurs.

There are two methods to add a string to a combo box, depending on your desired outcome. The easiest way is to use AddString().

```
int AddString(LPCTSTR lpszString );
```

This adds the NULL-terminated string lpszString to the combo box. If the CBS_SORT style was used, the string is inserted to the listbox portion of the combo box, and the list is sorted. The new string is added in alphabetical order. If the CBS_SORT style was not used, the string is added to the end of the list. The return value is the zero-based index of the string into the combo box, or one of the following error codes.

CB_ERR. A general error occurred.

CB_ERRSPACE. There was insufficient space available for adding the new string.

The second method for adding a string is to use InsertString().

```
int InsertString(int nIndex, LPCTSTR lpszString);
```

The parameter nIndex is the zero-based index where you want the string inserted. The parameter lpszString is the added string. The return values are the same as described for AddString(). If you set nIndex to –1, the string is added to the end of the list. Unlike AddString(), this member function doesn't sort the list even if CBS_SORT was specified.

To remove a string from the listbox portion of a combo box, use DeleteString().

```
int DeleteString(UINT nIndex);
```

The parameter nIndex is the zero-based index of the string to delete. The return value is the count of the remaining strings in the list, or CB_ERR if you set nIndex to a value greater than the number of items in the list, minus 1. For example,

Right:

```
m_SomeCombo.DeleteString(m_SomeCombo.GetCount()-1);
```

Wrong:

```
m_SomeCombo.DeleteString(m_SomeCombo.GetCount());
```

Remember, GetCount() is not zero-based, so you have to subtract 1 to convert the index to zero-base.

If you want to completely flush the listbox portion of the combo box, use ResetContent().

```
void ResetContent( );
```

This not only deletes all the strings from the listbox, but also clears the edit box portion of the combo box.

Searching a Combo Box

Searching for a string in a combo box is a complicated process. There is a distinct difference between searching for a string and selecting a string. *Searching* for a string indicates if the string is present somewhere in the listbox portion of the control, while *selecting* a string means that you not only found the string, but you placed it in the edit box portion. Let's take a look at the member functions available for these purposes.

The FindString() method is prototyped as follows:

```
int FindString(int nStartAfter, LPCTSTR lpszString) const;
```

This method finds, but does not select, the first string in the listbox that contains the prefix indicated by the parameter lpszString. The parameter nStartAfter is the zero-based index of the string from where the search is to begin. If this is –1, the entire listbox is searched from the beginning. For example, suppose a combo box contained the following three strings:

```
John
Johnson
Johnston
```

Then assume you called FindString() as follows:

```
m_SomeComboBox.FindString(-1,"Johns");
```

The return value would be 1, since this is the first string in the listbox that matches all five characters.

Closely related to FindString() is FindStringExact().

```
int FindStringExact(int nIndexStart, LPCTSTR lpszFind) const;
```

The parameters and their meanings are the same as for FindString(). Using the same data as in the previous example, the call

```
m_SomeComboBox.FindStringExact(-1,"Johns");
```

would now return CB_ERR, since there is no string "Johns" in the listbox. But, the following would return zero.

```
m_SomeComboBox.FindStringExact(-1,"JOHN");
```

Notice the string is in uppercase; the searching is thus case-insensitive. Both of these methods find, but they don't select, the target string. To select the target string, you must use SelectString().

```
int SelectString(int nStartAfter, LPCTSTR lpszString);
```

This method is almost identical to FindString() in the manner in which it operates, except that if the string is found, it is copied into the edit box portion of the combo box. But you need to be careful—if you want to find an exact match, and select it, you must first call FindStringExact() to get its index, then use SelectString().

To delete or clear the current selection (if any) from the edit box portion of the combo box, use the Clear() method.

For example:

```
m_SomeComboBox.Clear();
```

When this statement executes, whatever string was in the edit box side of the combo box will be erased. Of course, searching a combo box is not the end of the story. You may want to use the Windows Clipboard with them too.

Clipboard Methods

The combo box class methods include two functions that can be used to move text from the current selection to the Clipboard.

The Copy() method copies the current selection (if any) from the edit box portion of the combo box to the Clipboard. The text is copied in CF_TEXT format. The second method is Cut(). This method cuts or deletes the current selection (if any), and copies the text onto the Clipboard in CF_TEXT format.

The Sample Program

The sample code on the companion Web site includes an owner-drawn combo box example. The project is called Example1, and the pertinent files are ComboDlg.cpp and ComboDlg.h. This demo program populates an owner-drawn combo box with all the disk drives found on the user's PC. The output, based on my machine, is shown in Figure 6.1.

The dialog box consists of an owner-drawn combo box and an invisible listbox that is used to hold the sorted list of drives. I chose to demonstrate the Dir() class method simply because it was the most utilitarian, and offered the most details. For example, there are five types of disk drives that can be installed.

- A floppy drive
- A hard drive
- A CD-ROM drive
- A network drive
- A RAM drive

To be completely accurate, there are seven possible values that can be returned when interrogating the system configuration. They are defined as follows:

```
#define DRIVE_UNKNOWN      0
#define DRIVE_NO_ROOT_DIR  1
#define DRIVE_REMOVABLE    2
#define DRIVE_FIXED        3
#define DRIVE_REMOTE       4
#define DRIVE_CDROM        5
#define DRIVE_RAMDISK      6
```

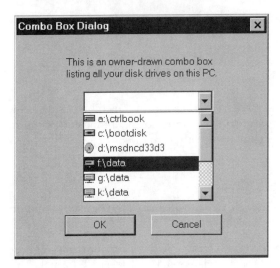

Figure 6.1 Sample output from the combo box example.

After locating the drive, the sample program also gets the volume label, converts it to lowercase, and adds it to the string identifier. Using my machine (which is on a network) as an example, the C: drive is displayed as

```
C:\bootdisk
```

(I labeled my C drive BOOTDISK for this example). But there's more to it than that: What if there's no disk in the floppy or CD-ROM drives? In this case, the call to Get-VolumeInformation() would fail, causing a system message box to appear. Not a desirable effect! To work around this problem, I first shut off all critical errors, loop through all the drives, and then restore the default error mode when I'm finished.

```
UINT uiPrevErrMode = SetErrorMode(SEM_FAILCRITICALERRORS);
//
for (i=0; i < numDrives;  i++)
{
    // loop thru all disk drives, etc
}
SetErrorMode(uiPrevErrMode); // restore default error mode
```

The reason I bring this up is that you *always* have to think through what you're doing when you build your user interface, and nip potential errors in the bud.

There are three major components to the sample program. The method DriveType() is used to identify the type of disk drive that was found. This method has one parameter, a string representing the drive letter. This parameter is in the format [-x-], where x is the drive letter. The drive letter is stripped out and converted to the format x:\; it is this new format that is passed to GetDriveType() to identify the drive type. The two other major players are InitDriveList() and OnDrawItem(). Since these do all the heavy lifting, let me walk you through them now.

The InitDriveList() Method

The InitDriveList() method does the work of finding the disk drives and saving them in an invisible listbox. The method takes two parameters, a pointer to the combo box and a pointer to the invisible listbox. The method is called from OnInitDialog(), which also creates the CImageList object that has all the necessary bitmaps. The bitmaps are presented in order, beginning with DRIVE_REMOVEABLE described previously . As a disk and its type is found, the type is piggybacked into the 32-bit item data of the listbox item using SetItemData(). Later, the disk drive's corresponding bitmap can be located in the CImageList object simply by subtracting 2 (the value of DRIVE_REMOVEABLE) when the process is reversed with GetItemData(). I'll discuss this in more detail later in the section on the OnDrawItem() method. Now, here is the InitDriveList() method in its entirety:

```
void CComboDlg::InitDriveList(CComboBox* hCombo,CListBox* hTempList)
{
    UINT           i, iItem;
    UINT           numDrives;
    UINT           iDrive, iType;
    UINT           iCurDrive;       // the current, active disk
    char           szDrive[32];
    //
    // -------------- end variable declarations ----------------------
    //
    //Clear out all the lists.
    hCombo->ResetContent();          // the combo box
    hTempList->ResetContent();       // the invisible list box
    //
    //Install available drive letters in the invisible list box
    //
    hTempList->Dir(DDL_DRIVES | DDL_EXCLUSIVE,"*" );
    iCurDrive=_getdrive()-1;         //Fix for zero-based drive indexing
    //
    //Drives are returned in format "[-A-]", etc.  I now remove the
    //brackets & dash, get the volume ID, and determine what kind of
    //disk I have--floppy, hard, etc.  I select the appropriate disk
    //icon for the drive & add the entire thing to the combo box
    //
    numDrives= hTempList->GetCount();// get number of disk drives
    //
    char lpVolumeNameBuffer[16];// hold volume name
    memset(lpVolumeNameBuffer,0,16);// flush it; set error mode
    UINT uiPrevErrMode = SetErrorMode(SEM_FAILCRITICALERRORS);
    char szFullSpec[32];
    memset(szFullSpec,0,sizeof(szFullSpec));
    //
    for (i=0; i < numDrives;  i++)// loop thru all disk drives
    {
        hTempList->GetText(i, (LPSTR)szDrive);// get each string
        AnsiLower(szDrive);//  make lower case
        //
        iType=DriveType(szDrive);     //  Get drive type: floppy,etc
```

```
        if(iType == DRIVE_UNKNOWN)// not likely, but trap it anyway
            continue;
        //---- add volume label, if any
        strcpy(szFullSpec,szDrive);
        if(GetVolumeInformation(szDrive, lpVolumeNameBuffer,
          16,NULL,NULL,NULL,NULL,NULL))
           strcat(szFullSpec,AnsiLower(lpVolumeNameBuffer));
        else
            strcpy(szFullSpec,szDrive);
        //
        //  All set, add new string to combo box here
        //
        iItem= m_Combo.AddString(szFullSpec);
        //
        //
        m_Combo.SetItemData(iItem,MAKELONG(iItem, iType));
        //
        //  Set the current selection to the current disk
        if (iDrive==iCurDrive)
        m_Combo.SetCurSel(iItem);

    }// end loop thru all the disk drives
    SetErrorMode(uiPrevErrMode);// restore previous error mode
    return;
}               // end InitDriveList()
```

This takes care of finding all the drives, the drive types, and volume labels. The method for drawing the combo box is as follows:

```
void CComboDlg::OnDrawItem(int nIDCtl,
    LPDRAWITEMSTRUCT lpDrawItemStruct)
{
    COLORREF crText, crBack;
    DWORD dw;
    //
    CDC* pDC = CDC::FromHandle(lpDrawItemStruct->hDC);
    if (!pDC)
        return;
    //
    if ((ODA_DRAWENTIRE | ODA_SELECT) & lpDrawItemStruct->itemAction)
    {
        //
        // Get colors-selected disk shown with blue background, etc
        //
        if (ODS_SELECTED & lpDrawItemStruct->itemState)
        {
            //Select the appropriate text colors
            crText=SetTextColor(lpDrawItemStruct->hDC,
                GetSysColor(COLOR_HIGHLIGHTTEXT));
            crBack=SetBkColor(lpDrawItemStruct->hDC,
                GetSysColor(COLOR_HIGHLIGHT));
```

```
        }
        //
        // now draw the drive letter/spec...
        //
        char szItem[32];
        memset(szItem,0,sizeof(szItem));
        m_Combo.GetLBText(lpDrawItemStruct->itemID, (LPSTR)szItem);
        //
        //Draw the text & bounding rectangles with proper colors
        //  NOTE: ALWAYS draw the text first, then the bitmap!!
        //
        ExtTextOut(lpDrawItemStruct->hDC,
            lpDrawItemStruct->rcItem.left+20,
            lpDrawItemStruct->rcItem.top, ETO_OPAQUE,
            &lpDrawItemStruct->rcItem, szItem,
            lstrlen(szItem), (LPINT)NULL);
        //
        //get combo box item's data
        //
        dw= m_Combo.GetItemData(lpDrawItemStruct->itemID);
        //
        //Get the bitmap associated with the TYPE of disk drive
        //
        UINT iType=(int)HIWORD(dw);
        iType -= 2;// FD is 2, HD = 3, etc. Convert to 0-base
        //
        // now draw the bitmap
        //
        m_ImageList.Draw(pDC,iType,CPoint(lpDrawItemStruct->rcItem.left,
            lpDrawItemStruct->rcItem.top), ILD_TRANSPARENT);
        //
        //Restore original colors if we changed them above.
        //
        if(ODS_SELECTED & lpDrawItemStruct->itemState)
        {
            SetTextColor(lpDrawItemStruct->hDC, crText);
            SetBkColor(lpDrawItemStruct->hDC,    crBack);
        }
    }
    //
    return;
}    // end OnDrawItem()
```

The OnDrawItem() method begins by checking if the item in the combo box is selected. If it is, the system's highlight colors are used to draw the item. Next, the disk drive letter and volume label (if any) are drawn. The type of the drive is saved in the 32 bits of extra data which is a part of the combo box entry. By subtracting the value of 2 from this, the index into the image list is returned. The image list was prudentially set up such that the images appear in the same order as they are indexed by the framework. Note that the line

```
iType -= 2;
```

could have been written as

```
iType -= DRIVE_REMOVABLE;
```

After drawing the bitmap, the colors are restored back to the default if the item was selected.

Summary

That does it for the combo box. As you can see, it's very similar to the listbox, with which it shares many of its properties and methods. Owner-drawn combo boxes like the one demonstrated in this chapter are specially suited for those applications that have a narrow set of options from which to choose. If your list of options starts getting fairly long, you may be better off using a listbox. The combo box will appear in Chapter 7, "Toolbars."

CHAPTER 7

Toolbars

A toolbar is a horizontal ribbon of buttons located at the top of a window. These objects belong to class CToolBarCtrl, and are often used as shortcuts to menu options by way of command buttons. But buttons are not the only control you can place in a toolbar; you can also add other controls such as combo boxes and listboxes, among others. This chapter demonstrates how to add controls to a toolbar, and includes code taken from the sample application. Figure 7.1 illustrates the toolbar created in this chapter. This is the same dialog box used in Chapter 5, "Status Bars."

Class CToolBarCtrl gives an application the functionality of the Windows toolbar common control. This class is only available for 32-bit applications developed for Windows 95/98, and NT v3.51 and above. The toolbar buttons can display images, strings, or both, and tool tips are also supported. Clicking a button generates a WM_COMMAND message that is sent to the parent window that owns the toolbar. These command messages are trapped and the code corresponding to the button's purpose (open a file, save a file, and so on) is added. Class CToolBarCtrl makes use of several internal data structures that you must configure before using the toolbar. But before we get under the hood and hammer out some code, let's look at the different styles, properties, and class members available for this class. After all, you need to know *what* you can create before you learn *how* to create it.

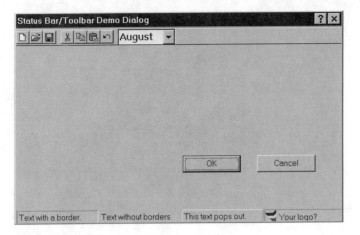

Figure 7.1   The sample program toolbar.

Toolbar Styles

Toolbars and child windows that must be explicitly created using the Create() function must be assigned the WS_CHILD property. You'll usually apply the WS_VISIBLE style, and on rare occasions the WS_DISABLED style. These are combined with the following styles for the CToolBarCtrl class:

CCS_ADJUSTABLE. This style allows the toolbar to be customized by the user. The owner window must process the notification messages that are sent by the toolbar.

CCS_BOTTOM. This style places the toolbar at the bottom of the parent window's client area. The toolbar's width is the same as the parent's. This style is rarely used because toolbars are usually placed at the top of the client area.

CCS_NODIVIDER. A CToolBarCtrl object can have a 2-pixel highlight that is drawn at the top of the control; this style prevents this highlight from being drawn.

CCS_NOHILITE. The control bar can also have a 1-pixel highlight at the top of the control; this style prevents it from being drawn.

CCS_NOMOVEY. This style forces the toolbar to resize and move itself horizontally in response to a WM_SIZE message. There is no change in the vertical direction. When the toolbar is created using the CCS_NORESIZE style, this style has no effect.

CCS_NOPARENTALIGN. When this style is used, the toolbar maintains its position inside the parent window despite changes to the size of the parent window. That is, it does not automatically move to the top or bottom of the parent window. If the CCS_TOP or CCS_BOTTOM styles are used, the height is adjusted to the default, but the position and width remain the same.

CCS_NORESIZE. This style keeps the control from using the default width and height values when setting or resetting its size. Instead, it uses the values specified in the request for creation or sizing.

CCS_TOP. This is the default style—it causes the toolbar to position itself at the top of the parent window's client area with its width the same as that of the parent window.

TBSTYLE_TOOL TIPS. This style causes the toolbar to create and manage a tool tip control. If you use this style, your application must process the tool tip notification messages.

TBSTYLE_WRAPABLE. This style allows the toolbar to have multiple lines of buttons that wrap to the next line when the window becomes too narrow to show all the buttons on the same line.

So, there you have it. These styles give you control over a wide range of features. Now let's look at the structures that work behind the scenes.

Toolbar Structures

The first structure we'll examine is the TBBUTTON structure. This structure associates the toolbar button with the button's style, image and/or string, command ID, state, and any user-defined data. Its members are as follows:

```
typedef struct _TBBUTTON
{
    int iBitmap;      // zero-based index of button image
    int idCommand;    // command to be sent when button pressed
    BYTE fsState;     // button state
    BYTE fsStyle;     // button style
    DWORD dwData;     // application-defined value
    int iString;      // zero-based index of button label string
} TBBUTTON;
```

The iBitmap member is the index into the image list of available bitmaps. Set it to NULL if an image is not used. The idCommand member is the command identifier that is sent in a WM_COMMAND message when the user clicks the button. If the fsStyle member includes the TBSTYLE_SEP style, this must be zero. The fsState member is the state of the button, and can be a combination of the values shown in Table 7.1. The fsStyle member is the button's style, and can be a combination of the values shown in Table 7.2.

The dwData member is a 32-bit value reserved for your private use, as shown with listboxes and combo boxes. The iString member is the zero-based index of the string to use for the button label. Set it to NULL if there is no string. You will always need to use the TBBUTTON structure to create a toolbar.

The next structure, TBBUTTONINFO, is used to read or write button information.

Table 7.1 Meaning of the fsState Member

FSSTATE VALUE	MEANING
TBSTATE_CHECKED	The button has the TBSTYLE_CHECKED style and is being pressed.
TBSTATE_ENABLED	The button accepts user input; without this, the button is grayed.
TBSTATE_HIDDEN	The button is invisible and cannot receive user input.
TBSTATE_INDETERMINATE	The button is grayed.
TBSTATE_PRESSED	The button is pressed.
TBSTATE_WRAP	A line break follows the button; must have the TBSTATE_ENABLED state.

```
typedef struct
{
    UINT cbSize;
    DWORD dwMask;
    int idCommand;
    int iImage;
    BYTE fsState;
    BYTE fsStyle;
    WORD cx;
    DWORD lParam;
    LPTSTR pszText;
    int cchText;
} TBBUTTONINFOA, *LPTBBUTTONINFOA;
```

The cbSize member is the size, in bytes, of the structure. This must be filled in prior to sending a message to the toolbar button. You can simply set it to sizeof(TBBUTTON-INFO).

Table 7.2 Meaning of the fsStyle Member

FSSTYLE VALUE	MEANING
TBSTYLE_BUTTON	Creates a standard push button.
TBSTYLE_CHECK	The button toggles between pressed and unpressed with each click.
TBSTYLE_CHECKGROUP	The check button stays pressed until another button is pressed.
TBSTYLE_GROUP	The button stays pressed until another button is pressed.
TBSTYLE_SEP	Creates a separator similar to those used with menus—a small gap.

Table 7.3 The dwMask Member Values

DWKMASK VALUES	MEANING
TBIF_COMMAND	The idCommand member has valid information or is being requested.
TBIF_IMAGE	The iImage member has valid information or is being requested.
TBIF_LPARAM	The lParam member has valid information or is being requested.
TBIF_SIZE	The cx member has valid information or is being requested.
TBIF_STATE	The fsState member has valid information or is being requested.
TBIF_STYLE	The fsStyle member has valid information or is being requested.
TBIF_TEXT	The pszText member has valid information or is being requested.

The dwMask member is a set of flags specifying which of the other members contain valid information. This must be filled in prior to sending a message to the toolbar with one or more of the values shown in Table 7.3.

The idCommand member is the command identifier of the button. The iImage member is the index of the button's image. If this is set to I_IMAGECALLBACK, the toolbar sends a TBN_GETDISPINFO notification message to fetch the image index when it is needed. The fsState is the state flag, and can be one or more of the values shown in Table 7.1. The fsStyle member is the style flags for the button, and can be one or more of the values shown in Table 7.2. The cx member is the button's width, in pixels. The lParam member is the application-defined 32-bit value associated with the button. The pszText is the character buffer that will contain, or receive, the button's text. The cchText member is the size of this buffer.

The sister companion to the TBBUTTON structure is the TBADDBITMAP structure. This structure maintains information regarding the bitmaps to use with the toolbar. It is prototyped as

```
typedef struct
{
    HINSTANCE hInst;
    UINT nID;
} TBADDBITMAP, *LPTBADDBITMAP;
```

The hInst member is the handle to the instance that contains the bitmaps (that is, your application). The nID member is the bitmap's resource identifier. If hInst is NULL, then nID must contain the handle of the bitmap. You can also define hInst to be HINST_COMMCTRL. Doing so allows you to use the system-defined bitmaps. However, you must also set the nID member to be one of the values shown in Table 7.4.

Table 7.4 Using System-Defined Bitmaps

VALUE	MEANING
IDB_STD_LARGE_COLOR	Use the large, color standard bitmaps.
IDB_STD_SMALL_COLOR	Use the small, color standard bitmaps.
IDB_VIEW_LARGE_COLOR	Use the large, color view bitmaps.
IDB_VIEW_SMALL_COLOR	Use the small, color view bitmaps.

Using the system-defined bitmaps also means you have access to the system-defined indexes to the bitmaps. These are

- STD_COPY
- STD_PASTE
- STD_CUT
- STD_PRINT
- STD_DELETE
- STD_PRINTPRE
- STD_FILENEW
- STD_PROPERTIES
- STD_FILEOPEN
- STD_REDOW
- STD_FILESAVE
- STD_REPLACE
- STD_FIND
- STD_UNDO
- STD_HELP
- VIEW_LARGEICONS
- VIEW_SORTNAME
- VIEW_SMALLICONS
- VIEW_SORTSIZE
- VIEW_LIST
- VIEW_SORTDATE
- VIEW_DETAILS
- VIEW_SORTTYPE

These indexes make it very easy to take advantage of the images that ship with Windows, should your application need them. Now let's see how to use the images with the member functions for the toolbar class.

CToolBarCtrl Member Functions

Sending a message to the control can duplicate the functionality of a member function. In this section, I'll give you the member function, with the corresponding messages covered in a separate section. You'll see these used in the sample program.

The first member function is Create(), prototyped as follows:

```
BOOL Create(DWORD dwStyle, const RECT& rect, CWnd* pParentWnd, UINT nID);
```

The parameters are the same as those you've seen before: the toolbar style, size and position rectangle, parent window, and resource ID, respectively. You must include WS_CHILD in the dwStyle parameter. Here is an example of the Create() method taken from the sample code on the companion Web site:

```
BOOL bToolBar= FALSE;
bToolBar = m_Toolbar.Create(WS_CHILD | WS_BORDER | WS_VISIBLE |
    CCS_ADJUSTABLE,rect,this ,NULL);
```

The return value is zero if an error occurs; any other value signifies success.

There is a plethora of member functions for determining a single button's state. These all share the same parameter and return value. They are

BOOL IsButtonEnabled(int nID) const; This method is used to determine if a button is enabled. The parameter nID is the command identifier of the button to check. The return value is nonzero if the button is enabled, or zero if it is not.

BOOL IsButtonChecked(int nID) const; This determines if the button is checked.

BOOL IsButtonPressed(int nID) const; This method determines if the button has been pressed.

BOOL IsButtonHidden(int nID) const; This determines if the button is hidden.

BOOL IsButtonIndeterminate(int nID) const; This method is used to determine if the specified button is indeterminate. Indeterminate buttons are displayed as grayed, similar to the way the bold button on a word processor toolbar would look when the text contains both bold and nonbold characters. In other words, the framework cannot say exactly if it's bold or not, since it contains elements of both.

Another method that is actually a combination of the five previous methods is GetState(), prototyped as follows:

```
int GetState(int nID) const;
```

The parameter nID is the command identifier of the button for which the state is to be retrieved. The return value is the button's state if the call was successful, or –1 if it failed. This method is the only way to detect the TBSTATE_WRAP state.

The opposite of the GetState() method is SetState().

```
BOOL SetState(int nID, UINT nState);
```

This method lets you set the state of a button. The nID parameter is the command identifier and nState is the new state, which can be a combination of the values shown in Table 7.1. The return value is nonzero if successful; otherwise, zero.

To retrieve information about a specific button, use GetButton().

```
BOOL GetButton(int nIndex, LPTBBUTTON lpButton) const;
```

The parameter nIndex is the zero-based index of the button that you wish to read, and lpButton is the address of a TBBUTTON structure that receives the button information.

To count the number of buttons on a toolbar, use

```
int GetButtonCount() const;
```

The return value is the number of buttons on the toolbar.

There are six methods that are useful for working with toolbar bitmaps. The first is the GetItemRect() method.

```
BOOL GetItemRect(int nIndex, LPRECT lpRect) const;
```

This method retrieves the bounding rectangle of the toolbar button indicated by nIndex. The parameter lpRect is the address of a RECT or CRect structure that receives the coordinates. The return value is nonzero if successful; otherwise, zero. This method does not work if the state is set to TBSTATE_HIDDEN.

The second method dealing with toolbar bitmaps is the SetBitmapSize() method.

```
BOOL SetBitmapSize(CSize size);
```

The parameter size indicates the width and height of the images in pixels. This function *must* be called before adding bitmaps to the toolbar. If it isn't called, the bitmap size defaults to 16 × 15 pixels.

The third method is SetButtonSize()f.

```
BOOL SetButtonSize(CSize size);
```

This sets the size of the buttons (not the bitmaps) on the toolbar. The size, indicated by the parameter *size*, must be at least as big as the bitmap it encloses. This function must be called only before adding bitmaps to the toolbar. If it isn't called, the default button size is 24 × 22 pixels.

You can add one or more button images to the list of images stored in the toolbar control by using one of the two varieties of AddBitmap().

```
int AddBitmap(int nNumButtons, UINT nBitmapID);
int AddBitmap(int nNumButtons, CBitmap* pBitmap);
```

The parameter nNumButtons is the number of button images in the bitmap. Parameter nBitmapID is the resource identifier of the new image(s) to add. Likewise, pBitmap is a pointer to a CBitmap object containing the new image or images. The return value is the zero-based index of the first new image if successful, or zero if the call failed. To map colors before adding the bitmap, use the API CreateMappedBitmap().

```
HBITMAP CreateMappedBitmap
(
    HINSTANCE hInstance,      // handle to your app instance
    int idBitmap,             // resource ID of the bitmap
    UINT wFlags,              // bitmap flag, 0 or CMB_MASKED
    LPCOLORMAP lpColorMap,    // address of a COLORMAP structure
    int iNumMaps              // number of color maps in lpColorMap
);
```

Another bitmap function is GetBitmapFlags( ).

```
UINT GetBitmapFlags( ) const;
```

This function retrieves the bitmap flags from the toolbar. The GetBitmapFlags() method should be called after the toolbar is created but before bitmaps are added. The return value indicates whether the display supports large bitmaps. If it does, the return value includes the TBBF_LARGE flag. If you want your application to use large bitmaps, call SetBitmapSize() and SetButtonSize() before calling AddBitmap().

To add buttons to the toolbar, use the AddButtons() method.

```
BOOL AddButtons(int nNumButtons, LPTBBUTTON lpButtons);
```

The parameter nNumButtons is the number of buttons to add, and lpButtons is the address of an array of TBBUTTON structures that have been configured as described in the "Toolbar Structures" section. The size of this array must be the same as nNumButtons.

You can also dynamically add new buttons to the toolbar using the InsertButton() method.

```
BOOL InsertButton(int nIndex, LPTBBUTTON lpButton);
```

The parameter nIndex is the zero-based index of the new button, and lpButton points to a TBBUTTON structure containing the information about the new button.

To remove a button, use DeleteButton().

```
BOOL DeleteButton(int nIndex);
```

The parameter nIndex is the zero-based index of the button to remove.

The next method is SetOwner().

```
void SetOwner(CWnd* pWnd);
```

This method is used to set the owner window for the toolbar, which receives the notification messages from the toolbar. The parameter pWnd is a pointer to the owner window.

CToolBarCtrl Messages

As mentioned previously, you can send messages to a toolbar instead of calling a member function. This is sometimes necessary, and sometimes simply expedient. The following is a look at these messages, their meaning, and some examples. For the sample code, the variable pToolbar is assumed to be a pointer to the toolbar, and hWndToolbar is its handle.

TB_BUTTONSTRUCTSIZE. This message is used to obtain the size of the TBBUTTON structure, and *must* be called before adding any buttons to the toolbar when using CreateWindowEx() to create the toolbar control. The TB_BUTTONSTRUCTSIZE message is not required (it's sent automatically) if you're using CreateToolBarEx() to create the toolbar. The size information obtained is used by the system to ascertain what version of COMMCTRL.DLL is being used. The wParam parameter is the size of the TBBUTTON structure; the lParam parameter is not used and is set to zero. There is no return value. For example,

```
pToolbar->SendMessage(TB_BUTTONSTRUCTSIZE,(WPARAM) sizeof(TBBUTTON),0L);
```

TB_ADDBITMAP. This message is used to add a bitmap to the toolbar with non-WIN32 applications. The wParam parameter is the number of buttons in the bitmap. lParam has the handle of the bitmap in the high-order word; the low-order word is NULL. The return value is 32-bit quantity that has the index of the first button bitmap in the low-order word. The high-order word is not used if the call succeeds; if not, the low-order word is a –1. Here is an example:

```
TBADDBITMAP tbStruct;// bitmap structure for buttons
tbStruct.hInst = HINST_COMMCTRL;// using system resources
tbStruct.nID   = IDB_STD_SMALL_COLOR;
pToolbar->SendMessage(TB_ADDBITMAP,(WPARAM) 8,(LPARAM) &tbStruct);
```

This example assumes you are using system-defined resources to add bitmaps to a toolbar with eight buttons. If you wanted to create your own bitmap and use it, follow this example:

```
TBADDBITMAP tbStruct;// bitmap structure for buttons
HBITMAP hBitmap;// handle to bitmap
hBitmap = ::LoadBitmap(hInstance, MAKEINTRESOURCE(IDR_MYBITMAP));
tbStruct.hInst = NULL;// using application-defined bitmap
tbStruct.nID = (UINT)hBitmap;
pToolbar->SendMessage(TB_ADDBITMAP, (WPARAM) 8,(LPARAM) &tbStruct);
```

where hInstance is the application instance, and IDR_MYBITMAP is the resource identifier for your bitmap in the .RC file. You could also set lParam as follows:

```
lParam = (MAKELONG)(hBitmap, NULL);
```

TB_ADDBITMAP32. This message is identical to TB_ADDBITMAP, except it is used with WIN32 applications only. Everything is the same, except lParam is a long pointer to a LPTBADDMBITMAP32 structure.

TB_ADDBUTTONS. This message adds the buttons to the toolbar. The wParam parameter is the number of buttons to add, and the lParam is the address of the array of TBBUTTON structures regarding the buttons. The size of this array must be the same as the wParam. The return value is TRUE if the call is successful; FALSE if not. For example,

```
PToolbar->SendMessage(TB_ADDBUTTONS, (WPARAM)8,
    (LPARAM)(LPTBBUTTON)&tbButtons);
```

TB_ADDSTRING. This message adds a string or strings to a toolbar. These strings are used with the tool tip help, or can be displayed under the button. The wParam parameter is the handle to the application instance; but if the high-order word of lParam points to one or more strings to add, wParam is zero. The lParam parameter is either the identifier of the string resource, or the address of a buffer containing the strings to add to the toolbar list. The last string must be terminated using two NULL terminators. The return value is the index of the first new string if the call was successful, or −1 if an error occurs.

TB_AUTOSIZE. This message is used to automatically resize the toolbar whenever an action has changed the size of the toolbar; for example, when changing the size of the bitmap, or adding strings. The wParam and lParam parameters are not used and should be set to zero. There is no return value.

TB_BUTTONCOUNT. This message returns the number of buttons in a toolbar. The wParam and lParam parameters are not used and should be set to zero. For example,

```
int nButtons = pToolbar->SendMessage(TB_BUTTONCOUNT,0,0L);
```

TB_CHECKBUTTON. This message is used to check, or uncheck, a button. A checked button appears in the depressed state. The wParam parameter is the command identifier of the button to check or uncheck. The high-order word of lParam is set to TRUE to check the button; FALSE to uncheck. The low-order word of lParam should be set to zero. For example, to check a button using the system-defined File Save command, follow this example:

```
pToolbar->SendMessage(TB_CHECKBUTTON, (WPARAM)IDM_SAVE,
    MAKELONG(TRUE,0));
```

The return value is TRUE if successful; FALSE if not. A button must first be enabled before it can be checked (see TB_ENABLEBUTTON later in this list).

TB_COMMANDTOINDEX. This message retrieves the index for the button associated with a given command identifier. The wParam parameter is the command identifier for the button in question; the lParam is not used and should be set to zero. Assuming you have a standard toolbar with the first three buttons used for File New, File Open, and File Save, the following example would return the index for the File Open button.

```
int nIndex = pToolbar->SendMessage(TB_COMMANDTOINDEX, IDM_FILE_OPEN, 0L);
```

The value for nIndex in this example would be 1 (the button indexes are zero-based).

TB_CUSTOMIZE. This message displays the Customize Toolbar dialog box. Both parameters are zero, and there is no return value. Examples of the Customize Toolbar dialog box can be found in many Microsoft applications, including Visual C++ version 6.0.

TB_DELETEBUTTON. Use this message to remove a button from the toolbar. The wParam parameter specifies the index of the button to delete. The lParam parameter is not used and is set to zero. To delete the File Save button in the example described previously for the TB_COMMANDTOINDEX message, follow this example:

```
pToolbar->SendMessage(TB_DELETEBUTTON, 2, 0L);
```

The return value is TRUE for success; FALSE for an error.

TB_ENABLEBUTTON. This message is identical in all respects to the TB_CHECK-BUTTON message, except this message causes the button to be enabled. A button must first be enabled before it can be pressed or checked.

TB_GETBUTTON. This message gets the TBBUTTON structure information about a button. The wParam parameter is the index of the button, and the parameter lParam is the address of a TBBUTTON structure that receives the information. The return value is TRUE if the call is successful. For example, to get the information associated with the File Open button used in the previous examples,

```
TBBUTTON tbHold;
pToolbar->SendMessage(TB_GETBUTTON,1, (LPARAM) &tbHold);
```

TB_GETITEMRECT. This message is used to find the bounding rectangle of a toolbar button. The button in question must not have its state set to TBSTATE_HIDDEN. The wParam parameter is the index of the button and the lParam parameter is the address of a RECT object. The return value is TRUE if the call is successful. For example, to find the rectangle for the "File New" button from the previous examples,

```
RECT rRect;
pToolbar->SendMessage(TB_GETITEMRECT, 0, (LPARAM)&rRect);
```

TB_GETSTATE. This message is used to determine the state of a button. The wParam parameter is the index of the button. The lParam parameter is not used. The return value is one of the values listed in Table 7.1, or −1 if the call failed. For example, to get the state of the third button (index is 2) on the toolbar,

```
int iState= pToolbar->SendMessage(TB_GETSTATE, 2, 0L);
```

TB_HIDEBUTTON. This message is used to hide or show a button. The wParam parameter is the command identifier of the button. The high-order word of lParam is set to TRUE to hide a button, FALSE to show it. For example, to hide the first button from our previous example ("File New"), follow this example:

```
pToolbar->SendMessage(TB_HIDEBUTTON, IDM_FILE_NEW, MAKELONG(TRUE,0));
```

The return value is TRUE if the call succeeds; FALSE on error.

TB_INDETERMINATE. This message is used to set, or clear, the indeterminate state of a button. Its parameters and return values are identical in every respect to those described for TB_HIDEBUTTON.

TB_INSERTBUTTON. This message is used to insert a button into a toolbar. The wParam parameter is the index of the button at which the new button will be inserted; that is, the new button is placed in front of the button indicated by wParam. The lParam parameter is the address of a TBBUTTON structure containing information about the button. The return value is TRUE if the call is successful, FALSE if the call has failed. For example, suppose you have a toolbar with three buttons, and you want to insert a button in front of the second button. The following example demonstrates this.

```
TBBUTTON tb;
// initialize tb members here
pToolbar->SendMessage(TB_INSERTBUTTON, 1, (LPARAM) &tb);
```

TB_ISBUTTONCHECKED. This message is used to determine if a button is checked. The wParam parameter is the command identifier of the button. The lParam is not used and is set to zero. The return value is TRUE if the call is successful.

TB_ISBUTTONENABLED. This message is used to determine if a button is enabled. The wParam parameter is the command identifier of the button. The lParam is not used and is set to zero. The return value is TRUE if the call is successful.

TB_ISBUTTONHIDDEN. This message is used to determine if a button is hidden. The wParam parameter is the command identifier of the button. The lParam is not used and is set to zero. The return value is TRUE if the call is successful.

TB_ISBUTTONINDETERMINATE. This message is used to determine if a button is indeterminate. The wParam parameter is the command identifier of the button. The lParam is not used and is set to zero. The return value is TRUE if the call is successful.

TB_ISBUTTONPRESSED. This message is used to determine if a button is pressed. The wParam parameter is the command identifier of the button. The lParam is not used and is set to zero. The return value is TRUE if the call is successful.

TB_PRESSBUTTON. This message is used to press, or release, a button. The wParam parameter is the command identifier of the button. The high-order word of the lParam parameter is set to TRUE for a button press, and FALSE for a button release. The return value is TRUE if the call is successful. For example,

```
pToolbar->SendMessage(TB_PRESSBUTTON, IDM_FILE_SAVE,MAKELONG(1,0));
```

This would press the File Save button, using our previous example of a toolbar with the standard three file options.

TB_SAVERESTORE. Use this message to save or restore the state of the toolbar. The wParam parameter is set to TRUE to save the state of the toolbar, and FALSE to restore it. The lParam parameter is the address of two consecutive, NULL-terminated strings. The first indicates the name of a section in the application's .INI file, and the second is the name of the .INI file. If the second string is NULL, the WIN.INI file is used. There is no return value. This message is generally used to allow the user to cancel a TB_CUSTOMIZE message. You can save the state of the toolbar before the user begins the customization, and restore it if he or she cancels the operation.

TB_SETBITMAPSIZE. This message is used to set the size of the bitmap images to be used with a toolbar. This message should be used before you add any bitmaps to the toolbar. Failure to use this message will set the default size of the bitmap image or images to 16 × 15 pixels. The wParam parameter is not used and is set to zero. The high-order word of the lParam parameter contains the width of the bitmap, in pixels. The low-order word holds the width. The return value is TRUE if the call is successful.

TB_SETBUTTONSIZE. This message sets the size of the toolbar buttons; you can only set their size before they are created, not after. If you do not use this message, the default size is 24 × 22 pixels. If the toolbar was created using the CreateWindow() or CreateWindowEx() API calls, refer to the TB_BUTTONSTRUCTSIZE message discussed previously. The wParam parameter is not used and is set to zero. The high-order word of the lParam parameter contains the width of the bitmap, in pixels. The low-order word holds the width. The return value is TRUE if the call is successful.

TB_SETSTATE. This message is used to set the state of a button. The wParam parameter specifies the command identifier of the button. The high-order word of the lParam parameter is one of the states listed in Table 7.1, and the low-order word is set to zero. The return value is TRUE if the call is successful.

The Sample Program

The companion Web site contains the sample program, Example1, which includes a simple toolbar example. I combined it with the status bar demo dialog; look for the code in StatDlg.cpp and StatDlg.h. The example creates a customizable toolbar with the standard file operations (open, save, and so on) buttons. This allowed me to use the standard bitmap for these operations, so I didn't have to create a new bitmap. After the toolbar is created, a combo box is added to it to demonstrate how easy it is to add little touches like this to your interface. This combo box is filled with the names of the months of the year, and scrolled to the month to which your computer's clock is set.

The work begins in the OnInitDialog() method found in StatDlg.cpp; I've added some prominent comments where the toolbar portion begins to make it easier for you to spot it. The code is fairly short—here it is in its entirety.

```
HWND hWndToolbar;          // handle to toolbar
TBADDBITMAP tbStruct;      // bitmap structure for buttons
//
// populate button array with values (8 buttons, using MFC supplied)
//
TBBUTTON tbButtons[] =
{
    { STD_FILENEW, IDM_NEW, TBSTATE_ENABLED, TBSTYLE_BUTTON, 0L, 0},
    { STD_FILEOPEN, IDM_OPEN, TBSTATE_ENABLED, TBSTYLE_BUTTON, 0L, 0},
    { STD_FILESAVE, IDM_SAVE, TBSTATE_ENABLED, TBSTYLE_BUTTON, 0L, 0},
    { 0, 0, TBSTATE_ENABLED, TBSTYLE_SEP, 0L, 0},
```

```
        { VIEW_LARGEICONS, 200, TBSTATE_ENABLED, TBSTYLE_BUTTON, 0L, 0},
        { VIEW_SMALLICONS, 210, TBSTATE_ENABLED, TBSTYLE_BUTTON, 0L, 0},
        { VIEW_LIST, 220, TBSTATE_ENABLED, TBSTYLE_BUTTON, 0L, 0},
        { VIEW_DETAILS, 230, TBSTATE_ENABLED, TBSTYLE_BUTTON, 0L, 0},
    };
    //
    // Create a toolbar using CreateWindow()
    //
    BOOL bToolBar= FALSE;
    bToolBar = m_Toolbar.Create(WS_CHILD | WS_BORDER | WS_VISIBLE |
        CCS_ADJUSTABLE,rect,this ,NULL);
    //
    if(!bToolBar)
    {
        AfxMessageBox ("Toolbar not created!", NULL, MB_OK );
    }
    //
    hWndToolbar = m_Toolbar.GetSafeHwnd();
    //
    // Add the bitmap containing button images to the toolbar.(MFC default)
    //
    tbStruct.hInst = HINST_COMMCTRL;// defined in commctrl.h
    tbStruct.nID   = IDB_STD_SMALL_COLOR;// ditto...
    m_Toolbar.SendMessage(TB_ADDBITMAP, (WPARAM) 8,
        LPARAM) &tbStruct);
    //
    // Now add the buttons
    //
    m_Toolbar.AddButtons(8, tbButtons);
    //
    //Now lets add a combobox to the toolbar
    //
    char *szComboStr[] = { "January", "February", "March", "April", "May",
        "June","July","August","September","October","November","December"};
    //
    HWND hWndCombo;// handle to the combobox
    hWndCombo = CreateWindowEx(0L,      // no extended styles
        "COMBOBOX",                     // class name
        "",                             // default text
        WS_CHILD | WS_VISIBLE | WS_VSCROLL |
        CBS_HASSTRINGS | CBS_DROPDOWN,  // styles and defaults
        176, 0, 100, 150,              // size and position
        hWndToolbar,                   // parent window
        NULL,                          // ID
        AfxGetInstanceHandle(),        // current instance
        NULL);

    if (hWndCombo)
    {
        // Add strings to combo box.
        for (int k=0; k < 12; k++)
```

```
        ::SendMessage(hWndCombo, CB_INSERTSTRING,(WPARAM)-1,
            (LPARAM)szComboStr[k]);
    //
    //select the string for the current month
    //
    CTime t = CTime::GetCurrentTime();
    int iMon = (t.GetMonth())-1;
    ::SendMessage(hWndCombo, CB_SETCURSEL,iMon, 0L);
}
else
{
    AfxMessageBox ("Combo box not created!", NULL, MB_OK );
}
```

As you can see, none of this is rocket science. The TBBUTTON array is filled with the necessary values, and then the toolbar is created. The steps to create and fill the combo box follow, and is initialized to the current month. Along the way some very weak error traps are added—you should probably shore these up or remove them completely before using this code.

Message Handlers

The next question that comes to mind is, "How do I know when the user has clicked on one of my toolbar buttons?" You can't use Class Wizard, but you can still add message handlers. All you need to do is patch the AFX-generated message map, and add your function to the source code and header file. The previous sample code responds to a click on the first button, File New. If you click this, the following handler is called.

```
void CStatDlg::OnClickNew()
{
    AfxMessageBox("You clicked the File New button.",MB_OK);
}
```

This is do-nothing code that simply lets you know that the File New button was clicked. After adding the handler to StatDlg.cpp, I modified the message map (in the same file) as follows:

```
BEGIN_MESSAGE_MAP(CStatDlg, CDialog)
    //{{AFX_MSG_MAP(CStatDlg)
    ON_WM_DRAWITEM()
    ON_COMMAND(IDM_NEW, OnClickNew)// my message handler
    //}}AFX_MSG_MAP
END_MESSAGE_MAP()
```

The only other thing you need to do is edit your header file. Here are the changes made to StatDlg.h:

```
// Implementation
protected:
    // Generated message map functions
    //{{AFX_MSG(CStatDlg)
```

```
virtual BOOL OnInitDialog();
    afx_msg void OnDrawItem(int nIDCtl,LPDRAWITEMSTRUCT
lpDrawItemStruct);
    afx_msg void OnClickNew(); // My message handler
    //}}AFX_MSG
    DECLARE_MESSAGE_MAP()
```

Repeat this process for all the buttons on your toolbar. Remember, just because Visual C++ generated the code doesn't mean it's a sacred cow—it's okay to edit the message map to suit your purpose. There are more examples of this later in this book, like in Chapter 16, "The Find-Replace Dialog."

Summary

Toolbars, used judiciously, can enhance your user interface. Users are comfortable with them—the graphical elements provide a visual cue to the button's underlying meaning. They're easy to embellish with things like combo boxes and edit boxes. Also, as you've seen in the sample program in this chapter, you can avail yourself of elements that ship with MFC, obviating the need to reinvent the wheel. Now, let's move on to the next item of discussion, list views and header controls.

CHAPTER 8

New Common Controls

B eginning with Microsoft Internet Explorer 4.0, several new common controls were introduced that can also be used in generic MFC applications. Many of these controls support a new technology called *custom draw*. The beauty of this technology lies in its simplicity—you can customize the appearance of the control without having to implement it as owner-drawn. Other enhancements include the addition of the ListView control, which allows you to display literally millions of items instantly. Improvements have also been made to the ListView control's report mode. The custom draw feature has also been added to the combo box, allowing images now to appear in the edit box portion of the control. But be warned—this information is highly volatile and is subject to change. You should consult Microsoft's Web site for more information before jumping in too deeply.

Another feature of the new common controls is something called *hot tracking*. This feature displays an item, such as a combo box entry, as selected whenever the mouse cursor is over the item for roughly one second, eliminating the need for clicking the mouse button.

This chapter is an introduction to the new common controls and their features, and contains some functional code to help you get started. The code can be found on the companion Web site under Example3 link. You'll need the new COMCTL32.DLL, version 4.70, which ships with Internet Explorer 4.0. If you don't have COMCTL32.DLL, you can download it by following the link on the companion Web site. Let's begin with an overview of some fundamental topics that apply to all the new controls, as well as the existing controls that support custom draw.

The Basics

The underlying principle of the new controls is that they must be registered before you can use them. This is made possible by the InitCommonControlsEx() function, prototyped as follows:

```
BOOL InitCommonControlsEx(LPINITCOMMONCONTROLSEX lpInitCtrls);
```

The parameter lpInitCtrls is the address of an INITCOMMONCONTROLEX structure that contains the information regarding the control you're registering. The return value is TRUE if the call succeeded, and FALSE if it failed. The INITCOMMONCONTROLEX structure looks like this:

```
typedef struct tagINITCOMMONCONTROLSEX
{
    DWORD dwSize;
    DWORD dwICC;
} INITCOMMONCONTROLSEX, *LPINITCOMMONCONTROLSEX;
```

The first member is simply the size of the structure, and the second member is a set of bit flags indicating which of the common controls should be loaded from COMCTL32.DLL. The list of possible values can be found in Table 8.1.

Table 8.1 The New Common Control Classes

DWICC VALUE	CONTROL(S) LOADED
ICC_ANIMATE_CLASS	Animation control class.
ICC_BAR_CLASSES	Loads the ToolBar, Status Bar, Track Bar, and Tool Tip classes.
ICC_COOL_CLASSES	Loads the rebar control.
ICC_DATE_CLASSES	Loads the date/time picker control.
ICC_HOTKEY_CLASS	Loads the hot key control.
ICC_INTERNET_CLASSES	Loads the IP (Internet Protocol) class.
ICC_PAGESCROLLER_CLASS	Loads the pager control class.
ICC_PROGRESS_CLASS	Loads the progress bar control.
ICC_LISTVIEW_CLASSES	Loads the ListView and Header control classes.
ICC_TREEVIEW_CLASSES	Loads the TreeView and Tool Tip control classes.
ICC_TAB_CLASSES	Loads the Tab control and Tool Tip control classes.
ICC_UPDOWN_CLASS	Loads the Spin Control class.
ICC_USEREX_CLASSES	Loads the new, extended Combo Box class.
ICC_WIN95_CLASSES	Loads all but Pager, Date Picker, Rebar, and IP classes.

Figure 8.1 A rebar control.

You're probably familiar with all of these except for ICC_COOL_CLASSES. This control behaves like a container for other controls, and contains one or more bands. In turn, each band can contain one child window or control, which can even be a toolbar that contains additional controls. If you've used Microsoft's Internet Explorer, you've seen a rebar control. If not, it may help you to think of them as the customizable tool bars that can be added to the Visual C++ workbench. Figure 8.1 shows a rebar control from Internet Explorer.

The rebar control is discussed in more detail later in this chapter when we get some hands-on experience with this control in the sample code for the extended combo box. But first, let's talk a little more about custom drawing.

Custom Draw

The custom draw technology gives the developer complete, extendible control over the manner in which items are drawn. For example, imagine a combo box with several different string entries. Custom draw allows you to draw one of the strings using the Arial font, and another using the Times New Roman font. One could be drawn in red, the other in blue. One could be in bold, the other in italic. Just about any combination is possible, but again, you must be consistent and keep it simple.

Custom draw begins when the control sends its owner a new notification message called NM_CUSTOMDRAW and a pointer to a new structure, NMCUSTOMDRAW.

```
typedef struct tagNMCUSTOMDRAWINFO
{
    NMHDR hdr;
    DWORD dwDrawStage;
    HDC hdc;
    RECT rc;
    DWORD dwItemSpec;
    UINT uItemState;
    LPARAM lItemlParam;
} NMCUSTOMDRAW, FAR * LPNMCUSTOMDRAW;
```

The hdr member is an NMHDR structure that contains information about the notification message. The dwDrawStage member specifies the current drawing stage. The stage is essentially a designated portion of the entire drawing process. The dwDraw-Stage member can be one of the following four *global* values:

CDDS_POSTERASE. After the erasing cycle is complete.

CDDS_POSTPAINT. After the painting cycle is complete.

CDDS_PREERASE. Before the start of the erasing cycle.

CDDS_PREPAINT. Before the start of the painting cycle.

The CDDS_PREPAINT member can also be one of the following *item-specific* values:

CDDS_ITEM. The dwItemSpec, uItemState, and lItemlParam members are valid.

CDDS_ITEMPOSTERASE. After an item has been erased.

CDDS_ITEMPOSTPAINT. After an item has been drawn.

CDDS_ITEMPREERASE. Before an item is erased.

CDDS_ITEMPREPAINT. Before an item is drawn.

CDDS_SUBITEM. For COMCTL32.DL version 4.71, a subitem is being drawn that has the CDDS_ITEMPREPAINT or CDDS_ITEMPOSTPAINT flags set. This subitem will be set only when CDRF_NOTIFYSUBITEMDRAW is returned from CDDS_PREPAINT.

The hdc member of NMCUSTOMDRAW is the handle to the given control's device context and should be used for any GDI functions. The rc member is a RECT structure that defines the bounding rectangle of the area that is being drawn. The dwItemSpec member is the item number and depends on the type of control sending the notification message. Refer to the documentation for the NM_CUSTOMDRAW message to ascertain what value, if any, to assign this member.

The uItemState member of NMCUSTOMDRAW indicates the current state of the item. Possible values are described in Table 8.2.

Finally, the lItemlParam is a 32-bit value that you can use to piggyback data about the item onto the structure.

Table 8.2 The uItemState Member

UITEMSTATE VALUE	MEANING
CDIS_CHECKED	The item is checked.
CDIS_DEFAULT	The item is in its default state.
CDIS_DISABLED	The item is disabled.
CDIS_FOCUS	The item is in focus.
CDIS_GRAYED	The item is grayed.
CDIS_HOT	The item is currently under the pointer (or hot).
CDIS_INDETERMINATE	The item is in an indeterminate state.
CDIS_MARKED	The item is marked. The meaning of this varies with the item.
CDIS_SELECTED	The item is selected.

The Custom Draw Cycle

The custom drawing cycle for a control begins when the control processes its WM_PAINT message. At the onset of the drawing cycle, the control sends the NMCUSTOMDRAW notification message with dwDrawStage set to CDDS_PRE-PAINT. This message signals the beginning of the cycle. You don't have to make any assumptions regarding the order of custom draw messages, other than the fact that CDDS_PRExxx messages always arrive ahead of CDDS_POSTxxx messages. If the owner window returns CDRF_DODEFAULT (zero) in response to the NMCUSTOM-DRAW notification message, custom drawing is disabled for the drawing cycle and no additional notifications will be sent until the next cycle. If a nonzero value is returned, the control will send additional notification messages.

As an example, suppose you want to draw a particular item in a CTreeCtrl object (for example, the tree control) such that it has a different font and color from the other items. When you add the item to the control, you can use its lParam to piggyback the information needed to determine how each item should be drawn. After returning CDRF_NOTIFYITEMDRAW in response to the CDDS_PREPAINT notification message, you'll get a separate NM_CUSTOMDRAW notification with dwDrawState set to CDDS_ITEMPREPAINT for each tree control item being drawn. As you process the CDDS_ITEMPREPAINT notification messages, you can check the item's lParam to see how to draw the item. If the item is the one for which you want to change the font and color, you can change the font by selecting the desired HFONT into the hdc member of your NMCUSTOMDRAW structure. Whenever you change the font, your return value will need to set the CDRF_NEWFONT bit. Setting CDRF_NEWFONT forces the control to recalculate the text extent using the new font. To modify the item's color, just call SetTextColor() using the hdc member of your NMCUSTOMDRAW structure. Likewise, to change the background color, call SetBkColor() using this same hdc. Because changing the color doesn't force the control to recalculate anything, any return value is acceptable. However, you cannot override the colors used for *selected* items—these are always displayed using the host machine's configuration. If you want to handle all of the drawing for all or some of the items, do so when you get the CDDS_ITEMPRE-PAINT message. You can then return CDRF_SKIPDEFAULT, which tells the control not to perform any painting for the item. Because no portion of the item will be drawn, you'll have to draw the item images as demonstrated earlier in the section "Custom Draw." There are two special controls that are a little different.

Special Cases

There are two special cases involving custom draw.

- Custom draw in a ListView control
- Custom draw and tool tips

When using custom draw in a ListView control (i.e., class ICC_LISTVIEW_CLASSES), the lParam points to a special structure, NMLVCUSTOMDRAW, and not the regular NMCUSTOMDRAW structure. This structure is prototyped as follows:

```
typedef struct tagNMLVCUSTOMDRAW
{
    NMCUSTOMDRAW nmcd;
    COLORREF clrText;
    COLORREF clrTextBk;
    #if (_WIN32_IE >= 0x0400)
        int iSubItem;
    #endif
} NMLVCUSTOMDRAW, *LPNMLVCUSTOMDRAW;
```

The only difference is that you don't call SetTextColor() and SetBkColor(). Instead, you put the colors into the clrText and clrTextBk members of this structure to change these properties.

The second special case involves the Tool Tips class (i.e., ICC_BAR_CLASSES) and (you guessed it) another structure. When the Tool Tip object sends a NM_CUSTOM-DRAW notification message, lParam now points to an NMTTCUSTOMDRAW structure prototyped as follows:

```
typedef struct tagNMTTCUSTOMDRAW
{
    NMCUSTOMDRAW nmcd;
    UINT uDrawFlags;
} NMTTCUSTOMDRAW, FAR * LPNMTTCUSTOMDRAW;
```

The nmcd member is an NMCUSTOMDRAW structure that contains the general draw information. The uDrawFlags member is a value that specifies the format of the tool tip text when it is displayed. How many ways are there? Well, take a peek at the DrawText() function in the Visual C++ documentation, and check out the uFormat parameter. Any and all of these are good (DT_BOTTOM, DT_CENTER, DT_CALCRECT, and so on).

A Tool Tip class only uses the CDDS_PREPAINT step of the drawing cycle, and sends the NM_CUSTOMDRAW notification twice. The first message is used to get the bounding rectangle needed by the tool tip. You'll recognize this because the DT_CAL-CRECT bit will be set in uDrawFlags. If you need to adjust this rectangle, do so now. After the first NM_CUSTOMDRAW message, it's also safe to modify the uDrawFlags so long as you *always* set the DT_CALCRECT bit.

The second NM_CUSTOMDRAW message sent by the control is identified by the fact that DT_CALCRECT is not set (see why you need to manage it in uDrawFlags?). In other words, the tool tip is about to be painted. Don't make any changes to the bounding rectangle now, but you can change the HDC and the uDrawFlags parameter by setting the DT_CALCRECT bit.

Now you understand what custom draw is all about. As you can see, you have to do a little more work in setting up structures and sending messages, but the end result is a very impressive user interface. I realize that this section contained a lot of information to digest; nothing helps to make things more clear than some examples. Let's start by looking at one of the new controls, the date and time picker.

The Date Picker

The date picker control makes working with dates and times almost pleasant because so much of the burden of calculating days of the month, leap years, and so on, has been removed. Also, the control is presented in a compact, easy-to-use format and allows the user to select a value rather than key it in, which can lead to errors. Figure 8.2 shows the date picker from the example on the companion Web site.

As you can see in the figure, the date and time appear as the entry in the edit box portion of a combo box. Figure 8.3 shows the date picker when the drop-down arrow is pressed.

The date picker control acts a lot like the Calendar application that ships with Windows—you can click the left or right arrows to move to the next or previous month, where you can click on a specific day in the month. This control, also called a *DTP control*, is completely capable of being customized so that you can work with long or short formats, dates only, time only, and so on. To create a DTP, you call InitCommonControlsEx() first, then CreateWindow(). Here is the code that created the DTP shown in Figures 8.2 and 8.3:

```
INITCOMMONCONTROLSEX commctrlStruct;
commctrlStruct.dwSize = sizeof(INITCOMMONCONTROLSEX);
commctrlStruct.dwICC = ICC_DATE_CLASSES;
InitCommonControlsEx(&commctrlStruct);
//
HWND hWnd = this->GetSafeHwnd();
HINSTANCE hHandle = AfxGetInstanceHandle();
LPVOID lpParam;
m_hWndDP = CreateWindow(DATETIMEPICK_CLASS,"Date Picker",
    WS_VISIBLE | WS_CHILD |
    DTS_LONGDATEFORMAT,10,50,230,25,hWnd,NULL,hHandle,lpParam);
```

Since you've seen CreateWindow() before, the only new material here is the DTP control style, DTS_LONGDATEFORMAT. The format styles, and their meanings, are summarized in Table 8.3.

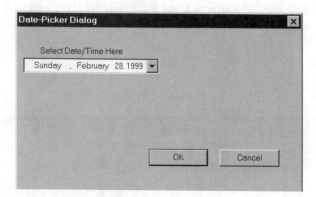

Figure 8.2 The example date picker control.

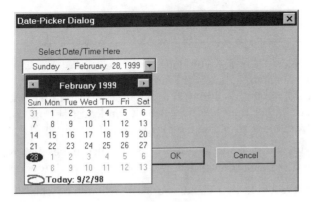

Figure 8.3 The date picker control expanded.

Figure 8.4 shows the exact same DTP but with the DTS_TIMEFORMAT style. Notice that the up-down control used to change the time is located on the right side of the control. The actual format displayed depends on the values used for the user's locale as given by the LOCALE_SLONGDATEFORMAT, LOCALE_SSHORTDATE, and LOCALE_STIME-FORMAT values, respectively.

There are, however, additional styles that you can apply to the DTP control. These are summarized as follows:

DTS_APPCANPARSE. This style allows the user to edit within the client area of the DTP when the F2 key is pressed; the parent window can parse the user's input and take action as necessary. The control sends a DTN_USERSTRING notification message when the user finishes.

DTS_RIGHTALIGN. This style forces the drop-down month calendar to be right-aligned with the DTP instead of left-aligned (the default).

DTS_SHOWNONE. It is possible to have no date in the control. When this style is applied, the DTP displays a checkbox that the user can check after he or she has entered or selected data. Until this is checked, no date can be retrieved from the control. This state can be verified with the DTM_GETSYSTEMTIME message, or set with the DTM_SETSYSTEMTIME message.

Table 8.3 DTP Styles

DTP STYLE	MEANING
DTS_LONGDATEFORMAT	The date is shown using a long format.
DTS_SHORTDATEFORMAT	The date is shown using a short format.
DTS_TIMEFORMAT	Only the time is shown.

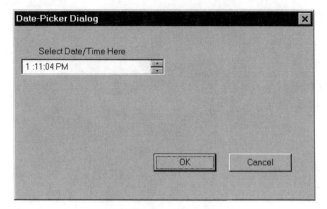

Figure 8.4 The date-time picker control.

DTS_UPDOWN. This style causes an up-down control to appear on the right of the DTP that allows the user to modify date values. This can be used to replace the drop-down month calendar, which is the default.

That takes care of the styles—you really do have a lot of flexibility when it comes to using them. Now let's see how to get our hands on the date-time selected by the user.

Retrieving DTP Selection

So, you have a DTP control inside your application and everything is working fine. The next question is, how do you retrieve the user's selection into your program's variables? The answer is simple—just send the control a DTM_GETSYSTEMTIME message with the lParam parameter as a pointer to a SYSTEMTIME structure. In the sample program, you'll find the following code when the OK button is pressed.

```
SYSTEMTIME sysTime;
static CWnd* pDTP;
pDTP = CWnd::FromHandle(m_hWndDP);
pDTP->SendMessage(DTM_GETSYSTEMTIME,NULL,(long)(&sysTime));
```

Figure 8.5 shows the value of the SYSTEMTIME structure in a Quick watch window. You now have the day, month, and so on, as numerical values that can be validated or manipulated at will.

That's it for the new DTP control. This little gadget is a really cool way to enhance any user interface that needs to do date/time processing, such as database query applications, project/schedule management software, and product and inventory management. Another cool gadget available from the common controls is the extended combo box. Let's take a look at it.

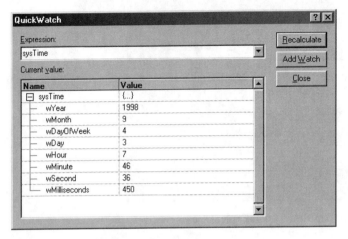

Figure 8.5 The SYSTEMTIME structure.

The Extended Combo Box

The new extended combo box control, or ComboBoxEx, is essentially a regular combo box except that it supports item images and indenting. The module Example3 on the companion Web site includes an example of this control embedded in a CoolBar object. Figure 8.6 shows the dialog box from this example.

As always, there are styles, messages, and structures to consider, so let's begin.

Extended Combo Box Styles

The ComboBoxEx control can use any of the regular styles of class CComboBox except for the following:

- CBS_OWNERDRAWFIXED
- CBS_OWNERDRAWVARIABLE
- CBS_HASSTRINGS

In addition to the regular styles, ComboBoxEx has a set of extended styles. These must not be confused with the extended window styles that can be used in CreateWindowEx(), SetWindowLong(), and GetWindowLong(). The extended styles are detailed in Table 8.4.

After you create the ComboBoxEx control, you can set the extended styles by sending it a CBEM_SETEXSTYLE message. This message, and the others, are discussed later in this chapter. First let's look at the structures used by the control.

The ComboBoxEx Structures

The first structure, ComboBoxExItem, is used to contain information about a ComboBoxEx item, and is prototyped as

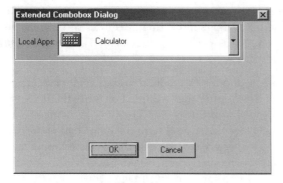

Figure 8.6   The Extended combo box example.

```
typedef struct
{
    UINT     mask;
    int      iItem;
    LPTSTR   pszText;
    int      cchTextMax;
    int      iImage;
    int      iSelectedImage;
    int      iOverlay;
    int      iIndent;
    LPARAM   lParam;

} COMBOBOXEXITEM, *PCOMBOBOXEXITEM;
```

Table 8.4   ComboBoxEx Extended Styles

EXTENDED STYLE	MEANING
CBES_EX_NOEDITIMAGE	The edit control will not display an image for selected items.
CBES_EX_NOEDITIMAGEINDENT	The edit control will not indent text to make room for an item image.
CBES_EX_PATHWORDBREAKPROC	**NT Only**. The edit control of the ComboBoxEx will use the forward slash, backslash, and period as word delimiters. This makes keyboard shortcuts for word-by-word cursor movement effective in path names and URLs.
CBES_EX_CASESENSITIVE	Search strings will be case sensitive.
CBES_EX_NOSIZELIMIT	Allows the control to be sized smaller vertically than its contained combo box; the combo box is also clipped in this case.

Like a lot of the other structures you've seen, this one contains a lot of familiar members. The *mask* member is a set of bit flags indicating attributes of the structure or of some operation using the structure. The possible values, which can be ORed together, are listed in Table 8.5.

The iItem member is the zero-based index of the item in the combo box. The pszText member is the address of a character buffer that will read or write the item's text. The cchTextMax member specifies the size of this buffer. The iImage member is the zero-based index into the CImageList object associated with the item. This is the image that is displayed when the item is not selected. Conversely, the iSelectedImage member is the index of the image to display when the item is selected. The iOverlay member is the one-based index into the image list of an overlay image. These images are drawn transparently over the regular image and are used in drag-and-drop operations. The iIndent member is the number of indent spaces to draw for the item; each indentation is 10 pixels. Finally, the lParam is the 32-bit value you get for free and can be used to provide additional information about the item.

This structure is used when adding, deleting, or inserting items into the ComboBoxEx control. To perform these kinds of operations, you fill in the members with the values you want, and send the control a message. There's more ground to cover before we see some examples.

Another structure called NMCBEENEDIT is used with the notification messages. The CComboBoxEx control makes considerable use of notification messages, so this structure is used frequently. It is prototyped as follows:

```
typedef struct
{
    NMHDR   hdr;
    BOOL    fChanged;
    int     iNewSelection;
    TCHAR   szText[CBEMAXSTRLEN]; // CBEMAXSTRLEN is 260
    int     iWhy;
} NMCBEENDEDIT, *PNMCBEENDEDIT;
```

Table 8.5 The Mask Member of ComboBoxExItem

MASK VALUES	MEANING
CBEIF_DI_SETITEM	Store the item data and do not ask for it again.
CBEIF_IMAGE	The iImage member is valid or must have a value.
CBEIF_INDENT	The iIndent member is valid or must have a value.
CBEIF_LPARAM	The lParam member is valid or must have a value.
CBEIF_OVERLAY	The iOverlay member is valid or must have a value.
CBEIF_SELECTEDIMAGE	The iSelectedImage member is valid or must have a value.
CBEIF_TEXT	The pszText member is valid or must have a value.

The hdr member contains information about the notification message. fChanged is a flag indicating if the edit box contents have been modified. The iNewSelection member is the zero-based index for the item selected upon completion of the edit operation. The string containing the edit box contents is in the szText member. Finally, the iWhy member is a value specifying what action triggered the message.

Another important structure, also used with the notification messages, is NMCOM-BOBOXEX, prototyped as follows:

```
typedef struct
{
    NMHDR hdr;
    COMBOBOXEXITEM ceItem;
} NMCOMBOBOXEX, *PNMCOMBOBOXEX;
```

The hdr member contains information related to the notification message for the combo box item. The ceItem member is a COMBOBOXEXITEM structure that contains specific information about the current notification message. This structure contains information needed by the parent window to respond to the message. Its members often can be used as fields for the owner to return values back to the combo box item.

There are two more ComboBoxEx structures used with drag-and-drop operations, NMCBEDRAGBEGIN and NMCBEENDEDIT. These are not covered in this book. Consult the documentation if you need specific information about these activities.

That's a wrap on the structures you'll see with the extended combo box object. In the next section, you'll see how these structures are used with the messages to drive the combo box.

Extended Combo Box Messages

Like its cousin CComboBox, the ComboBoxEx control responds to messages sent by the developer to accomplish discrete programming tasks. As the programmer, you'll need to add new items to this combo box, search for strings, or delete items. As with any other control, simply fill in the appropriate structure with the values you want, and use SendMessage() to operate on the combo box. There are 13 different messages altogether and all have the prefix CBEM_. Here is a quick overview of what these are, and what they're used for.

CBEM_INSERTITEM. This message is used to insert an item into the combo box. The wParam is 0, the lParam is the address of a COMBOBOXEXITEM structure that contains the item information. The iItem member of this structure must be the zero-based index in which the item is inserted. If iItem is –1, the item is inserted at the end of the list. The return value from SendMessage() is the index of the new item inserted if it succeeded, or –1 if the call failed. Here's an example that assumes you've created a ComboBoxEx control and have a handle to it called hWndCombo:

```
COMBOBOXEXITEM exItem;
CWnd * pCombo = CWnd::FromHandle(hWndCombo);
```

```
//
// set up structure with item to add
//
exItem.mask = CBEIF_TEXT | CBEIF_LPARAM | CBEIF_IMAGE |
    CBEIF_SELECTEDIMAGE;
exItem.pszText = "Hello world!";
exItem.cchTextMax = sizeof(exItem.pszText);
exItem.lParam = (LPARAM)rgApps[idx].szProg;
exItem.iItem = -1; // insert at end of combo box
exItem.iImage = idxImage;// Image to display
exItem.iSelectedImage = idxImage;// Image to display
LRESULT lRet; // return value
lRet = pCombo->SendMessage(CBEM_INSERTITEM, 0L,(LPARAM)&exItem);
```

All the messages work like this—set up a structure and send a message—so this code acts as a template. Upcoming examples will use these variables for the sake of brevity.

CBEM_DELETEITEM. This message deletes an item from the combo box. The wParam parameter is the index of the item to delete. The lParam is zero. For example,

```
pCombo->SendMessage(CBEM_DELETEITEM, 3 ,0L);
```

This would remove the fourth item (3 is zero-based!) from the hypothetical combo box. The return value is the number of items left in the control, or CB_ERR (–1) if an error occurs.

CBEM_SETIMAGELIST. This message associates a CImageList object with the extended combo box. You should give careful thought to how you organize your image lists, as this can make it easier to program the control. For example, if the item needs an image showing the icon as disabled, you could make the first entry into the list the normal graphic and the second the disabled. If you need more (for drag-and-drop, and so on), keep them together as a *group* in the CImageList object so that you can use offsets from the default image: i, i+1, i+2, and so forth. The wParam of the CBEM_SETIMAGELIST message needs to be zero, and the lParam is the handle to the control's image list. The return value is the handle to any previous image list, or NULL if no previous list exists. One very important note: The height of your images might change the size requirements of the control. You should resize the ComboBoxEx control after sending this message to make sure it displays correctly.

CBEM_GETIMAGELIST. The return value for this message is the control's image list. Both wParam and lParam are zero. For example,

```
CImageList ciList;
ciList = pCombo->SendMessage(CBEM_GETIMAGELIST,0,0L);
```

When this code executes, the return value will be the CImageList object associated with the list of items in the combo box.

CBEM_GETEDITCONTROL. This message gets the handle to the combo box's edit box. Both wParam and lParam are zero. The return value is the handle to the edit box. This is NULL if the combo box does not have the CBS_DROPDOWN style.

CBEM_HASEDITCHANGED. This message detects if the contents of the edit box were changed by typing. Both wParam and lParam are zero. The return value is nonzero if the contents changed, or zero otherwise. For example,

```
LRESULT lrChanged;
lrChanged = pCombo->SendMessage(CBEM_HASEDITCHANGED,0,0L);
```

When this code executes, the programmer can determine if the user has changed the text in edit box portion of the combo box.

There are a few more messages (for reading/writing the extended styles, etc.), but the ones just described are used most frequently. In the next section, we'll examine the notification messages.

Notification Messages

A lot of the heavy lifting with the extended combo box is done with notification messages. There are seven notification messages for ComboBoxEx.

- CBEN_BEGINEDIT
- CBEN_ENDEDIT
- CBEN_INSERTITEM
- CBEN_DELETEITEM
- CBEN_DRAGBEGIN
- CBEN_GETDISPINFO
- NM_SETCURSOR

No doubt you can guess the functionality behind these messages, but if you get stuck, they're in the documentation. They're handled like any other garden-variety notification.

That does it for the extended combo box for now. We'll look at the sample code after the next new control, the rebar or CoolBar control.

The CoolBar Control

The CoolBar control is one of the latest common controls. You've probably seen these before—they're something like menu strips, although they're formally known as a tool container control. Each CoolBar control contains a set of functionally related tools organized into bands. These embedded tools can be controls or even additional toolbars. The bands can be configured to consume an entire row or share a row. The CoolBar with Microsoft's Internet Explorer even has an animation control in the upper right-hand corner. As with the other extended controls, you set up certain system structures and send messages to configure the CoolBar. I should point out that the real name for this control is the rebar control. But, since CoolBar seems to be the more widely accepted term in colloquial use, it is referred to as CoolBar in this chapter, except where rebar is required for class names and structures.

CoolBar Styles

The CoolBar control supports the standard common control styles (i.e., those with pre-fix CCS_XXX) in addition to the values shown in Table 8.6.

The CoolBar is created like the other extended controls—set up and call InitCommon-ControlsEx(), then create the CoolBar with CreateWindow() or CreateWindowEx(). But first, you'll need to use the system structures to give the CoolBar the properties you want.

CoolBar Structures

There are a few structures that can be used with a CoolBar, depending on your purpose. The first of these is REBARINFO, and it is prototyped as follows:

```
typedef struct tagREBARINFO
{
    UINT        cbSize;
    UINT        fMask;
    HIMAGELIST  himl;
} REBARINFO, FAR *LPREBARINFO;
```

The structure contains information regarding the characteristics of the CoolBar control. The cbSize member is the size of this structure, in bytes. You'll need to fill this in before firing off any messages to the control—set it to sizeof(REBARINFO). The fMask member is a flag that describes the characteristics of the CoolBar control. Presently, there is only one value for this, RBIM_IMAGELIST, which means the himl member is valid or must be supplied. The himl member is the handle to an image list to use with the control.

After you configure this structure to tell the framework that you're using an image list, you need to add the bands to the CoolBar via the RB_INSERTBAND message and the REBARBANDINFO structure.

```
typedef struct tagREBARBANDIFNO
{
    UINT cbSize;
    UINT fMask;
    UINT fStyle;
    COLORREF clrFore;
    COLORREF clrBack;
    LPTSTR lpText;
    UINT cch;
    int iImage;
```

Table 8.6 The CoolBar Styles

STYLE FLAG	DESCRIPTION
RBS_BANDBORDERS	Each band has a border drawn around its controls.
RBS_VARHEIGHT	Each row can be a different height.
RBS_FIXEDORDER	Prevents user from reordering the bands.

```
    HWND hwndChild;
    UINT cxMinChild;
    UINT cyMinChild;
    UINT cx;
    HBITMAP hbmBack;
    UINT wID;
    #if (_WIN32_IE >= 0x0400)
        UINT cyChild;
        UINT cyMaxChild;
        UINT cyIntegral;
        UINT cxIdeal;
        LPARAM lParam;
        UINT cxHeader;
    #endif
}REBARBANDINFO, FAR * LPREBARBANDINFO;
```

This structure defines a band in a CoolBar control. The cbSize member is the size of this structure and must be filled in before using the structure; for example, in a message. The fMask member is a flag that indicates which structure members are valid or which must be filled. It can be a combination of the values shown in Table 8.7.

Notice that some of the values depend on the version of Internet Explorer—the RBBIM_HEADERSIZE, RBBIM_IDEALSIZE, and RBBIM_LPARAM all require version 4.71 or above of COMCTL32.DLL. The fStyle member specifies the style of the band, and can be a combination of the values shown in Table 8.8.

Table 8.7   The fMask Values for the REBARBANDINFO Structure

FMASK VALUE	DESCRIPTION
RBBIM_BACKGROUND	The hbmBack member is valid or must be filled.
RBBIM_CHILD	The hwndChild member is valid or must be filled.
RBBIM_CHILDSIZE	The cxMinChild and cyMinChild members are valid or must be filled.
RBBIM_COLORS	The clrFore and clrBack members are valid or must be filled.
RBBIM_HEADERSIZE	The cxHeader member is valid or must be filled.
RBBIM_IDEALSIZE	The cxIdeal member is valid or must be filled.
RBBIM_ID	The wID member is valid or must be filled.
RBBIM_IMAGE	The iImage member is valid or must be filled.
RBBIM_LPARAM	The lParam member is valid or must be filled.
RBBIM_SIZE	The cx member is valid or must be filled.
RBBIM_STYLE	The fStyle member is valid or must be filled.
RBBIM_TEXT	The lpText member is valid or must be filled.

Table 8.8 The fStyle Flag of the REBARBANDINFO Structure

FSTYLE FLAG VALUE	DESCRIPTION
RBBS_BREAK	The band is on a new line.
RBBS_CHILDEDGE	The band has an edge at the top and bottom of the child window.
RBBS_FIXEDBMP	The background bitmap doesn't move when the band is resized.
RBBS_FIXEDSIZE	The band can't be sized. With this style, the sizing grip is not displayed on the band.
RBBS_GRIPPERALWAYS	The band will always have sizing grip, even if it is the only band.
RBBS_HIDDEN	The band will not be visible.
RBBS_NOGRIPPER	The band will never have sizing grip, even if there is more than one band in the rebar.
RBBS_NOVERT	The band won't be displayed when the rebar control uses the CCS_VERT style.
RBBS_VARIABLEHEIGHT	The band can be resized by the rebar control. cyIntegral and cyMaxChild affect how the rebar will resize the band.

The RBBS_GRIPPERALWAYS, RBBS_NOGRIPPER, and RBBS_VARIABLEHEIGHT flags all require version 4.71 or higher of COMCTL32.DLL. The clrFore and clrBack members of this structure are the band foreground and background colors, respectively. If the hbmBack member specifies a background bitmap, then clrFore and clrBack are ignored.

The lpText member of the REBARBANDINFO structure is the address of a buffer containing the text to be displayed for the band. If the fMask member includes RBBIM_TEXT and you request information from the control, initialize this member with the address of a buffer that will receive the text. The cch member is the size of this buffer, in bytes.

The iImage member is the zero-based index into the image list for the image to display in the band (if any). The hwndChild member is the handle to the child window contained in the band (if any). The cxMinChild is the minimum width, in pixels, of the child windows on the band. The band cannot be resized to a value smaller than the value in cxMinChild. The cyMinChild is the minimum height, in pixels, of the child windows on the band. The cx member is the length, in pixels, of the band, and hbmBack is the handle to a background bitmap for the band.

The wID member is a unique value that the control uses to identify the band for custom draw notification messages. This member could be changed in the future to support additional features.

The cyChild member is the initial height, in pixels, of the band. It is ignored unless you specify the RBBS_VARIABLEHEIGHT style. The cyMaxChild member is also in pixels—this is the maximum height of the band and is also ignored without the RBBS_VARIABLEHEIGHT style.

The cyIntegral member is a step value that governs how the band can grow or shrink in size, and is also in pixels. It is ignored without the RBBS_VARIABLEHEIGHT style. The cyIdeal member is a pixel measurement specifying the ideal width of the band. The lParam is 32 bits of data that you can use as you will—the same piggyback demonstrated in earlier chapters.

The cxHeader member is the pixel size of the band's header, which is the area between the band edge and the control. When this value is specified, it overrides all the normal header dimensions as calculated by the control.

In closing on this structure, keep in mind that the cx, cxMinChild, cyMinChild members are relative to the CoolBar's orientation. If it's a horizontal control, cx and cxMin-Child are horizontal measurements, and cyMinChild is a vertical measurement. But if the control is vertical, the opposite is true: cx and cxMinChild are vertical measurements and cyMinChild is a horizontal quantity. Be careful.

Before I give you the messages, be advised that the CoolBar shares a unique property with the toolbar control, and only this control. That is, the toolbar control is transparent to any image used as a background bitmap on a CoolBar. This is really great for creating unique visual effects that add a nice touch to the user interface.

CoolBar Messages

Like all the other controls, working with the CoolBar control is simply a matter of configuring some structures, and sending messages to the control. The following is an overview of the messages that you can use with this control.

RB_INSERTBAND. This message inserts a new band into the control. The wParam of SendMessage() is the position where the band should be inserted. Use –1 to add a new band. If this value is greater than the number of bands already in the rebar control, the band is added at the end of the list. The lParam is a pointer to the REBAR-INFO structure. The return value is TRUE if the call was a success. This is the case for all the messages, and is not repeated in the list that follows.

RB_SETBARINFO. This sets the general information about the control. The wParam is not used, lParam is a pointer to a REBARINFO structure.

RB_GETBARINFO. This retrieves the general information into the REBARINFO structure pointed to by lParam (wParam is not used).

RB_SETBANDINFO. This sets the information for a band in the CoolBar control. The wParam is the zero-based index of the band, and lParam is a pointer to a REBAR-BANDINFO structure.

RB_GETBANDINFO. This gets the information for a band into the REBARBAND-INFO structure pointed to by lParam. Set wParam to the index of the band.

RB_GETBANDCOUNT. This message gets the number of bands currently in the control. Neither wParam nor lParam are used. Unlike the other messages, the return value is not a BOOL; it's the number of bands in the control.

RB_GETROWCOUNT. The return value of this message is the number of rows in the CoolBar control. Neither wParam nor lParam are used.

RB_GETROWHEIGHT. The return value of this message is the height of a row in the CoolBar control. Set wParam to the index of the band you're querying. lParam is not used.

RB_DELETEBAND. This deletes a band from the control. Set wParam to the index of the band to delete; lParam is not used. The return value is a BOOL.

That does it for the messages. There are a few more details that need to be addressed.

CoolBar Details

Before we get into the sample code, here are a couple of tidbits to consider regarding the CoolBar control. When your application exits, you most likely want to save the current layout of the control in your .INI file or another location. To do this, first get the number of bands using the RB_GETBANDCOUNT message, and loop through all the bands. As you loop, get the information about each band (use RB_GETBANDINFO) and save what you need. You should use the wID and cx values as a minimum, since these are the order of the bands and their size, respectively. When it comes time to rebuild the CoolBar, read these values back in and reverse the process.

The CoolBar doesn't destroy its own image list, so you need to get the handle to the image list by using RB_GETBARINFO and then manually destroy the list. Also, there is only one notification message for the CoolBar control, RBN_HEIGHTCHANGE. This message is routed to your application by WM_NOTIFY. The message is sent whenever the control is resized in any direction, or has the CCS_VERT style. The lParam of the message points to a vanilla-flavored NMHDR structure if you need it.

That's a wrap for all the details. Now I'll show you some code that puts them into action.

The Sample Program

The sample program for this material is simple but functional. You'll find the code in the Example3 project on the companion Web site. The code creates a CoolBar control, then adds an extended combo box. The combo box is populated with applications that ship with Windows. Not all the entries in the combo box may work on your installation, but there are enough for you to get the idea. Figure 8.7 shows the dialog box with the controls.

The code can be found in the ExCombo.cpp and header files. A lot is going on in OnInit-Dialog(). For example, the names of various Windows programs that *should* be on your machine are hard-coded. An array of structures (rgApps) is used to store item information for the combo box entries. Here is the code for one item, the Windows Calculator:

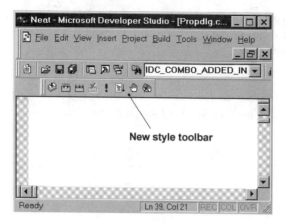

Figure 8.7 The CoolBar/Combo box dialog box.

```
memset(szWinDir,0,sizeof(szWinDir));
memset(szBufr,0,sizeof(szBufr));
//
GetWindowsDirectory(szWinDir,MAX_PATH);
strcpy(szBufr,szWinDir);
strcat(szBufr,"\\");
strcat(szBufr,"calc.exe");
//
// set up the array of applications from which to choose
//
strcpy(rgApps[0].szName,"Calculator");
strcpy(rgApps[0].szProg,szBufr);
rgApps[0].iBmp = IDB_CALC;
rgApps[0].i = 0;
```

This code is an example of what programming information you need to manage for each item that goes into the combo box. In the code, you can see the name of the program (i.e., the item in the combo box) that is executed when the item is selected, the bitmap identifier (e.g., IDB_CALC), and the item's position in the list. In this example, it is zero as indicated by the last line of code. This code repeated for each item in the combo box. Next, set up the INITCOMMONCONTROLSEX structure by specifying the classes for both the CoolBar and the extended combo box. You create an images list for the combo box, and then create the CoolBar control.

```
hWndRebar = CreateWindowEx(0L,REBARCLASSNAME,
            NULL,WS_VISIBLE | WS_BORDER | WS_CHILD | WS_CLIPCHILDREN |
            WS_CLIPSIBLINGS | CCS_NODIVIDER | CCS_NOPARENTALIGN |
            RBS_VARHEIGHT | RBS_BANDBORDERS,0, 0, 350, 375,hWndParent,
            NULL,hInst,NULL );
```

Next, create an extended combo box and add it to the CoolBar control. You loop through all the local applications going into the combo box and add them with the CBEM_INSERTITEM message.

```
m_pCombo->SendMessage(CBEM_INSERTITEM, 0L,(LPARAM)&cbI);
```

This is where all the heavy lifting is done. The CoolBar and combo box have both been created, so it's time to configure a REBARBANDINFO structure and glue on the combo box.

```
// Initialize REBARBANDINFO
rbBand.cbSize = sizeof(REBARBANDINFO);
rbBand.fMask = RBBIM_COLORS |       // clrFore and clrBack are valid
               RBBIM_CHILD |        // hwndChild is valid
               RBBIM_CHILDSIZE |    // cxMinChild and cyMinChild are valid
               RBBIM_STYLE |        // fStyle is valid
               RBBIM_ID |           // wID is valid
               RBBIM_TEXT |         // lpText is valid
               RBBIM_BACKGROUND;    // hbmBack is valid

rbBand.clrFore = GetSysColor(COLOR_BTNTEXT);
rbBand.clrBack = GetSysColor(COLOR_BTNFACE);
rbBand.fStyle = RBBS_NOVERT |       // do not display in vert. orientation
                RBBS_CHILDEDGE |
                RBBS_FIXEDBMP;
rbBand.hbmBack = LoadBitmap(hInst, MAKEINTRESOURCE(IDB_BACK));
rbBand.lpText = TEXT("Local Apps:");
rbBand.hwndChild = hWndCombo;
rbBand.cxMinChild = MIN_COMBOCX;
rbBand.cyMinChild = MIN_CY;
//
// Add the combo box band to the end
//
m_pRebar->SendMessage(RB_INSERTBAND, (WPARAM)-1, (LPARAM)&rbBand);
```

The process of sending a message to a control should be familiar to you by now. The next thing to look at is how the combo box item runs when selected. To do this, you trap the DefWindowProc() call.

```
CExCombo::DefWindowProc(UINT message,WPARAM wParam,LPARAM lParam)
{
    int iSelect; // index of combo selection

    if((message == WM_COMMAND) && (HIWORD(wParam)==CBN_SELCHANGE))
    {
        // Get, and run, the currently selected item
        iSelect = ::SendMessage(hWndCombo, CB_GETCURSEL, 0, 0);
        ShellExecute( NULL, TEXT("open"), rgApps[iSelect].szProg,
                      NULL, NULL, SW_SHOWNORMAL );
    }
    return CDialog::DefWindowProc(message, wParam, lParam);
}   // End DefWindowProc()
```

There you have it. As you can see, the CoolBar control is pretty snappy, and really easy to use. You can expect to see more and more user interfaces sporting these features in the near future. This direction is heavily influenced by the "Web-centric" trend in contemporary software development.

The Progress Bar

The extended progress bar control supports full 32-bit ranges instead of 16. To set the 32-bit range, send it a PBM_SETRANGE32 message. Set the wParam to the low end of the range and lParam to the high end. The return value is a DWORD value containing the previous 16-bit low range in its low-order word, and the high limit will be in the high-order word. Here's some code that assumes pProg is a pointer to the progress bar control:

```
DWORD dwRet;
int iLo, iHi;  // previous 16-bit values
// now set range
dwRet = pProg->SendMessage(PBM_SETRANGE32, 0x0000, 0xffff);
// get previous hi/lo limits
iLo = LOWORD(dwRet); // get previous 16-bit low limit
iHi = HIWORD(dwRet); // previous 16-bit high limit
```

If the previous ranges were already set to 32-bit values by a PBM_SETRANGE32 message, the return value consists of the low words of both 32-bit limits. If you need the entire high and low 32-bit range, send the control a PBM_GETRANGE message and set wParam to TRUE or FALSE, and send lParam a pointer to a PBRANGE structure. When wParam is FALSE, the message returns the previous 32-bit high limit; when TRUE, the low limit. The PBRANGE structure is prototyped as follows:

```
typedef struct
{
    int iLow;
    int iHigh;
} PBRANGE, *PPBRANGE;
```

The iLow and iHigh members of this structure receive the 32-bit values you're looking for. When using the PBM_GETRANGE for other purposes, the lParam parameter can be NULL.

The Tool Tip Control

You've already glimpsed at this control from the previous discussion of custom drawing. The extended tool tip control (that is, ICC_BAR_CLASSES from Table 8.1) lets the tip float above the mouse as it moves, not just when it's stationary over the object to which it is linked. This behavior is called *hot tracking*. Combining the TTM_TRACKACTIVATE and TTM_TRACKPOSITION messages allows you to do this. The first message sets wParam to nonzero to indicate if tracking is being enabled, and zero to disable. Prior to sending the message, you'll need to set up the TOOLINFO structure as follows:

```
typedef struct tagTOOLINFO
{
    UINT cbSize;
    UINT uFlags;
    HWND hwnd;
    UINT uId;
    RECT rect;
    HINSTANCE hinst;
    LPTSTR lpszText;
    #if (_WIN32_IE >= 0x0300)
        LPARAM lParam;
    #endif
} TOOLINFO, NEAR *PTOOLINFO, FAR *LPTOOLINFO;
```

The cbSize member is the size of this structure and must be set to sizeof(TOOLINFO). The uFlags member is a set of bit flags indicating how the tool tips will behave and be displayed. These can be a combination of the values listed in Table 8.9.

The hwnd member is the handle of the window containing the tool. The uId member is the identifier you assign to the tool, and rect is its bounding rectangle. The hinst member of this structure is the handle to the instance containing the string resource for the tool, and lpszText is the text that appears as tool tip help. The lParam member is 32 bits that you can use as necessary.

Table 8.9 The TOOLINFO uFlags

UFLAGS VALUE	DESCRIPTION
TTF_ABSOLUTE	Tool tip window positioned at coordinates provided by TTM_TRACKPOSITION. Requires TTF_TRACK flag and version 4.70+ of COMCTRL32.DLL.
TTF_CENTERTIP	Tool tip centered below the tool given by the uId member.
TTF_IDISHWND	Indicates the uId member is handle to the tool when set. When not set, it's the tool identifier.
TTF_RTLREADING	Tool tip text displayed right-to-left for Arabic/Hebrew systems.
TTF_SUBCLASS	The tool tip control must subclass the tool's window to intercept messages like WM_MOUSEMOVE. If you don't set this, you must use the TTM_RELAYEVENT message to send messages to the tool tip control.
TTF_TRACK	Tool tip window positioned next to the tool it tracks, and moves according to coordinates from the TTM_TRACKPOSITION message. Requires the TTM_TRACKACTIVATE message and version 4.70+.
TTF_TRANSPARENT	The tool tip forwards mouse messages to the parent window except for mouse events inside the tool tip window.

To enable hot tracking, set up a TOOLINFO structure with the cbSize, hwnd, and uId members filled in with the necessary values, and send the TTM_TRACKACTIVATE message followed by the TTM_TRACKPOSITION message. The wParam is not used, and the lParam contains the x and y screen coordinates where the tip will be displayed. For example,

```
DWORD dwLoc =  MAKELONG(50,100);
pToolTip->SendMessage(TTM_TRACKPOSITION,0,(LPARAM)dwLoc);
```

When this code executes, your application can take advantage of hot tracking.

Note that tool tip tracking is not supported for windows that have the tool tip control as a subclass. To allow tracking for other windows, you must subclass the window yourself and then send the TTM_TRACKPOSITION message where appropriate.

Tool Tip Properties

In addition to supporting custom draw, the extended Tool Tip class gives you more control over various properties, such as the margins and colors. You set the margins with the TTM_SETMARGIN message. This message takes a pointer to a RECT that specifies the distance between the edges of the Tool Tip window and the edges of the text. The margins are set in the lParam. The RECT is used to maintain spacing between the various edges. The *left* member is the space for the left margin and the text; the *right* is used for the right edge. The *top* and *bottom* members are for the top and bottom edges. The values you supply are measured in pixels. For example,

```
RECT rect;
rect.top = 5;
rect.bottom= 15;
rect.right= 100;
rect.left= 10;
pToolTip->SendMessage(TTM_SETMARGIN,0,(LPARAM)(&rect));
```

This code creates a margin for the text that is displayed in the tool tip window.

Use the TTM_GETMARGIN message to retrieve the current margins.

You can also change the width of the tool tip using the TTM_SETMAXTIPWIDTH message. This value does not reflect the tool tip's actual width; rather, it is a relative amount used to segment lengthy text into multiple lines. The message is used as follows:

```
int iMaxWidth = 300;
int iOldWidth = pToolTip->SendMessage(TTM_SETMAXTIPWIDTH,
                      0,(LPARAM)iMaxWidth);
```

The return value is the previous maximum tool tip width. If the text string exceeds the maximum width, the control tries to break the text into multiple lines, using spaces as the breaking points. If the text cannot be segmented into multiple lines, it is displayed on a single line whose length may exceed the maximum tool tip width.

It's also easy to set the background and text colors that are displayed in the tool tip— use the TTM_SETTIPBKCOLOR and TTM_SETTIPTEXTCOLOR messages, respectively. Here is the code to set the background color to yellow and the text color to black:

```
COLORREF clr = (0xffff00); // yellow
pToolTip->SendMessage(TTM_SETTIPBKCOLOR,(WPARAM)clr,0);
Clr = (0x000000);// black
pToolTip->SendMessage(TTM_ SETTIPTEXTCOLOR,(WPARAM)clr,0);
```

To adjust the delay time for a tool tip, use the TTM_SETDELAYTIME message. The delay time is the amount of time that will elapse between when the mouse moves over the tool boundary and when the tool tip text appears. The wParam is a flag specifying the duration value, and can be one of the following values:

TTDT_AUTOPOP. This retrieves the amount of time the tool tip window remains visible when the cursor is stationary within a tool's bounding rectangle.

TTDT_INITIAL. This retrieves the amount of time the cursor must remain stationary over a tool before the tip text appears.

TTDT_RESHOW. This retrieves the amount of time it takes for subsequent tool tip windows to appear as the cursor moves from one tool's bounding rectangle to another.

The lParam is the delay time to be set, measured in milliseconds. The following example sets the delay time to 250 milliseconds.

```
pToolTip->SendMessage(TTM_SETDELAYTIME,TTDT_INITIAL,(LPARAM)(INT)
    ( MAKELONG(250,0));
```

The new version of the common control library now includes a message to retrieve the delay time, which was missing under Windows95. This message is TTM_GETDELAY-TIME, prototyped as follows

```
int iDelay;
iDelay = pToolTip->SendMessage(TTM_GETDELAYTIME,(DWORD)(TTDT_INI-
TIAL),0);
```

You can use any of the duration flags described earlier for TTM_SETDELAYTIME for the wParam parameter. The return value is the delay, in milliseconds.

The ListView Control

Another new common control that has extended features is the ListView control. A new feature of this control is that items can now be indented when the control is in report view. Although you would surely never want to do this, the control can now have up to 100,000,000 items. Also, the control can be given both horizontal and vertical lines, making it look and behave like a grid control.

Styles

The ListView control also supports extended styles. These should not be confused with extended window styles. After you create the ListView control, you can set the extended styles by sending it the LVM_SETEXTENDEDLISTVIEWSTYLES message. The lParam contains the styles. Table 8.10 summarizes the extended styles.

Table 8.10 The New ListView Extended Styles

EXTENDED STYLE FLAG	DESCRIPTION
LVS_EX_CHECKBOXES	The control contains checkboxes for each item.
LVS_EX_FULLROWSELECT	Selecting an item also selects its subitems. Requires LVS_REPORT style.
LVS_EX_GRIDLINES	Dashed lines are placed around all items and subitems.
LVS_EX_HEADERDRAGDROP	Enables drag-and-drop reordering of the control's columns.
LVS_EX_SUBITEMIMAGES	Images may be displayed for subitems.
LVS_EX_TRACKSELECT	Hot tracking is enabled.

That wraps up the styles, now we need some messages. That's next.

Extended ListView Messages

There are some new messages available for use with the extended ListView control. Like virtually every other control, there are system structures available for use with the messages. The following is an overview of the new messages.

LVM_GETEXTENDEDLISTVIEWSTYLES. This message returns the extended ListView styles in the return value. Neither the wParam or lParam parameters are used in the call to SendMessage() and should be set to zero.

LVM_SETEXTENDEDLISTVIEWSTYLES. This message sets the extended styles for a ListView control. The wParam parameter is not used. The lParam contains the extended style flags that are to be set. There is no return value.

LVM_GETCOLUMNORDERARRAY. This message retrieves the current column ordering information. The wParam parameter is the zero-based index of the column in the control to retrieve, and the lParam is a pointer to an array of integers that receive the column ordering information. This array must be at least the number of columns multiplied by the size of an integer. For example, if you have four columns in the control:

```
int iArraySize = 4 * sizeof(int);
int iTheArray[iArraySize];
```

As every C/C++ programmer knows from experience, failing to properly allocate space for an array is an easy way to cause your program to crash.

The return value from SendMessage() is a BOOL value indicating success or failure for the call.

LVM_SETCOLUMNORDERARRAY. The converse of the LVM_GETCOLUMN-ORDERARRAY message, this message sets the column ordering information. Set wParam to the size of the array that will contain the new column ordering information as described previously in the LVM_GETCOLUMNORDERARRAY message description, and set lParam to a pointer to the array. The return value is a BOOL indicating success or failure.

LVM_GETSUBITEMRECT. This message gets the bounding rectangle for an item's subitem. Set wParam to the index of the parent item for the subitem, and lParam is a pointer to a RECT. Before sending the message, set the *top* member of this RECT structure to the one-based index of the subitem in question, and the *left* member to one of the following flag values:

- LVIR_BOUNDS This returns the bounding rectangle for the entire subitem, including the icon and label.
- LVIR_ICON This returns the bounding rectangle for the subitem's icon only.
- LVIR_LABEL This returns only the bounding rectangle for the subitem's label.
- The return value from this message is a BOOL value indicating success or failure.

LVM_SUBITEMHITTEST. This message determines what item or subitem (if any) is at the given point. The wParam is not used. The lParam parameter is a pointer to an LVHITTESTINFO structure, which is prototyped as follows:

```
typedef struct _LVHITTESTINFO
{
    POINT pt;
    UINT flags;
    int iItem;
    int iSubItem;
} LVHITTESTINFO;
```

Prior to sending the message to the ListView control, set the pt member to the client coordinates of the point to be tested. After sending the message, if the hit was successful and the point falls on an item, the iItem member of this structure will have the index of the item. If it falls on a subitem, the iSubItem member will contain the one-based index of the subitem, and the iItem member will have the subitem's parent index. The return value from the message is the index of the item or subitem if the hit test was successful, or –1 if it failed.

LVM_SETICONSPACING. This message sets the icon spacing for a ListView that has the LVS_ICON style. The wParam is not used; lParam is a DWORD value containing the new horizontal spacing in the low word and the vertical spacing in the high word. The return value is a DWORD containing the previous spacing in the low and high words.

That's all for the ListView control. This control is usually used in tandem with the next topic of discussion, the header control.

The Enhanced Header Control

The extended header control now comes with some cool enhancements. These include hot tracking, drag-and-drop capabilities, image lists, item ordering, among others. You can also place text, bitmaps, and images directly into a header item. The following is a closer look at the header control's styles and structures.

Styles

You specify the styles for the header control when you create it. These styles can be retrieved and changed later by using the GetWindowLong() and SetWindowLong() functions. In addition to the styles available prior to the release of the enhanced header control, there are some new ones. The following is a list of styles currently available for the header control.

HDS_BUTTONS. With this style, every item in the header looks and acts like a push-button. This is generally used to allow the user to carry out some operation relative to the items in that column. For example, if the header control is for a list of files, you may allow the user to sort them by date, or type.

HDS_DRAGDROP. This is a new style for version 4.70 of the Microsoft common controls DLL and higher. It allows drag-and-drop reordering of header items.

HDS_FULLDRAG. This is also new for version 4.70. The style causes the header control to display the contents of the column while it is being resized.

HDS_HIDDEN. This style points out one of the features that is also included with the listbox and combo box. Sometimes you want to hide a control and use it as an information container and not as a visual element. This style indicates the header control is intended to be hidden. The style doesn't hide the control until you adjust its size. When you send the HDM_LAYOUT message to a header with this style, the control returns zero in the cy member of the WINDOWPOS structure. You could then hide the control by setting its height to zero.

HDS_HORZ. This style simply creates a header control with a horizontal orientation instead of a vertical one.

HDS_HOTTRACK. This is a new style that is applied to allow hot tracking with the header control.

That takes care of the header control's styles. As you suspect, there are some system structures for you to play with, so let's take a look at them.

Structures

Information about an item in a header control is contained in an HDITEM structure. This structure supersedes the old HD_ITEM structure, and is prototyped as follows:

```
typedef struct _HDITEM
{
    UINT    mask;
    int     cxy;
    LPTSTR  pszText;
    HBITMAP hbm;
    int     cchTextMax;
    int     fmt;
    LPARAM  lParam;
    #if (_WIN32_IE >= 0x0300)
        int     iImage;
```

```
        int     iOrder;
    #endif
} HDITEM, FAR * LPHDITEM;
```

The mask member indicates which of the other members are valid or which must be filled in. It can be a combination of the values shown in Table 8.11.

The cxy member is the width or height of the item. The pszText is the address of an item string containing text for the header item. The hbm member is a handle to the item's bitmap. The cchTextMax is the length of the pszText member, and fmt is a set of bit flags specifying the format of the item. There are several ways you can set this up. First, you can use the following text justification flags.

- **HDF_CENTER.** The item's contents are centered.

- **HDF_RIGHT.** The item's contents are right-aligned.

- **HDF_LEFT.** The item's contents are left-aligned.

- **HDF_RTLREADING.** Text is read from right to left in support of Hebrew or Arabic. This flag can be combined with one of the following to further specify the fmt member.

  - **HDF_BITMAP.** The item displays a bitmap.

  - **HDF_IMAGE.** The item displays an image from its image list. Requires version 4.70 or higher of COMCTL32.DLL.

  - **HDF_BITMAP_ON_RIGHT.** The bitmap appears to the right of the text; it has no effect on an image from the image list. Version 4.70 or higher is required.

- **HDF_OWNERDRAW.** The header control's parent draws the item.

- **HDF_STRING.** The header control item displays a string.

Table 8.11   The Mask Flags

MASK FLAG	DESCRIPTION
HDI_BITMAP	The hbm member is valid.
HDI_FORMAT	The fmt member is valid.
HDI_HEIGHT	The cxy member is valid and indicates the item's height.
HDI_IMAGE	The iImage member specifies the image for the item. Requires version 4.70 or higher of the Microsoft common controls DLL.
HDI_LPARAM	The lParam member is valid.
HDI_ORDER	The iOrder member specifies the item's order value. Requires version 4.70 or higher of the Microsoft common controls DLL.
HDI_TEXT	The pszText and cchTextMax members are valid.
HDI_WIDTH	The cxy member is valid and specifies the width of the item.

The lParam member of the structure is application-defined data which you can use to piggyback extra information about the item. The iImage member is the zero-based index of an image within the header's image list. Finally, the iOrder member sets the order in which the item will appear within the header control, moving from left to right, where the extreme left item is 0, the item to its right is 1, and so on.

That's it for the header control. I've omitted a review of the messages since there isn't anything really earth shattering or new with them. The enhanced header is created just like the other controls. You then set up your item structure and send the control the desired message.

The Enhanced Tab Control

The new, enhanced tab control now supports hot tracking, and you can place the tabs along any side of the control. Specifying the TCS_HOTTRACK style for the control enables hot tracking, which highlights the entire tab when the mouse hovers above it.

By default, tabs are placed at the top of the control. To have them placed at the bottom, specify the TCS_BOTTOM style when creating the control. To place them on the left side of the control, specify the TCS_VERTICAL style. Specify both the TCS_VERTICAL and TCS_RIGHT styles to place them on the right side of the control.

Another feature of the enhanced tab control is that unused rows of tabs can be displayed on the opposite side of the control. Just specify the TCS_SCROLLOPPOSITE style when you create the control.

Like the original tab control, the new one uses the TC_ITEM and TC_ITEMHEADER structures. However, these have been renamed to TCITEM and TCITEMHEADER to follow current naming conventions. The old names can still be used, but any new projects should use the new names.

The Enhanced TreeView Control

The TreeView control has only one enhancement besides the support for custom draw explained previously in this chapter: A parent item can now be partially expanded. This means the plus sign symbol (+) in the button next to the parent item remains visible when the tree is expanded. This property can be established by specifying the TVIS_EXPANDPARTIAL style for the parent item. To support partial expanding, send the control a TVE_EXPAND message with wParam set to TVE_EXPANDPARTIAL and lParam the parent item, as follows:

```
ptr->SendMessage(TVE_EXPAND,TVE_EXPANDPARTIAL,
    (LPARAM)(HTREEITEM)hItem);
```

When and where might you use this feature? Well, suppose you're reading in a list of sales regions from a database: North, South, East, and West. But, suppose an error occurs after reading in the first two. The + symbol will still be present for the other two regions, giving the user a visual cue that more data is available. You could allow the user to click the + symbol again, resulting in another attempt to read the data source. Exercise caution when using this feature—you don't want to add the same data twice!

The Enhanced TrackBar

The new TrackBar control now supports two buddy windows and tool tips. The TrackBar automatically places the buddy windows centered around the control at the TrackBar's extents, but it won't make any other modifications to them.

To assign a control as a buddy window, send the TrackBar control a TBM_SETBUDDY message. The wParam is a BOOL value. If FALSE, the buddy window will be placed to the right of the TrackBar if it has the TBS_HORZ style. If it has the TBS_VERT style, the buddy window will be positioned below the TrackBar. If wParam is TRUE, the placement is reversed. The lParam for the message is the handle to the control that is being assigned as the new buddy window.

To add tool tips to the TrackBar, specify the TBS_TOOLTIPS style when you create the control. Or, you can send the control a TBM_SETTOOLTIPS message.

```
pTrak->SendMessage(SBM_SETTOOLTIPS,hWndTips,0L);
```

The wParam is the handle to the tool tip control. By default, the tool tip control will display the current position of the TrackBar.

The New ToolBar

The last new control is the ToolBar. You can now give your applications the Internet Explorer version 4.0 style toolbar, which has many new features. This control now sports two new styles that provide different ways to display the toolbar. These are

- TBSTYLE_FLAT
- TBSTYLE_LIST

Another property of the TBSTYLE_FLAT style is that it renders the ToolBar control transparent. This causes the buttons to be displayed on the client area of the window that is beneath the toolbar. For either style, hot tracking is supported by default. Image lists are also supported for either new style. Figure 8.8 illustrates the new ToolBar control.

The new extended ToolBar provides four new features, summarized in Table 8.12.

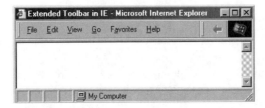

Figure 8.8 The extended ToolBar control.

Table 8.12   New ToolBar Features

FEATURE	DESCRIPTION
Transparent style	Using the TBSTYLE_FLAT style, the control displays buttons while allowing the client area under the ToolBar to show through.
Image list support	The ToolBar can use up to three image lists to dis play buttons as normal, hot, and disabled.
Drop-down toolbar buttons	The ToolBar now supports drop-down buttons with the TBSTYLE_DROPDOWN style.
Insertion marks	The ToolBar now supports insertion marks. An insertion mark provides a visual indication of where an item will be inserted (useful with drag-and-drop).

A lot of functionality has been provided in the way of ToolBar messages. Some of these are new—the following is a quick peek at what you get.

ToolBar Messages

Just like all the other controls you've seen, the new extended ToolBar can be manipulated via messages. The following are some of the more salient messages at your disposal. In the sample code found sprinkled in the upcoming text, it is assumed that pTool is a pointer to the ToolBar control.

TB_SETSTYLE. Use this message to dynamically change the style of the ToolBar. The wParam is not used. lParam is the new style flag. The return value is not used. For example,

```
PTool->SendMessage(TB_SETSTYLE,0,(LPARAM)TBSTYLE_FLAT);
```

TB_GETSTYLE. Use this message to retrieve the ToolBar's style. wParam and lParam are not used. The style is retrieved into the return value from SendMessage().

TB_GETRECT. This message is used to obtain the rectangle of a ToolBar item. The parameter wParam is the item identifier for which you wish to obtain the rectangle, and lParam is a pointer to a RECT structure that will receive the rectangle coordinates. For example,

```
RECT rect;
PTool->SendMessage(TB_GETRECT,1,(LPARAM)(&rect));
```

This gets the rectangle for the second item on the ToolBar (i.e., items are zero-based). The return value is TRUE or FALSE, indicating the success or failure of the message.

TB_SETIMAGELIST. There are three image lists that the ToolBar can use. The first image list is for displaying normal or default images on the ToolBar. Use the TB_SETIMAGELIST message to associate the buttons with their images. The wParam parameter is not used and is set to zero. The lParam is the HIMAGELIST of the image list to use. The return value is the HIMAGELIST of the previous image list, or NULL if no default image list has been set.

TB_SETDISABLEDIMAGELIST. This message sets the image list to be used for displaying the ToolBar items in a disabled state. It is used exactly like the TB_SETIMAGELIST message.

TB_SETHOTIMAGELIST. This message sets the image list to be used for displaying hot-tracking images when the mouse cursor is over an item on the ToolBar, or when the mouse button is clicked on an item. It is used exactly like the TB_SETIMAGELIST message. You can also retrieve the current hot-tracking image list, if any, by sending the control a TB_GETHOTIMAGELIST message.

TB_LOADIMAGES. This message is used to load bitmaps into a ToolBar's image list. The wParam is the identifier of the bitmap to be loaded, and lParam is your application's instance handle. You can also use system-defined images by setting lParam equal to HINST_COMMCTRL. The return value is an INT representing the count of images in the list, excluding the one just added. It returns zero if the control has no image list or if the existing list is empty. Table 8.13 lists the bitmaps available.

TB_SETBUTTONWIDTH Use this message to set the minimum and maximum widths of the ToolBar's buttons. The wParam is not used and set to zero. The lParam is a long word containing the minimum and maximum values. For example,

```
int cxMin = 75;
int cxMax = 100;
pTool->SendMessage(TB_SETBUTTONWIDTH,0,
      LPARAM)(DWORD)MAKELONG(cxMin,cxMax));
```

The return value is nonzero if the call succeeded, or zero if it failed. The value cxMin is the minimum button width, in pixels. The ToolBar buttons will never be smaller than this value. The value cxMax is the maximum width, in pixels. If the button text is too wide for this value, the control displays it using ellipsis points.

TB_SETMAXTEXTROWS. This message sets the maximum number of text rows that will be displayed on a ToolBar button. The wParam parameter is an integer containing the number of rows. The lParam is not used and is set to zero. The return value of the message is nonzero if the call was successful; zero otherwise. You can use the TB_GETTEXTROWS message to find the number of text rows currently displayed.

Table 8.13 Standard ToolBar Button Bitmaps

BITMAP ID	DESCRIPTION
IDB_HIST_LARGE_COLOR	Explorer bitmaps in large size.
IDB_HIST_SMALL_COLOR	Explorer bitmaps in small size.
IDB_STD_LARGE_COLOR	Standard bitmaps in large size.
IDB_STD_SMALL_COLOR	Standard bitmaps in small size.
IDB_VIEW_LARGE_COLOR	View bitmaps in large size.
IDB_VIEW_SMALL_COLOR	View bitmaps in small size.

TB_SETINDENT. You can now adjust the starting location for all buttons on the Tool-Bar by sending it this message. Set wParam to the number of pixels to indent before the first button is displayed on the ToolBar. The lParam is not used and should be zero. For example,

```
pTool->SendMessage(TB_SETINDENT,50,0L);
```

That does it for the messages. There are lots more, of course, but these will help get your interface off the ground in short order. Now for some coding examples.

The Sample Program

The first example is based on the default toolbar created by App Wizard. You'll find the code on the companion Web site in the Example3 project—look in the file mainfrm.cpp. When OnCreate() is called, the framework creates the window's toolbar and status bar. Here is that function:

```
int CMainFrame::OnCreate(LPCREATESTRUCT lpCreateStruct)
{
    if (CFrameWnd::OnCreate(lpCreateStruct) == -1)
        return -1;

    if (!m_wndToolBar.Create(this) ||
        !m_wndToolBar.LoadToolBar(IDR_MAINFRAME))
    {
        TRACE0("Failed to create toolbar\n");
        return -1;      // fail to create
    }
    //
    //  Change the toolbar style here!
    //
    m_wndToolBar.ModifyStyle(0, TBSTYLE_FLAT);
    // set indent
    CWnd *pTool = CWnd::FromHandle(m_wndToolBar);
    pTool->SendMessage(TB_SETINDENT,25,0L); // Set indent

    if (!m_wndStatusBar.Create(this) ||
        !m_wndStatusBar.SetIndicators(indicators,
        sizeof(indicators)/sizeof(UINT)))
    {
        TRACE0("Failed to create status bar\n");
        return -1;      // fail to create
    }
    //
    m_wndToolBar.SetBarStyle(m_wndToolBar.GetBarStyle() |
        CBRS_TOOLTIPS | CBRS_FLYBY | CBRS_SIZE_DYNAMIC);

    // TODO: Delete these three lines if you don't want the toolbar to
    // be dockable
    m_wndToolBar.EnableDocking(CBRS_ALIGN_ANY);
```

```
        EnableDocking(CBRS_ALIGN_ANY);
        DockControlBar(&m_wndToolBar);
        //
        return 0;
    }
```

This sample application now has the new, flat-style toolbar thanks to this one line of code:

```
    m_wndToolBar.ModifyStyle(0, TBSTYLE_FLAT);
```

Directly after this call, indent the toolbar using the TB_SETINDENT message. Voilà! You now have the new, flat-style toolbar in your application's main view.

The last example creates a ToolBar control in a dialog box. You'll also find this in the Example3 project in the file ToolDlg.cpp. It is virtually identical to the example given in Chapter 7, "Toolbars." All the work is done in OnInitDialog().

```
    BOOL CToolDlg::OnInitDialog()
    {
        CDialog::OnInitDialog();

        // TODO: Add extra initialization here
        HWND hwndTB;
        INITCOMMONCONTROLSEX icex; // Register the toolbar classes
        HINSTANCE hInst = AfxGetInstanceHandle();
        HWND hwndParent = this->GetSafeHwnd();
        icex.dwSize = sizeof(INITCOMMONCONTROLSEX);
        icex.dwICC = ICC_BAR_CLASSES;
        InitCommonControlsEx(&icex); // Create the toolbar control.
        //
        CRect rect;
        this->GetWindowRect(&rect);
        rect.bottom = rect.top+50;

        HWND hWndToolbar;// handle to toolbar
        TBADDBITMAP tbStruct;// bitmap structure for buttons
        //
        // populate button array with values (8 buttons, using MFC supplied)
        //
        TBBUTTON tbButtons[] = {
        { STD_FILENEW, IDM_NEW, TBSTATE_ENABLED, TBSTYLE_BUTTON, 0L, 0},
        { STD_FILEOPEN, IDM_OPEN, TBSTATE_ENABLED, TBSTYLE_BUTTON, 0L, 0},
        { STD_FILESAVE, IDM_SAVE, TBSTATE_ENABLED, TBSTYLE_BUTTON, 0L, 0},
        { 0, 0, TBSTATE_ENABLED, TBSTYLE_SEP, 0L, 0},
        { VIEW_LARGEICONS, 200, TBSTATE_ENABLED, TBSTYLE_BUTTON, 0L, 0},
        { VIEW_SMALLICONS, 210, TBSTATE_ENABLED, TBSTYLE_BUTTON, 0L, 0},
        { VIEW_LIST, 220, TBSTATE_ENABLED, TBSTYLE_BUTTON, 0L, 0},
        { VIEW_DETAILS, 230, TBSTATE_ENABLED, TBSTYLE_BUTTON, 0L, 0},
        };
        //
```

```
// Create a toolbar using Create()
//
BOOL bToolBar= FALSE;
bToolBar = m_Toolbar.Create(WS_CHILD | WS_BORDER | WS_VISIBLE |
    CCS_ADJUSTABLE | TBSTYLE_FLAT,rect,this ,NULL);

if(!bToolBar)
{
    AfxMessageBox ("Toolbar not created!", NULL, MB_OK );
}
//
hWndToolbar = m_Toolbar.GetSafeHwnd();
//
// Add the bitmap containing button images to the toolbar.
// Use MFC default buttons
//
tbStruct.hInst = HINST_COMMCTRL;// defined in commctrl.h
tbStruct.nID   = IDB_STD_SMALL_COLOR;// ditto...
m_Toolbar.SendMessage(TB_ADDBITMAP, (WPARAM) 8,
    (LPARAM) &tbStruct);
//
// Now add the buttons
//
m_Toolbar.AddButtons(8, tbButtons);
//
return TRUE;  // return TRUE unless you set the focus to a control
              // EXCEPTION: OCX Property Pages should return FALSE
}
```

As you can see, you just register the ToolBar class, and set up the buttons the way you want them. You might try replacing the line

```
tbStruct.nID   = IDB_STD_SMALL_COLOR;
```

with some of the values listed in Table 8.13 on page 150, just to get a feel for how the different bitmaps look.

Summary

The new common controls look to usher in an era of even more Web-centric applications. Regardless of the philosophy of their usage, these controls can greatly enhance your user interface. In the future, it won't be necessary to register the controls prior to using them. This was the path taken in earlier releases of MFC—you may recall having to explicitly load new common controls in past releases of Visual C++. For example,

```
::LoadLibrary("COMCTL32.DLL");
```

was necessary when 32-bit controls were first released.

The registration will probably get wrapped in an MFC class, eventually. Regardless, you should try to incorporate these new common controls where possible in order to energize your interface and extend your application's shelf life.

Now let's look at another way to enhance the user interface, adding multimedia enhancements.

CHAPTER 9

Multimedia Enhancements

This chapter explores two of the more interesting controls for Windows 95/98, the animation control and the multimedia control.

The animation control, which is a big brother to the progress gauge control, displays silent Audio Video Interleaved (AVI) files. The keyword here is *silent*—the control will not load, or play, an AVI file containing sound. However, since the control does display a series of bitmap frames just like a video, you can do some pretty creative things with it. You've already seen this control in use in the Windows95 Explorer program. The Find file or folder dialog box displays a moving magnifying glass in the lower right-hand corner while the search is being conducted. Even though the features of an animation control are somewhat limited, and likely to change in the future, you're sure to find plenty of uses for it. The primary purpose of this control, besides providing for some intriguing visual appeal, is to give the user a sense of movement. For example, if your application is about to perform some lengthy or time-consuming operation, a small animation clip provides some reassurance that the program has not somehow locked up. Most users will only tolerate a few seconds of static inactivity, so the animation control can greatly enhance their sense of interaction.

If you want to take things a step further, you can team the animation control with the multimedia control, which is capable of playing sound. Sample code for both is included on the companion Web site—the first can be found in Example1 and the second is in Example3. Let's start things off with the animation control.

Animation Control Styles

There are only four styles you can use with animation controls. These are as follows:

ACS_AUTOPLAY. This style causes the control to start playing the animation when the AVI file is opened. The user does not have to click any Start buttons. This style is useful when you need to give the user instant feedback that an operation has started.

ACS_CENTER. This style centers the animation within the animation control.

ACS_TRANSPARENT. This style displays the AVI file using a transparent background instead of the background color present in the animation clips.

ACS_BORDER. This style draws a border around the control.

The style properties are few and simple, as you have just seen. The style you assign to the animation control has an impact on the way it behaves when it receives a message.

Animation Control Messages

Like the styles, there aren't that many messages for the animation control. This section explores these messages and describes their purpose. Basically, the messages are used to open, play, stop, and close an AVI file. The messages also have macros that can be used instead of the message. In the examples, assume a CWnd pointer to the control (for example, pAnim) has been obtained elsewhere.

ACM_OPEN. This message is used to open an AVI clip and displays its first frame in the animation control. The wParam parameter is not used and is set to zero. The lParam parameter is the name of the .AVI file and path. It can also be a DWORD that has the AVI resource identifier in the low-order word and zero in the high-order word. You can use the MAKEINTRESOURCE macro for this purpose. The return value is TRUE if the call is successful. For example,

```
pAnim->SendMessage(ACM_OPEN,0,(LPARAM)"SAMPLE.AVI");
```

The associated macro for this message is

```
Animate_Open(hWnd, szName)
```

where hWnd is the handle to the animation control, and szName is the name of the .AVI file.

If the animation control has the ACS_AUTOPLAY style, this message also causes the file to be played as soon as it is opened.

ACM_PLAY. This message plays an AVI file in the animation control in the background while the thread of your application continues executing. The wParam parameter indicates the number of times to play the clip—use –1 to play the clip endlessly. The lParam parameter is a long word as follows:

```
lParam = (LPARAM) MAKELONG(wFrom, wTo)
```

where wFrom is the zero-based index of the frame where playing is to begin. This value must be less than 65,536. The wTo parameter is the index of the frame where playing is to end. It too must be less than 65,536. Use a value of –1 to play to the end of the AVI file. The return value is TRUE if the call is successful, FALSE if not. For example, to play an entire AVI file one time:

```
pAnim->SendMessage(ACM_PLAY,1,MAKELONG(0,-1));
```

The corresponding macro for this message is

```
BOOL Animate_Play(hWnd, wFrom, wTo, cRepeat);
```

where hWnd is the handle to the animation control, wFrom and wTo the starting and ending frames, and cRepeat is the number of times to repeat playing the AVI file.

There is another macro associated with this message.

```
BOOL Animate_Seek(hWnd, wFrame);
```

This macro plays a particular frame (wFrame) in the animation control. Note this is the same as using Animate_Play(), with the wFrom and wTo parameters having the same value.

ACM_STOP. This message stops playing an AVI clip in an animation control. The wParam and lParam parameters are not used and are set to zero. The return value is TRUE if the call succeeds. For example,

```
pAnim->SendMessage(ACM_STOP,0,0L);
```

The associated macro is

```
BOOL Animate_Stop(hWnd);
```

where hWnd is the handle to the animation control.

That covers the properties and messages for the animation control; now for a look at actually creating the control.

Creating Animation Controls

You can create animation controls using the CreateWindow() function, but there is also a macro for this purpose called Animate_Create(). This macro is called CreateWindow(). It is prototyped as follows:

```
HWND Animate_Create(HWND hWndP,UINT id,DWORD dwStyle,HINSTANCE hInst);
```

where hWndP is the handle to the parent window, id is the child window identifier for the animation control, dwStyle is the style, and hInst is the handle to the application instance. The return value is the handle to the animation control.

If dwStyle is ACS_CENTER, this macro sets the height and width of the animation control to zero. Otherwise, the height and width are based on the frame dimensions in the AVI file.

Animation Control Sample Code

You'll find a very simple demonstration of an animation control in the Example1 project on the companion Web site in the file AnimDlg.cpp. To run the example, build the project, then select Animation control... from the menu item Controls. This will start the dialog box shown in Figure 9.1.

When the dialog box opens, it automatically plays the AVI file prism.avi endlessly. All the code can be found in the OnInitDialog() function.

```
BOOL CAnimDlg::OnInitDialog()
{
    CDialog::OnInitDialog();

    // TODO: Add extra initialization here
    PlaySound("ding.wav",NULL,NULL); // play Windows "ding" sound
    m_Animation.Open("prism.avi");
    m_Animation.Seek(0);
    m_Animation.Play(0,-1,-1);
    return TRUE;  // return TRUE unless you set the focus to a control
                  // EXCEPTION: OCX Property Pages should return FALSE
}
```

The call to PlaySound() is part of the demonstration that will be presented for playing sound in your application later in this chapter and should be ignored for the present. The animation control opens the prism.avi, moves the file pointer to the beginning of the file, and then plays the file endlessly.

Creating AVI Files

As you can see from the preceding material, there's not much to using the animation control. Which leads to the obvious question: Just how do you create AVI files? Fortunately, there is an easy answer. There are several freeware and shareware programs available

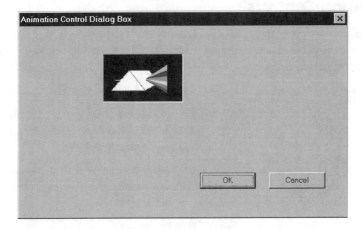

Figure 9.1 The animation control example.

from various Internet sites that you may wish to preview or purchase. Microsoft offers a free tool called VidEdit, which will be described shortly. This toolkit is available from the companion Web site as a link.

In addition to this toolkit, you'll need a graphics package to draw the individual frames of the AVI file. The Paintbrush program that ships with Windows will do just fine, but if you're going to be doing a lot of work in this area, you'll want to invest in a more powerful drawing tool. There are commercial software packages available for creating AVI files, with prices generally starting at about $50 U.S. If you are going to be creating a lot of multimedia files, you'd be well-advised to invest in one of these tools. Otherwise, VidEdit and Paintbrush will see you through.

Fundamentals of Animation

Before we look at an overview of VidEdit, it is necessary to say a few words about animation in general. As you probably know, animation is achieved by a series of still images chained together. Each image is changed slightly to give the appearance of motion. This is the exact technique you'll use to create AVI files for playback in the animation control. For some sequences, you may find it easier to draw the last frame first, and work backwards from it, erasing and replacing regions of the image. Save each frame as it is created, and give it a numerical suffix. When you've created all your images, you may need to rename and renumber your files, particularly if you're working backwards from the final frame. It also helps to know how many frames with which you plan to end. For example, suppose you want an animation sequence that starts with a blank background, and then draws the characters MFC in a popup fashion. In this case, you'll need four frames, one for the blank screen, and one for each letter in MFC. This is illustrated in Figure 9.2.

If the frames shown in Figure 9.2 were placed in an AVI file, it would seem as if the letters were being drawn on the screen. This example was created using the technique of working backwards from the end image. By starting with the final frame and erasing each letter in sequence, all the letters stay on the same horizontal line. This prevents the screen from flickering as each frame is drawn. These are small details, but they go a long way toward making your animation appear as desired.

Additional Considerations

There are a few common sense things to be aware of when creating AVI files. Your use of color should be kept to a minimum, and you need to be consistent in its use.

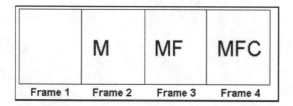

| Frame 1 | Frame 2 | Frame 3 | Frame 4 |

Figure 9.2　Sequential frames of an AVI file.

Color schemes with a lot of contrast work best, such as dark letters on a light-colored background. Also, don't forgot to add shadows where possible—these are simple to add and greatly enhance your final product.

When creating your frames, pick some point as the light source—this will make it easier to figure out where shadows will fall and what parts of the screen will be darker. For example, take a look at Figure 9.3.

With the light source assumed to be above and to the left of the image, the shadows and shading need to be behind and to the right of the image. The image on the left is correct—the shadows are properly placed. But for the image on the right, the shadows are not consistent, so the quality and realism of the 3-D effect is lost.

The VidEdit Tool

Before we look at the actual gadgets that support the Media Control Interface (MCI, or the multimedia windows you can use in your applications), let's take the 10-cent tour of VidEdit. This is a free utility available from Microsoft that lets you create AVI files. A link to the VidEdit tool can be found on the companion Web site. Although it is a bare-bones program, you can still use it as part of your multimedia studio.

After you download and install VidEdit, start it up and you'll see the window shown in Figure 9.4.

The menu options are all pretty much what you'd expect—you can open new files, save them, and so on. To create silent AVI files to be played with the animation control, you need to click the middle button on the lower right-hand side of the window. There are three buttons; these are for creating audio/video files, video-only files, or audio-only files. As you click the button, the mode is displayed in a small window under the tool buttons. In Figure 9.4, the middle button is clicked and the window displays Video. The tool is now configured for creating a silent animation series.

There is also a series of buttons on the bottom-left side of the window, on the same line as the mode buttons. These should be recognizable to you as the universal icons used

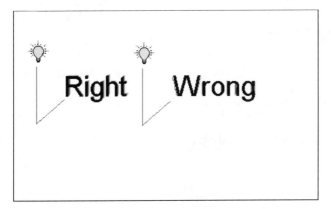

Figure 9.3 Right and wrong uses of a light source.

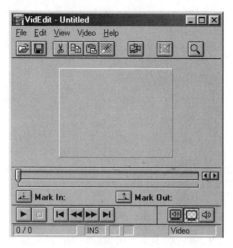

Figure 9.4 The VidEdit main window.

with tape players: play, stop, rewind, fast rewind, fast forward, and forward. In the center of the VidEdit window is a rectangle—this is the screen where your AVI frames are displayed as you build your file. You can also insert frames into your project using this screen by dragging and dropping files.

Just below the screen is a slider control terminated by left-right arrow buttons. This lets you drag forward to a frame, or step through them using the arrow buttons. The Mark In and Mark Out buttons mark the beginning and end of frame selection. You'll find more information about these in the VidEdit Help file that comes with the tool.

You can insert your individual frames by using the Insert command under the File menu, but it's easier just to drag-and-drop them into the VidEdit frame rectangle. Just be sure you insert them in the proper order. Once you insert your frames, you can save the entire sequence as an AVI file.

That's it for the VidEdit tool—now you can create AVI files. The next thing you need is something to play them on—enter the MCIWnd control.

The MCIWnd Control

MFC supports an API window class called MCIWnd. Although not a true control in the classical sense, you can think of it as such, and I'll call it player for ease of reference. Because it's not a C++ class, you cannot derive your own class from it, but the MCI-Wnd class will probably suit most of your needs. An example of the player is shown in Figure 9.5.

The player can be controlled using the controls provided, or you can right-click it, as shown in Figure 9.4, to display a popup menu with several options. If you choose the Command option, the dialog box shown in Figure 9.6 appears.

Figure 9.5 The MCIWnd window.

Unlike the animation control, the player will play any device that uses the Media Control Interface (MCI). These include audio CD, MIDI, video, and waveform-audio devices. You can use the player to play true AVI files; that is, files in which video and audio are mixed together. Another option is to use the animation control to play the video, and the player to play the audio (the approach used in the sample program).

The control can easily be added to your MFC application, and from there you can control it using class members, messages, or macros. There are lots and lots of these—I'm only going to discuss the ones you're likely to use the most. Let's start with the fundamental step of creating and using the MCIWnd player in your applications.

MCIWnd Functions

To use the MCIWnd player, you first have to do two things to your MFC application or project.

1. Include vfw.h
2. Link with vfw32.lib

This gives your application access to the MCIWnd player. Now all you need to do is create the window, position it, and use it as desired. The player is an entity unto itself— it is a self-contained, moveable window. In other words, just because you place it at a certain location in a dialog box or window doesn't mean the user can't move it by dragging with the mouse.

To create the multimedia player, use the MCIWndCreate() function, prototyped as follows:

```
HWND MCIWndCreate(HWND hwndParent, HINSTANCE hInstance, DWORD dwStyle,
                  LPSTR szFile);
```

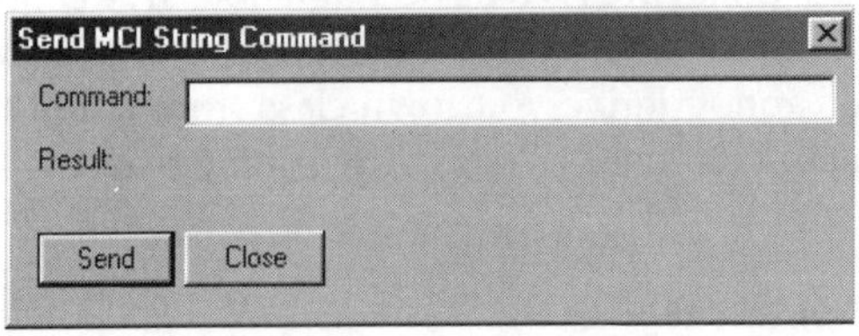

Figure 9.6 The MCIWnd Command dialog.

This function registers the MCIWnd window class, creates the window, and makes it available for using MCI services. The return value is the handle to the MCIWnd window if successful, or zero if there was an error. The hwndParent parameter is the handle of the parent window. The hInstance parameter is your application's instance handle. The third parameter, dwStyle, is a set of flags that specify the window's style. In addition to the standard styles available for use with Create-WindowEx(), the MCIWnd player has the following styles:

MCIWNDF_NOAUTOSIZEWINDOW. This style specifies that the dimensions of the player window will not change if the image size changes.

MCIWNDF_NOAUTOSIZEMOVIE. This style specifies that the dimensions of the destination rectangle will not change if the MCIWnd window size is modified.

MCIWNDF_NOERRORDLG. This style suppresses the displaying of MCI errors to the user.

MCIWNDF_NOMENU. This style hides the menu button on the toolbar and prevents the user from accessing its popup menu.

MCIWNDF_NOOPEN. This style hides the Open and Close commands from the player's menu and prevents the user from accessing these in the popup menu.

MCIWNDF_NOPLAYBAR. This hides the toolbar and prevents the user from accessing it.

MCIWNDF_NOTIFYANSI. This style causes the player to use an ANSI string instead of a Unicode string when notifying its parent of any device mode changes. This style must be used with the MCIWNDF_NOTIFYMODE flag and is exclusive to Windows NT.

MCIWNDF_NOTIFYMODE. This style causes the player to notify its parent window with an MCIWNDM_NOTIFYMODE message whenever the device switches operating modes. The lParam parameter of SendMessage() specifies the new mode.

MCIWNDF_NOTIFYPOS. This style causes the player to notify its parent window with an MCIWNDM_NOTIFYPOS message when there is a change in the record or playback position. lParam specifies the new position.

MCIWNDF_NOTIFYMEDIA. This style causes the player to notify its parent window with an MCIWNDM_NOTIFYMEDIA message when a data file is opened or closed, or if a new device is used. The lParam parameter for the message contains a pointer to the new filename.

MCIWNDF_NOTIFYSIZE. This style causes the player to notify its parent window when it is resized.

MCIWNDF_NOTIFYERROR. This style causes the player to notify its parent window when an MCI error occurs.

MCIWNDF_NOTIFYALL. This style causes all MCIWNDF window notification styles to be used.

MCIWNDF_NOTIFYRECORD. This style adds a Record button to the player's toolbar and adds a new file command to the menu. The player must have recording capability.

MCIWNDF_SHOWALL. This style causes all MCIWNDF_SHOW styles to be used with the player's window.

MCIWNDF_SHOWMODE. This style causes the current mode of the device to be displayed in the window title bar.

MCIWNDF_SHOWNAME. This style causes the name of the open MCI device or data file to be displayed in the window title bar.

MCIWNDF_SHOWPOS. This style causes the current position within the content of the MCI device to be displayed in the window title bar.

The last parameter used in the call to MCIWndCreate() is szFile, and is a NULL-terminated string that is the name of the open data file or MCI device.

The MCI Sample Program

You'll find the sample code for the MCIWnd control on the companion Web site, in the Example3 project. The code is in the files MultiMed.cpp and MultiMed.h. The control is created in the OnInitDialog() function.

```
BOOL CMultiMed::OnInitDialog()
{
    CDialog::OnInitDialog();

    // TODO: Add extra initialization here
    CString filename("demo.avi"); // name of file to play, w/sound
    //
    // Create the MCIWnd child window
    //
    m_videoWnd = MCIWndCreate(this->GetSafeHwnd(),
        AfxGetInstanceHandle(), WS_CHILD | WS_CAPTION | WS_VISIBLE |
        MCIWNDF_SHOWPOS | MCIWNDF_SHOWNAME, filename);
    //
    CWnd *pMCI = CWnd::FromHandle(m_videoWnd);
    pMCI->MoveWindow( 200,60, 100, 120, TRUE ); // re-size it
    return TRUE;   // return TRUE unless you set the focus to a control
                   // EXCEPTION: OCX Property Pages should return FALSE
}
```

This snippet of code creates the MCIWnd control, and assigns the name of the file to play. When the "Play Demo" button is clicked, the following method is called which plays the AVI file.

```
void CMultiMed::OnDemoButton()
{
    // TODO: Add your control notification handler code here

    MCIWndPlay(m_videoWnd);
}
```

You could easily modify this example to include other buttons such as one for rewinding the file. Also, the AVI file can be played and rewound directly by the MCIWnd control itself—this example is purely for the sake of simplicity.

AVIFile Functions and Macros

Win32 provides you with many functions and macros for accessing files that use the Resource Information File Format (RIFF), like AVI and waveform-audio (WAV) files. For simplicity's sake, this discussion is limited to AVI files only. These functions and macros manage RIFF files, obviating your need to navigate through the RIFF architecture. These functions and macros handle the file data as one or more *data streams* instead of tagged data blocks called *chunks*. Data streams refer to the components of the file. For example, an AVI file can contain a video clip as well as an English soundtrack and a Spanish soundtrack. Using these functions and macros, your application can access each of these separately.

AVIFile functions and macros are contained in a Dynamic Link library (DLL). You must first initialize this library before you can use any of the functions and macros. The library is initialized with the AVIFileInit() function. When you're finished, you must release the library with a call to AVIFileExit(). AVIFile keeps a count of the applications that are using the DLL, but it doesn't count those that have released it. So make sure your application manages this step properly.

The AVIFile functions and macros can be used to perform the following types of operations:

- Open and close an AVI file
- Open streams in an AVI file
- Read streams from an AVI file
- Read one stream and write to another
- Edit an AVI file
- Put an AVI file on the Clipboard

The process of using the AVIFile functions can be simplified to a three-part operation: The file is opened, you do whatever it is you want to do, then you close and exit.

Here's a snippet of generic code that illustrates the basic steps to follow to use the AVI-File functions:

```
LPCSTR szFile; // file to open
HWND hWnd;  // window handle
LONG hr;
PAVIFILE pFile; // handle of AVI file
AVIFileInit(); // open DLL
hr = AVIFileOpen(&pFile, szFile, OF_SHARE_DENY_WRITE, 0L);
if(hr != 0)
{
```

```
        AfxMessageBox("Failed to open AVI file.",MB_OK);
        return;
    }
    //
    //  Insert AVIFile functions here to manipulate/edit the file
    //
    AVIFileRelease(pfile); // close the AVI file
    AVIFileExit();         // release the DLL
```

The use and content of all the AVIFile functions and macros are well beyond the scope of this book—consult the documentation for a complete list of all the functions available.

Sound

You can easily add sound to your applications. Brief sound clips provide a nice way to alert the user when some interaction on his or her behalf is required, such as cueing the user, to insert a floppy disk or CD, or to indicate low memory. As with visual elements, don't get carried away with sound—some users find superfluous feedback like this annoying. But for important cues, such as your application's About box, sound can give your application a very polished look.

You can create your own sound clips, or use those that ship with Windows. These are identified by their WAV file extension. To play the WAV file, use the PlaySound() API. This API requires that you add the following to your application:

1. Include mmsystem.h in your application

2. Link with winmm.lib

The PlaySound() function plays a sound file specified by the filename, resource, or system event. You can associate a sound with a system even in the registry or in the WIN.INI file. The PlaySound() API is prototyped as follows:

```
    BOOL PlaySound(LPCSTR pszSound, HMODULE hMod, DWORD dwSound);
```

The pszSound parameter is a string that contains the name of the WAV file to play. If this is NULL, any WAV file that is currently being played is stopped. You can stop a non-waveform sound by specifying SND_PURGE in the dwSound parameter. Three flags in dwSound determine whether pszSound is interpreted as a filename, an alias for a system event, or a resource identifier. These are, respectively,

- SND_FILENAME

- SND_ALIAS

- SND_RESOURCE

If none of these are specified (that is, the parameter is NULL), PlaySound() searches the registry or WIN.INI file to see if there is an association for the given sound name. If one is found, it is played. If no association is found in the registry, pszSound is assumed to be a filename.

The second parameter, hMod, is the handle of the executable file containing the resource to load. This must be NULL unless dwSound is set to SND_RESOURCE.

The last parameter, dwSound, is a set of flags for playing the sound. These are defined as follows:

SND_APPLICATION. The sound is played using an association specified by the application.

SND_ALIAS. The pszSound parameter is a system event alias in the WIN.INI file or registry. Do not combine this with the SND_FILENAME or SND_RESOURCE flags.

SND_ALIAS_ID. The pszSound parameter is a predefined sound identifier.

SND_ASYNC. The sound is played asynchronously. PlaySound() returns immediately after beginning the sound. You can stop an asynchronously played sound by calling PlaySound() with pszSound set to NULL.

SND_FILENAME. The pszSound parameter is a filename.

SND_LOOP. The sound is played repeatedly until PlaySound() is called again with pszSound set to NULL. You must also specify the SND_ASYNC flag with this value.

SND_MEMORY. The sound event's file is loaded into memory. The pszSound parameter must point to an image of the sound in memory.

SND_NODEFAULT. No default sound is used. If the sound cannot be found, PlaySound() returns silently and the default sound is not played.

SND_NOSTOP. The specified sound event will yield to another sound that is already playing. If the sound cannot be played because the sound card or audio device is busy playing another sound, then PlaySound() returns immediately with a FALSE value and doesn't play the requested sound. If this flag is not specified, PlaySound() tries to stop whatever sound is currently playing in order to play the new sound.

SND_NOWAIT. PlaySound() returns immediately without playing the sound when the driver is busy.

SND_PURGE. This flag indicates that sounds are to be stopped for the calling task. If pszSound is not NULL, all instances of the sound are stopped. If pszSound is NULL, all sounds currently playing on behalf of the calling task are terminated. You must also specify your application's instance handle in the hMod parameter to stop SND_RESOURCE events.

SND_RESOURCE. The pszSound parameter is the identifier of a resource. The hMod parameter must specify the application instance that owns the resource.

SND_SYNC. Specifies synchronous playback of the sound. PlaySound() returns after the sound finishes playing.

The return value for PlaySound() is TRUE if the call was successful, or FALSE if it failed. Also, the sound indicated by pszSound parameter must fit into available memory and be playable by the installed audio device driver. When playing sounds, this API searches the following directories for the sound in this order:

1. The current directory.

2. The Windows system directory.

3. Directories listed in the PATH environment variable.

4. The list of directories mapped in a network.

If the specified sound cannot be found anywhere, PlaySound() will use the default system event sound. If that can't be found, it doesn't play anything and returns FALSE.

There is an example of PlaySound() on the companion Web site in the Example1 project. When you run the example dialog for the animation control, the ding sound is played. This is in the OnInitDialog() method found in file AnimDlg.cpp.

```
PlaySound("ding.wav",NULL,NULL); // play Windows "ding" sound
```

If you don't hear this when you run the demo program, check your machine and make sure you have the ding.wav file. If not, you can substitute another valid WAV file and rebuild the project.

Summary

There are several approaches you can take to add animation to your application. The real challenge is using it judiciously. Once again, overkill is overwhelming to the user, so limit your animation sequences to something meaningful.

Animation sequences can also be played inside your application's help file. This will be demonstrated later in Chapter 22, "Adding Help to the Interface," but it does point out that you have a lot of power and flexibility at your disposal. Now let's look at another way to enhance your interface: spin controls.

CHAPTER 10

Spin Controls

This chapter takes a look at spin controls. A spin control (also known as an up-down control or a spinner) is a pair of arrow buttons that allows the user to increment or decrement a value, such as a scroll position or a number displayed in an edit box control. The value associated with a spin button control is called its *current position*. A spin button control is most often used in conjunction with a companion control, called a *buddy window*. The buddy window is almost always an edit box. When spin controls are used without a buddy window, they behave as nothing more than simplified scrollbars. This control is encapsulated in class CSpinButtonCtrl.

To the user, a spin button control and its buddy window appear as a single control. You can specify that a spin button control automatically position itself next to its buddy window, and that it automatically set the text in the buddy window to its current position. You generally use a spin button control with an edit control to prompt the user for numeric input across a predefined range of values. Spin controls can be oriented in both the vertical and horizontal directions. This discussion will assume the vertical orientation since it is easier to visualize a value as going up or going down.

By clicking the up arrow, the user moves the current position toward the maximum, and clicking the down arrow moves the current position toward the minimum. The default values are 100 for the minimum, and 0 for the maximum. Take heed—you would normally think the minimum would be 0 and the maximum 100, so you will probably need to adjust these for your application. Any time the minimum setting is greater than the maximum setting (for example, when the default settings are used), clicking the up arrow decreases the position value and clicking the down arrow increases it. You'll find an example of a spin control on the companion Web site in Example3. This example uses spin controls in a dialog box that allows the user to specify a date. The spinners can be used to change the value of the day and year fields. This dialog box is shown in Figure 10.1.

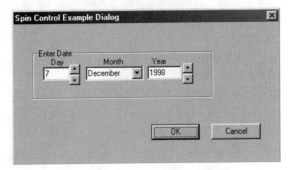

Figure 10.1 Example of a spin control.

Spin Control Styles

Because spin controls are nothing more than child windows, you can assign them various styles that influence their operating properties. These include providing text for the buddy control, positioning the arrows relative to the buddy control, and allowing the up and down arrows on the keyboard to navigate the control. The styles can be set in App Studio or by the use of messages. Figure 10.2 shows the Properties dialog box for spin controls in App Studio.

The following is an overview of these styles and how they affect both the spin control and the buddy control.

UDS_ALIGNLEFT. This style is used to align the spin control with the left side of the buddy control. If necessary, the buddy control is narrowed to make room for the spin control.

UDS_ALIGNRIGHT. Identical to the UDS_ALIGNLEFT, except the up-down arrows are aligned on the right side of the buddy control. For both of these styles, if the user resizes the buddy control, you will need to send a UDM_SETBUDDY message to the spin control in order to realign the arrows with the appropriate side of the buddy control.

UDS_ARROWKEYS. This style allows you to press the up and down arrow keys from inside the buddy control—the buddy control is incremented and decremented accordingly. This style actually subclasses the buddy control in order to trap these keys.

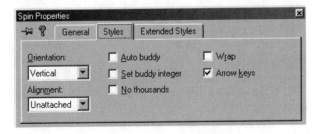

Figure 10.2 App Studio Properties dialog box spin controls.

UDS_AUTOBUDDY. This style indicates that the previously created window control is the buddy control for the spin control. If the spin control is not being used in a dialog resource, the GetWindow() function is called with GW_HWNDPREV to associate the spin control with the buddy control. Otherwise, the previous control in the dialog box definition in the resource file is assumed to be the buddy control.

UDS_HORZ. By default, the spin control arrows are arranged vertically; specifying this style draws them horizontally.

UDS_NOTHOUSANDS. By default, a separator is inserted after every third digit (for example, 29,512,256) in the buddy control. This style overrides this action.

UDS_SETBUDDYINT. This style is used to automatically update the buddy control whenever the value changes as a result of clicking the spin buttons. In effect, the text in the control is changed using the WM_SETTEXT message.

UDS_WRAP. This style causes the value displayed in the buddy control to wrap back to the minimum value if the maximum value is exceeded, and vice versa. If this style is not set, and the user attempts to exceed an upper or lower limit, the control draws grayed (that is, dimmed) arrows for both buttons.

That's it for the styles. Now let's look at the class members.

Class Member Functions

There are several member functions that you can use to change various properties of a spin control. In general, these are divided into the following categories:

- Acceleration—how fast the position changes
- Base—the numerical base (10 or 16) of the value displayed in the buddy control
- Buddy Control/Window—the control that displays the current position/value
- Position—the value in the buddy window
- Range—the maximum and minimum positions for the spin control

The methods discussed in this section will fall into one of these five categories. Let's begin by creating a spin control. You create an object of class CSpinButtonCtrl by using the Create() method, prototyped as follows:

```
BOOL Create(DWORD dwStyle,const RECT& rect, CWnd* pParentWnd,UINT nID);
```

The dwStyle parameter is a combination of the styles previously discussed. The rect parameter is the size and location of the spinner, and pParentWnd is a pointer to the parent window. This parameter will generally be a pointer to a dialog box—it must not be NULL. The nID parameter is the resource ID of the spin control. The return value is nonzero if it succeeded, zero if it failed.

To set the range or limits of a spin control, use SetRange().

```
void SetRange(int nLower, int nUpper);
```

The first parameter establishes the lower limit for the control, and the second is the upper limit. Neither parameter can be outside the range UD_MAXVAL and UD_MINVAL. These are defined in CommCtrl.h as follows:

```
#define UD_MAXVAL          0x7fff
#define UD_MINVAL          (-UD_MAXVAL)
```

Also, the difference between the nLower and nUpper parameters cannot exceed UD_MAXVAL.

Closely related to this method is GetRange(), which comes in two flavors.

```
DWORD GetRange() const;
void GetRange(int &lower, int& upper) const;
```

The first variety returns the limits in a 32-bit DWORD. The low-order word is the upper limit, and the high-order word is the lower limit. The second variety takes the reference to integers to receive the lower and upper range limits, respectively. Code examples for each are as follows:

```
DWORD dwRange;
int nLow, nHigh;
dwRange = m_SomeSpinner.GetRange();
nLow = HIWORD(dwRange);
nHigh= LOWORD(dwRange);
```

or

```
m_SomeSpinner.GetRange(&nLow, &nHigh);
```

The class provides two methods for manipulating the current position of the control. These are

```
int SetPos(int nPos);
```

The parameter nPos is the new position for the control; the return value is the previous position. This parameter must be in the range of UD_MINVAL and UD_MAXVAL. To get the current position, use the GetPos() function.

```
int GetPos() const;
```

The return value is the current position in the low-order word. The high-order word is nonzero if an error occurred while making the call. The spin control updates its current position based on the value in the buddy control when processing the return value. The return value is an error if there is no buddy control or if the value in the buddy window is out of range. Remember, the user is free to type a bogus value in the buddy window, so be sure and add sufficient error-checking when using this method.

Two additional methods are available for working with the buddy window. These are SetBuddy() and GetBuddy().

```
CWnd* SetBuddy(CWnd* pWndBuddy);
```

The parameter pWndBuddy is a pointer to the new buddy window. The return value is a pointer to the old one. This method is generally used when creating the control dynamically on the stack. To get the buddy window, call GetBuddy().

```
CWnd* GetBuddy( ) const;
```

The return value is a pointer to the current buddy window, or NULL if no buddy has been established.

There are two methods available for adjusting the acceleration properties of a spin control. The acceleration is a relative quantity that determines the rate at which the current position changes. For example, if the range of the control is fairly large, you may want the control to change its position quickly. Conversely, for a narrow range, the acceleration should be kept fairly slow. To set the acceleration, use SetAccel(), prototyped as follows:

```
BOOL SetAccel( int nAccel, UDACCEL* pAccel );
```

The parameter nAccel is the number of UDACCEL structures as indicated by the second parameter, pAccel. The pAccel parameter is a pointer to an array of UDACCEL structures that contain information about the acceleration properties. The structure is defined as follows:

```
typedef struct
{
    int nSec;
    int nInc;
} UDACCEL;
```

The nSec member of this structure is the time, in seconds, that the control waits before updating the current position. The nInc member is the amount to increment (or decrement) the control—usually 1. The return value of this method is nonzero if it succeeded, or zero if it failed.

Closely related is GetAccel().

```
UINT GetAccel(int nAccel, UDACCEL* pAccel) const;
```

The parameters are the same as for SetAccel(), except that values are returned into these structures. The return value is the number of accelerator structures retrieved.

The last two methods deal with setting the numerical base of the buddy window. These are SetBase() and GetBase().

```
int SetBase(int nBase);
```

The parameter nBase is the base to use. Acceptable values are 10 for decimal, and 16 for hexadecimal. The return value is the previous base value if successful, or 0 if a value other than 10 or 16 was specified. The base value controls how the buddy window displays numbers, in decimal or hex. Decimal numbers are signed, but hexadecimal numbers are always unsigned. The corresponding method to get the base is

```
UINT GetBase( ) const;
```

The return value is the current base for the spin control/buddy window combination.

Spin Control Messages

Messages can be sent to a spin control to read, and write, its styles and those of its buddy control. For example, you can change the range, or retrieve a handle to the buddy control.

Whenever the value of a spin control changes, it sends its parent window a WM_VSCROLL message. This is the case even if the UDS_HORIZ style was specified in the control's definition. In the following discussion of the spin control messages, I have assumed that a CWnd pointer to the control (pSpin) has been obtained prior to sending the message.

UDM_GETACCEL. This message, which will only work with Windows NT, retrieves information regarding the *accelerators* for a spin control. The acceleration of a spin control refers to the rate at which the value is changed in the buddy control as the user scrolls. It is defined by an array of structures of type UDACCEL. This structure type includes members for time interval between when the arrows are clicked and when the buddy control is updated. The structure is defined as

```
typedef struct
{
    UINT nSec;
    UINT nInc;
} UDACCEL;
```

This can be used to set the apparent speed of operation for the user—you could even allow the user to specify his or her own preference using a property sheet and the UDM_SETACCEL message (described later in this list).

The wParam parameter is set to the number of the accelerators to retrieve. If a value greater than the number of existing accelerators, the message returns information only for the existing accelerators. The lParam is the address of the array of UDACCEL structures with the same number of elements as declared in wParam. It is into this array of structures that the information is fetched (the values are read into the structure).

UDM_GETBASE. This message, which can be used with either Windows 95/98 or Windows NT, returns the current radix base for a spin control. The return value (a DWORD) is either 10 (indicating a decimal base) or 16 (hexadecimal). The wParam and lParam are not used and should be set to 0, as in the following example:

```
DWORD dwBase = pSpin->SendMessage(UDM_GETBASE,0,0L);
```

Refer to the UDM_SETBASE message later in this section.

UDM_GETBUDDY. This message returns the handle of the current buddy control as the low-order word of a 32-bit value. The wParam and lParam parameters are not used, and should be set to zero.

UDM_GETPOS. Use this message to find the current value of a spin control. Again, both parameters are not used and thus set to zero. The current value is returned as a 32 bit. The low-order word of this value is the current position or value. An example is

```
DWORD dwValue = pSpin->SendMessage(UDM_GETPOS,0,0L);
int nCurVal = dwValue & 0xffff;
```

If an error occurs, the high-order word will be nonzero. To test for this, simply change the bit mask as follows:

```
int nError = dwValue & 0xffff0000;
```

UDM_GETRANGE. This message is used to retrieve the current range of values for a spin control. The wParam and lParam parameters are not used and are set to zero. The return value is a 32-bit value with the upper limit in the low-order word, and the lower limit in the high-order word. For example,

```
DWORD dwValue = pSpin->SendMessage(UDM_GETRANGE,0,0L);
int nUpper = dwValue & 0xffff;
int nLower = dwValue & 0xffff0000;
```

UDM_SETACCEL. This message is only valid with Windows NT. It is used as described for the UDM_GETACCEL message. The return value is TRUE if the operation was successful; FALSE if otherwise.

UDM_SETBASE. This message sets the base value for a spin control—base 10 is the default. The base value refers to how the buddy control displays numbers—as decimal or hexadecimal. The wParam is the new base value, the lParam is not used and is set to zero. For example,

```
DWORD dwOldBase = pSpin->SendMessage(UDM_SETBASE,16,0L);
```

sets the radix to 16 for the spin control pointed to by pSpin. Base 10 numbers are signed, base 16 numbers are unsigned. If the buddy control is a listbox, this message sets the current selection instead of the text or value. The return value is the previous radix, or zero upon an error.

UDM_SETBUDDY. This message is used to designate a control as the buddy control for a spin control. The wParam is the handle of the control. The lParam is not used and is set to zero. The return value is a 32-bit value. The low-order word of this is the handle of the previous buddy control, if any. For example,

```
DWORD dwOldCtrl = pSpin->SendMessage(UDM_SETBUDDY,hWndNewCtrl,0L);
```

where hWndNewCtrl is the handle of the new control.

UDM_SETPOS. This message is used to set the value (the position) for the buddy control used with a spin control. The wParam is not used and is set to zero. The lParam is the new value, and must be within the range established for the control. The return value is the previous value. For example, to set the new value to 75:

```
DWORD dwNew = MAKELONG(75,0);
DWORD dwOldPos = pSpin->SendMessage(UDM_SETPOS,0,dwNew);
```

UDM_SETRANGE. This message is sent to a spin control to establish the range of upper and lower limits. The wParam is set to zero; lParam contains the upper limit of the range in the lower-order word of this parameter, and the lower limit is in the high-order word. For example, to set the range of a control to be 100–200, follow this example:

```
DWORD lParam = MAKELONG(200,100);
pSpin->SendMessage(UDM_SETRANGE,0,lParam);
```

There is no return value for this message. Also, the range cannot exceed 32,767 positions.

That covers it for the messages. Let's take a look at the sample program.

The Sample Program

The sample code for the spin control is on the companion Web site in the Example3 project. An illustration of the dialog box is shown in Figure 10.1. Here, spin controls are used as part of a date input gadget—the date's day and year values can be adjusted by using the spin controls. You'll find the code in the files SpinDlg.cpp and SpinDlg.h.

When the dialog box is opened, the date gadget is set to the current system date in OnInitDialog().

```
BOOL CSpinDlg::OnInitDialog()
{
    CDialog::OnInitDialog();
    //
    //  init. to today's date
    //
    CTime t = CTime::GetCurrentTime();
    m_Combo_Month.SetCurSel((t.GetMonth())-1 );
    char szText[8];
    memset(szText,0,sizeof(szText));     // init to all NULLs
    _itoa(t.GetDay(), szText, 10 );
    m_E_Day.SetWindowText(szText);
    _itoa(t.GetYear(), szText, 10 );
    m_E_Year.SetWindowText(szText);
    //
    return TRUE;  // return TRUE unless you set the focus to a control
                  // EXCEPTION: OCX Property Pages should return FALSE

}
```

The main point of interest is what happens when the spin control arrows are clicked; that is, the response to a UDN_DELTAPOS message that you can trap in Class Wizard. Here is a message handler for the spin control associated with the day value of the date gadget:

```
void CSpinDlg::OnDeltaposSpinDay(NMHDR* pNMHDR, LRESULT* pResult)
{
    NM_UPDOWN* pNMUpDown = (NM_UPDOWN*)pNMHDR;
    // TODO: Add your control notification handler code here
    char szBufr[4];
    memset(szBufr,0,sizeof(szBufr));
    m_E_Day.GetWindowText(m_csTmp);
    char *p = m_csTmp.GetBuffer(2);
    m_csTmp.ReleaseBuffer();
```

```
    m_iDay = atoi(p);
    //
    //  Days are different because of Feb. Must check for leap year
    //
    int iMon = m_Combo_Month.GetCurSel();

    if(iMon == 1)   // it's Feb!!
    {
        m_E_Year.GetWindowText(m_csTmp);
        char *p = m_csTmp.GetBuffer(4);
        m_csTmp.ReleaseBuffer();
        m_iYear = atoi(p);
        if( (m_iYear % 4 == 0) || ( m_iYear % 400 == 0 )  ) // leap
year!
            iMaxDays[1] = 29;
        else    // reset in case changed last time
            iMaxDays[1] = 28;
    }
    //
    if((pNMUpDown->iDelta < 0))// user clicked up
    {
        if(m_iDay < iMaxDays[iMon])
        {
            ++m_iDay;  // safe to increment day
            _itoa(m_iDay, szBufr, 10 );
            m_E_Day.SetWindowText(szBufr);
        }
    }
    else              // user clicked down
    {
        if(m_iDay > 1)
        {
            --m_iDay;  // safe to decrement day
            _itoa(m_iDay, szBufr, 10 );
            m_E_Day.SetWindowText(szBufr);
        }
    }
    *pResult = 0;
}
```

You can tell which way the user is adjusting the spin control by looking at the iDelta member of the NMHDR structure. If this value is less than zero, the user is increasing the position value. If greater than or equal to zero, the user is decreasing the value.

It's necessary to check in this method if the month is February, since its number of days can change. Although not directly related to spin controls, this example needs to "watch" for a change in the selected month, since the number of days in the month determine the range values for the spin control. Here is the method that handles changes to the month combo box:

```
void CSpinDlg::OnSelchangeComboMonth()
```

```
    {
        // TODO: Add your control notification handler code here
        //
        //  This code checks if the day value is greater than what is
allowed
        //  for the month. If it is, sets it to max days for that month
        //
        int iMon = m_Combo_Month.GetCurSel();
        if(m_iDay > iMaxDays[iMon])
        {
            char szBufr[8];
            memset(szBufr,0,sizeof(szBufr));
            _itoa(iMaxDays[iMon], szBufr, 10 );
            m_E_Day.SetWindowText(szBufr);
        }
    }
```

As you can see, this ensures that the user doesn't somehow end up with a month being displayed with more days than it actually has. For example, suppose a user selects January 31. That's fine, since there are 31 days in January. But what if the user selects a month that doesn't have 31 days, like February? Without this code, you'd end up with the gadget displaying February 31, which is nowhere near valid. So this illustrates something I spoke to in Chapter 1, "Controls and the User Interface"—build in your error traps and safety checks as you go. You'll get a much better interface out of the deal.

Summary

The spin control is a very easy-to-use device well-suited for certain tasks involving the user interface. Ideal candidates for using the spinner are those that have a fairly narrow range of values, such as the date gadget demonstrated in the sample program. For broad ranges, the spin control may not be so practical, since it forces the user to go through a lot of values. One feature that might ameliorate this condition would be to include a context menu for the spin control—the user could then be allowed to adjust the acceleration of the spinner from a popup window. This is similar to right-clicking the Desktop screen in Windows 95/98—a context menu appears that lets you adjust the visual aspects of the Desktop. While this might be overkill, it does demonstrate that you can add a lot of simple touches to your interface that can greatly extend its usability. In the next chapter, you'll see a distant cousin of the spin control, the slide control.

CHAPTER 11

Progress and Slider Controls

This chapter examines two similar controls, the progress gauge and the slider control. The progress control is used to indicate the progress of an operation. The slider control is used to adjust a setting, such as the amount of red to add to a color selection. The slider control, also called a *trackbar*, is similar to a sliding volume control on a stereo. Both controls are readily available in App Studio, and both can be used to add a nice touch to what could ordinarily be a drab user interface. Make sure your application can benefit from these controls and that another control, like a spinner, isn't better suited to your needs.

Progress Gauge

A progress gauge control is a child window of class CProgressCtrl used to indicate the relative progress of a lengthy or time-consuming operation. Figure 11.1 shows a progress gauge control, taken from the Example1 program on the companion Web site.

As you can see, the progress control is a rectangle that is gradually filled, from left to right, with the user's system highlight color. The progress gauge control has a range, a current position, and other properties that you can set or read. The range reflects the duration of the total operation, and the current position indicates the relative progress the application has made toward completing the operation. These values are unsigned integers, so the highest range and position value is 65,535.

The purpose of the progress gauge is to provide feedback to the user. It can be used to reflect the relative amount of a task, such as a file transfer, that has been completed, and provide visual assurance that the application has not stopped functioning. These controls are frequently used in setup or installation programs that copy a large number

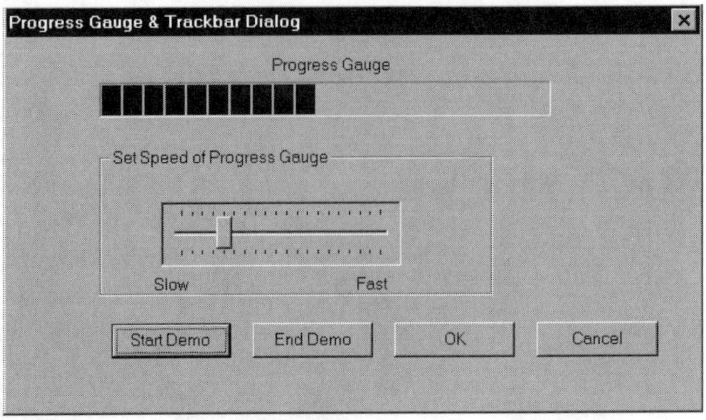

Figure 11.1   A progress gauge from the example program.

of files, or for other activities that consume system resources. You can set the range, and current position, of the progress gauge control much like a scrollbar.

A progress gauge control can include descriptive text that can be a reflection of the progress as either a percentage of the total or as current value. For example, a progress gauge for an operation that takes 10 seconds could indicate the 5-second point as either 50 percent or as 5 seconds.

The progress gauge control has only one property that can be set, although the other Window styles like WS_VISIBLE are still available to the Create() class method. This property is the border.

Let's examine the class methods associated with a progress gauge control.

Progress Gauge Class Methods

The first method is the ubiquitous Create() method. This is prototyped as follows:

```
BOOL Create(DWORD dwStyle, const RECT& rect, CWnd* pParentWnd, UINT nID);
```

The first parameter, dwStyle, is the style of the progress gauge child window. Usually, the basic styles WS_CHILD and WS_VISIBLE are included. The second parameter, rect, is the bounding rectangle for the control. The third parameter, pParentWnd, is the CWnd pointer to the window that owns the progress gauge. Generally, the this pointer is sufficient. The last parameter is the numerical ID of the control, which goes in the resource.h file.

The next method is SetRange(), prototyped as follows:

```
void SetRange(int nLower, int nUpper);
```

The first parameter is the lower limit of the range. The default is zero. The second parameter is the upper limit of the range. Its default is 100. The bar is redrawn after calling this method to reflect the new ranges imposed for the control.

While this method is used to set the range of the control, the SetPos() method sets the control to a new position. The prototype is

```
int SetPos(int nPos);
```

The return value is the previous position of the control. The parameter nPos is the new setting. The control is redrawn to reflect the change in the position.

Another method used quite often is SetStep().

```
int SetStep(int nStep);
```

This class method is used to specify the amount the progress gauge is incremented. The default is 10. The return value is the previous step increment. The parameter nStep is the amount by which a call to StepIt() will increase the progress bar's position.

The prototype for StepIt() is

```
int StepIt();
```

The return value is the previous position of the progress gauge; the control is redrawn after calling StepIt() to show the new position.

Closely related to this method is the OffsetPos() method, prototyped as

```
int OffsetPos(int nPos);
```

The return value is the previous position of the gauge. The parameter nPos is the amount to advance the position of the gauge. The control is redrawn after OffsetPos() is called to reflect the new position.

That's a wrap on the class methods. You can't do a lot with this control, but then again, you don't need much beyond what these methods can do for you. The real challenge comes in determining exactly how long something will take to complete in order to set the range and step increment of the control. A simple guideline is to quantify how many or how much has to be accomplished, use the CTime class methods to determine how long it takes to do one of the chosen task, then multiply this by how many tasks need to be completed. For example, if the user wants to update 1500 records in a database table, the application would calculate the amount of time needed for one update, then multiple the resulting value by 1500. Other examples include modem speeds and network throughput. Whatever the task, it is possible to calculate how long the task will take. Be sure to use variables that are big enough for the task —like floats and doubles (data types used and defined by the compiler).

The Slide Control

The *slide control* is also known as the *trackbar*. This control consists of a slider and optional tick marks, and is used to adjust a value in a range. Moving the slider generates notification messages. The slide control is very similar to the spin control, except the slide control doesn't have buddy controls. The slider can be used for adjusting the output volume of a sound device, adjusting color saturation, or setting the repeat rate of the keyboard.

The slider portion of the control moves in specified increments that are set when you create the control, or via the class method for this purpose. Let's take a quick look at the different styles that can be assigned to this control.

CSlideCtrl Styles

Unlike the progress gauge control, the slider has lots of properties that you can use. These are

TBS_HORZ. This gives the slider a horizontal orientation—TBS_HORZ is the default.

TBS_VERT. This gives the slider a vertical orientation.

TBS_AUTOTICKS. This style sets tick marks on the slider's face for each increment in its range of possible values. These marks are added automatically when the SetRange() member function is called. If you specify this style, you cannot use the SetTic() and SetTicFreq() member functions to specify the tick marks.

TBS_NOTICKS. This creates a slider without tick marks.

TBS_BOTTOM. This style displays tick marks on the bottom of a slider when it has the TBS_HORZ style.

TBS_TOP. This style displays tick marks on the TOP of a slider when it has the TBS_HORZ style. You can give a slider both the TBS_TOP and TBS_BOTTOM properties to display tick marks on both sides of the slider.

TBS_RIGHT. For a slider with the TBS_VERT style, this displays tick marks on the right side of the slider control.

TBS_LEFT. Sets the tick marks on the left for a slider with the TBS_VERT style. Use both the TBS_RIGHT and TBS_LEFT styles to display the tick marks on the left and right sides. An alternative, regardless of the orientation, is to use TBS_BOTH.

TBS_BOTH. Displays tick marks on both sides of a slider regardless of its orientation.

TBS_ENABLESELRANGE. This displays a selection range. When this style is applied, the tick marks at the beginning and ending positions of the range are displayed as triangles instead of vertical dashes, and the range is highlighted. You might find this useful in, say, a scheduling application. The user could select a range of tick marks that correspond to the hours in a day to allocate time for some task. Like all the other controls covered, there are lots of ways to make the user interface better by selecting the right tool for the job.

Let's take a look at the notification messages for the slide control. It is important to understand the notification messages in order to see how the control is implemented, but also how these messages are used with the class methods covered later in this chapter.

CSliderCtrl Notification Messages

Like a lot of other child windows, the slider control uses notification messages to inform the parent window when certain events occur. In reality, notification messages are nothing more than disguised command messages, just like WM_PAINT and WM_SIZE. This helps explain why the pParentWnd parameter of so many Create() methods can't be NULL. The slider control sends its parent WM_HSCROLL messages, so you can override the parent window's OnHScroll member function to trap and process these messages. The function is passed a notification code, the position of the slider, and a pointer to the slider control. This pointer is not of type CSliderCtrl as you might expect, but is instead of class CScrollBar. This can cause some problems in your coding, and you may need to cast the pointer in order to use it. In contrast to using scrollbar notification codes, the slider sends its own unique set of messages, which can be recognized by the prefix TB_. The control sends the following messages when the user manipulates the slider via the keyboard.

- TB_TOP
- TB_ BOTTOM
- TB_LINEUP
- TB_LINEDOWN

No doubt you can guess what these are: the Page Up/Page Down keys and the Up/Down arrow keys. The next two messages are sent only when the mouse is used.

- TB_THUMBPOSITION
- TB_THUMBTRACK

The next three messages are shared by keyboard and mouse input.

- TB_ENDTRACK
- TB_PAGEDOWN
- TB_PAGEUP

Table 11.1 lists the slider's notification messages and the events that cause them to fire.

Let's look at an example of how to trap these events. This example appears on the companion Web site in the Example1 project. Class Wizard is used to trap the WM_HSCROLL message, which is modified as follows:

```
void CProgTrak::OnHScroll(UINT nSBCode,UINT nPos,CScrollBar* pScrollBar)
{
    // TODO: Add your message handler code here and/or call default
    //CDialog::OnHScroll(nSBCode, nPos, pScrollBar);
    //
    if(pScrollBar->GetSafeHwnd() == m_Trackbar.GetSafeHwnd())
    {
        if(nSBCode == TB_LINEDOWN)  // right arrow key pressed
            TRACE("Right arrow key pressed in slider control.\n");
    }
}          // end OnHScroll()
```

The only change was to comment out the default handler (you can leave it in) and add a new one. The member variable m_Trackbar points to the slider control. Compare the window handle of this against the one passed in, and this code will recognize that the right arrow key was pressed.

Table 11.1   The Slider Control Notification Messages

NOTIFICATION MESSAGE	EVENT
TB_BOTTOM	VK_END
TB_ENDTRACK	WM_KEYUP (the user released a key that sent a relevant virtual-key code)
TB_LINEDOWN	VK_RIGHT or VK_DOWN
TB_LINEUP	VK_LEFT or VK_UP
TB_PAGEDOWN	VK_NEXT (the user clicked the channel below or to the right of slider pointer)
TB_PAGEUP	VK_PRIOR (the user clicked the channel above or to the left of slider pointer)
TB_THUMBPOSITION	WM_LBUTTONUP after a TB_THUMBTRACK notification message
TB_THUMBTRACK	Slider being dragged with mouse
TB_TOP	VK_HOME

That's it for the notification messages. Don't forget about these, for this or any control. The notification methods can be used to do a lot of neat things that can enhance the user interface, or at least make it a more pleasant experience. With this peek under the hood out of the way, it's time to look at the primary methods that accompany the slider control.

Primary CSlideCtrl Class Methods

This section provides an overview of those methods you'll probably use the most, what I call the *primary class methods*. Read the MFC documentation for a more detailed discussion.

The first method is Create(). Its prototype is the same as for the progress control.

```
BOOL Create(DWORD dwStyle, const RECT& rect, CWnd* pParentWnd,UINT nID);
```

All the parameters are the same, and used in the same way. The pParentWnd parameter must not be NULL. The return value is nonzero if the function was successful, and zero if it failed.

The next function is GetLineSize().

```
int GetLineSize() const;
```

This method returns the size of a line for the TB_LINEUP and TB_LINEDOWN notification messages. The default size is 1. The line size is a measure of how much the slider moves in response to these messages.

The sister method for GetLineSize()is SetLineSize().

```
int SetLineSize(int nSize);
```

The parameter nSize is the new line size of the control. The return value is the previous line size. There are identical methods for the page size; GetPageSize() to obtain the page size, for example. The page size is a measure of how much a TB_PAGEUP or TB_PAGEDOWN message moves the slider. For both the line and page methods, pressing the left arrow and right arrow keys and the Page Up and Page Down buttons generates a notification message when the slider control has the focus.

The next method is GetPageSize(), which is prototyped as follows:

```
int GetPageSize();
```

Use this method to find the size of a page for the slide control. The page size affects the amount that the slider moves when the user presses the Page Up and Page Down keys (the TB_PAGEUP and TB_PAGEDOWN notification messages). The return value is the page size.

The SetPageSize() method sets the size of a page for the slide control. It is prototyped as follows:

```
int SetPageSize(int nSize);
```

The return value is the previous page size.

The SetRange() method is used to set the range—the maximum and minimum positions—for the slider in the slide control. It is prototyped as

```
void SetRange( int nMin, int nMax, BOOL bRedraw = FALSE );
```

If the parameter bRedraw is TRUE, the slider will be redrawn after you set the range. You can get the current range by calling

```
void GetRange( int& nMin, int& nMax );
```

Notice that both parameters are passed by reference.

The GetPos() method is used to retrieve the current position of the slider in the slide control. It is prototyped as

```
int GetPos();
```

The following example is taken from the sample code on the Web site.

```
int nSlideSpeed = m_Trackbar.GetPos();
```

The opposite of this method is used to set the position.

```
void SetPos( int nPos );
```

The parameter nPos is the new position, which must be in the range set by an earlier call to SetRange().

The next method is GetNumTics(), which is prototyped as

```
UINT GetNumTics();
```

This method returns the number of tick marks in a slide control.

SetTicFreq() method, prototyped as

```
void SetTicFreq( int nFreq );
```

is used to set the frequency that tick marks are displayed in the slide control. The default frequency is 1; the slide control must have been created with the TBS_AUTOTICKS style. For example,

```
m_Trackbar.SetRange(1,20);
m_Trackbar.SetTickFreq(2);
```

gives the trackbar referred to by m_Trackbar a range of 20, with 10 tick marks (every second increment in the range).

The Sample Program

Two examples of the progress gauge control can be found on the companion Web site in the Example1 project. The first example demonstrates how to use your application's frame window and status bar to contain a progress gauge, and the second example is a progress gauge in a dialog box. The second example includes the code for the slide control.

Progress Gauge in the Status Bar

There are likely to be occasions when you'd want to use the progress gauge control in your view. If you specified a status bar in AppWizard when you first created your application, you can easily use one of the panes of your status bar as the container for a progress gauge. An application generated by AppWizard has the class CMainFrame, which contains a member variable m_wndStatusBar of type CStatusBar. This member variable is used as the parent window of the CProgressCtrl object. The following is the entire message handler that responds to the menu option Progress gauge in Status Bar.

```
void CMainFrame::OnProgStatbar()
{
    // TODO: Add your command handler code here

    // Create the CProgressCtrl as a child of the status bar.
    // Use the first pane of the status bar to display the progress
    //bar.
    //
    RECT rRect;
    m_wndStatusBar.GetItemRect (0, &rRect);
    CProgressCtrl cProgBar;
    VERIFY (cProgBar.Create(WS_CHILD | WS_VISIBLE, rRect,
            &m_wndStatusBar, 1));
    cProgBar.SetRange(0, 50);
    cProgBar.SetStep(1);
    //
    // This simulates a time-consuming operation by using Sleep()
    //
    for(int j=0; j < 50; j++)
```

```
    {
        Sleep(50);
        cProgBar.StepIt();
    }
}
```

In a real-world application, you would probably want to call this method from anywhere in your code. Because the member variable m_wndStatusBar is protected (by
default), you will need to make some adjustments so that other classes can access the
member function. Use the class descriptor *friend* to accomplish this task.

Progress Gauge in a Dialog Box

The next example is more restrictive in that it's in a dialog box, which is its parent window. This example also uses the progress gauge with the slide control. The speed of the
progress gauge can be set by using the slider, as shown in Figure 11.1. The following
code snippets can be found on the companion Web site in the Example1 project, in the
files ProgTrak.cpp and ProgTrak.h. Timers are used to mimic the time-consuming
operation, so some of the variables you'll see next will appear to be undefined because
they're global. Look at the entire source code file for all the gory details.

The trackbar is configured and initialized in OnInitDialog(), as shown here:

```
BOOL CProgTrak::OnInitDialog()
{
    CDialog::OnInitDialog();

    // TODO: Add extra initialization here
    m_Trackbar.SetPageSize(1);

    // Set the initial range.
    m_Trackbar.SetRange(1,20, FALSE);

    // Set the initial position.
    m_Trackbar.SetPos(1);

    // Set the selection.
    m_Trackbar.SetSelection(1,1);

    // Set the tick frequency.
    m_Trackbar.SetTicFreq(1);
    //
    return TRUE;    // return TRUE unless you set the focus to a control
                    // EXCEPTION: OCX Property Pages should return FALSE
} // end OnInitDialog()
```

The next thing to examine is what happens when you click the Start Demo button.
Here is that method:

```
void CProgTrak::OnStart()
{
```

```
        int nSlideSpeed = m_Trackbar.GetPos();
        m_Progress.SetStep(nSlideSpeed);
        m_Progress.StepIt();
        uTimeNow = uMin;
        uMax = 20;    // step counter
        uTimerID = this->SetTimer(uTimeNow,50,NULL);

    }    // end OnStart()
```

This method first looks at the trackbar to see how fast to update the progress gauge, which it then starts. It then starts a timer. Here is the message handler for the timer:

```
    void CProgTrak::OnTimer(UINT nIDEvent)
    {
        // comment out MFC default code
        //CDialog::OnTimer(nIDEvent);
        //
        if (uTimeNow < uMax)    // keep incrementing...
        {
            // Increment the progress gauge
            m_Progress.StepIt();
            uTimeNow++;
        }
        else
        {
            // At the end of the range - kill timer.
            this->KillTimer(uTimerID);
            uTimeNow = 0; // restart progress loop all over again
        }

    }       // end OnTimer()
```

While uTimeNow is less than 20 (that is, uMax), the progress gauge is stepped. Once this value is reached, the timer is killed, and uTimeNow is reset to zero to start the whole process again. WM_TIMER messages already in the message queue are not removed when KillTimer() is called. Finally, you can interrupt the whole process by clicking the End Demo button, which calls this method:

```
    void CProgTrak::OnEnddemo()
    {
        m_Progress.SetPos(0);
        uMax = 0;      // force OnTimer() to quit
        this->KillTimer(uTimerID);
    }    // end OnEnddemo()
```

That does it for the sample code for progress gauges and trackbars. In the real world, your code probably won't use WM_TIMER messages but instead will update the progress gauge based on some calculated value. Let's take a look at some additional issues and caveats concerning these controls and the user interface.

Additional Issues

If the progress gauge control is used for a lengthy operation, you might also want to change the cursor to the standard wait cursor, which looks like an hourglass. You can do this by using class CWaitCursor. This class doesn't have a base class, and there's not much to it. Simply define a CWaitCursor variable prior to beginning the time-consuming operation. The object's constructor automatically displays the wait cursor. When the object goes out of scope, its destructor automatically restores the cursor to its previous shape, eliminating cleanup on your part. Because of the way CWaitCursor's constructors and destructors operate, these objects are always local, never global, and cannot be allocated with the *new* operator.

If your application performs an operation that could change the wait cursor (for example, displaying a message box), use the Restore() member function to restore the wait cursor. For example, you might use a timer to ask the user if he or she would like to cancel every 5 or 10 minutes. This message box would cause the arrow cursor to be displayed. If the user elects to continue, call Restore() and the cursor changes back to a wait cursor. Here is a simple example of using the wait cursor:

```
void CSomeClass::MyLongOperation()
{
    CWaitCursor cHourGlass;  // display wait cursor    //
    // do lengthy operation here
    //
}   // end MyLongOperation()
// cursor restored here when MyLongOperation() returns
```

Summary

A lot of ground was covered in this chapter. The progress gauge and the slide control, or slider, have special places in the development of successful Windows applications, and should be used where appropriate. The progress gauge is an ideal candidate to be teamed with the animation control during long operations such as huge file transfers. Placing a progress gauge control in the status bar demonstrates out how easy it is to enhance your user interface by combining established elements. The next chapter looks at another extremely powerful and useful control for enhancing the user interface, the tree control.

CHAPTER 12

The Tree Control

D isplaying data in hierarchical fashion used to involved a lot of complicated drawing and linked list management. The tree control, an object of class CtreeCtrl, rescues the developer from this nightmare. This chapter introduces this control and shows you how to use it to extend and enhance your user interface. Tree controls can make considerable use of graphical images, and they have their own structures that allow you to add, edit, and delete the leaves on the tree.

CTreeCtrl versus CTreeView

MFC provides two classes that encapsulate tree controls, CTreeView and CTreeCtrl. Each class has specific properties that make it well-suited for certain situations.

Use CTreeCtrl when you need a plain, old-fashioned child window control, for example, in a dialog box. Especially use CTreeCtrl if there will be other child controls in the window, as in a dialog box.

Use CTreeView when you want the tree control to act like a view window in document/view architecture as well as a tree control. A CTreeView object consumes the entire client area of a frame window or splitter window. It is automatically resized when its parent window is resized, and it can process command messages from menus, accelerator keys, and toolbars. Because a tree control contains the data necessary to display the tree, the corresponding document object does not have to be complicated—you could even use a CDocument object as the document type in your document template. This chapter focuses on the CTreeCtrl class, and presents a sample program that uses it in a dialog box. The output of this program is shown in Figure 12.1.

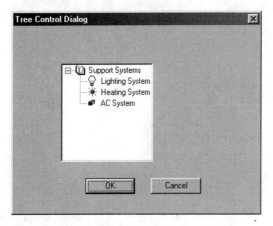

Figure 12.1 A CTreeCtrl object from the companion Web site.

Tree Control Styles

There are several different styles, each with their own properties, that you can assign to a tree control to change both its appearance and functionality. You can set these when you create a CTreeCtrl object by calling its Create() method, or by using the Properties dialog box in App Studio, as shown in Figure 12.2. Styles can be retrieved, and changed, after the control has been created by using the GetWindowLong() and SetWindowLong() APIs.

Here is an overview of the different styles that can be assigned to a tree control.

TVS_HASLINES. The TVS_HASLINES style draws lines that link child items to their corresponding parent. This gives the user a nice visual representation of a tree control's underlying hierarchy. Items at the root of the control are not drawn. To do so, combine the TVS_LINESATROOT style with this style.

TVS_LINESATROOT. With this style, the tree control displays lines linking child items to the root of the hierarchy.

TVS_HASBUTTONS. This style adds a button to the left of each parent item in the tree. Users can expand and collapse these items by clicking the button as an alternative to double-clicking the parent item itself.

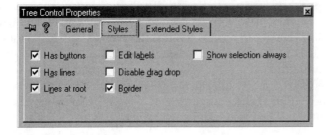

Figure 12.2 The CTreeCtrl styles in App Studio.

TVS_EDITLABELS. This style allows the user to edit the labels of tree control items.

TVS_SHOWSELALWAYS. This style causes a selected item to remain selected when the tree control loses the focus.

TVS_DISABLEDRAGDROP. This style prevents the tree control from sending TVN_BEGINDRAG notification messages.

That does it for the styles. You will almost always use the TVS_HASLINES and TVS_LINESATROOT styles; experiment with these to see the effect of the style(s) on the tree control.

Tree Control and Image Lists

One of the things that make tree controls user friendly is their ability to display data graphically. Data can be displayed with both a text label and a bitmap. You've seen these before in the Windows 95/98 Explorer, for example, which displays files and directories as a tree.

The data is represented using bitmaps that can be coded to give the user a visual cue to the underlying meaning. For example, a closed file-folder bitmap can be used to indicate a root directory and an open folder can be used for the current directory. These bitmaps are handled by defining an image list. An image list is not a control, but just another drawing tool that can be thought of as a glorified bitmap manager. Another analogy for image lists is to think of them as a roll of film. Just like a roll of film, image lists are a stream of bitmaps that come with their own APIs that you can call to perform most of the work for you. And just as a roll of film has a fixed size (for example, 35mm), the image list has a maximum height of 32K pixels. In other words, an image list can have one bitmap with a size of $32K \times 32K$ pixels, or it could have 32K bitmaps, each 1-pixel wide.

To determine the maximum number of images supported by an image list, divide 32K by the width of one image.

You can arrange the bitmaps that are associated with a tree control item in an image list so that they can be easily indexed. This allows you to change the bitmap that is displayed when the user changes the state of a tree item.

Image List Properties

The graphical images displayed from an image list will be either *masked* or *unmasked*. The masked flavor includes transparent pixels that allow the background to come through—just like an icon on the Windows 95/98 Desktop. The unmasked image list overwrites whatever is under it. When working with tree controls, you'll probably be using the masked version.

Another property supported by image lists is the ability to add images as necessary. Look back at the Windows Explorer example. When new files are added, new bitmaps appear in the control. The ability to insert new images and delete old ones is built in. Adding images is a matter of calling the right API and specifying the desired image list style.

The simple image list in a tree control is created later in this chapter that illustrates these concepts. First, let's get back to tree controls, and examine the structures needed to manipulate them.

Tree Control Structures

There are eight structures available for use with the tree control. These are

- TVITEM
- TVITEMEX
- TVINSERTSTRUCT
- NMTREEVIEW
- TVDISPINFO
- TVHITTESTINFO
- TVKEYDOWN
- TVSORTCB

Of these, the first two are the most commonly used. The following is a description of these structures.

TVITEM

The TVITEM structure describes the items or leaves of a tree control. This structure is required. Although it has been replaced by the TVITEMEX structure, certain applications can require it. The TVITEM structure is prototyped as

```
typedef struct tagTVITEM
{
    UINT mask;                \\ indicates which members are valid
    HTREEITEM hItem;          \\ the item to which this structure refers
    UINT state;               \\ current state of the item
    UINT stateMask;           \\ current state of the item mask
    LPSTR pszText;            \\ text for the item
    int cchTextMax;           \\ size of the item's text buffer
    int iImage;               \\ index of the image for this item
    int iSelectedImage;       \\ index of the selected image
    int cChildren;            \\ number of child nodes
    LPARAM lParam;            \\ application-defined item data
}   TVITEM, FAR *LPTVITEM;
```

When you create or modify tree control items, fill out this structure and pass it to a class member function, or use it in a call to SendMessage().

Table 12.1   Values of the Mask Member of a TVITEM Structure

MASK	MEANING
TVIF_CHILDREN	Indicates the cChildren member is valid.
TVIF_HANDLE	Indicates the hItem member is valid.
TVIF_IMAGE	Indicates the iImage member is valid.
TVIF_PARAM	Indicates the lParam member is valid.
TVIF_SELECTEDIMAGE	Indicates the iSelectedImage member is valid.
TVIF_STATE	Indicates the state and stateMask members are valid.
TVIF_TEXT	Indicates the pszText and cchTextMax members are valid.

The *mask* member indicates which of the other structure members contain valid data. If retrieving data, it reflects which members should be filled in. This can be a combination of the values shown in Table 12.1.

The hItem member is the item to which the structure is referring. Think of it as a complete leaf on the tree, which can be an icon or text label, for example. The state member indicates the current state of the item. This can be zero or any valid combination of the predefined constants (for example, TVIS_CUT, TVIS_DISABLED). The stateMask member describes which of these states are valid for the item in question. The pszText member is the address of a string that contains the item's text label (if text has been specified). This member is also used to receive text in certain calls that query the structure. The cchTextMax member is the size of the pszText string buffer when the structure is receiving item attributes. The iImage and iSelectedImage members are the indexes of the icon image and selected icon image in the image list. Recall that images can change their appearance when selected in a tree control (for example, a closed-book icon changes to an open-book icon in Windows Help). The cChildren member is the number of child items associated with the item referred to by the hItem member. Finally, the lParam member is a scratch pad for you to use with application-defined data. This is 32-bits, and is like the item data used for list and combo boxes.

TVITEMEX

The TVITEMEX structure is an enhancement to the TVITEM structure, and should be used where possible. It is prototyped as

```
typedef struct tagTVITEMEX
{
    UINT      mask;
    HTREEITEM hItem;
    UINT      state;
    UINT      stateMask;
    LPTSTR    pszText;
    int       cchTextMax;
    int       iImage;
    int       iSelectedImage;
```

```
      int      cChildren;
   LPARAM    lParam;
      int      iIntegral;
} TVITEMEX, FAR *LPTVITEMEX;
```

The structure is identical to TVITEM, except for the additional member called iIntegral. This member specifies the height of the item as increments of the standard item height. The default is one increment of item height. Setting it to 2 gives the items twice the standard height; 3 gives it three times, and so on. The control does not draw in this extra space—this is used by the application for drawing when using custom draw, discussed later in this chapter.

The state and stateMask members work together. The state member is a set of bit flags and image list indexes indicating the state of the item. When setting the state of a tree item, the stateMask member is used to specify which bits in the state member are valid. Conversely, when retrieving an item's state, the state member returns the current state for the bits specified in stateMask. Bits 0 through 7 are used for the item's state flags. The item states are covered in a separate section later in this chapter. Bits 8 through 11 are used to specify the one-based (not zero!) overlay image index. The overlay image is superimposed over the item's icon. If bits 8 through 11 are zero, then the item has no overlay image. To isolate these bits, you can use the TVIS_OVERLAYMASK bit mask. To set the overlay image index, use the INDEXTOOVERLAYMASK macro. This macro is prototyped as follows:

```
UINT INDEXTOOVERLAYMASK(UINT iOverlay);
```

This prepares the index of an overlay mask so the ImageList_Draw() function can use it. The macro is defined as

```
#define INDEXTOOVERLAYMASK(i) ((i) << 8)
```

Bits 12 through 15 of the state member specify the state image index. This is the image that is displayed next to an item's icon to indicate an application-defined state. If these are zero, then the item has no state image. You can isolate these bits using the TVIS_STATEIMAGEMASK bit mask. To set the image index, use the INDEXTO-STATEIMAGEMASK macro.

```
UINT INDEXTOSTATEIMAGEMASK(UINT i);
```

where i is the index of the state image. The macro is defined as

```
#define INDEXTOSTATEIMAGEMASK(i) ((i) << 12)
```

This index specifies the image in the state image list that should be drawn.

The stateMask member specifies what bits in the state member are valid. When retrieving the state of an item, set the bits of this member to indicate which bits you want returned into the state member. When setting the state, set the bits in stateMask to indicate which bits of the state member you wish to set.

The pszText member is the address of a NULL-terminated string containing the text for the item if the structure specifies item attributes. If this is LPSTR_TEXTCALLBACK, the parent window is responsible for storing the text. In this case, the tree control sends a TVN_GETDISPINFO notification message to the parent window whenever it needs the item text for displaying, editing, or sorting. It sends the parent a TVN_SET-DISPINFO message when the item text changes. If the TVITEMEX structure is receiving item attributes, then pszText is the address of the buffer that receives the item text.

The cchTextMax member is the size of the buffer pointed to by pszText, in characters. If the structure is being used to set item attributes, this member is ignored.

The iImage member is index into the control's image list for the icon to use whenever the item is in the nonselected state. If this is I_IMAGECALLBACK, the parent window is responsible for storing the index and a TVN_GETDISPINFO notification message is sent to retrieve the index when the image needs to be displayed.

The iSelectedImage is the index into the image list when the item is in the selected state. The action is the same as for iImage when this is set to I_IMAGECALLBACK.

The cChildren member is a flag indicating whether the item has any associated child items. It can be one of the following values: 0 if the item has no child items, 1 if it has at least one child, or I_CHILDRENCALLBACK, which means the parent window tracks the child items.

The last member of the TVITEMEX structure is lParam. This is a 32-bit value that you can use to associate with the item.

TVINSERTSTRUCT

The next frequently used tree control structure is TVINSERTSTRUCT. This structure is used to add new items to a tree control. It is prototyped as

```
typedef struct tagTVINSERTSTRUCT
{
    HTREEITEM hParent;
    HTREEITEM hInsertAfter;
    #if (_WIN32_IE >= 0x0400)
    union
    {
        TVITEMEX itemex;
        TVITEM item;
    } DUMMYUNIONNAME;
    #else
        TVITEM item;
    #endif
} TVINSERTSTRUCT, FAR *LPTVINSERTSTRUCT;
```

The TVINSERTSTRUCT structure is identical to the TV_INSERTSTRUCT structure, but has been renamed to follow current naming conventions. It contains information used to add a new item to the tree control. The hParent member is the handle to the parent item. If this is TVI_ROOT or NULL, the item is inserted at the root of the tree.

The hInsertAfter item is the handle of the item after which the item will be inserted, or one of the following values:

TVI_FIRST. Inserts the item at the beginning of the list.

TVI_LAST. Inserts the item at the end of the list.

TVI_SORT. Inserts the item into the list in alphabetical order.

The itemex member is a TVITEMEX structure containing information about the item to add. This requires version 4.71 or higher of the common control library. For lower versions, the item member is used, which is a TVITEM structure containing information about the item to add.

NMTREEVIEW

The NMTREEVIEW structure contains information about tree control notification message. It is prototyped as

```
typedef struct tagNMTREEVIEW
{
    NMHDR hdr;
    UINT action;
    TVITEM itemOld;
    TVITEM itemNew;
    POINT ptDrag;
} NMTREEVIEW, FAR *LPNMTREEVIEW;
```

The hdr member is another structure, the NMHDR structure.

```
typedef struct tagNMHDR
{
    HWND hwndFrom;
    UINT idFrom;
    UINT code;
} NMHDR;
```

This structure contains information about the notification message. The hwndFrom member is the Window handle of the control sending the message, and the idFrom is the identifier of the control. The code member is the notification code.

The next member of the NM_TREEVIEW structure is the action member. This member is a flag specifying an action related to the notification message. The itemOld member is also a structure of type TVITEM. It contains information about the old item state and is zero for notification messages that do not use it.

The itemNew member is a TVITEM structure containing information about the new state of the item and is also zero for notification messages that do not use it.

Finally, the ptDrag is a POINT structure that contains the client coordinates of the mouse when the event that fired the notification message occurred.

NMTVDISPINFO

The NMTVDISPINFO structure is identical to the TV_DISPINFO structure, but has been renamed to conform to naming conventions. It is prototyped as

```
typedef struct tagNMTVDISPINFO
{
NMHDR hdr;
TVITEM item;
}NMTVDISPINFO, FAR *LPNMTVDISPINFO
```

This structure is used as a read-write buffer for the visual aspects of a tree view item. The hdr member is an NMHDR structure containing information about the notification message. The item member is a TVITEM structure used to identify and store information about the tree item. The mask member of this structure indicates what is being set or retrieved, and be one of the values shown in Table 12.2.

TVHITTESTINFO

The TVHITTESTINFO structure is used to store the location of a point relative to the tree view control. This structure is used with the TVM_HITTEST message. It is prototyped as follows:

```
typedef struct tagTVHITTESTINFO
{
    POINT pt;
    UINT flags;
    HTREEITEM hItem;
} TVHITTESTINFO, FAR *LPTVHITTESTINFO;
```

The pt member is the point to test, in client coordinates. The flags member is used to tell you the results of the hit test, and can be one or more of the values shown in Table 12.3.

The hItem member is the handle to the item that occupies the point.

Table 12.2   Values of Mask in NMTVDISPINFO Structure

MASK VALUES	DESCRIPTION
TVIF_CHILDREN	The cChildren member specifies, or is to receive, a value that indicates whether the item has child items.
TVIF_IMAGE	The iImage member specifies, or is to receive, the index of the item's nonselected icon in the image list.
TVIF_SELECTEDIMAGE	The iSelectedImage member specifies, or is to receive, the index of the item's selected icon in the image list.
TVIF_TEXT	The pszText member specifies the new item text or the address of a buffer that is to receive the item text.

Table 12.3 The Mouse Hit Tests Results

VALUE OF FLAGS	MEANING
TVHT_ABOVE	Above the client area.
TVHT_BELOW	Below the client area.
TVHT_NOWHERE	In the client area, but below the last item.
TVHT_ONITEM	On the bitmap or label associated with an item.
TVHT_ONITEMBUTTON	On the button associated with an item.
TVHT_ONITEMICON	On the bitmap associated with an item.
TVHT_ONITEMINDENT	In the indentation associated with an item.
TVHT_ONITEMLABEL	On the label (text) associated with an item.
TVHT_ONITEMRIGHT	In the area to the right of an item.
TVHT_ONITEMSTATEICON	On the state icon for a tree view item that is in a user-defined state.
TVHT_TOLEFT	To the left of the client area.
TVHT_TORIGHT	To the right of the client area.

NMTVKEYDOWN

NMTVKEYDOWN is a structure used for keyboard events. It contains information used with the TVN_KEYDOWN notification message. The hdr member is an NMHDR structure containing information about the message. The wVKey member is the virtual key code that was pressed, and the flags member is always zero.

TVSORTCB

The TVSORTCB structure is used to store information used to sort child items in a tree control. This structure is used with the TVM_SORTCHILDRENCB message. It is identical to the TV_SORTCB structure, but has been renamed to follow naming conventions. It is prototyped as follows:

```
typedef struct tagTVSORTCB
{
HTREEITEM hParent;
PFNTVCOMPARE lpfnCompare;
LPARAM lParam;
}TVSORTCB, FAR * LPTVSORTCB;
```

The hParent member is the handle to the parent item of the children to be sorted. The lpfnCompare member is the address of a callback function defined in your application. It is called during a sort operation whenever the relative order of two list items requires comparison. This function must be defined as in the following prototype:

```
int CALLBACK MyCompareFunc(LPARAM lParam0, LPARAM lParam1, LPARAM lpSort);
```

The return value must be a negative value if the first item should come before the second, a positive value if the first should follow the second, or zero if the two items are identical. The lParam0 and lParam1 parameters correspond to the lParam member of the TVITEM structure of the items being compared. The lpSort parameter corresponds to the lParam member of this structure (the TVSORTCB structure).

Tree Item States

One of the cool things about the TreeView control is that it can have many different states, which can be represented visually with the image list or by changing the properties of the control. Sending messages to the control can set these states. The following is a quick look at the various state flags that are available.

TVIS_BOLD. The TreeView control item is bold.

TVIS_CUT. The item has been selected as part of a cut-and-paste operation.

TVIS_DROPHILITED. The item has been selected as the target of a drag-and-drop operation.

TVIS_EXPANDED. The child items in the list are shown expanded (that is, visible). This value only applies to parent items.

TVIS_EXPANDEDONCE. The child items in the list have been expanded at least once. This value only applies to parent items. When this state is set, a TVM_EXPAND message does not generate TVN_ITEMEXPANDING or TVN_ITEMEXPANDED notification messages for the parent items. Refer to the Expand() class member in the section on class members later in this chapter for more information.

TVIS_EXPANDPARTIAL. This state is valid only when using version 4.70 or higher of the common control library. It produces a partially expanded tree view item in which some, but not all, of the child items are visible and the parent's plus symbol is displayed.

TVIS_SELECTED. The item is in the selected state. Its visual properties depend on whether or not it has the focus.

That takes care of the various states that the TreeView control can have—now I'll give you a look at the class members.

CTreeCtrl Class Members

Between the tree control's class member functions and its messages, you can exert a great deal of control over the properties and behavior of the control. This section looks at the most commonly used class member functions. Although there are a lot of functions at your disposal, you'll only need to use a few.

BOOL Create(DWORD dwStyle, const RECT& rect, CWnd* pParentWnd, UINT nID);
This method creates a tree control. First call the constructor, then Create(), which creates the control and attaches it to the CTreeCtrl object. The dwStyle parameter indicates the

tree control style(s), discussed earlier in this chapter. The rect parameter specifies the control's size and position. The pParentWnd parameter is the tree control's parent window, usually a CDialog or CWnd object. It cannot be NULL. The nID parameter is the control's ID in your resource.h file. The return value is nonzero if the call was successful, or zero if it failed.

BOOL Expand(HTREEITEM hItem, UINT nCode); Use this class member function to expand, or collapse, the list of child items under its parent. The hItem parameter is the handle of the tree item being expanded. The nCode parameter is a flag specifying the type of action to be taken, and can be one of the following:

- **TVE_COLLAPSE.** Collapses the list of items.
- **TVE_COLLAPSERESET.** Collapses the list and removes the child items.
- **TVE_EXPAND.** Expands the list of items.
- **TVE_TOGGLE.** Expands the list if it's collapsed, or collapses it if it's expanded.

HTREEITEM InsertItem(LPTV_INSERTSTRUCT lpInsertStruct); There are actually four flavors of this function, but this one is probably the simplest and easiest to use. The lpInsertStruct parameter is the address of a TV_INSERTSTRUCT structure that you configure. The return value is the handle of the item just inserted if successful, or NULL if the call failed. I've found it best to wrap this function in a class method and pass it the handle of the parent, the text of the item, and its image. This makes it very easy to use the control when you have a lot of items to insert. An example of this is provided in the section, "The Sample Application," later in this chapter.

BOOL DeleteItem(HTREEITEM hItem); This function deletes an item from the tree control. The hItem parameter is the handle of the item to be deleted. If this is TVI_ROOT, all the items in the tree are deleted. The return value is nonzero if the call was successful.

UINT GetCount(); This method returns the number of items in the tree control, or –1 if the call fails.

HTREEITEM GetSelectedItem(); This function retrieves the handle of the currently selected item in the tree. The return value is NULL if no item is selected.

HTREEITEM GetParentItem(HTREEITEM hItem); This method helps the user find the parent of a tree item identified by the hItem parameter. This method is useful for walking up a tree given any leaf. The return value is the handle of the parent, or NULL if the call failed.

HTREEITEM GetRootItem(); This returns the handle of the root item, or NULL if the call failed. This method can be used in conjunction with GetParentItem() to determine if you've walked up the tree to the root.

CString GetItemText(HTREEITEM hItem) const; This method is used to find the text string associated with the parameter hItem.

TIP

To safely delete all items from a tree, use GetRootItem() to find the root, and pass this to DeleteItem().

TIP

To avoid ambiguity and to facilitate searching a tree, try to give each item a unique text label where possible.

BOOL ItemHasChildren(HTREEITEM hItem); This method is used to determine if an item identified by hItem has any children. If it does, you can use the GetChildItem() method to retrieve them.

HTREEITEM GetChildItem(HTREEITEM hItem); This method retrieves the handle to the first child item of the parent identified by hItem. Once you have this handle, you can use the next function to find all the siblings of the item.

HTREEITEM GetNextSiblingItem(HTREEITEM hItem); The return value is the handle of the next sibling, or NULL when there are no more siblings found.

Although there are additional class methods, these are the ones you'll use most frequently. Hopefully, you've noticed a pattern here: The methods are implemented such that the tree control can be changed dynamically by your application, but you can interrogate the tree control to find out where and how items are situated. For example, you'll often populate a tree with data from external sources—you cannot predict or hard-code in certain values. For example, suppose your tree control lists all the states, and under each state you list the counties. In a case like this, you simply read the data source, insert the parents (the state's name) followed by its children (the names of the counties). Clearly, this data will vary from state to state, but you can use the class methods described previously to find out how many counties a state has, and sort them in alphabetical order.

Tree Control Messages

This section looks at the messages you can use with tree control. Like the structures, some are used more than others, but all follow the same basic pattern. In the following examples, the variable pTreeCtrl is a hypothetical pointer to the tree control which has been obtained prior to calling SendMessage().

TVM_CREATEDRAGIMAGE. This message is used when you want to change the bitmap for an object when your program supports dragging. This message creates the dragging bitmap and its image list, then adds the bitmap to the list. The wParam parameter is not used and is set to zero. The lParam parameter is the handle to the HTREEITEM object that receives the new dragging bitmap. The return value is NULL if the message fails; otherwise, it is the handle of the image list to which the dragging bitmap was added.

TVM_DELETEITEM. This message is used to delete an item from a tree control. The wParam parameter is not used and is set to zero. The lParam parameter is the handle to the HTREEITEM object to be deleted. The return value is TRUE if the item is successfully deleted.

TVM_EDITLABEL. This message is used to edit the text labels associated with tree control items. The wParam parameter is not used and is set to zero. The lParam parameter is a pointer to the HTREEITEM object that is to be edited. The return value is the handle of the edit control used to edit the text if successful, or NULL if the call fails. You must first set the focus to the tree control *before* sending this message.

TVM_ENDEDITLABELNOW. This message ends the editing of an item in a tree control. The wParam parameter is set to TRUE to cancel the editing and to ignore the changes. If FALSE, the changes are saved. The lParam parameter is not used and is set to zero. The return value is TRUE if the message was successful, FALSE if not.

TVM_ENSUREVISIBLE. This message makes sure that a given item in the control is visible. The parent item is expanded, and the control is scrolled, if necessary. The wParam parameter is not used and is set to zero. The lParam parameter is the HTREEITEM object to be made visible. The return value is TRUE if the control was scrolled in order to ensure the item was made visible. Otherwise, the return value is FALSE.

TVM_EXPAND. This message is used to expand, or collapse, the list of child items associated with a given parent. The wParam parameter is a flag that can have one of the following values:

- **TVE_COLLAPSE.** Collapses the list of items.
- **TVE_EXPAND.** Expands the list of items.
- **TVE_TOGGLE.** Toggles the list from expanded/collapsed and vice versa.
- **TVE_COLLAPSERESET.** Collapses the list and removes any child items. You must also specify TVE_COLLAPSE.

The lParam parameter is the handle to the HTREEITEM object that is to be expanded or collapsed. The return value is TRUE if any changes occurred to the list; FALSE otherwise.

TVM_GETCOUNT. This message is used to determine the number of items in a tree control. The wParam and lParam parameters are not used and are set to zero. The return value is the number of items in the control. For example,

```
int nItems;
nItems = pTreeCtrl->SendMessage(TVM_GETCOUNT,0,0L );
```

TVM_GETEDITCONTROL. This message is used to fetch the handle of the edit control that is being used to edit the text associated with a tree control item. The wParam and lParam parameters are not used and are set to zero. The return value is the handle of the edit control if the call is successful, or NULL if it fails.

TVM_GETIMAGELIST. This message is used to retrieve the handle to the image list associated with a tree control. It can be used to fetch both the normal and state image lists. The wParam parameter is set to TVSIL_NORMAL to retrieve the normal state, and to TVSIL_STATE for the state. The lParam parameter is not used and is set to zero. The return value is the handle to the image list.

TVM_GETINDENT. This message is used to determine the number of pixels that child items are indented in a tree control, relative to their parent's position. The wParam and lParam parameters are not used and are set to zero. The return value is the amount of indentation being used.

TVM_GETISEARCHSTRING. This message is used to fetch the incremental search string for a tree control. Recall that an incremental search string is the string entered by the user as the characters are being typed. The wParam parameter is not used and is set to zero. The lParam parameter is a pointer to a buffer that receives the search string. The return value is the length of this string; if the tree control is not in incremental search mode, the return value is zero.

TVM_GETITEM. This message is used to retrieve the attributes of a tree control item. The wParam parameter is not used and is set to zero. The lParam parameter is a pointer to a TV_ITEM structure that specifies what attributes to retrieve and that also stores the attributes. The hItem member of this structure indicates the item for which the information is to be retrieved, and the mask member indicates which attributes are to be found. If mask is TVIF_TEXT, you must also set the pszText and cchTextMax members of the structure accordingly. The return value is TRUE if the call is successful; FALSE otherwise.

TVM_GETITEMRECT. This message is used to find the bounding rectangle for a tree control item, and indicates if the item is currently visible. The wParam parameter is a flag; if TRUE, the bounding rectangle is only for the text of the item. If FALSE, it means the entire line occupied by the item is to be retrieved. The lParam parameter is a pointer to a RECT object that receives the coordinates of the boundary rectangle. These coordinates are relative to the upper-left corner of the tree control. The return value is TRUE if the item is visible, in which case the bounding rectangle is also retrieved. Otherwise, this value is FALSE, and the rectangle is not retrieved.

TVM_GETNEXTITEM. This message is used to retrieve the item in a tree control that has a specified relationship to a given item (the lParam parameter). The wParam parameter indicates the item in question, and can be one of the following:

- **TVGN_PARENT.** Retrieves the parent of the specified item.
- **TVGN_CARET.** Retrieves the currently selected item.
- **TVGN_CHILD.** Retrieves the first child. The hitem parameter must be NULL.
- **TVGN_DROPHILITE.** Retrieves the item that is the target of a drag-and-drop operation.
- **TVGN_FIRSTVISIBLE.** Retrieves the first item that is visible.
- **TVGN_NEXT.** Retrieves the next sibling item.
- **TVGN_NEXTVISIBLE.** Retrieves the next visible item that follows the specified item. The specified item must be visible.
- **TVGN_PREVIOUS.** Retrieves the previous sibling item.
- **TVGN_PREVIOUSVISIBLE.** Retrieves the first visible item that precedes the specified item. The specified item must be visible.
- **TVGN_ROOT.** Retrieves the topmost item of the TreeView control. The return value is the handle to the item if successful or NULL if the call fails.

TVM_GETVISIBLECOUNT. This message returns the number of items that are fully visible in the client area of the tree control. The wParam and lParam parameters are not used and are set to zero. The return value is the number of items that are *completely* visible. For example,

```
int nVisible;
nVisible = pTreeCtrl->SendMessage(TVM_GETVISIBLECOUNT,0,0L );
```

TVM_HITTEST. This message is used to determine if a tree control item is at a given point, relative to the client area of the control. The wParam parameter is not used and is set to zero. The lParam parameter is a pointer to a TV_HITTESTINFO structure; the pt member of this structure indicates the coordinates of the point to test. After the message returns, the hItem member of the TV_HITTESTINFO structure contains the handle of the item at the point, or NULL if no item is present at the point. The return value is the same as the hItem member of the TV_HITTESTINFO structure.

TVM_INSERTITEM. This message is used to insert a new item into a tree control. The wParam parameter is not used and is set to zero. The lParam parameter is a pointer to a TV_INSERTSTRUCT structure that contains the attributes of the new item. The return value is the handle of the new item if the call is successful, or NULL otherwise.

TVM_SELECTITEM. This message is used to select a tree control item. The item is scrolled into view if necessary; if it is the target of a drag-and-drop operation, the item is redrawn in that style. If the control is collapsed, it is expanded in order to bring the item into view. The wParam parameter is a flag that can be one of the following values:

- **TVGN_CARET.** Selects the specified item.

- **TVGN_DROPHILITE.** Redraws the item in the style used as the target of a drag-and-drop operation.

- **TVGN_FIRSTVISIBLE.** Scrolls the tree such that the item is the first visible one.

The lParam parameter is the handle to the tree control item. If this is NULL and an item is currently selected, the selection state is removed. The return value is TRUE if the call is successful; FALSE otherwise.

TVM_SETIMAGELIST. This message sets the state image list for a tree control, and redraws it using that image. The wParam parameter is a flag indicating which state to use—TVSIL_NORMAL for the normal state, and TVSIL_STATE for the state. The lParam parameter is the handle to the image list. If this is NULL, all images are removed from the control. The return value is the handle of the previous image list (if any) if the call was successful; NULL otherwise.

TVM_SETINDENT. This message is used to set the width, in pixels, of the amount of indentation to use between a parent and child items. The control is redrawn after this message is sent. The wParam parameter is the number of pixels to use. If this value is less than the system-defined minimum, the system value is used. The lParam parameter is not used and should be set to zero. There is no return value.

TVM_SETITEM. This message sets the attributes of an item in a tree control. The wParam parameter is not used and is set to zero. The lParam parameter is a pointer to a TV_ITEM structure that specifies the attributes. The return value is zero if the call is successful; –1 otherwise.

TVM_SORTCHILDREN. This message sorts the child items of a given parent item in a tree control. The wParam parameter is not used (it is reserved for future use) and *must* be zero. The lParam parameter is the handle to the parent item whose child items are to be sorted. The return value is TRUE if the call is successful; FALSE otherwise.

TVM_SORTCHILDRENCB. This message is identical to TVM_SORTCHILDREN, except the sort is based on a callback function that you define for your application. Again the wParam parameter must be zero. The lParam parameter is a pointer to a TV_SORTCB structure. the lpfnCompare member points to your callback function. The return value is TRUE if the call is successful; FALSE otherwise.

You have now seen the TreeView control's styles, messages, and other accessories. The next step is to put it all together in a working example.

The Sample Application

Now that you've seen what's available, let's put it to work with an example. You'll find the tree control example on the companion Web site, in the Example1 project (TreeDlg.cpp and .h). The example consists of a simple tree control and an edit box that is read-only. The edit box is used as feedback. It displays the tree item you select (this will be covered in the next section). The tree control has been assigned a member variable in Class Wizard, m_TreeCtrl. As usual, everything begins in OnInitDialog().

```
BOOL CTreeDlg::OnInitDialog()
{
CDialog::OnInitDialog();
// TODO: Add extra initialization here
//
m_ImageList.Create(IDB_TREEIMAGES, 16, 1, RGB(255, 0, 255));
m_TreeCtrl.SetImageList(&m_ImageList, LVSIL_NORMAL);
HTREEITEM hTRoot,hTItem;
//
hTRoot = AddOneItem((HTREEITEM)NULL,"Support Systems",(HTREEITEM)
        TVI_ROOT,0);
hTItem = AddOneItem(hTRoot,"Lighting System",(HTREEITEM)TVI_FIRST, 2);
hTItem = AddOneItem(hTRoot,"Heating System", (HTREEITEM)TVI_LAST,4);
hTItem = AddOneItem(hTRoot,"AC System", (HTREEITEM)TVI_LAST,6);
m_TreeCtrl.Expand(hTRoot ,TVE_EXPAND);
return TRUE;  // return TRUE unless you set the focus to a control
            // EXCEPTION: OCX Property Pages should return FALSE
}
```

This method creates the image list that will be associated with the tree control, adds some text for the root, then adds three items under this parent. It displays the tree in expanded mode, making all the choices visible to the user.

To facilitate adding items to your tree control, you may want to write a class method similar to the one used here, AddOneItem(). This method takes four parameters:

- Handle to the parent
- Text that accompanies the item
- Where to insert the item
- The image that accompanies the item

Here is the method from the sample program that is responsible for inserting items into the tree control shown in Figure 12.1, on page 192:

```
HTREEITEM CTreeDlg::AddOneItem( HTREEITEM hParent, LPSTR szText,
    HTREEITEM hInsAfter,int iImage)
{
    HTREEITEM hItem;
    TVITEM tvI;                    // tree control structures
    TVINSERTSTRUCT tvIns;
    //
    //  set mask to text and images
    //
    tvI.mask = TVIF_TEXT | TVIF_IMAGE;
    tvI.iImage = iImage;  // associate the image
    tvI.pszText = szText; // associate the text
    tvI.cchTextMax = lstrlen(szText);
    //
    tvIns.item = tvI;
    tvIns.hInsertAfter = hInsAfter;      // where to insert
    tvIns.hParent = hParent;
    //
    // insert this item into the tree
    //
    hItem = m_TreeCtrl.InsertItem(&tvIns);
    //
    //     make selected image index+1
    //
    m_TreeCtrl.SetItemImage( hItem, iImage, (iImage+1));
    return (hItem);
}    // end AddOneItem()
```

By using a class method like this, it's easier to adjust the tree from various places in your application. Next, you need to determine if the user has clicked or selected an item in the control.

Detecting a Selection

By overriding the TVN_SELCHANGED message in Class Wizard, you can determine if the user has clicked on one of your tree's items. This can be used to launch additional processing, such as opening property dialog boxes. Here is the method from the sample program:

```
void CTreeDlg::OnSelchangedTree1(NMHDR* pNMHDR, LRESULT* pResult)
{
    NM_TREEVIEW* pNMTreeView = (NM_TREEVIEW*)pNMHDR;
    // TODO: Add your control notification handler code here
    HTREEITEM htreeItemSel = m_TreeCtrl.GetSelectedItem();
    CString csTmp =  m_TreeCtrl.GetItemText( htreeItemSel );
    CString csStr = "You clicked ";
    csStr += csTmp;
    m_E_Edit.SetWindowText(csStr);
```

```
            //
            *pResult = 0;
    }       // end OnSelchangedTree1()
```

The call to GetSelectedItem() tells you which item was selected. Once you have that, you can get its text label (using GetItemText()), and identify the user's selection. In this example, the edit box is simply updated with the name of the string you select. You could easily modify these using if statements to take specific action when the item is selected.

Summary

The tree control provides an outstanding way to manage, and present, hierarchical data. It can give a big boost to any interface that needs to show data in a parent-child relationship. The most important thing you'll need to keep in mind is image management. The images need to be kept in synch with the current state of the control to provide consistency. For example, if you're displaying the files found on a floppy disk that is also marked as write-protected, you might wish to show the disk icon, but with a red circle and slash superimposed, or some other recognizable symbol to reflect this state.

Chapter 13, "The RTF Edit Control," switches to text-based issues and takes a look at a completely encapsulated editor, the Rich Text Format (RTF) edit control.

The RTF Edit Control

T he RTF Edit control is the mother of all edit box controls. It has features and properties that far exceed those of class CEdit. Whereas the text in those edit boxes is limited and cannot be formatted, the text in this control (which is more like a miniature word-processor) is formatted in the Rich Text Format (RTF). This is a special formatting protocol that makes it easy for multiple editors that support the RTF format to read and write documents created in the RTF format. The RTF control uses as its interchange format a subset of the RTF formatting tokens. As such, it does not do everything a full-blown RTF editor can, but it comes pretty close. As long as the document is in the RTF format, this control can read it. However, it will ignore any formatting commands it doesn't understand.

The text you enter into a CRichEditCtrl object can be given both character formatting (bold, italic, and so on) and paragraph formatting (center, right align, and so on), and can include embedded Component Object Model (COM) objects. The control provides a programming interface, but it's up to you to implement any interface components to support formatting. The sample code for this chapter demonstrates paragraph formatting by creating a toolbar with three buttons that allow you to align the text right, center, or left. It also includes combo boxes already set up with the host machine's installed fonts. You can use this as a starting point to implement character formatting.

Finally, the RTF control supports virtually all the messages and notification messages that multiline edit controls use, allowing you to easily change existing applications from CEdit objects to CRichTextCtrl objects. There are some unique messages and notifications available for the CRichTextCtrl object that give you access to the unique features of the RTF edit control. Naturally, there are a number of system structures to contend with, so let's begin with them.

RTF Structures

This section looks at the structures maintained by Windows 95/98 for use with the RTF control. Unlike the previous chapters, this chapter does not have a section for Styles. For this control, there aren't any styles, per se. You can assign character formatting or paragraph formatting, but you don't assign a style. Let's look at the structures.

PARAFORMAT Structure

The PARAFORMAT structure is used to format a paragraph in the RTF control. It is used with the EM_GETPARAFORMAT and EM_SETPARAFORMAT messages, covered later in this chapter. The following is the prototype for this structure.

```
typedef struct _paraformat
{
    UINT cbSize;
    _WPAD _wPad1;
    DWORD dwMask;
    WORD wNumbering;
    WORD wReserved;
    LONG dxStartIndent;
    LONG dxRightIndent;
    LONG dxOffset;
    WORD wAlignment;
    SHORT cTabCount;
    LONG rgxTabs[MAX_TAB_STOPS];
} PARAFORMAT;
```

The cbSize member is the size of the structure, which can be set to Sizeof(PARAFORMAT). The next member, _wPad1, is not really a member at all, but is simply byte padding added to make the structures that are passed between 16- and 32-bit versions of Windows compatible. You'll find this defined in RichEdit.h in the MFC source directory as

```
#ifdef _WIN32
    #define_WPAD/##/
#else
    #define_WPADWORD #endif
```

The dwMask member is used to indicate which of the other structure members are valid. It can be zero or one of the values shown in Table 13.1.

If both PFM_STARTINDENT and PFM_OFFSETINDENT are specified for dwMask, PFM_STARTINDENT takes precedence.

The wNumbering member specifies numbering options. This can be zero or PFN_BULLET. The dxStartIndent member is the amount of indentation, in *twips*, of the first line of the paragraph. A twip is a Windows unit of measurement based on how a document would appear if printed. It is 1/20 of a printer's point. One inch equals 1440 twips. The dxRightIndent member is the size, in twips, of the indentation from the

Table 13.1 Values of dwMask in PARAFORMAT Structure

DWMASK VALUE	MEANING
PFM_ALIGNMENT	The wAlignment member is valid.
PFM_NUMBERING	The wNumbering member is valid.
PFM_OFFSET	The dxOffset member is valid.
PFM_OFFSETINDENT	The dxStartIndent member is valid and specifies a relative value.
PFM_RIGHTINDENT	The dxRightIndent member is valid.
PFM_STARTINDENT	The dxStartIndent member is valid.
PFM_TABSTOPS	The cTabStops and rgxTabStops members are valid.

right margin. The dxOffset member is the twips indentation of all the lines after the first, relative to the starting indentation. The first line is indented if dxOffset is negative, or outdented if it is positive.

The wAlignment member specifies how the paragraph is aligned. It can be one of the following:

PFA_LEFT. The paragraph is aligned with the left margin.

PFA_RIGHT. The paragraph is aligned with the right margin.

PFA_CENTER. The paragraph is centered between margins.

Finally, the cTabCount member is the number of tab stops, and the rgxTabs member is an array of absolute tab stop positions. An example of formatting a paragraph in the RTF control by adjusting the PARAFORMAT structure is presented later in this chapter.

CHARFORMAT Structure

The CHARFORMAT structure applies to the character properties. It is prototyped as follows:

```
typedef struct _charformat
{
    UINT      cbSize;
    _WPAD     _wPad1;
    DWORD     dwMask;
    DWORD     dwEffects;
    LONG      yHeight;
    LONG      yOffset;
    COLORREF  crTextColor;
    BYTE      bCharSet;
    BYTE      bPitchAndFamily;
    TCHAR     szFaceName[LF_FACESIZE];
    _WPAD     _wPad2;
} CHARFORMAT;
```

The cbSize member is the size of this structure and must be set before using the structure with the RTF control. The dwMask member specifies the character formatting to apply. It can be zero or one or more of the values shown in Table 13.2.

The dwEffects member determines the character effects. This can be a combination of the values shown in Table 13.3.

The yHeight member is the character height, in twips. The yOffset member is the amount of superscripting or subscripting applied to the character. It is measured in twips, from the baseline. If it is positive, the character is superscripted. The character is subscripted if yOffset is negative.

The crTextColor member is the color of the text and is ignored if CFE_AUTOCOLOR is specified in dwEffects. The bCharSet member is the character set value and can be one of the following:

- ANSI_CHARSET
- BALTIC_CHARSET
- CHINESEBIG5_CHARSET
- DEFAULT_CHARSET
- EASTEUROPE_CHARSET
- GB2312_CHARSET
- GREEK_CHARSET
- HANGUL_CHARSET
- MAC_CHARSET
- OEM_CHARSET
- RUSSIAN_CHARSET

Table 13.2   Values of dwMask in CHARFORMAT Structure

DWMASK VALUE	MEANING
CFM_BOLD	The CFE_BOLD value of the dwEffects member is valid.
CFM_CHARSET	The bCharSet member is valid.
CFM_COLOR	The crTextColor member and the CFE_AUTOCOLOR value of the dwEffects member are valid.
CFM_FACE	The szFaceName member is valid.
CFM_ITALIC	The CFE_ITALIC value of the dwEffects member is valid.
CFM_OFFSET	The yOffset member is valid.
CFM_PROTECTED	The CFE_PROTECTED value of the dwEffects member is valid.
CFM_SIZE	The yHeight member is valid.
CFM_STRIKEOUT	The CFE_STRIKEOUT value of the dwEffects member is valid.
CFM_UNDERLINE	The CFE_UNDERLINE value of the dwEffects member is valid.

Table 13.3 Values of dwEffects in CHARFORMAT Structure

DWEFFECTS VALUE	MEANING
CFE_AUTOCOLOR	Text has color returned by GetSysColor(), or COLOR_WINDOWTEXT.
CFE_BOLD	Characters are shown in bold.
CFE_ITALIC	Characters are shown in italic.
CFE_STRIKEOUT	Characters are shown as struck out.
CFE_UNDERLINE	Characters are shown as underlined.
CFE_PROTECTED	Characters are protected; modifying them causes an EN_PROTECTED notification message to be generated.

- SHIFTJIS_CHARSET
- SYMBOL_CHARSET
- TURKISH_CHARSET

There are additional values for Korean, mid-Eastern, and Thai Windows installations.

The bPitchAndFamily member is the font family and its pitch. The two low-order bits indicate the pitch and can be of the following:

```
DEFAULT_PITCH
FIXED_PITCH
VARIABLE_PITCH
```

Bits 4 through 7 indicate the font family and can be in the following:

```
FF_DECORATIVE
FF_DONTCARE
FF_MODERN
FF_ROMAN
FF_SCRIPT
FF_SWISS
```

The proper value is obtained by ORing the pitch constant with the family constant. Lastly, the szFaceName member is a NULL-terminated character array containing the name of the font face.

CHARRANGE Structure

The CHARRANGE structure is used to obtain, or set, the starting and ending character positions for a highlighted selection in an RTF control, and also can be used for finding text. It is prototyped as follows:

```
typedef struct _charrange
{
```

```
        LONG cpMin;
        LONG cpMax;
} CHARRANGE;
```

The cpMin member is the starting position, and cpMax is the ending. If *cpMin* is 0, and *cpMax* is –1, the entire text is used for the search. For example, suppose the user highlights the substring "bar" in the word "beerbarrel". If you use this structure to obtain what was highlighted, the cpMin member would contain 4 and the cpMax would contain 6, since "bar" starts at position 4 and runs through position 6 in the string being searched.

REQRESIZE Structure

The REQRESIZE structure contains the size of an RTF control. It is used with the EN_REQUESTRESIZE message for resizing an RTF control. It is prototyped as follows:

```
typedef struct _reqresize
{
    NMHDR nmhdr;
    RECT rc;
} REQRESIZE;
```

The nmhdr member is the notification header, and rc is the requested new size.

EDITSTREAM Structure

The EDITSTREAM structure is used to hold information about a data stream for an RTF control. It is prototyped as

```
typedef struct _editstream
{
    DWORD dwCookie;
    DWORD dwError;
    EDITSTREAMCALLBACK pfnCallback;
} EDITSTREAM;
```

The dwCookie member is an application-defined value passed to the callback function. The dwError member is used as an error trap while streaming. This member is set to zero if no error occurred.

The pfnCallback member is a pointer to an application-defined function called by the RTF control to transfer data.

The EDITSTREAM structure is used with the EM_STREAMIN and EX_STREAMOUT messages. These messages move data into and out of an RTF control. When streaming, the RTF control repeatedly calls the specified callback function. If the call is successful, data is transferred in either direction with each call. The callback function has the following form:

```
DWORD CALLBACK YourFunction (DWORD dwCookie,LPBYTE pbBuff, LONG cb,
LONG FAR *pcb);
```

where dwCookie is the value of the dwCookie member of the EDITSTREAM structure. The pbBuff parameter is a pointer to the read/write buffer, cb is a count of the bytes to move, and pcb is a pointer to a variable that contains the actual number of bytes transferred. The return value, a DWORD, is related to the direction of the streaming. If reading, it represents the number of bytes copied to the buffer during the call and is zero when the transfer is complete. If writing, it is a nonzero value to continue the write, or zero to abort it.

ENDDROPFILES Structure

The ENDDROPFILES structure contains information for use with an EN_DROPFILES message. This message is used to drop a file into the RTF edit control just as in the Microsoft Explorer. It is prototyped as

```
typedef struct _endropfiles
{
    NMHDR nmhdr;
    HANDLE hDrop;
    LONG cp;
    BOOL fProtected;
} ENDROPFILES;
```

The nmhdr member is the notification header. The hDrop member is the handle to the dropped files list. The cp member is the character position at which the files are to be dropped. The fProtected member is set to TRUE if the specified position is protected, or FALSE if it is not.

ENPROTECTED Structure

The ENPROTECTED structure contains information associated with an EN_PROTECTED message, which is sent if a user attempts to edit protected text. It is prototyped as

```
typedef struct _enprotected
{
    NMHDR nmhdr;
    _WPAD _wPad1;
    UINT msg;
    _WPAD _wPad2;
    WPARAM wParam;
    LPARAM lParam;
    CHARRANGE chrg;
} ENPROTECTED;
```

The nmhdr member is the notification header. The msg member is the message that caused the notification. The wParam and lParam members are the associated WPARAM and LPARAM of the message, msg. The chrg member is the current selection.

FINDTEXT Structure

The FINDTEXT structure contains information regarding the text for which to search in an RTF control. It is prototyped as

```
typedef struct _findtext
{
    CHARRANGE chrg;
    LPSTR lpstrText;
} FINDTEXT;
```

The chrg member is the range to search; lpstrText is the string to find. It is used with the EM_FINDTEXT message.

FINDTEXTEX Structure

The FINDTEXTEX structure is used with the EM_FINDTEXTEX message, and contains information about the text to find in an RTF control. It is prototyped as

```
typedef struct _findtextex
{
    CHARRANGE chrg;
    LPSTR lpstrText
    CHARRANGE chrgText
} FINDTEXTEX;
```

The chrg member is the range to search, the lpstrText member is the string to find, and chrgText receives the range in which the text is found (–1 if no more matches are found).

FORMATRANGE Structure

The FORMATRANGE structure contains information that an RTF control uses to format its output to a given device. It is prototyped as

```
typedef struct _formatrange
{
    HDC hdc;
    HDC hdcTarget;
    RECT rc;
    RECT rcPage;
    CHARRANGE chrg;
} FORMATRANGE;
```

The hdc member is the handle to the device context to which output is directed. The hdcTarget is the target device. Usually, the hdc and hdcTarget members will be set to the same value. The member rc is the rectilinear area, in twips, to render. The rcPage member is the entire area of the rendering device, in twips. The chrg member is the range of text to format.

MSGFILTER Structure

The MSGFILTER structure contains information about a keyboard or mouse event. It is commonly used to trap an event and to prevent a particular action from being taken on the RTF control. It is prototyped as

```
typedef struct _msgfilter
{
    NMHDR nmhdr;
    UINT msg;
    WPARAM wParam;
    LPARAM lParam;
} MSGFILTER;
```

The nmhdr member is the notification header. The msg member is the message. The next two parameters are the WPARAM and LPARAM parameters of the msg, respectively.

PUNCTUATION Structure

The PUNCTUATION structure contains information regarding the punctuation used in an RTF control. It is prototyped as

```
typedef struct _punctuation
{
    UINT    iSize;
    LPSTR   szPunctuation;
} PUNCTUATION;
```

The iSize member is the size, in bytes, of a buffer pointed to by the szPunctuation member. The szPunctuation member is the address of a buffer containing the punctuation characters.

REOBJECT Structure

The REOBJECT structure contains information about an object in an RTF control. It is prototyped as

```
typedef struct _reobject
{
    DWORD   cbStruct;
    LONG    cp;
    CLSID   clsid;
    LPOLEOBJECT poleobj;
    LPSTORAGE pstg;
    LPOLECLIENTSITE polesite;
    SIZEL sizel;
    DWORD dvaspect;
    DWORD dwFlags;
    DWORD dwUser;
} REOBJECT;
```

The cbStruct member is the size of this structure, in bytes. The cp member is the character position of the object. The clsid member is the class identifier for the object. The poleobj member is the address of an OLEOBJECT structure that specifies the OLE interface for the object. The pstg member is the address of a STORAGE structure that specifies the associated storage interface for the object. The polesite member is the address of an OLECLIENTSITE structure for an associated client-site interface of the object. This address must have been obtained from the GetClientSite() function. The sizel member is a SIZEL structure specifying the zsize of the object. A value of 0,0 on insert means that an object is free to determine its size until the modify flag is turned off. The dwAspect member is the display aspect to use. The dwFlags member is the object status flag. Finally, the dwUser member is reserved for user-defined values.

REPASTESPECIAL Structure

The REPASTESPECIAL structure contains information that specifies whether the display properties of a pasted object should be based on the content of the object, or on an icon representing the object. It is prototyped as

```
typedef struct _repastespecial
{
    DWORD   dwAspect;
    DWORD   dwParam;
} REPASTESPECIAL;
```

The dwAspect member is set to DVASPECT_CONTENT if the properties of the pasted object are to be based on the content of the object, or DVASPECT_ICON if based on the icon view of the object. The dwParam member is the aspect data. If dwAspect is set to DVASPECT_ICON, it means dwParam is the handle to a metafile with the icon view of the object.

SELCHANGE Structure

The SELCHANGE structure contains information for use with the EN_SELCHANGE message. It is prototyped as

```
typedef struct _selchange
{
    NMHDR nmhdr;
    CHARRANGE chrg;
    WORD seltyp;
} SELCHANGE;
```

The nmhdr member is the notification header. The chrg member is the new selection range, and seltyp is a value indicating the contents of the new selection. It can be one (or more) of the following values:

SEL_EMPTY. The selection is empty.

SEL_TEXT. Text.

SEL_OBJECT. At least one OLE object.

SEL_MULTICHAR. More than one character of text.

SEL_MULTIOBJECT. More than one OLE object.

TEXTRANGE Structure

The TEXTRANGE structure receives a range of text from an RTF control as a result of an EM_GETTEXTRANGE message. It is prototyped as

```
typedef struct _textrange
{
    CHARRANGE chrg;
    LPSTR lpstrText;
} TEXTRANGE;
```

The chrg member is the range of characters to get; lpstrText is a buffer that receives the text.

RTF Messages

The messages that can be sent to the edit control can be used with the RTF control. Because there are over 70 such messages, this section only covers those messages that are unique to RTF controls, and only for those in the English language version. For example, the EM_GETPUNCTUATION message is only available for Asian language versions of Windows 95/98. Unless otherwise stated, consult the documentation for using the regular edit control messages (EM_CANUNDO, EM_EMPTYUNDOBUFFER, and so on).

For the examples of the SendMessage() API call, I have once again assumed that a CWnd pointer to the control called pRtf has been obtained elsewhere.

EM_CANPASTE. This message is used to determine if an RTF control can paste a specified clipboard format. The wParam parameter is a value that identifies the format of the contents to try. It is set to zero to use the format of the current contents of the clipboard. The lParam parameter is not used and should be set to zero. The return value is zero if the format is not supported, or any nonzero value if it is. For example, to see if an RTF control supports the CF_BITMAP format, follow this example:

```
BOOL bOk;
bOk = pRtf->SendMessage(EM_CANPASTE, (WPARAM) CF_BITMAP, 0L);
```

If bOk is nonzero, the RTF control pointed to by pRtf supports the CF_BITMAP format.

EM_DISPLAYBAND. Use this message to display a portion of an RTF control's contents that has already been formatted for a DC using the EM_FORMATRANGE message. The wParam parameter is not used and is set to zero. The lParam parameter is a pointer to a RECT structure for the area of the device to display. The return value is TRUE if the operation succeeds, or FALSE if it fails. Text and OLE objects are automatically clipped by the lParam parameter rectangle, eliminating a need to define a clipping region.

EM_EXGETSEL. Use this message to retrieve the starting and ending character positions of a selection in an RTF control. The wParam parameter is not used and is set to zero. The lParam parameter is a pointer to a CHARRANGE structure that receives the selection range. There is no return value. For example, suppose the user has highlighted some text in an RTF control. The starting and ending positions can be found as follows:

```
CHARRANGE FAR * lpChr;
pRtf->SendMessage(EM_EXGETSEL, 0, (LPARAM) lpChr);
```

Now, lpChr.cpMin contains the starting position, and lpChr.cpMax contains the ending position.

EM_EXLIMITTEXT. This message sets the upper limit for the amount of text in an RTF control. The default is 32K. The wParam parameter is not used and is set to zero. The lParam parameter is set to the maximum, or use 0L to specify the default. There is no return value. For example, to set the maximum amount of text to be 128K, follow this example:

```
dwMaxText = 128000;
pRtf->SendMessage(EM_EXLIMITTEXT,0,(LPARAM) dwMaxText);
```

EM_EXLINEFROMCHAR. This message is used to find a line in an RTF control that contains a specified character. The wParam parameter is not used and is set to zero. The lParam parameter is the zero-based index of the character for which to search. The return value is the zero-based index of the line containing the character.

EM_EXSETSEL. This message is used to select a range of characters in an RTF control. The wParam parameter is not used and is set to zero. The lParam parameter points to a CHARRANGE structure containing the indexes for the characters. The return value is the zero-based index of the line.

EM_FINDTEXT. This message finds text in an RTF control. The wParam parameter can be zero, or one or more of the FT_WHOLEWORD or FT_MATCHCASE values. The lParam parameter is a pointer to a FINDTEXT structure for the text to find. The return value is the zero-based character position of the next match, or –1 if there are no more matches. For example, to find the string "Hello!" in an RTF controls, respecting case sensitivity, follow this example:

```
FINDTEXT lpFindText;
CHARRANGE chrg;
chrg.cpMin = 0L;
chrg.cpMax = -1L;            // search entire text
lpFindText.chrg = chrg;      // initialize the FINDTEXT structure
lpFindText.lpstrText = "Hello!";
pRtf->SendMessage(EM_FINDTEXT, (WPARAM)
( FT_WHOLEWORD | FT_MATCHCASE),
    (LPARAM)&lpFindText);
```

EM_FINDTEXTEX. This message is also used to find text within an RTF control. The wParam parameter can be zero, or one or more of the FT_WHOLEWORD or FT_MATCHCASE values. The lParam parameter is a pointer to a FINDTEXTEX structure containing information about the find operation. The return value is the zero-based character position of the next match or –1 if there are no more matches.

EM_FINDWORDBREAK. This message finds the next word break before or after a specified position. It can also be used to fetch information about the character at that position. The wParam parameter can have any one of the following values:

- **WB_CLASSIFY.** This returns the character class and word break flags of the character at the position.

- **WB_ISDELIMITER.** This returns TRUE if the character at the position is a delimiter, or FALSE if it isn't.

- **WB_LEFT.** This finds the nearest character before the position which begins a word.

- **WB_LEFTBREAK.** This finds the next word end before the position.

- **WB_MOVEWORDLEFT.** This finds the next character that begins a word before the indicated position. This value is useful for processing a CTRL+LEFT key combination.

- **WB_MOVEWORDRIGHT.** This finds the next character that begins a word after the indicated position. This value is useful for processing a CTRL+RIGHT key combination.

- **WB_RIGHT.** This finds the next character that begins a word after the position specified.

- **WB_RIGHTBREAK.** This finds the next end-of-word delimiter after the position.

The lParam parameter is the zero-based position from which the search is to start. The return value is the character index of the word break, unless the wParam parameter is WB_CLASSIFY or WB_ISDELIMITER. These values refer to where the RTF control determines to perform a break. Consult the documentation for more information on this subject.

EM_FORMATRANGE. Use this message to format a range of text in an RTF control for a specific output device. The wParam parameter is a flag indicating whether rendering is to be performed. If it is nonzero, the text is rendered; otherwise, it is just measured. The lParam parameter is a pointer to a FORMATRANGE structure that contains information about the output device. Set it to NULL to free information cached by the RTF control. In fact, it is necessary to do this after the last time you use this message, and once again before using it with a different device. The return value is the index of the last character that fits in the rendering region, plus 1.

EM_GETCHARFORMAT. This message is used to find the current character formatting in an RTF control. The wParam parameter is a flag indicating whether the default character formatting, or the current selection's formatting, is to be found. If wParam is zero, the default formatting is returned; otherwise, the current selection's character formatting is returned. The lParam parameter is a pointer to a CHARFORMAT which is filled in by the message. If wParam is nonzero (that is, the selection formatting is being retrieved), the CHARFORMAT structure receives the attributes of the first character, and the dwMask member indicates which attributes are consistent for the entire selection. The return value is the value of the dwMask member.

EM_GETEVENTMASK. This message retrieves the event mask associated with an RTF control. Both the wParam parameter and lParam parameters are not used and are set to zero. The return value is the event mask for the control.

EM_GETOLEINTERFACE. This message retrieves an IRichEditOle object that will allow an OLE client to access an RTF control's OLE functionality. The wParam parameter is not used and is set to zero. The lParam parameter is the address at which the RTF control stores a pointer to the IRichEditOle object. The return value is nonzero if the call was successful; zero if not. Because the RTF control calls the AddRef() function before returning, you must call the Release() function when your application is finished with the IRichEditOle object. An example of this message is

```
LPVOID FAR * pOleObject;
pRtf->SendMessage(EM_GETOLEINTERFACE 0, (LPARAM) pOleObject);
```

EM_GETPARAFORMAT. This message gets the paragraph formatting of the current selection of an RTF control. The wParam parameter is not used and is set to zero. The lParam parameter is a pointer to a PARAFORMAT structure. The return value is the value of the dwMask member of the PARAFORMAT structure. If more than one paragraph was selected, the PARAFORMAT structure receives the attributes of the first paragraph, and the dwMask member indicates which formatting attributes are consistent for the entire selection.

EM_GETSELTEXT. This message fetches the selected text from an RTF control. The wParam parameter is not used and is set to zero. The lParam parameter is a pointer to a buffer to hold the text. You must size the buffer to ensure it is large enough to hold the selected text. The return value is the number of characters fetched, not counting the NULL terminator.

EM_GETTEXTRANGE. Use this message to retrieve a range of characters from an RTF control. The wParam parameter is not used and is set to zero. The lParam parameter is a pointer to a TEXTRANGE structure that specifies the range of characters to retrieve. The return value is the number of characters retrieved, not counting the NULL terminator.

EM_HIDESELECTION. This message hides or shows the selection characters in an RTF control. The wParam parameter is set to zero to hide the characters, nonzero to show them. The user can highlight characters in the control, or the programmer can force them to be highlighted without user intervention. The lParam parameter is a Boolean value that indicates whether or not to change the control's ES_NOHIDESEL style. If it is zero, the selection characters are temporarily shown or hidden. If nonzero, the style is changed (that is, toggled on/off). There is no return value.

EM_PASTESPECIAL. This message pastes a specific clipboard format in an RTF control. The wParam parameter is the clipboard format (CF_BITMAP) to paste. The lParam parameter is not used and is set to zero. There is no return value.

EM_REQUESTRESIZE. This message causes an RTF control to send an EN_REQUEST-RESIZE message to its parent window. The wParam and lParam parameters are not used and are set to zero. There is no return value.

EM_SELECTIONTYPE. This message retrieves the selection type for an RTF control. Both the wParam and lParam parameters are set to zero. The return value can be one of the following values:

- **SEL_EMPTY.** Nothing selected
- **SEL_TEXT.** Text
- **SEL_MULTICHAR.** More than one character of text
- **SEL_OBJECT.** At least one OLE object
- **SEL_MULTIOBJECT.** More than one OLE object

EM_SETBKGNDCOLOR. This message sets the background color for an RTF control. The wParam parameter is set to nonzero to set the background color of the control to the window background system color. If zero, the color specified in the lParam parameter is used. The return value is the old background color. For example, to set the background color to cyan, follow this example:

```
pRtf->SendMessage(EM_SETBKGNDCOLOR,0,(LPARAM)(COLORREF(0,255,255 )));
```

EM_SETCHARFORMAT. This message sets the character formatting of an RTF control. The wParam parameter is a flag indicating the character format to apply. The wParam parameter can be zero or one of the following:

```
WParam = (UINT) uFlags;
lParam = (LPARAM) (CHARFORMAT FAR *) lpFmt;
```

uFlags is the character formatting that applies to the control. This parameter can be zero or more of these values:

- **SCF_SELECTION.** This specifies the formatting should be applied to the current selection. It also sets the default formatting if the selection is empty.
- **SCF_WORD.** This applies the formatting to selected words. If the selection is empty, but the insertion cursor is inside a word, the formatting is applied to that word. This value must be used with the SCF_SELECTION value.

The lParam parameter is a pointer to a CHARFORMAT structure that specifies the character formatting. Only the attributes indicated by the dwMask member are modified. The return value is nonzero if successful; zero if not.

EM_SETEVENTMASK. This message sets the event mask for an RTF control. An event mask specifies what notification messages are to be sent on to the parent window. The wParam parameter is not used and is set to zero. The lParam parameter is the new event mask for the RTF control. The return value is the previous event mask.

EM_SETOLEINTERFACE. This message gives an RTF control an IRichEditOleCallback object that the control uses to get OLE-related information from the client. The wParam parameter is not used and is set to zero. The lParam parameter is a pointer to an IRichEditOleCallback object. The return value is nonzero if the call is successful, or zero if it fails.

EM_SETOPTIONS. This message sets the options for an RTF control. The wParam parameter is a flag indicating the operations, and can be one of the following values:

- **ECOOP_SET.** Set the options to those specified by the lParam parameter
- **ECOOP_OR.** Combine the current options with the specified options
- **ECOOP_AND.** Retain only those current options that are specified by lParam
- **ECOOP_XOR.** Retain only those current options that are not specified by lParam

The lParam parameter indicates the options, which can be one or more of the following:

- **ECO_AUTOWORDSELECTION.** Automatic selection of word on double-click
- **ECO_AUTOVSCROLL.** Same as ES_AUTOVSCROLL style
- **ECO_AUTOHSCROLL.** Same as ES_AUTOHSCROLL style
- **ECO_NOHIDESEL.** Same as ES_NOHIDESEL style
- **ECO_READONLY.** Same as ES_READONLY style
- **ECO_WANTRETURN.** Same as ES_WANTRETURN style
- **ECO_SAVESEL.** Same as ES_SAVESEL style
- **ECO_SELECTIONBAR.** Same as ES_SELECTIONBAR style

The return value is the current option of the RTF control.

EM_SETPARAFORMAT. This message sets the paragraph formatting for the current selection in an RTF control. The wParam parameter is not used and must be set to zero. The lParam parameter is a pointer to a PARAFORMAT structure. Only the attributes specified by the dwMask member are modified. The return value is nonzero upon success; zero if it fails.

EM_SETTARGETDEVICE. This message sets the target device and line width used with WYSIWYG formatting in an RTF control. The wParam parameter is the handle to the device context for the target output device. The lParam parameter is the line width to use for formatting. The return value is nonzero if successful; zero if it fails.

EM_STREAMIN. This message replaces the contents of an RTF control with the specified data stream. The wParam parameter indicates the data format, which can be combined with the SFF_SELECTION flag, and is one of the following:

- SF_TEXT Text
- SF_RTF Rich text format

If the SFF_SELECTION flag is used, the incoming stream replaces the contents of the current selection. If not, the entire contents of the control are replaced by the stream. The lParam parameter is a pointer to an EDITSTREAM structure. The RTF control reads the incoming data stream by repeatedly calling the function indicated by the structure's pfnCallback member. The return value is the number of characters read.

EM_STREAMOUT. This message writes the contents of an RTF control to the indicated data stream. The wParam parameter is a value specifying one of the following data formats, which can be combined with the SFF_SELECTION flag:

- **SF_TEXT.** Text with spaces in place of OLE objects
- **SF_RTF.** Rich Text Format (RTF)
- **SF_RTFNOOBJS.** RTF with spaces in place of OLE object
- **SF_TEXTIZED.** Text with a text representation of OLE objects

If the SFF_SELECTION flag is used, only the contents of the current selection are streamed out. Otherwise, the entire contents of the control are streamed out.
The return value is the number of characters written to the output stream.

That's a wrap for the messages than you can use with the RTF control—next up I'll give you a look at some of its limitations as well as other considerations.

Limitations, Properties, and Backward Compatibility

While the RTF control can add a lot of sparkle to your applications, it doesn't have all the bells and whistles. Table 13.4 lists what you can and can't do with the RTF control.

If your application needs to do any special formatting beyond what is shown in Table 13.4, you'll have to resort to inserting an OLE 2-enabled Word document (or, create a new control—ouch!).

There is a limit on the amount of text the RTF control can hold. The RTF control can hold more than 64K of text. But, some of the older multiline edit control messages use indexes which are data-typed as WORDs, meaning these will only get you the first 64K of text in the control. If you are converting an application from an old-style edit control to an RTF control, don't forget to change all your messages too. Use the new messages discussed earlier in this chapter to get all the text.

The Sample Application

The sample code containing the RTF edit control can be found on the companion Web site in the Example1 project. The RTF edit control is inserted in a dialog box that has a toolbar. The toolbar has three buttons that allow you to left-align, right-align, or center-align text in the control. An illustration of the output is shown in Figure 13.1.

Because this toolbar also supports tool tips, the dialog box's message map had to be manually modified to trap the notification message and to add the message handlers for the buttons on the toolbar. Here is the message map after adding these features:

```
BEGIN_MESSAGE_MAP(CRtfDlg, CDialog)
    //{{AFX_MSG_MAP(CRtfDlg)
    //}}AFX_MSG_MAP
    ON_COMMAND(IDC_LEFT, OnLeft)// manually added these 4 items
    ON_COMMAND(IDC_CENTER, OnCenter)
```

Table 13.4 RTF Limitations

PROPERTY	SUPPORTED IN RTF CONTROL?
OLE 2 client support	Yes
Find and replace	Yes
Simple bullet lists	Yes
Over 64k of text	Yes
Multiple fonts, sizes, styles, and colors	Yes
Superscript, subscript, strikethrough	Yes
Left/right alignment	Yes
Full justification	No
Ruler	No
Left tabs	Yes
Header/footer support	No
Decimal tabs	No
Paragraph spacing	No
Top/bottom margins	No
Automatic page numbering	No
Printing	Yes
RTF to text to RTF conversion	Yes
Previewing	Yes
Streaming	Yes

```
    ON_COMMAND(IDC_RIGHT, OnRight)
    ON_NOTIFY_EX( TTN_NEEDTEXT, 0, MyToolTips )
END_MESSAGE_MAP()
```

To keep things simple, a lot of global variables are used. If you don't see a variable defined locally, check the source files (RtfDlg.cpp and RtfDlg.h). As usual, all the work begins when the dialog box is initialized.

```
BOOL CRtfDlg::OnInitDialog()
{
    CDialog::OnInitDialog();
    // TODO: Add extra initialization here
    RECT rDlg;          // size of dialog box
    HWND hDlg;          // handle to dialog box
    //
    this->GetWindowRect(&rDlg);    // for creating toolbar,etc.
    this->ScreenToClient(&rDlg);
    rDlg.top += 80;
```

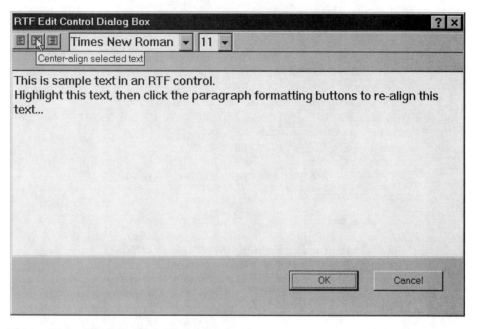

Figure 13.1 The RTF edit control example.

```
rDlg.bottom -= 80;
int nWidth = rDlg.right-rDlg.left;      // width of dialog box
hDlg = this->GetSafeHwnd();             // get handle to dialog box
HWND hWndRtf;
m_RtfCtrl.Create(WS_CHILD | WS_VISIBLE | WS_BORDER |
    ES_MULTILINE,rDlg, this, 0x222 );
hWndRtf = m_RtfCtrl.GetSafeHwnd();
//
// add a toolbar so we can show fonts, etc.
//
TBBUTTON tbButtons[] = {
{ 0, IDC_LEFT, TBSTATE_ENABLED, TBSTYLE_BUTTON, 0L, 0},
{ 1, IDC_CENTER, TBSTATE_ENABLED, TBSTYLE_BUTTON, 1L, 0},
{ 2, IDC_RIGHT, TBSTATE_ENABLED, TBSTYLE_BUTTON, 2L, 0},
};
//
HWND hWndToolBar;
TBADDBITMAP tbStruct;            // bitmap structure for buttons
RECT rRect;
rRect.top = 0;
rRect.left= 0;
rRect.bottom = 18;
rRect.right = nWidth;
m_ToolBar.Create(WS_CHILD | WS_BORDER |
    WS_VISIBLE | TBSTYLE_TOOLTIPS,  rRect,this,0);
//
```

```
hWndToolBar = m_ToolBar.GetSafeHwnd();
CWnd *pToolbar= m_ToolBar.FromHandle(hWndToolBar);
//
// Add the bitmap containing button images to the toolbar
//
HBITMAP hBitmap;
HINSTANCE hInstance = AfxGetInstanceHandle();
hBitmap = ::LoadBitmap(hInstance,MAKEINTRESOURCE(IDR_PARA_ATTR));
tbStruct.hInst = NULL;
tbStruct.nID   = (UINT)hBitmap;
//
pToolbar->SendMessage(TB_ADDBITMAP, (WPARAM) 3,
    (LPARAM) &tbStruct);
//
// Now add the buttons
//
pToolbar->SendMessage(TB_ADDBUTTONS, (WPARAM)3,
    (LPARAM) (LPTBBUTTON) &tbButtons);

// Create the combo box for the font facenames.
hWndComboFont = CreateWindowEx(0L,  // no extended styles
  "COMBOBOX",                       // class name
  "",                               // default text
  WS_CHILD | WS_VISIBLE | WS_VSCROLL |
    CBS_HASSTRINGS | CBS_DROPDOWN,  // styles and defaults
  80, 0, 180, 150,                  // size and position
  hWndToolBar,                      // parent window
  NULL,                             // ID
  hInstance,                        // current instance
  NULL);
//
// now make a combo box for the point sizes
//
hWndComboPoint = CreateWindowEx(0L, // no extended styles
   "COMBOBOX",                      // class name
   "",                              // default text
  WS_CHILD | WS_VISIBLE | WS_VSCROLL |
    CBS_HASSTRINGS | CBS_DROPDOWN,  // styles and defaults
  265, 0, 50, 150,                  // size and position
  hWndToolBar,                      // parent window
  NULL,                             // ID
  hInstance,                        // current instance
  NULL);
//
//  get all the fonts, put into font combobox
//
pComboSize = CWnd::FromHandle(hWndComboPoint);
pComboFont = CWnd::FromHandle(hWndComboFont);
InitFonts();  // this fills both combo boxes
//
//  get pointer to RTF edit control just created, add some text
```

```
    //
    pRtf= CWnd::FromHandle(hWndRtf);
    pRtf->SetWindowText("This is sample text in
    an RTF control.\nHighlightthis text, then
    click the paragraph formatting buttons to
    re-align this text...");
    //
    return TRUE;   // return TRUE unless you set the focus to a control
                   // EXCEPTION: OCX Property Pages should return FALSE
}   // end OnInitDialog()
```

This method starts by getting the size of the window in order to size the toolbar that is added. Next, the RTF edit control is created by calling the class's Create() method. After this, the toolbar is created. Notice that it has the TBSTYLE_TOOLTIPS style. Once the toolbar is created, two combo boxes are added. One combo box will store all the enumerated fonts on the host machine, and the second contains font sizes. These aren't functional, but you might wish to modify this code and make them operational. You can easily add character-formatting buttons to the toolbar for characteristics such as bold or italic.

The next two methods enumerate the system's fonts and provide the callback function for the EnumFonts() method.

```
void CRtfDlg::InitFonts()
{
    CDC *pDC = this->GetDC();
    EnumFonts(pDC->GetSafeHdc(),NULL,(FONTENUMPROC)
        EnumFontProc,(LPARAM)this);//Enumerate
}

BOOL CALLBACK CRtfDlg::EnumFontProc (LPLOGFONT lplf, LPTEXTMETRIC lptm,
    DWORD dwType, LPARAM lpData)
{
    if (dwType == TRUETYPE_FONTTYPE) //Add only TrueType Fonts
    {
        ((CComboBox*)(pComboFont))->AddString(lplf->lfFaceName);
    }
    //
    char szSize[10];
    for (int idx=0; idx < NUM_POINTS; idx++)
    {
        wsprintf(szSize, "%d", aPoints[idx]);
        ((CComboBox*)(pComboSize))->SendMessage( CB_ADDSTRING, 0,
(LPARAM)
            (LPCSTR) szSize);
    }
    ((CComboBox*)(pComboSize))->SetCurSel(3); // set to something
    ((CComboBox*)(pComboFont))->SetCurSel(3); // set to something
    return TRUE;
}
```

Even if you don't use the RTF edit control, this code might come in handy if you ever need to find all the installed fonts. The only other piece of code to examine is what happens when you select some text and click one of the paragraph-formatting buttons. All three work the same way, so I'll just give you one.

```
void CRtfDlg::OnCenter()
{
    // TODO: Add your command handler code here
    PARAFORMAT pf;
    // Fill in the PARAFORMAT structure with the mask and size.
    pf.cbSize = sizeof(pf);
    pf.dwMask = PFM_ALIGNMENT;
    pf.wAlignment = PFA_CENTER;
    // Set the new paragraph alignment.
    pRtf->SendMessage(EM_SETPARAFORMAT, 0, (LPARAM)&pf);
}    // end OnCenter()
```

The only other piece of code that is not covered here is the message handler for the tool tips, because these are fairly straightforward. As for the formatting buttons, all you have to do is set up the PARAFORMAT structure as described earlier, and send it to the RTF edit control using SendMessage().

Summary

Windows text programming has come a long way, and the new RTF editor promises to take it even further. Coupled with OLE, and word processing packages that support the RTF format, you can now deliver some impressive text-editing capabilities with your applications. Gone too are the size restrictions of the past. This control gives you a lot more real estate in addition to its features. Don't forget, you can use this control not just in a dialog box as I've shown, but in your view too. If you ever have to write a mini text editor, you might want to think about using the RTF control as your main interface element.

The next several chapters address some of the common dialogs that ship with MFC, including the color dialog, file open/save, and find-replace. This material may at first seem out of place in a book on user interfaces, but because they save you so much work and are often under-documented, I've included them in the interest of completeness. First up will be the common color dialog.

CHAPTER 14

The Common Color Dialog

O ne of the nice advantages gained from object-oriented programming is reusability. Evidence of this feature can be found in the common dialog classes that ship with Visual C++/MFC. Beginning with this chapter, I'll give you a more detailed look at these objects, and show you how to customize or extend their properties.

The common dialog classes give you a quick jump on developing certain portions of your applications. Examples of these include things like opening a file, saving a file, and searching for text. By using the common dialogs, you don't have to write as much code or create new resources in App Studio's dialog box editor. Many of these classes provide structures that you can manipulate to modify the given dialog box's behavior or appearance. Again, this removes a lot of work from your shoulders. Furthermore, the Microsoft Foundation Class library includes an error trapping API, called CommDlgExtended-Error() API for use with the common dialogs. This API, discussed later in the chapter, helps cut development time further through superior error detection and resolution—you spend time writing your application, not debugging it.

There are five dialog boxes, each with its own class, that constitute the common dialogs. These are

- CColorDialog
- CFileDialog
- CFindReplaceDialog
- CFontDialog
- CPrintDialog

CFileDialog, CFindReplaceDialog, CFontDialog, and CPrintDialog will be covered in subsequent chapters. This chapter takes a look at the Common Color dialog, CColorDialog.

CColorDialog

Your GDI (Graphics Device Interface—a subsystem of Windows)-intensive applications will need to use the CColorDialog class. This class gives you a fully functional, customizable Color Selection dialog box, shown in Figure 14.1.

Clicking the Define Custom Colors >> button expands the CColorDialog box and allows you to access the RGB values and adjust the amount of saturation, luminosity, and hue. The expanded Color dialog box is shown in Figure 14.2.

Notice in Figure 14.2 that expanding the dialog box gives you control over color selection. Recall that color selection consists of three values: red, green, and blue. Each of these can have a value in the range of 0–255, giving rise to over 16 million different color combinations. A color can be constructed using the COLORREF() or RGB() macros. The COLORREF() takes a 32-bit, hexadecimal integer as its parameter. The low-order byte specifies the relative intensity of red, the second byte the green, and the third the blue. The high-order byte must be zero. Here are some examples that create commonly used colors:

```
COLORREF(0x000000ff);        // red
COLORREF(0x0000ff00);        // green
COLORREF(0x00ff0000);        // blue
COLORREF(0x00ffff00);        // yellow
```

You'll probably find it easier to use the RGB() macro.

```
RGB(255,0,0)   or RGB(0xff,0,0);     // red
RGB(0,255,0)   or RGB(0,0xff,0);     // green
RGB(0,0,255)   or RGB(0,0,0xff);     // blue
RGB(255,255,0) or(RGB(0xff,0xff,0);  // yellow
```

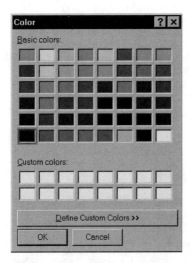

Figure 14.1 The CColorDialog box.

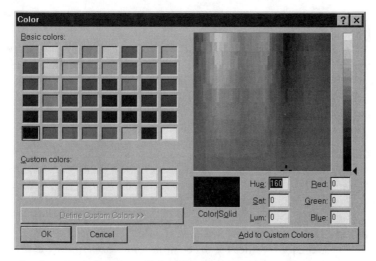

Figure 14.2   The expanded Color dialog.

The Common Color dialog returns color values as a COLORREF() object. These can be used in a variety of ways, including to create brushes and pens, and text colors, all based on selections made by the user from this dialog box. The class CColorDialog includes the CHOOSECOLOR structure that allows you to initialize the Common Color dialog box. The following is a closer look at this structure, and how you can use it when instantiating a CColorDialog object.

CHOOSECOLOR Structure

The CHOOSECOLOR structure contains information used by the ChooseColor() function to initialize the Common Color dialog box. The ChooseColor() function accepts a pointer to the CHOOSECOLOR structure. First configure the CHOOSECOLOR structure, then call ChooseColor() before the Color dialog box opens to do any customization. An example of this can be found in the sample code for Example2 on the companion Web site. After the user closes the dialog box, the system returns information about the user's selection (if any) in this structure. The following is the prototype for the CHOOSE-COLOR structure followed by a brief explanation of the members.

```
typedef struct {    // cc
    DWORD          lStructSize;
    HWND           hwndOwner;
    HWND           hInstance;
    COLORREF       rgbResult;
    COLORREF*      lpCustColors;
    DWORD          Flags;
    LPARAM         lCustData;
    LPCCHOOKPROC   lpfnHook;
    LPCTSTR        lpTemplateName;
} CHOOSECOLOR;
```

The lStructSize member is the size of the structure—it can be set to sizeof(CHOOSE-COLOR). The hwndOwner member is the handle of the window that owns the dialog box, or NULL if it has no owner. The value of the hInstance member depends on the Flags member. When the Flags includes the CC_ENABLETEMPLATEHANDLE value, hInstance is the handle of a memory object with a dialog box template. If the CC_ENABLETEMPLATE flag is set, then hInstance is the identifier of a module containing a dialog box template named by the lpTemplateName member. If neither one of these flags is set, the hInstance member is ignored.

The rgbResult member of the CHOOSECOLOR structure indicates the color initially selected when the dialog box is created. In this case, the CC_RGBINIT flag must be set in the Flags member. This is useful when you want to steer the user toward a particular color or shade. The framework estimates the color if a given value is not available on the system, and picks a suitable substitute. Examine this structure member when the user clicks the OK button to close the dialog. The lpCustColors member is a pointer to an array that holds the RGB values for the custom color boxes that are exposed when the Define Custom Colors >> button is clicked, as shown in Figures 14.1 and 14.2. If you aren't going to save the new custom colors between successive calls to the Choose-Color() function, allocate static memory for this array. This will preserve the values in memory until the next call is made.

The Flags member is one of the most important members. Recall the discussion of this concept in the controls discussed earlier in the book, where Flags was generally called a *mask member*. This member specifies how the Common Color dialog box will be initialized. This member is simply a set of bit flags that can be ORed together. Table 14.1 lists the different flags and their meanings.

Table 14.1   Flags Used with CHOOSECOLOR Structure

FLAG	MEANING
CC_ANYCOLOR	Displays all available colors in the set of basic colors in dialog box.
CC_ENABLEHOOK	Enables a hook procedure for the dialog box.
CC_ENABLETEMPLATE	Specifies a dialog box template for the dialog box.
CC_ENABLETEMPLATEHANDLE	Template data block.
CC_FULLOPEN	Opens Color dialog box as expanded.
CC_PREVENTFULLOPEN	Disables the Define Custom Colors >> button that expands the box.
CC_RGBINIT	Initializes with the color specified in the rgbResult member.
CC_SHOWHELP	Displays a Help button.
CC_SOLIDCOLOR	Displays only solid colors in the set of basic colors.

The remaining members of the CHOOSECOLOR structure pertain to the use of hook procedures and templates. The lCustData member is the data passed to your hook function (identified by the lpfnHook member). The lpfnHook member is a pointer to a CCHookProc() procedure that can intercept and process messages intended for the Common Color dialog box. Finally, the lpTemplateName member is the string value of a dialog box template resource. Only in the rarest of cases are you likely to need these capabilities from class CColorDialog.

Useful CColorDialog Class Methods

Besides the CHOOSECOLOR structure, the CColorDialog class has all the utility features commonly required to meet your color needs. Let's look at some of the ones you'll use most often, and how they can solve some user interface problems.

The GetColor() class member is used to get the color value selected by the user, or return the value back to the default if the user clicked OK when the Color dialog box is closed. The prototype is

```
COLORREF GetColor()const;
```

The opposite of this class member is SetCurrentColor().

```
void SetCurrentColor(COLORREF clr);
```

Call this function after a DoModal() to force the current color selection to the color value specified by the clr parameter. This function is called from within OnColorOK() or a message handler. The Color dialog box will automatically update the user's selection based on the value of the clr parameter.

To provide custom validation of the color the user selects, use the method OnColorOK().

```
virtual BOOL OnColorOK();
```

Override this class method and set the return value to zero if the color was valid, or nonzero to reject the entry and leave the dialog box open. Youíll rarely need to override a color selection, but the capability is here. If you don't override the selection, the framework provides a default message box should an invalid color be entered.

The last class member is GetSavedCustomColors(), prototyped as follows:

```
static COLORREF * GetSavedCustomColors();
```

This is used when your application allows the user to define up to 16 custom colors. This method returns a pointer to an array that contains the custom colors. Each of the entries in this array is initialized to all white, or RGB(255,255,255). These colors are only saved while the application is in a running process. If you need to save and restore them when the application runs, you will need to save them somewhere. If you don't serialize these values, you could add an entry to your application's INI file, then use GetPrivateProfileString()to reload the custom values in your OnInitInstance() routine.

CommDlgExtendedError

The CommDlgExtendedError() function is available for use with the following common dialog box functions.

- ChooseColor()
- ChooseFont()
- FindText()
- ReplaceText()
- GetOpenFileName()
- GetSaveFileName()
- PrintDlg()
- PageSetupDlg()

The CommDlgExtendedError() function returns a common dialog box error code that indicates the most recent error to occur during one of the functions listed. This function is prototyped as follows:

```
DWORD CommDlgExtendedError(void);
```

If the call to one of these functions succeeds, the return value is undefined. If the user closes the common dialog box or clicks the Cancel button, the return value is zero. If an error occurs, the return value is a nonzero error code. All the error codes are listed in the CDERR.H file. Table 14.2 lists the general error codes for all common dialog boxes.

There are many specific error codes for the list of functions. These will be covered in subsequent chapters. Notice there are no specific errors for the Common Color dialog box.

The Sample Application

The sample code for the Common Color dialog can be found on the companion Web site in the Example2 project. The message handler for the Color dialog menu item is located in file MainFrm.cpp.

```
void CMainFrame::OnColorDlg()
{
    // TODO: Add your command handler code here
    CColorDialog cColor;
    cColor.m_cc.lStructSize = sizeof(CHOOSECOLOR);
    cColor.m_cc.Flags = CC_FULLOPEN | CC_ENABLEHOOK;
    cColor.DoModal();
}
```

Table 14.2   General Common Dialog Box Error Codes

ERROR CODE	MEANING
CDERR_DIALOGFAILURE	The dialog box could not be created. The common dialog box function's call to the DialogBox() function failed. For example, this error occurs if the common dialog box call specifies an invalid window handle.
CDERR_FINDRESFAILURE	The common dialog box function failed to find a specified resource.
CDERR_INITIALIZATION	The common dialog box function failed during initialization. This error often occurs when sufficient memory is not available.
CDERR_LOADRESFAILURE	The common dialog box function failed to load a specified resource.
CDERR_LOADSTRFAILURE	The common dialog box function failed to load a specified string.
CDERR_LOCKRESFAILURE	The common dialog box function failed to lock a specified resource.
CDERR_MEMALLOCFAILURE	The common dialog box function was unable to allocate memory for internal structures.
CDERR_MEMLOCKFAILURE	The common dialog box function was unable to lock the memory associated with a handle.
CDERR_NOHINSTANCE	The ENABLETEMPLATE flag was set in the Flags member of the initialization structure for the corresponding common dialog box, but there is no corresponding instance handle.
CDERR_NOHOOK	The ENABLEHOOK flag was set in the Flags member of the initialization structure for the corresponding common dialog box, but there is no pointer to a corresponding hook procedure.
CDERR_NOTEMPLATE	The ENABLETEMPLATE flag was set in the Flags member of the initialization structure for the corresponding common dialog box, but you omitted a corresponding template.
CDERR_REGISTERMSGFAIL	The RegisterWindowMessage() function returned an error code when it was called by the common dialog box function.
CDERR_STRUCTSIZE	The lStructSize member of the initialization structure for the corresponding common dialog box is invalid.

The class data member m_cc is a structure of type CHOOSECOLOR. This has been adjusted prior to calling the Color dialog box to show it fully expanded, as in Figure 14.2. Add a call to GetColor() after the dialog box is closed to determine the RGB values of the color selected.

Summary

This has been an easy chapter—the Common Color dialog box isn't complicated, although it does support a lot of functionality. Your primary interest will likely be in initializing the box, retrieving the user's selection with GetColor(), and taking action accordingly in your application. This common dialog is useful for setting text and background colors and other preferences supplied by the user. The next chapter looks at another useful common dialog, the File dialog.

CHAPTER 15

The Common File Dialog

This chapter looks at the Common File dialog class, CFileDialog. This class gives you an easy way to prompt the user for a file to open or to save. The OPENFILENAME structure can be manipulated to filter files or specify extensions. It may not be necessary to use the CFileDialog class, particularly if all you want to do is restrict the user to opening and saving files of your document type (for example, project files). When you use Visual C++ to create a new application, it automatically creates an entry into your string table. You can then modify this to restrict files to a certain type. For example, when I created the Example2 project on the companion Web site, the string IDR_EXAMPLETYPE was created, with the following value:

```
\nExampl\nExampl\n\n\nExample2.Document\nExampl Document
```

This produces the result shown in Figure 15.1.

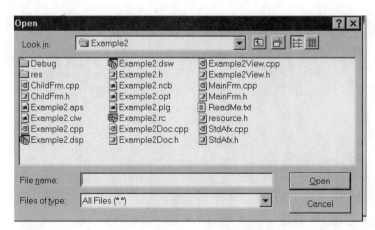

Figure 15.1   Example CFileDialog without restrictions.

If I wanted to allow this application to open only files having the extension .cpp, and to fill the file list control with only files having that extension, I could modify this string so that it appears as follows:

```
\nExampl2-Untitled\nProject\nProjects (*.cpp)\n.cpp\n Project
   \nExample2 Project
```

This is seen in Figure 15.2. Modifying IDR_EXAMPLETYPE is a quick-and-easy way to restrict files to a certain type without resorting to using CFileDialog. This is not always possible. Let's look at the CFileDialog class.

Creating a CFileDialog Object

To begin, first create the dialog box, which will be used for both opening and saving files. The following is the prototype for the constructor.

```
CFileDialog(
    BOOL bOpenFileDialog,
    LPCTSTR lpszDefExt = NULL,
    LPCTSTR lpszFileName = NULL,
    DWORD dwFlags = OFN_HIDEREADONLY | OFN_OVERWRITEPROMPT,
    LPCTSTR lpszFilter = NULL,
    CWnd* pParentWnd = NULL );
```

The bOpenFileDialog parameter is a flag set to indicate if the box is used for opening or saving a file. A value of TRUE will create a File Open dialog box, while FALSE creates a File Save As dialog. The lpszDefExt parameter is the default extension to use with the file. If the user omits the extension in the filename edit box, the string specified by lpszDefExt will automatically be added to the filename. If this parameter is NULL, no extension will be appended to the filename. The lpszFileName parameter is the name of the file that initially appears in the filename edit box. If this is NULL, no name appears. The dwFlags parameter is a combination of one or more flags used to customize the CFileDialog box object. These will be discussed in the upcoming section

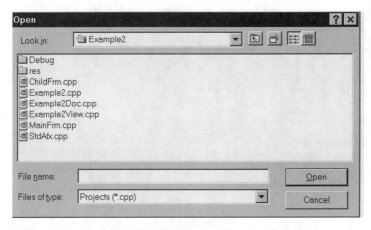

Figure 15.2 Example CFileDialog with file type restrictions.

regarding the OPENFILENAME structure. The lpszFilter parameter is a series of string pairs that let you restrict the dialog box to only certain file extension types, filtering out the filenames, so to speak. Essentially, the first string describes the filter, and the second describes the file extension to use. You can have multiple extensions by using a semicolon delimiter. The strings ends with two | characters, followed by a NULL. The lpszFilter parameter can also be a CString. The following is an example of specifying a filter that can be used with text files that have the extension .txt or .rtf.

```
static char BASED_CODE szFilter[] = "Text Files (*.txt)|
    *.rtf|RTF Files (*.rtf)|*.rtf|
    All Files (*.*)|*.*||";
```

Here is a complete example based on the Example2 program from the companion Web site. The output is shown in Figure 15.3.

```
static char BASED_CODE szFilter[] = "Text Files (*.txt)|
    *.rtf|RTF Files (*.rtf)|*.rtf|All Files (*.*)|*.*||";
CFileDialog cMyFileOpen(TRUE, "*.txt",NULL,
    OFN_HIDEREADONLY |
    OFN_OVERWRITEPROMPT,szFilter, this);
cMyFileOpen.DoModal();
```

When the file type's combo box is expanded, only three choices are available: files with extension *.txt, *.rtf, and *.*.

Before discussing the CFileDialog class and examining the system structure, it's a good idea to quickly review some of the constants available for use with files. These are the path field limit constants.

Path Field Limits

As you begin working with files and the CFileDialog class, you need to be mindful of the fact that the user may be accessing files on different drives and in different directories.

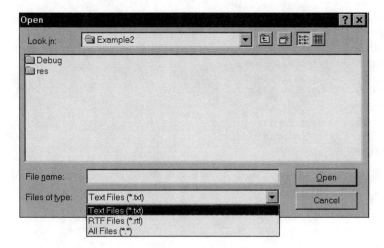

Figure 15.3 Filtering file types with CFileDialog.

The following constants, which are defined in stdlib.h, define the maximum length for the path and fields within the path. Here is a quick review:

_MAX_DIR. Maximum length of directory component

_MAX_DRIVE. Maximum length of drive component

_MAX_EXT. Maximum length of extension component

_MAX_FNAME. Maximum length of filename component

_MAX_PATH. Maximum length of full path

The sum of the fields should not exceed _MAX_PATH, or 512 bytes.

The CFileDialog class can be further customized using the OPENFILENAME structure.

OPENFILENAME Structure

The OPENFILENAME structure works like a door that swings both ways. You can manipulate it to customize the dialog box, and you can examine its member after the user closes the box to see what was entered. The class methods GetOpenFileName() and GetSaveFileName() make use of this structure for opening and saving files. The structure is prototyped as follows:

```
typedef struct tagOFN {  // ofn
    DWORD            lStructSize;
    HWND             hwndOwner;
    HINSTANCE        hInstance;
    LPCTSTR          lpstrFilter;
    LPTSTR           lpstrCustomFilter;
    DWORD            nMaxCustFilter;
    DWORD            nFilterIndex;
    LPTSTR           lpstrFile;
    DWORD            nMaxFile;
    LPTSTR           lpstrFileTitle;
    DWORD            nMaxFileTitle;
    LPCTSTR          lpstrInitialDir;
    LPCTSTR          lpstrTitle;
    DWORD            Flags;
    WORD             nFileOffset;
    WORD             nFileExtension;
    LPCTSTR          lpstrDefExt;
    DWORD            lCustData;
    LPOFNHOOKPROC    lpfnHook;
    LPCTSTR          lpTemplateName;
} OPENFILENAME;
```

The lStructSize member is the length, in bytes, of the structure. This member can be initialized by setting it to

```
OPENFILENAME myOfn;    // instantiate structure
MyOfn. LStructSize = sizeof(OPENFILENAME);  // init. LStructSize member
```

The hwndOwner member is the handle of the window that owns the CFileDialog box. Set it to NULL if it has no owner (the most common case). The hInstance member is dependent upon the Flags member. If you're creating a CFileDialog box based on a template such that the OFN_ENABLETEMPLATEHANDLE flag is set, this member is the handle to the memory object of that template. If the OFN_ENABLETEMPLATE flag is set, this member identifies a module containing the dialog box template. If neither of these flags is set, this member is ignored. If the OFN_EXPLORER flag is set, the framework uses the specified template to create a dialog box that is a child of the default Explorer-style dialog box. If this flag isn't set, the template is used to create the old-style (for example, pre-Windows95) dialog box.

The lpstrFilter member is a pointer to a buffer containing pairs of NULL-terminated filter strings like those shown earlier in this chapter. The last string in the buffer must be terminated by two NULL characters. Make sure there are no spaces in the pattern string, and that the filters are in the desired order, as the File Types combo box is not sorted—it just inserts the types in the order in which it finds them in the lpstrFilter member. Set this member to NULL if you don't want to display any filters.

The lpstrCustomFilter member is a pointer to a static buffer containing a pair of NULL-terminated filter strings for preserving the filter pattern chosen by the user. The first string is the display string that describes the custom filter, and the second string is the filter pattern selected by the user. The first time your application creates the CFileDialog box, specify the first string, which can be any (nonempty) string. When the user selects a file, the dialog box copies the current filter pattern to the second string. The preserved filter pattern can be one of the patterns specified in the lpstrFilter buffer, or it can be a filter pattern typed by the user. The system uses the strings to initialize the user-defined file filter the next time the dialog box is created. If the nFilterIndex member is zero, the dialog box uses the custom filter. Set this member to NULL if you don't want to preserve user-defined filter patterns. If lpstrCustomFilter member is not NULL, then the value of the nMaxCustFilter member must specify the size of the lpstrCustomFilter buffer. If you're writing an ANSI version application, this size is in bytes. If using Unicode, these are 16-bit characters (2 bytes).

The nMaxCustFilter member is the size (8 or 16 bits, ANSI or Unicode) of the lpstrCustomFilter buffer. The nMaxCustFilter member is ignored if lpstrCustomFilter is NULL or points to a NULL string. Otherwise, make nMaxCustFilter at least 40 characters long.

The nFilterIndex member specifies the index into the combo box of file types (pointed to by the lpstrFilter member). The first pair of strings has an index value of 1, the second 2, and so on. An index of zero indicates the custom filter that was specified by lpstrCustomFilter. You can set this member of the structure to initialize the dialog box with an initial file type. If this member is zero and the lpstrCustomFilter is NULL, the framework uses the first filter in the lpstrFilter buffer. In the event the nFilterIndex member is zero, and lpstrCustomFilter and lpstrFilter are NULL, the framework ignores any filters and does not show any files in the file list control of the CFileDialog box.

The lpstrFile member points to a buffer that holds a filename used to initialize the File Name edit control in the dialog box. Make sure you set this to NULL if you don't want to initialize the box with a specific filename (as for a file open operation). This member is used by GetOpenFileName() and GetSaveFileName(). When these functions return successfully, the lpstrFile member contains the full file spec, including the path and extension, of the file. If the OFN_ALLOWMULTISELECT flag is set and multiple files are selected, the buffer contains the current directory followed by the filenames of the selected files. For Explorer-style dialog boxes, the directory and filename strings are NULL separated, with an extra NULL character after the very last filename. For pre-Windows 95/98 dialog boxes, the strings are delimited by a space and the function uses short filenames for filenames with spaces. The FindFirstFile() function can be used to convert between long and short filenames in this situation. If the buffer isn't large enough to hold all the filenames, FindFirstFile() returns FALSE and the CommDlg-ExtendedError() function returns FNERR_BUFFERTOOSMALL. When this happens, the first 16 bits of the lpstrFile buffer contain the required size, in bytes or characters (ANSI or Unicode).

The nMaxFile member is the size of the buffer pointed to by lpstrFile. The documentation recommends that the buffer size be at least 256 bytes, although I personally use _MAX_PATH (512 bytes). The lpstrFileTitle member is a pointer to a buffer that receives the filename and extension of the file selected by the user. It does not include path information, and can be NULL. The nMaxFileTitle member is the size of the buffer pointed to by lpstrFileTitle, and is ignored when this is NULL.

The lpstrInitialDir member points to a string that specifies the initial file directory from which the user can select or save files. For Windows NT version 5.0 and Windows98 (and later versions of both), there are additional considerations. If lpstrInitialDir is NULL, and the current directory contains files matching the filter types, the initial directory becomes the current directory. If it is NULL but the directory does not contain files of the type specified, the initial directory instead becomes the personal files directory of the user. To set the user's personal files directory as the initial directory, set this member to the path returned by calling SHGetSpecialFolderLocation(), passing it the CSIDL_PERSONAL flag. For earlier flavors of Windows (for example, 95) and NT, the initial directory is the current directory when this member is NULL. Refer to the material in the upcoming section for more information on this function—there are all sorts of possibilities with this flag.

The lpstrTitle member points to the string text for the dialog box caption. If NULL, the framework uses the default values of Save As or Open.

When the dialog box returns, the Flags members are set to reflect the user's input. It can be a combination of the following 23 flags.

OFN_ALLOWMULTISELECT. This flag means the list box allows multiple selections. Combine this with the OFN_EXPLORER flag to use the Windows98 Explorer-style interface.

OFN_CREATEPROMPT. This flag causes the dialog box to ask the user if it should create the file when a nonexistent file is specified. If the user answers "Yes," the dialog box closes and the function returns the specified name. If the OFN_ALLOW-MULTISELECT flag is also set, the dialog still only allows the user to specify just one non-existent file.

OFN_ENABLEHOOK. This flag enables the hook function specified with the lpfn-Hook member.

OFN_ENABLESIZING. This flag is necessary only when you specify a hook procedure or custom template. For Windows NT version 5.x and Windows98, this allows the Explorer-style dialog box to be resized.

OFN_ENABLETEMPLATE. This flag indicates that the lpTemplateName member points to the name of a dialog template resource. The template is in the module identified by the hInstance member. If the OFN_EXPLORER flag is set, the framework creates a dialog box that is a child of the default Explorer-style dialog box. If the OFN_EXPLORER flag is not set, a pre-Windows95 dialog box is created based on the template.

OFN_ENABLETEMPLATEHANDLE. This flag means the hInstance member identifies a data block that contains a preloaded dialog box template. The system ignores the value of lpTemplateName if this flag is specified. If the OFN_EXPLORER flag is set, the framework creates a dialog box that is a child of the default Explorer-style dialog box. If the OFN_EXPLORER flag is not set, a pre-Windows95 dialog box is created based on the template.

OFN_EXPLORER. This flag means that any customizations made to the dialog box will use the new Explorer-style customization methods.

OFN_EXTENSIONDIFFERENT. This flag means that the user typed a filename extension that differs from the extension specified by lpstrDefExt. The function does not use this flag if lpstrDefExt is NULL.

OFN_FILEMUSTEXIST. This flag means that the user can type only names of existing files in the File Name entry field. If this flag is specified and the user enters an invalid name, the dialog box procedure displays a warning in a message box. The OFN_PATHMUSTEXIST flag must also be used with this flag.

OFN_HIDEREADONLY. This hides the Read Only checkbox on the File dialog box.

OFN_LONGNAMES. For old-style dialog boxes, this flag causes the dialog box to use long filenames. If this flag is not specified, or if the OFN_ALLOWMULTISELECT flag is also set, old-style dialog boxes use short filenames (8.3 format; for example, xxxxxxxx.ext) for filenames with spaces. Explorer-style dialog boxes ignore this flag and always display long filenames.

OFN_NOCHANGEDIR. This flag restores the current directory to its original value if it was changed by the user as a result of searching for files.

OFN_NODEREFERENCELINKS. This flag causes the dialog box to return the path and filename of a shortcut (.LNK file). If this flag is not set and the user selects a shortcut, the dialog box returns the path and filename that the shortcut references.

OFN_NOLONGNAMES. For old-style dialog boxes, short filenames (8.3 format) are used. Explorer-style dialog boxes always ignore this flag and display long filenames.

OFN_NONETWORKBUTTON. This flag causes the Network button to be hidden and disabled.

OFN_NOREADONLYRETURN. This specifies that the returned file is not write-protected and does not have the Read Only checkbox checked.

OFN_NOTESTFILECREATE. This specifies the file is not created before the dialog box is closed. Use this flag if your application is allowed to save files on a create-nonmodify network share point. When this flag is set, the library does not check for write protection, an open disk drive door, network protection error, or a full disk.

OFN_NOVALIDATE. This specifies that the File dialog box allows invalid characters in the filename that is returned. Usually, the calling procedure uses a hook procedure to check the filename via the FILEOKSTRING message. If the filename edit box is empty or only contains spaces, the lists of files and directories are updated. If the edit box contains anything else, the nFileOffset and nFileExtension members are set to values created by parsing the text. No default extension is appended, and the text is not copied to the lpstrFileTitle buffer. If nFileOffset is less than zero, the filename is invalid. Otherwise, the nFileOffset and nFileExtension members can be used if the OFN_NOVALIDATE flag has not been specified.

OFN_OVERWRITEPROMPT. This flag controls whether existing files can be overwritten. When set, a message prompts the user to confirm overwriting the file.

OFN_PATHMUSTEXIST. This flag means the user can only enter valid paths and filenames. A warning is displayed if an invalid filename or path is entered.

OFN_READONLY. Specifying this flag causes the Read Only checkbox to be checked when the dialog box is created. When the box is closed, check for this flag to get the state of the checkbox.

OFN_SHAREAWARE. This flag causes network sharing violations to be ignored. The dialog box returns with the name of the selected file. If the flag is not set, the dialog box notifies your hook procedure when network sharing violations occur. If you also set the OFN_EXPLORER flag, the dialog box sends the CDN_SHAREVIOLATION message to your hook procedure. If the OFN_EXPLORER flag is not set, the box sends the SHAREVISTRING registered message to the hook procedure.

OFN_SHOWHELP. This flag causes the dialog box to display a Help button. The hwndOwner member must specify the window to receive the HELPMSGSTRING registered messages that the dialog box sends when the Help button is clicked. If the OFN_EXPLORER flag is set, the dialog box sends a CDN_HELP notification message to your hook procedure when the Help button is clicked.

The nFileOffset member of the OPENFILENAME structure specifies the zero-based index, in bytes (ANSI) or 16-bit characters (Unicode) from the beginning of the path to the filename referenced by the lpstrFile member. For example, if lpstrFile contains the string

C:\VC\MFC\SRC\DLGCOMM.CPP

the nFileOffset member would contain the value 14 to indicate the offset to dlgcomm.cpp. When used with multiple selections, this points to the first filename.

The nFileExtension member is like nFileOffset, except it points to the extension. Using the preceding example, it would contain 22, the offset to the c in .cpp. This member is set to zero if the user types the period without the file extension. For example,

C:\VC\MFC\SRC\DLGCOMM

The lpstrDefExt member is a pointer to a buffer containing the default extension. The default extension can be any string not containing a period, but only the first three characters are used.

The lCustData member specifies application-defined data that the system passes to the hook procedure. When the framework sends the WM_INITDIALOG message to the hook procedure, the lParam parameter is a pointer to the OPENFILENAME structure specified when the dialog box was created.

Lastly, the lpfnHook member is a pointer to a hook procedure, and the lpTemplate-Name member points to a NULL-terminated string naming a dialog box resource.

There's a lot of abstract information to absorb here, so let's look at an example.

A CFileDialog Example

The following example shows how to customize your CFileDialog class object. This example can be found on the companion Web site as Example2. Build and run the program—you'll need to close the child MDI window that is opened to get to the menu with CFileDialog. This brings up the dialog shown in Figure 15.4.

Besides demonstrating how to restrict the files to certain types, I've customized the dialog box caption and connected the Help button to a topic. Clicking the Help button launches WinHelp, and opens the help file to a specific topic. The output is shown in Figure 15.5.

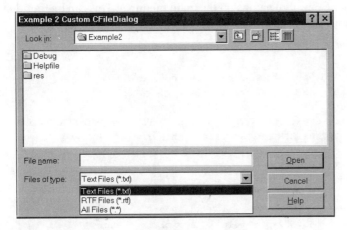

Figure 15.4   The sample CFileDialog program.

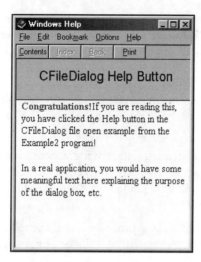

Figure 15.5 The Help topic for the sample program.

I'm a big believer in adding lots of help to your application. It's a simple way to enhance the user interface while providing the user with a comfortable cushion for his or her uncertainty about how to navigate and use your application. Although my Help topic doesn't do anything special, a real-world application would include help text instructing the user as to what types of files can be opened or saved, and why this dialog box was displayed. From a purely technical standpoint, the sample demonstrates the use of the CALLBACK function to trap the CBN_HELP notification message.

The following is the message handler that is called when you click on the menu option Open File… under CommonDialogs on the main menubar. This can be found in Mainfrm.cpp for Example2.

```cpp
void CMainFrame::OnFileDialog()
{
    // TODO: Add your command handler code here
    static char BASED_CODE szFilter[] = "Text Files (*.txt)|*.rtf|RTF
        Files (*.rtf)|*.rtf|All Files (*.*)|*.*||";
    CFileDialog cMyFileOpen(TRUE, "*.txt",NULL,OFN_HIDEREADONLY |
        OFN_OVERWRITEPROMPT,szFilter, this);
    cMyFileOpen.m_ofn.Flags |= OFN_SHOWHELP | OFN_ENABLEHOOK |
        OFN_EXPLORER;
    cMyFileOpen.m_ofn.hInstance = AfxGetInstanceHandle();
    //
    cMyFileOpen.m_ofn.lpfnHook = MyHookProc;
    cMyFileOpen.m_ofn.lpstrTitle = "Example 2 Custom CFileDialog";
    cMyFileOpen.DoModal();
}
```

The file type combo box is restricted to files with an extension of .txt or .rtf. As a safety catch, the user can open any file (the *.* filter). Next, the CFileDialog is created. Note the first parameter is TRUE, which creates a file open box, not a file save. Then, adjust the OPENFILENAME structure for the dialog box. The class includes a data member, m_ofn, for just this purpose. The flags (note the OFN_SHOWHELP), the hInstance, and the lpfnHook members are set. Change the text of the caption, and call DoModal() to show the dialog box.

The heavy lifting is done in the hook function, so let's look at it.

```
UINT APIENTRY MyHookProc( HWND hdlg, UINT uiMsg, WPARAM wParam,
    LPARAM lParam )
{

    LPNMHDR pnmh;
    switch (uiMsg)
    {
        case WM_NOTIFY:
            pnmh = (LPNMHDR) lParam;
            if (pnmh->code == CDN_HELP)
                AfxGetApp()->WinHelp(IDH_FILE_HELP,HELP_CONTEXT);
            break;
    }
    return 1; //
}   // end hook proc
```

The hook function traps WM_NOTIFY messages and, if it finds the CDN_HELP message, opens the Help file to the topic identified by the IDH_FILE_HELP context string. The hook procedure's lParam parameter is a pointer to a NMHDR structure—the code member of this structure has the notification message. Use this same technique to trap other notification messages besides CDN_HELP.

The CommDlgExtendedError() Function

As promised in Chapter 14, "The Common Color Dialog," this section is an overview of the specific errors for each common dialog returned by CommDlgExtendedError(). Recall that the general errors, which apply to all the common dialogs, were presented in the previous chapter. The errors shown in Table 15.1 apply only to the Common File dialog.

Table 15.1 File Dialog Common Error Codes

ERROR CODE	MEANING
FNERR_BUFFERTOOSMALL	The buffer pointed to by the lpstrFile member of the OPENFILENAME structure is too small for the filename specified.
FNERR_INVALIDFILENAME	A filename is invalid.
FNERR_SUBCLASSFAILURE	An attempt to subclass a list box failed because sufficient memory was not available.

The SHGetSpecialFolderPath() Function

The SHGetSpecialFolderPath() API can be used to retrieve the path of special folders such as those used in Windows98 and NT 5.x. This function is prototyped as follows:

```
WINSHELLAPI HRESULT WINAPI SHGetSpecialFolderPath(
    HWND hwndOwner,
    LPTSTR lpszPath,
    int nFolder,
    BOOL fCreate
);
```

The return value is NOERROR if successful, or one of the OLE-defined error codes if it failed. The hwndOwner parameter is the handle to the owner window the client should specify when it displays a dialog or message box. The lpszpath parameter receives the drive and path of the specified folder. This must be at least MAX_PATH characters in size.

The nFolder parameter indicates the folder of interest. This must be a real folder and not a virtual one, which causes the function to fail. There are 30 possible values—refer to the documentation for the SHGetSpecialFolderLocation() to see them all. Lastly, the fCreate parameter is a flag indicating if the folder should be created if it doesn't exist. If nonzero, the folder is created; otherwise, it isn't.

Summary

The Common File dialog is truly a timesaving addition to MFC. It completely obviates the need to create your own File Open/Save dialog boxes. Furthermore, it can be subclassed and customized at your discretion. If you have an MDI application, you can specify these types in your resource file, then call CMultiDocTemplate() in your application's InitInstance() method. As a result, your File Open/Save dialog box will prompt the user for the type (for example, file extension) to use. For example,

```
CMultiDocTemplate* pDocTemplate;
pDocTemplate = new CMultiDocTemplate(
    IDR_MYDOC_TYPE1,             // first type/extension
    RUNTIME_CLASS(CMyAppDoc),
    RUNTIME_CLASS(CChildFrame),  // custom MDI child frame
    RUNTIME_CLASS(CMyAppView));
    AddDocTemplate(pDocTemplate);
//
pDocTemplate = new CMultiDocTemplate(
    IDR_MYDOC_TYPE2,             // second type/extension
    RUNTIME_CLASS(CMyAppDoc),
    RUNTIME_CLASS(CChildFrame),  // custom MDI child frame
    RUNTIME_CLASS(CMyAppView));
    AddDocTemplate(pDocTemplate);
```

In your .RC file's string table, you would define the types something like this:

```
IDR_MYDOC_TYPE1 \nMy App Type 1-Untitled\nMyApp Project\nType 1
   (*.xyz)\n.xyz\n
```

Here, only documents having an extension of xyz will be opened/saved for IDR_MY_TYPE1. This takes a lot of work and aggravation out of providing the user with different document types.

Now, let's move on to the next common dialog, the Find-Replace dialog box.

CHAPTER 16

The Find-Replace Dialog

T his chapter takes an in-depth look at a powerful common dialog, the Find-Replace dialog. If you generate any applications that do a lot of text or document management, you're probably going to find a use for this class. This dialog is found in other software packages, such the Visual C++ file editor, shown in Figure 16.1.

This dialog can be an intimidating dialog at first glance, but hopefully, the sample program will help you with the difficult concepts. The most challenging portion of using class CFindReplaceDialog is that fact that it is a modeless dialog. Recall that a *modeless* dialog box can lose the focus at any time, while a *modal* dialog forces you to close the dialog box yourself. The modal dialog box has its own DefWinProc(), which locks out all messages except for those in the dialog's message pump. Before looking at the code, here is a brief overview of some of the more salient points to keep in mind when using this common dialog.

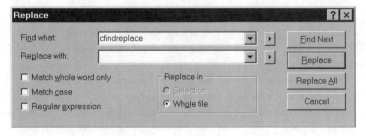

Figure 16.1 The Find-Replace common dialog.

Overview

The purpose of the CFindReplaceDialog class is to allow you to search for or search and replace for a string, in the CDocument() class object. The style of the dialog to use is specified via special flags that permit you to present the user with the search-only or the search-replace functionality. Actually creating and using the find-replace dialog is pretty easy. The difficult part is the option to draw the search string in a special color scheme to cue the user. Your application does not have to take this option; instead, it can scroll the line containing the string into view or something similar.

The implications of your design considerations when using the Find-Replace dialog are fairly extensive. If you use all the bells and whistles of this class you greatly extend the power of the interface by giving the user more power and control, including the ability to search up or down in the document and specify a case-sensitive or case-insensitive search. Choosing to use the text replace feature entails adjusting the document view to account for more or less characters in the document's lines. The point is, decide early what functionality your application will support and code your algorithms accordingly. Avoiding the replace feature will make coding easier.

NOTE

Keep in mind that the sample code, found on the companion Web site in Example1, is not a full-blown editor. It is intended for demonstration purposes only.

The purpose of this dialog is to search for text in a document and possibly replace it with something new. You need some way to switch between the messages for the Find-Replace dialog and those for the file you're reading. The application must be able to let you know if the search string is found. There is a special message that is used with objects of class CfindReplaceDialog that does this, as well as a class system structure that you can adjust.

FINDMSGSTRING Message

When a text document is opened in order to search and invoke a Find-Replace dialog, the Find-Replace dialog gets ready to communicate with the window in which you're viewing the document. When one of the command buttons on the box is clicked, it sends a FINDMSGSTRING message to its parent window. This message can't be found anywhere in Class Wizard. You have to register it yourself in your application's frame window. The key word here is *frame*, as in the document-view-frame troika upon which MFC Windows development is founded. All your heavy surgery will be in your application's MainFrm.cpp and its Header file. In turn, this message is checked to see what action to take. If necessary, the view window is notified to search for a string or take some other action.

This message is registered using the RegisterWindowMessage() API. For example, in the MainFrm.cpp file for this example, the following statement is located at beginning of the file.

```
static UINT NEAR WM_FINDREPLACE = RegisterWindowMessage(FINDMSGSTR);
```

This statement defines a special message called WM_FINDREPLACE. This message can be renamed as long as the name you choose is unique and doesn't conflict with an existing message, such as WM_PAINT or WM-SIZE.

The Find-Replace works by trapping the WM_FINDREPLACE message, and passing control to a special handler called a *Callback function* that you provide. The Find-Replace dialog box can also be customized to include, for example, checkboxes that specify case sensitivity in the search. In order to customize the Find-Replace dialog box, you need a system structure.

FINDREPLACE Structure

Class CFindReplaceDialog includes a data member called m_fr. This is a structure of type FINDREPLACE, and is used not only to customize your Find-Replace dialog, but also to pass your search and replacement string (if any) to the owner window or view. This structure is prototyped as follows:

```
typedef struct
{
    DWORD          lStructSize;
    HWND           hwndOwner;
    HINSTANCE      hInstance;
    DWORD          Flags;
    LPTSTR         lpstrFindWhat;
    LPTSTR         lpstrReplaceWith;
    WORD           wFindWhatLen;
    WORD           wReplaceWithLen;
    LPARAM         lCustData;
    LPFRHOOKPROC   lpfnHook;
    LPCTSTR        lpTemplateName;
} FINDREPLACE;
```

The lStructSize member is the length, in bytes, of the structure. You can initialize this member to

```
sizeof(FINDREPLACE);
```

The hwndOwner member is the handle of the window that owns the dialog box. The window procedure of this window receives FINDMSGSTRING messages from the dialog box. It can be any valid window handle, but it cannot be NULL.

The meaning of the hInstance member depends on the next member, Flags. If *Flags* includes the FR_ENABLETEMPLATEHANDLE bit, then hInstance is the handle of a memory object that contains a dialog box template. If the FR_ENABLETEMPLATE bit flag is set, it identifies a module containing a template identified by the lpTemplate-Name member. If neither flag is set, this member is ignored.

The Flags member is a set of bit flags used to initialize the Find-Replace dialog box. This can be a combination of the values shown in Table 16.1.

Table 16.1   The Flags Member Values of the Find-Replace Structure

FLAGS VALUE	MEANING
FR_DIALOGTERM	The Find-Replace dialog box is closing.
FR_DOWN	Sets the Down direction radiobutton for the search direction.
FR_ENABLEHOOK	Enables the hook function specified in the lpfn-Hook member.
FR_ENABLETEMPLATE	The hInstance and lpTemplateName members specify a template.
FR_ENABLETEMPLATEHANDLE	The hInstance member identifies a data block that contains a template.
FR_FINDNEXT	The user clicked the Find Next button.
FR_HIDEUPDOWN	If set when initializing the dialog box, hides the search direction radiobuttons.
FR_HIDEMATCHCASE	If set when initializing the dialog box, hides the Match Case checkbox.
FR_HIDEWHOLEWORD	If set when initializing the dialog box, hides the Match Whole Word Only checkbox.
FR_MATCHCASE	The Match Case checkbox is checked indicating that the search should be case sensitive.
FR_NOMATCHCASE	If set when initializing the dialog, disables the Match Case checkbox.
FR_NOUPDOWN	If set when initializing a Find dialog box, disables the search direction radiobuttons.
FR_NOWHOLEWORD	If set when initializing the dialog, disables the Whole Word checkbox.
FR_REPLACE	The user clicked the Replace button.
FR_REPLACEALL	The user clicked the Replace All button.
FR_SHOWHELP	The dialog box displays a Help button.
FR_WHOLEWORD	Search for whole words, not fragments.

The lpstrFindWhat member points to a buffer containing the NULL-terminated search string that the user entered in the Find What: edit control of the Find-Replace dialog. You must dynamically allocate this buffer or use a global/static array to prevent the buffer from going out of scope before the dialog box is closed. The buffer should be at least 80 characters long. You can also insert a value into this member in order to initialize the Find-Replace dialog with a default value.

The lpstrReplaceWith member points to a buffer containing the NULL-terminated replacement string that the user entered in the Replace With: edit control of the Find-Replace dialog. This buffer must have the same properties as the lpstrFindWhat buffer.

The wFindWhatLen member is length, in bytes, of the buffer pointed to by lpstrFind-What. The wReplaceWithLen member is the length, in bytes, of the buffer pointed to by lpstrReplaceWith.

The lCustData member is application-defined data that the system passes to a hook procedure indicated by the lpfnHook member. The lpnHook member is a pointer to a FRHookProc hook procedure that can process messages destined for the Find-Replace dialog box. This member is ignored unless you specify the FR_ENABLEHOOK flag in the Flags member of the structure. If the hook procedure returns FALSE when it gets a WM_INITDIALOG message, your hook procedure must display the dialog box or it won't be visible. To show it, first perform any paint operations, then call Show-Window() and UpdateWindow().

The last member is lpTemplateName. This member is a pointer to a string that names the dialog box template resource in the module identified by the hInstance member.

Class Methods

The Find-Replace dialog box isn't exactly a trivial exercise. Fortunately, once you get past the grunt work of registering the FINDMSGSTRING message and setting up the structure, the class methods make short work of the other chores. You can use these to specify the string for which to search, if the search is case sensitive, or any replacement string.

The first and foremost method is Create(), prototyped as follows:

```
BOOL Create(BOOL bFindDialogOnly, LPCTSTR lpszFindWhat,
    LPCTSTR lpszReplaceWith = NULL,
    DWORD dwFlags = FR_DOWN,
    CWnd* pParentWnd = NULL);
```

A TRUE value for the bFindDialogOnly parameter will create a standard Windows Find dialog box. FALSE creates the Find-Replace variety. The lpszFindWhat member is the string for which to search, and lpszReplaceWith is the default string to use if in replacement mode. The dwFlags member is one or more flags that customize the dialog. These are the same as the values listed in Table 16.1. The pParentWnd member is a pointer to the dialog box's parent or owner window. This is the same window that will receive the FINDMSGSTRING message indicating that a find/replace action was requested. If NULL, your application's main window is the default.

The next method, GetNotifier(), is the next most important class method. This is used to retrieve the FINDREPLACE structure in your registered message handler, or callback function. This function, which is the next main topic of discussion, is code you must write to interact with the Find-Replace dialog. The method is prototyped as follows:

```
static CFindReplaceDialog* PASCAL GetNotifier(LPARAM lParam);
```

The cool thing about this method is that it returns a pointer to the Find-Replace dialog box! This makes calling the other member functions easy as you'll see in the sample code section later. The lParam parameter is a value passed to your frame window's callback function.

To determine if the user wants to find the next occurrence of the search string, use FindNext().

```
BOOL FindNext() const;
```

The return is nonzero if the user clicks the Find Next button; otherwise, it is zero. The user can also click the Cancel button. Use IsTerminating() to detect this.

```
BOOL IsTerminating() const;
```

The return value is nonzero if the Cancel button was clicked, or zero if it was not. When the user does cancel, you need to call the dialog box's DestroyWindow() function and set any dialog box pointer variables to NULL. This is also a good time to save, either on the heap or in your application's INI file, the last entered find-replace text. The next time the user starts Find-Replace, these can be restored as the defaults. This is a subtle enhancement that makes the user interface a little more pleasing.

The GetFindString() method returns the default search string. It is prototyped as

```
CString GetFindString() const;
```

Because the default should have already been set, it's not clear to me when you would want to retrieve it. It should already be stored in another variable somewhere.

A close cousin to this method is GetReplaceString().

```
CString GetReplaceString() const;
```

This gets the default replacement string.

One method you're sure to use is MatchCase().

```
BOOL MatchCase() const;
```

When the return value is nonzero, it means the user has checked the case sensitivity box in the Find-Replace dialog. This means you'll have to change your searching algorithm, so think ahead. That advice goes for the next method, MatchWholeWord().

```
BOOL MatchWholeWord() const;
```

When the return value is nonzero, it means to ignore word fragments; that is, the string searched for must be a delimited word. For example, if the search string is "tar", words like target and tardy should be skipped.

To find the direction of the search, up or down, use the SearchDown() class method.

```
BOOL SearchDown() const;
```

When the return value is nonzero, the user wishes to search in a downward direction for the current text insertion point. If zero, search up from the current text insertion point.

To replace the current word found in the search, use the ReplaceCurrent() method.

```
BOOL ReplaceCurrent() const;
```

A return value that is nonzero means you should replace the currently selected string with the replacement string.

Closely related to the ReplaceCurrent() method is ReplaceAll().

```
BOOL ReplaceAll( ) const;
```

A return value of nonzero means the user wants to replace all occurrences of the search string in the document. Otherwise, the return value is zero.

There you have it for the class methods. As you can see, you'll need to write some pretty tight code to cover all the bases in the most efficient manner.

At this point, an application has registered the FINDMSGSTRING message, implying that a function has been specified in the MainFrm.h file to process all transactions with the Find-Replace dialog. Keep in mind that this is a modeless dialog. Your application needs to be able to communicate with the dialog box. It does this using the registered message's callback function.

Callback Function

All the heavy lifting performed by the Find-Replace dialog box occurs in its callback function. This is the routine you defined when you registered the message. Look at it again.

```
ON_REGISTERED_MESSAGE(WM_FINDREPLACE,OnFindReplaceHandler) // my handler
```

Inside Example3's Mainfrm.cpp file on the companion Web site is a function called OnFindReplaceHandler(), or the callback function. This function interacts with the Find-Replace dialog, and contains a lot of code. This function also determines if the user is closing the dialog box, changing the search and/or replacement strings, or clicking the Find Next button. Whatever functionality you plan to support will have to be implemented in the callback function, using one of the member functions covered in the previous section.

View Considerations

I've saved the worst for last—updating your view when using the Find-Replace dialog. The code so far is not rocket science, just a matter of creating a CFindReplace object and using its member functions. But you need some way to show the user you've found the search string. This gives the user the opportunity to replace it. A common method is to highlight the string using the system text highlight color.

When a string is found, use the default Windows configuration. For example, to draw the search string, you might want to use the following, taken from the sample code.

```
pDC->SetTextColor(GetSysColor(COLOR_HIGHLIGHTTEXT));
pDC->SetBkColor(GetSysColor(COLOR_HIGHLIGHT));
pDC->SetBkMode(OPAQUE);
// call TextOut(),TabbedTextOut(), etc
```

Likewise, when you're ready to display any remaining text, switch back to the default.

```
pDC->SetBkColor(GetSysColor(COLOR_WINDOW));
```

This keeps the user interface consistent with the user's Windows installation, and saves you a lot of work and worry.

The Sample Program

The program that demonstrates the Find-Replace dialog box can be found on the companion Web site in the Example1 project. This program lets you open any ASCII file and display it in your view window. You can then select Find-Replace... from the Edit menu option to display the Find-Replace dialog. This dialog box is shown in Figure 16.2.

Most of the work takes place in the project files MainFrm.cpp and MainFrm.h. A public variable is defined for use in instantiating the Find-Replace dialog in the header file.

```
// Attributes
public:
    CFindReplaceDialog * cFind;  // the Find-Replace dialog box object
```

A message handler is also added to the message map in MainFrm.h for interfacing with the dialog box.

```
afx_msg LONG OnFindReplaceHandler(UINT message, LONG lParam);
```

In MainFrm.cpp, the FINDMSGSTRING message is registered in the class declaration.

```
static UINT NEAR WM_FINDREPLACE = RegisterWindowMessage(FINDMSGSTRING);
```

The method OnFindReplace() is called after a file is opened and the Find-Replace option is clicked in the menu. This creates the Find-Replace dialog box.

```
void CMainFrame::OnFindReplace()
{
    // TODO: Add your command handler code here
    CWnd *pWnd = GetActiveWindow();
    cFind = new CFindReplaceDialog();
    cFind->Create(FALSE,NULL,NULL,FR_DOWN | FR_FINDNEXT, pWnd);
    cFind->CenterWindow();
}
```

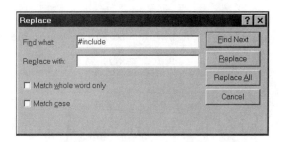

Figure 16.2   The Find-Replace dialog in the sample program.

The pointer to the active window (i.e., the frame window) is required to create the CFind-ReplaceDialog object. The Create() method was discussed earlier in this chapter. Refer back to it if you need to refresh your memory as to the meaning of the different parameters.

The last piece of code we need to look at in MainFrm.cpp is the message handler that responds to messages from the CFindReplaceDialog object, as follows. Note that all it really does is use the GetNotifier() method to determine if the user clicked the Find Next or Cancel button.

```cpp
LONG CMainFrame::OnFindReplaceHandler(UINT message, LONG lParam)
{
    static CFindReplaceDialog * pFindDlg;
    pFindDlg = pFindDlg->GetNotifier(lParam);
    CRect rRect;
    //
    BOOL bTerm = pFindDlg->IsTerminating();
    BOOL bNext = pFindDlg->FindNext();
    CExample1View *pView, *pMyView;
    //
    if(bTerm)
    {
        //
        //   inform the view we're done searching
        //
        pMyView = pView->GetView();
        pMyView->SetSearchFlag(FALSE);
        //
        //   refresh the view, remove  highlighting, etc
        //
        pMyView->GetClientRect(&rRect);
        pMyView->InvalidateRect(&rRect);
        delete pFindDlg;    // free allocated memory
        //return 0L;
    }
    //
    //
    if(bNext)    // user clicked "Find Next" button
    {
        CString csStr = pFindDlg->GetFindString();
        pMyView = pView->GetView();
        pMyView->SetSearchFlag(TRUE);
        pMyView->SetSearchStr(csStr);

        pMyView->SetActiveWindow();
        //
        //   refresh view
        //
        pMyView->GetClientRect(&rRect);
        pMyView->InvalidateRect(&rRect);
    }
    return 0L;
}
```

As you can glean from this piece of code, there is considerable interaction with the project's view class. The lines

```
pMyView->SetSearchFlag(TRUE);
pMyView->SetSearchStr(csStr);
```

call member functions added to class Example1View. The first method sets a flag that indicates if searching is enabled. This tells the view to highlight the text when it is found. The second method passes the view the string that is to be found. This is where all the heavy lifting is done when using a Find-Replace dialog box. Remember, this is not a full-featured editor, so this code isn't ready for prime time. To give you some idea of the type of things involved, look at the following snippet of code. This is taken from the OnDraw() method and is executed when the search string is at the start of a line.

```
if(iFound == 0) // search string starts the line!!
{
    pDC->SetTextColor(GetSysColor(COLOR_HIGHLIGHTTEXT));
    pDC->SetBkColor(GetSysColor(COLOR_HIGHLIGHT));
    pDC->SetBkMode(OPAQUE);
    pDC->TabbedTextOut( 2 * GetCharSize().cx, nYPos, csStr, 4,
        nTabPositions, 2 * GetCharSize().cx );
    //
    pDC->SetBkColor(GetSysColor(COLOR_WINDOW));
    pDC->SetTextColor(m_RGBFontColor);    // text color
    //
    nXPos =   (2 * GetCharSize().cx)+((csStr.GetLength()-1) *
        GetCharSize().cx );
    nXPos += 2 * textMet.tmInternalLeading;
    csPart2 = csCurLine.Right((csCurLine.GetLength()-
        (iFound+(csStr.GetLength()) )));
    //
    pDC->TabbedTextOut( nXPos, nYPos, csPart2, 4, nTabPositions, nXPos
);
}
```

That's a lot of work just to show a string highlighted. You have to account for margins, internal spacing between the characters, the size of the characters, among other things. For the record, the example editor has a small margin on the left side of the screen that is two characters wide. The following statement reflects this in the code.

```
2 * GetCharSize().cx
```

The best advice I can give you is to implement your own string highlighting algorithms. However, you can safely use the CFindReplaceDialog code to get you started.

Summary

The Find-Replace dialog box is complicated. If your application requires this capability, there are some special things you have to do (like registering the message and setting up the callback function) to get going. These things pale in comparison to updating the view. You may even find it more efficacious to simply use a third-party editing tool as an add-on.

Let's move on to the next topic, the font and print common dialog boxes.

CHAPTER 17

CFontDialog and CPrintDialog

T his chapter concludes the common dialogs available that cannot only enhance your interface, but minimize your efforts as well. These are CFontDialog and CPrintDialog. The CFontDialog class lets you include a Font-Selection dialog box in your applications that lists all the fonts currently installed. The CPrintDialog class encapsulates the services provided by the Windows common dialog box for printing. This is the same dialog you see when Print is selected from the File menu option. This provides an easy way to implement Print and Print Setup dialog boxes in a manner consistent with the Windows standard.

The chapter ends with sample code for the font dialog. The code can be found on the companion Web site in the Example1 project. This application is actually the beginning of a text editor, as discussed in Chapter 16, "The Find-Replace Dialog." Figure 17.1 shows the CFontDialog object from the Web site.

Class CFontDialog

The CFontDialog class allows you to include a Font-Selection dialog box in your application. A CFontDialog object is a dialog box that contains a list of all the *logical* fonts that are currently installed in the system. A logical font is an ideal description of a font. Before your application can begin drawing text using a logical font, it has to find the closest match from among the physical fonts known to the operating system. This chore is handled by a system utility known as the *font mapper*.

The user can select a particular font from this list, and this selection is then reported back to the application. This provides your application with a great deal of independence because it relieves you of the burden of shipping fonts with your application and configuring your install/uninstall utilities. The class maintains a rich repertoire of

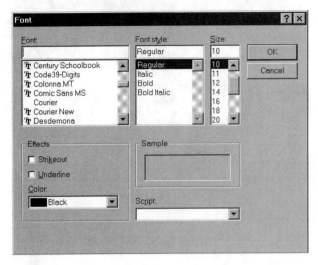

Figure 17.1 A CFontDialog object.

member functions at your disposal to determine font characteristics, such as bold or font color. The CHOOSEFONT system structure can be customized to include additional features related to fonts. After the CFontDialog object has been constructed, you can initialize its states or data values. Construction is a breeze (as compared to the CFileDialog). Use the default constructor or derive a new subclass and call your own. The code for the default constructor is the following:

```
CFontDialog cFontDlg;    // instantiate class
cFontDlg.DoModal();      // open the dialog box
```

If you cut your programming teeth on the old SDK, you know that displaying text can be time-consuming. The beauty of the CFontDialog class is that it makes displaying text easier. There are member functions that deliver the properties of the selected font. By using this class, you not only give the user a professional-looking font dialog but you can combine the property values with other CDC class methods to manage all your text painting.

To get these property values (for example, the font name, size, color, weight) you'll need to set up a CHOOSEFONT system structure and LOGFONT structure.

LOGFONT Structure

Fonts can be a confusing. Let's start with a quick overview of how fonts are measured. Fonts consist of both vertical and horizontal components. The vertical components consist of the following properties:

- *External leading.* The amount of space between two rows of text.
- *Internal leading.* Space reserved above character for accent mark.

- *Ascent*. Distance from the baseline to the top of most characters.

- *Descent*. Distance below the baseline reserved for most characters.

- *Height*. Number of pixels in the vertical portion of the character cell.

The horizontal components are ranged values called *escapement* and *orientation*. Figures 17.2 and 17.3 illustrate the vertical and horizontal elements, respectively.

The LOGFONT structure is used to define the attributes of the font. It is prototyped as follows:

```
typedef struct tagLOGFONT { /* lf */
   LONG lfHeight;
   LONG lfWidth;
   LONG lfEscapement;
   LONG lfOrientation;
   LONG lfWeight;
   BYTE lfItalic;
   BYTE lfUnderline;
   BYTE lfStrikeOut;
   BYTE lfCharSet;
   BYTE lfOutPrecision;
   BYTE lfClipPrecision;
   BYTE lfQuality;
   BYTE lfPitchAndFamily;
   CHAR lfFaceName[LF_FACESIZE];
} LOGFONT;
```

The lfHeight member is the height of the font in logical units. This can be set in one of three ways. When strictly greater than zero, it is transformed into device units and matched against the cell height of the available fonts. If equal to zero, a default size is set by the font mapper. If less than zero, it is transformed into device units and the absolute value is matched against the character height of the available fonts. When attempting to find a match, the mapper searches for the largest font that does not exceed the requested size. If none is found, it looks for the smallest available font. This mapping occurs when the font is actually used for the first time.

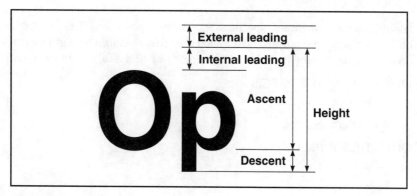

Figure 17.2 Vertical font measurements.

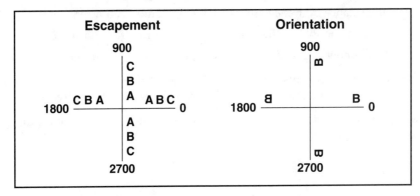

Figure 17.3 Horizontal font measurements.

The lfWidth member is the average width, in logical units, of characters in the font. The lfEscapement member indicates the angle, in tenths of a degree, of each line of text written using the font, relative to the bottom of the page. The lfOrientation member is the angle, in tenths of degrees, of each character's base line relative to the bottom of the page. Figures 17.2 and 17.3 show a visual representation of these members.

The lfWeight member is the weight of the font and is a value in the range of 0–1000. If lfWeight is zero, a default weight is assigned by the font mapper. This member consists of all the constants defined in Table 17.2, which appears later in this chapter.

The next three members are related to the visual effects for the font. The lfItalic member specifies an italic font when set to TRUE. If lfUnderline is TRUE, it indicates an underlined font. If lfStrikeOut is TRUE, a strikeout font is indicated.

The lfCharSet member defines the character set. The following values are predefined:

- ANSI_CHARSET
- OEM_CHARSET
- SYMBOL_CHARSET
- UNICODE_CHARSET

The lfOutPrecision member specifies the output precision. The output precision defines how closely the output must match the requested font's height, width, character orientation, escapement, and pitch. It can be one of the following values:

- OUT_CHARACTER_PRECIS
- OUT_DEFAULT_PRECIS
- OUT_STRING_PRECIS
- OUT_STROKE_PRECIS

The lfClipPrecision member specifies the clipping precision, which defines how to clip characters that are partially outside the clipping region. It can be one of the following values:

- CLIP_CHARACTER_PRECIS

- CLIP_DEFAULT_PRECIS

- CLIP_STROKE_PRECIS

lfQuality specifies the output quality. The output quality defines how carefully the graphics device interface must attempt to match the logical-font attributes to those of an actual physical font. It can be one of the following values:

DEFAULT_QUALITY. The appearance of the font does not matter.

DRAFT_QUALITY. The appearance of the font is less important than when PROOF_QUALITY is used. For GDI fonts, scaling is enabled, which means that more font sizes are available, but the quality may be decreased. Bold, italic, underline and strikeout fonts are generated if necessary.

PROOF_QUALITY. Character quality of the font is more important than exact matching of the logical-font attributes. For GDI fonts, scaling is disabled and the font closest in size is chosen. Although the chosen font size may not be mapped exactly when PROOF_QUALITY is used, the quality of the font is high and there is no distortion of appearance. Bold, italic, underline, and strikeout fonts are generated if necessary.

The lfPitchAndFamily member indicates the pitch and family of the font. The two low-order bits specify the pitch of the font and can be one of the following values:

- DEFAULT_PITCH

- FIXED_PITCH

- VARIABLE_PITCH

Bits 4 through 7 of the member specify the font family and can be one of the following values:

- FF_DECORATIVE

- FF_DONTCARE

- FF_MODERN

- FF_ROMAN

- FF_SCRIPT

- FF_SWISS

The proper value is obtained by using the Boolean OR operator to join one pitch constant with one family constant. Font families describe the look of a font in a general way. They are intended for specifying fonts when the exact typeface you want is not available. The values for font families are as follows:

FF_DECORATIVE. Novelty fonts. Old English is an example.

FF_DONTCARE. Don't care or don't know.

FF_MODERN. Fonts with constant stroke width (fixed pitch), with or without serifs. Fixed-pitch fonts are usually modern. Pica, Elite, and Courier New are examples.

FF_ROMAN. Fonts with variable stroke width (proportionally spaced) and with serifs. MS Serif is an example.

FF_SCRIPT. Fonts designed to look like handwriting. Script and Cursive are examples.

FF_SWISS. Fonts with variable stroke width and without serifs. MS Sans Serif is an example.

The last member, lfFaceName, points to a NULL-terminated string that specifies the typeface name of the font. The length of this string must not exceed 32 characters. The Windows EnumFonts() function can be used to enumerate the typeface names of all currently available fonts. If lfFaceName is NULL, GDI uses a default typeface.

The LOGFONT structure is used just about everywhere fonts are used. For the common font dialog box, this structure is itself the member of another structure, the CHOOSEFONT structure.

CHOOSEFONT Structure

The CHOOSEFONT structure is the system structure used both to initialize the font common dialog box, and to get the user's selections. Here is the prototype for the structure:

```
typedef struct {      // cf
    DWORD          lStructSize;
    HWND           hwndOwner;
    HDC            hDC;
    LPLOGFONT      lpLogFont;
    INT            iPointSize;
    DWORD          Flags;
    DWORD          rgbColors;
    LPARAM         lCustData;
    LPCFHOOKPROC   lpfnHook;
    LPCTSTR        lpTemplateName;
    HINSTANCE      hInstance;
    LPTSTR         lpszStyle;
    WORD           nFontType;
    WORD           ___MISSING_ALIGNMENT__;
    INT            nSizeMin;
    INT            nSizeMax;
} CHOOSEFONT;
```

The first member, lStructSize, is the size of the CHOOSEFONT structure. Initialize it to sizeof(CHOOSEFONT). The hwndOwner member is the handle of the parent window, or NULL if it has no owner. The hDC member is generally ignored, but its meaning is tied to the Flags member. When Flags indicates the CF_PRINTERFONTS or CF_BOTH flag, then hDC is the handle to the device context of the printer whose fonts will be listed in the dialog box.

The lpLogFont member is also tied to the Flags member. Here it is a pointer to a LOGFONT structure. When Flags includes CF_INITTOLOGFONTSTRUCT, use this LOGFONT structure to initialize the font dialog box. The font to which it is the closest match will be used to perform the initialization. When the OK button is clicked to close the box, the members of this LOGFONT structure are set based on properties set by the user.

The iPointSize member is the size of the selected font. The font is measured in increments of 1/10 of a printer's point. This member is set with the point size specified by the user when the dialog box is closed.

The Flags member is like all the others you've seen so far—it runs the whole shooting match. Because of their importance and complexity, these are reviewed in more detail in a separate section later in this chapter. Certain Flags member values can have an effect in relation to the remaining members.

The rgbColors is used to set and retrieve the text color. The Flags member must include the CF_EFFECTS flag to initialize the font dialog box. The lCustData member is 32-bits' worth of free data you can have to pass to a hook procedure used with this common dialog (identified by the lpfnHook member; you must include the CF_ENABLEHOOK value in Flags). When a WM_INITDIALOG message gets routed to the hook procedure, the lParam parameter of the message is a pointer to the CHOOSEFONT structure specified when the dialog was created.

The lpTemplateName member is also used for extreme customization (as with a hook procedure). This is the string that names the dialog box template resource in the module specified by the hInstance member. This member is ignored without the CF_ENABLETEMPLATE flag. The hInstance member is ignored unless the CF_ENABLETEMPLATEHANDLE or CF_ENABLETEMPLATE flags are set. Otherwise, it's the handle of a memory object containing a dialog box template.

The lpszStyle member is a pointer to a buffer that contains optional style data. The CF_USESTYLE flag is required. The nFontType member specifies the type of selected

Table 17.1 Values for the nFontType Member

NFONTTYPE VALUE	MEANING
BOLD_FONTTYPE	The font weight is bold.
ITALIC_FONTTYPE	The italic font attribute is set.
PRINTER_FONTTYPE	The font is a printer font.
REGULAR_FONTTYPE	The font weight is normal.
SCREEN_FONTTYPE	The font is a screen font.
SIMULATED_FONTTYPE	The font is simulated by the Graphics Device Interface (GDI).

font when the ChooseFont() function returns. This member can be a combination of the values shown in Table 17.1.

The last two members are nSizeMin and nSizeMax. They specify the minimum and maximum point sizes, respectively. These are only recognized by the ChooseFont() function if the CF_LIMITSIZE flag is specified.

The Flags

This section examines only the most commonly used flag values. If you see something that's not covered, check out your Visual C++ Help file.

The first is CF_APPLY flag. When you OR this bit mask into Flags, it causes the Apply button to appear on the dialog box. You'll need to supply a hook procedure to process the WM_COMMAND message sent by clicking this button. This hook procedure can send a WM_CHOOSEFONT_GETLOGFONT message to the font dialog box to obtain the address of the LOGFONT structure that stores the current font properties.

The next flag is CF_BOTH. This causes the font dialog box to list both the printer and screen fonts. This flag is equivalent to

```
CF_SCREENFONTS | CF_PRINTERFONTS
```

Closely related is the CF_WYSIWYG flag. This indicates that the ChooseFont() function should allow both printer and screen fonts. However, it also requires that both the CF_BOTH and CF_SCALABLEONLY flags be included. The CF_SCALABLEONLY flag means the ChooseFont() function should allow only the selection of scalable fonts. Scalable fonts include TrueType fonts, vector fonts, scalable printer fonts, and various others.

To limit the dialog box to only those screen fonts supported by the host system, specify the CF_SCREENFONTS flag.

To restrict the CFont dialog box to TrueType fonts only, you can specify the CF_TTONLY flag. To have the dialog box display the text property controls (for example, strikeout, underline, and text color), use the CF_EFFECTS flag. When this flag is set, you can set the rgbColors member to specify the initial text color. You can set the lfStrikeOut and lfUnderline members of the LOGFONT structure (as pointed to by lpLogFont) to specify the initial settings of the strikeout and underline checkboxes. The ChooseFont() function uses these members to return the user's selections.

The next three flags relate to using a hook procedure. Specify the CF_ENABLEHOOK flag to enable the hook procedure specified by the lpfnHook member. If you're using a custom dialog template, include the CF_ENABLETEMPLATE flag. If using a pre-loaded dialog template, include the flag CF_ENABLETEMPLATEHANDLE.

The CF_FIXEDPITCHONLY flag restricts the ChooseFont() function to fixed-pitch fonts only. The CF_FORCEFONTEXIST flag means the ChooseFont() function should return an error condition if an attempt is made to select a font or style that does not exist. Remember, you can use the CommDlgExtendedError() function to retrieve errors with the common dialogs.

For initializing the CFont dialog box when it opens, include the CF_INITTOLOG-FONTSTRUCT flag. The lpLogFont member points to a LOGFONT structure that you must also initialize.

To initialize a font dialog box's controls such that there is no initial font name selected in the combo box, specify the CF_NOFACESEL flag. This is helpful if there is no single font name that applies to the text selection.

Another initialization flag is CF_NOSCRIPTSEL. This disables the Script combo box. When set, the lfCharSet member of the LOGFONT structure is set to DEFAULT_CHARSET when the ChooseFont() function returns. This flag is only used to initialize the Font dialog box.

To prevent the Font dialog box from displaying an initial selection in the Font Style combo box, include the CF_NOSTYLESEL flag. This flag is useful when there is no single font style that applies to the text selection. Closely related is the CF_NOSIZESEL flag. This prevents a font size from being initially selected in the dialog box This flag is used when there is no single font size that applies to the text selection.

The CF_NOSIMULATIONS flag is used to signal the ChooseFont() function that it should not allow fonts to be simulated by the GDI. Vector fonts can also be disallowed by including the CF_NOVECTORFONTS flag. To force the Font dialog box to list only horizontally oriented fonts, use the CF_NOVETFONTS flag.

To give the font dialog box a Help button, include CF_SHOWHELP with the Flags member. You'll have to register the HELPMSGSTRING message, and hwndOwner must indicate the window that will receive this message when the Help button is clicked.

The flag CF_PRINTERFONTS will force the dialog box to only list those fonts that are supported by the printer associated with the hDC member (for example, the device context). To allow font selection for non-OEM, ANSI, and Symbol character sets, include the CF_SCRIPTSONLY flag. This flag supersedes the CF_ANSIONLY flag used in previous versions of MFC. Compare it to the CF_SELECTSCRIPT flag—this flag restricts the fonts to those of the character set identified by the lfCharSet member of the LOGFONT structure. The user cannot change the character set specified in the Scripts combo box on the dialog.

The last flag is CF_USESTYLE. This flag indicates that the lpszStyle member points to a buffer that contains style data that the ChooseFont() function should use to initialize the Style combo box. When the Font dialog box is closed, the ChooseFont() function copies this style data into this buffer.

That's a wrap for the flags. Let's take a closer look at the ChooseFont() function.

ChooseFont() Function

The ChooseFont() function is used to create a CFont dialog box that allows the user to choose properties for a logical font, such as the typeface name, style (bold, italic, and so on), or size. The prototype is simply

```
BOOL ChooseFont(LPCHOOSEFONT lpcf);
```

The parameter lpcf is a pointer to a CHOOSEFONT structure containing the data needed to initialize the dialog box. When the dialog box is closed, this structure is populated with the user's font selection properties. The return value is nonzero if the user closes the dialog by clicking the OK button. If the Cancel button is clicked instead, or if an error occurs, the return value is zero. You can then call CommDlg-ExtendedError() to retrieve the error information. The error codes and their meanings are as follows:

CDERR_FINDRESFAILURE. The CFont dialog could not find a specified resource (such as a custom template).

CDERR_NOHINSTANCE. The CF_ENABLETEMPLATE flag was set, but no corresponding instance handle (the hInstance member) was found.

CDERR_INITIALIZATION. The Font dialog box function failed during initialization. This error generally occurs when sufficient memory is not available.

CDERR_NOHOOK. The CF_ENABLEHOOK flag was set in the Flags member of the initialization structure for the corresponding common dialog box, but there is no pointer to a corresponding hook procedure.

CDERR_LOCKRESFAILURE. The Font dialog box failed to lock a specified resource.

CDERR_NOTEMPLATE. The Flags member indicated a template, but none was found.

CDERR_LOADRESFAILURE. The font dialog box failed to load a specified resource.

CDERR_STRUCTSIZE. An invalid value was given for the lStructSize member.

CDERR_LOADSTRFAILURE. The font dialog box failed to load a specified string.

CFERR_MAXLESSTHANMIN. The size specified in the nSizeMax member of the CHOOSEFONT structure is less than the size specified in the nSizeMin member.

CDERR_MEMALLOCFAILURE. The common dialog box function failed to allocate memory for internal structures.

CFERR_NOFONTS. No fonts exist.

CDERR_MEMLOCKFAILURE. The Font dialog box function was unable to lock the memory associated with a handle.

This ends our look at the ChooseFont() function—now let's look at the hook procedure.

The Hook Procedure

There are some situations when you'll want to use a hook procedure with the Font common dialog box. For example, if you include the Apply button, the hook procedure acts like a traffic cop for your application and the Font dialog box. As discussed earlier, a hook procedure is enabled by specifying the CF_ENABLEHOOK flag in the Flags member of the CHOOSEFONT structure, and the address of the hook procedure in the lpfnHook member.

In order to get and set the current values and flags for a Font dialog box, the hook procedure can send it the following messages:

- WM_CHOOSEFONT_GETLOGFONT
- WM_CHOOSEFONT_SETFLAGS
- WM_CHOOSEFONT_SETLOGFONT

The WM_CHOOSEFONT_GETLOGFONT message is used to retrieve information from the CFont dialog regarding the user's font selection. To send the message, set wParam to zero and lParam to the address of a LOGFONT structure that will store the font data. For example,

```
PMyFontDlg->SendMessage(WM_CHOOSEFONT_GETLOGFONT,0,(LPLOGFONT) lplf);
```

This message does not return a value.

The WM_CHOOSEFONT_SETFLAGS is used to set the display options for the font dialog box. The parameters are the same as for the WM_CHOOSEFONT_GETLOGFONT message except that the LOGFONT structure is used to write data and not read it. Again, there is no return value.

The last message you can use is WM_CHOOSEFONT_SETLOGFONT. This is used to set the current logical font information. The parameters are identical to the previous two messages, and there is no return value.

It gets easier from here on out, thanks in part to the class members. The following section provides a quick look at these functions and their usage.

Class Members

Now that you've seen how simple it is to create the common dialog box for fonts, it's time to put the class members to work. These tell you all about the properties the user assigned to a font (for example, bold, font size). The first one you'll want to see is GetCurrentFont(), prototyped as follows:

```
void GetCurrentFont(LPLOGFONT lplf);
```

The parameter lplf is a pointer to a LOGFONT structure. Call this function to load the user's selections into the structure. For example, the next four lines of code demonstrate how to create and display a CFont dialog box, then call GetCurrentFont() to retrieve the settings.

```
CFontDialog cFontDlg;
cFontDlg.DoModal();      // show CFont dialog box
LOGFONT logFont;         // a LOGFONT structure to hold values
cFontDlg.GetCurrentFont(&logFont); // get log. Font values
```

If this function is called during a call to DoModal(), the structure is populated with the values at that instant (what the user sees or has changed in the dialog). If called after DoModal(), the structure has what the user actually selected.

The next method is used to fetch the face name of the selected font.

```
CString GetFaceName()const;
```

The return value is the face name of the font that was selected. For example, if Courier New was selected from the Font dialog shown in Figure 17.1, then GetFaceName() would return Courier New. This is the same value returned into the lfFaceName member of the LOGFONT structure.

To get the style name of the font, use GetStyleName().

```
CString GetStyleName()const;
```

To find the size of the selected font, call GetSize().

```
int GetSize()const;
```

The return value is the font size, in tenths of a point. Getting the color selected is easy, too.

```
COLORREF GetColor()const;
```

The return value is the 24-bit color value. The weight of the font is much like the rest.

```
int GetWeight()const;
```

The return value is the weight of the selected font. It can be one the values shown in Table 17.2.

Table 17.2   Font Weights

FONT WEIGHT CONSTANT	VALUE
FW_DONTCARE	0
FW_THIN	100
FW_EXTRALIGHT	200
FW_ULTRALIGHT	200
FW_LIGHT	300
FW_NORMAL	400
FW_REGULAR	400
FW_MEDIUM	500
FW_SEMIBOLD	600
FW_DEMIBOLD	600
FW_BOLD	700
FW_EXTRABOLD	800
FW_ULTRABOLD	800
FW_BLACK	900
FW_HEAVY	900

To ascertain if the selected font has the strikeout characteristic enabled, use IsStrikeOut().

```
BOOL IsStrikeOut()const;
```

The return value is nonzero if the user selected the strikeout property; otherwise, it is zero. The same return values are used to determine if the underline, italic, and bold properties were selected.

```
BOOL IsUnderline()const;
BOOL IsBold()const;
BOOL IsItalic()const;
```

That takes care of the CFontDialog class. There is one more common dialog you can use, the common print dialog.

Class CPrintDialog

The CPrintDialog class encapsulates the services provided by the Windows common dialog box for printing. Common print dialog boxes give your application an easy way to implement the Print and Print Setup dialog boxes in a manner consistent with Windows standards.

If you like, you can let the framework handle most aspects of the printing process for your application. In this case, the framework automatically displays the Windows common dialog box for printing. You can also have the framework handle printing for your application but override the common Print dialog box with your own Print dialog box. If you want your application to handle printing without the framework's involvement, use the CPrintDialog class as is with the constructor provided, or derive your own dialog class from CPrintDialog and write a constructor to suit your needs. In either case, these dialog boxes will behave like standard MFC dialog boxes because they are derived from class CCommonDialog.

To use a CPrintDialog object, first create the object using the CPrintDialog constructor. Once the dialog box has been constructed, set or modify any values in a system structure to initialize the values of the dialog box's controls. This structure is of type PRINT-DLG. Class CPrintDialog includes a data member called m_pd that is a structure of this type. Just as CHOOSEFONT has an embedded structure (for example, the LOGFONT structure), so the PRINTDLG has a similar member. The next section takes a closer look at this structure; this will set up a look at the "mother" structure, PRINTDLG.

DEVMODE Structure

Anything you would ever want to tweak with a printer can probably be found in the DEVMODE structure. It contains information concerning the printer's environment and initialization. Here is the prototype:

```
typedef struct _devicemode {    /* dvmd */
    TCHAR   dmDeviceName[32];
    WORD    dmSpecVersion;
```

```
    WORD    dmDriverVersion;
    WORD    dmSize;
    WORD    dmDriverExtra;
    DWORD   dmFields;
    short   dmOrientation;
    short   dmPaperSize;
    short   dmPaperLength;
    short   dmPaperWidth;
    short   dmScale;
    short   dmCopies;
    short   dmDefaultSource;
    short   dmPrintQuality;
    short   dmColor;
    short   dmDuplex;
    short   dmYResolution;
    short   dmTTOption;
    short   dmCollate;
    TCHAR   dmFormName[32];
    WORD    dmUnusedPadding;
    USHORT  dmBitsPerPel;
    DWORD   dmPelsWidth;
    DWORD   dmPelsHeight;
    DWORD   dmDisplayFlags;
    DWORD   dmDisplayFrequency;
} DEVMODE;
```

The dmDeviceName member is the name of the device the driver supports; for example, PCL/HP LaserJet. This string is unique among device drivers.

The dmSpecVersion member specifies the version number of the initialization data specification on which the structure is based. The dmDriverVersion member is the printer driver version number assigned by the printer driver developer.

The dmSize member is the size of the DEVMODE structure, in bytes. The dmDriverExtra member is the number of bytes of private driver-specific data that follows this structure. If a device driver does not use device-specific information, set this to zero.

The dmFields member indicates which of the remaining structure members have been initialized. Bit 0 of this DWORD (defined as DM_ORIENTATION) corresponds to the dmOrientation member. Bit 1 (defined as DM_PAPERSIZE) specifies dmPaperSize, and so on. Consult the MFC documentation if you want to see the meaning of each bit.

The dmOrientation member determines the paper orientation. This can be either 1 (DMORIENT_PORTRAIT) or 2 (DMORIENT_LANDSCAPE). The dmPaperSize member is the size of the paper used to print. This can be zero if the paper's dimensions have been set by the dmPaperLength and dmPaperWidth members. Just about every size imaginable is defined as a constant. For example,

```
DMPAPER_LETTER (8 1/2 x 11 inches)
DMPAPER_LEGAL (8 1/2 X 14 inches)
```

Refer to the DEVMODE documentation for the complete list.

The dmPaperLength member is used to override the length of the paper specified by the dmPaperSize member, either for custom paper sizes or for devices such as dot-matrix printers, which can print on a page of arbitrary length. These values, along with all other values in this structure that specify a physical length, are in tenths of a millimeter. The same is true of the dmPaperWidth member, except this is for the paper's width.

The dmScale member is basically a factor by which the printed output will be scaled. The apparent page size is scaled from the physical page size by a factor of dmScale/100. For example, a letter-sized page with a dmScale value of 50 would contain as much data as a page of 17 by 22 inches because the output text and graphics would be one-half the original height and width.

The dmCopies member is the number of copies to be printed (assuming the printer supports multiple-page copies). The dmDefaultSource member is reserved and must be set to zero. The dmPrintQuality member is the printer resolution and can be one of the following values:

- DMRES_HIGH
- DMRES_MEDIUM
- DMRES_LOW
- DMRES_DRAFT

The dmColor member is used to indicate a color or monochrome printer. Possible values are

- DMCOLOR_COLOR
- DMCOLOR_MONOCHROME

The dmDuplex selects duplex or double-sided printing for printers capable of duplex printing. Possible values are

- DMDUP_SIMPLEX
- DMDUP_HORIZONTAL
- DMDUP_VERTICAL

The dmYResolution member is a measure of the dots per inch in the y or vertical direction. If the printer initializes this member, the dmPrintQuality member specifies the x resolution (horizontal direction).

The dmTTOption member specifies how TrueType fonts should be printed. This member can be one of the following values:

DMTT_BITMAP. Print TrueType fonts as graphics

DMTT_DOWNLOAD. Print TrueType fonts as soft fonts

DMTT_SUBDEV. Substitute device fonts for TrueType fonts

The first value is the default for dot-matrix printers, the second is the default for Hewlett-Packard printers that use Printer Control Language (PCL), and the third is the default for PostScript printers.

The dmCollate member indicates whether multiple copies should be collated. A value of DMCOLLATE_FALSE causes the data to be sent only once to the printer, regardless of the number of copies requested. Multiple copies are not collated. A value of DMCOLLATE_TRUE collates when printing multiple copies.

The dmFormName member specifies the name of the form to use; for example, Letter or Legal. All names can be found using the EnumForms() API. The dmUnusedPadding member is used to align the DEVMODE structure on a DWORD boundary. This should not be used or referenced as it is reserved and may change in future releases.

The dmBitsPerPel member specifies the color resolution in bits per pixel; for example, 4 bits for 16 colors, 8 bits for 256, or 16 for 65,536 colors. The dmPelsWidth and dmPelsHeight members are the width and height, in pixels, of the visible device surface.

The dmDisplayFlags member specifies the device's display mode. The following values are valid.

DM_GRAYSCALE. The device is a noncolor device.

DM_INTERLACED. The device is interlaced.

The dmDisplayFrequency member is the frequency (in cycles per second) of the device when in a particular mode.

That takes care of the DEVMODE structure. Now you're ready to use it with its cousin, the PRINTDLG structure.

PRINTDLG Structure

The PRINTDLG structure is used to store information used by the PrintDlg() function to initialize the common print dialog. After the user closes the dialog box, the system uses this structure to return information about what was selected. Here is the structure's prototype:

```
typedef struct tagPD {     //  pd
    DWORD       lStructSize;
    HWND        hwndOwner;
    HANDLE      hDevMode;
    HANDLE      hDevNames;
    HDC         hDC;
    DWORD       Flags;
    WORD        nFromPage;
    WORD        nToPage;
    WORD        nMinPage;
    WORD        nMaxPage;
    WORD        nCopies;
    HINSTANCE   hInstance;
    DWORD       lCustData;
    LPPRINTHOOKPROC lpfnPrintHook;
    LPSETUPHOOKPROC lpfnSetupHook;
    LPCTSTR     lpPrintTemplateName;
```

```
      LPCTSTR    lpSetupTemplateName;
      HANDLE     hPrintTemplate;
      HANDLE     hSetupTemplate;
  } PRINTDLG;
```

The lStructSize member is the structure's size, in bytes. The hwndOwner member is the handle of the window that owns the dialog. It can be NULL.

The hDevMode member is a handle to a movable global memory object that contains a DEVMODE structure. This structure contains information about the device initialization and environment of a printer. If you don't set this member to NULL, you'll have to allocate a movable block of memory for the DEVMODE structure and initialize its members. When the print dialog box is closed, this structure contains the user's input. If you do set it to NULL, the PrintDlg() function allocates memory for the DEVMODE structure, initializes its members to indicate the user's input, and returns a handle that identifies it. If the printer does not support extended device modes, hDevMode is set to NULL when PrintDlg() returns (the dialog box is closed).

The hDevNames member is a handle to a movable global memory object that contains a DEVNAMES structure. This is a brief system structure that contains strings used to identify the driver, device, and output port names for the printer. It is used to initialize members in the system-defined Print dialog box. When the user closes the dialog box, information about the selected printer is returned in this structure. Refer to the documentation for more information on this structure. If this member is NULL, PrintDlg() allocates memory for the DEVNAMES structure, initializes it, and returns a handle.

The hDC member is the device context or an information context, depending on whether the Flags member specifies the PD_RETURNDC or PC_RETURNIC flag. If neither flag is specified, the value of this member is undefined. If both flags are specified, PD_RETURNDC takes priority.

Next comes the Flags member, and as usual, there are a lot of them. These are used to initialize the Print dialog box, and to determine what the user selected when it closes. The following is an overview of the various values you can use for Flags.

PD_ALLPAGES. This is a default flag that indicates that the All radiobutton is initially selected. It is used as a placeholder to indicate that the PD_PAGENUMS and PD_SELECTION flags are not specified.

PD_COLLATE. This flag causes the Collate checkbox to be initially checked (or is checked when the box is closed).

PD_DISABLEPRINTTOFILE. This flag disables the Print to File checkbox on the Print dialog box. The flag PD_HIDEPRINTTOFILE hides this checkbox completely.

PD_ENABLEPRINTHOOK. This enables the hook procedure specified in the lpfnPrintHook member.

PD_ENABLEPRINTTEMPLATE. Used for a custom print dialog; hInstance and lpPrintTemplateName members specify a replacement for the default Print dialog box template.

PD_ENABLEPRINTTEMPLATEHANDLE. This flag means the hPrintTemplate member identifies a data block that contains a preloaded dialog box template.

PD_ENABLESETUPHOOK. Enables the hook procedure specified in the lpfn-SetupHook member.

PD_ENABLESETUPTEMPLATE. Indicates that the hInstance and lpSetupTemplate-Name members specify a replacement for the default Print Setup dialog box template.

PD_ENABLESETUPTEMPLATEHANDLE. This flag means the hSetupTemplate member identifies a data block that contains a preloaded dialog box template.

PD_NONETWORKBUTTON. This flag hides and disables the Network button on the Print dialog box.

PD_NOPAGENUMS. Disables the Pages radiobutton and the associated edit controls.

PD_NOSELECTION. Disables the Selection radiobutton.

PD_NOWARNING. Prevents the warning message from being displayed when there is no default printer.

PD_PAGENUMS. If this flag is set, the Pages radiobutton is selected. When the dialog box is closed, the nFromPage and nToPage members contain the starting and ending pages entered by the user.

PD_PRINTSETUP. This flag causes the Print Setup dialog box to be displayed instead of the Print dialog.

PD_PRINTTOFILE. This flag causes the Print to File checkbox to be checked on initialization and is returned if selected by the user when the box is closed.

PD_RETURNDC. A device context matching the user's selections is returned in the hDC member.

PD_RETURNDEFAULT. If this flag is set, the PrintDlg() function does not display the dialog box. Instead, it sets the hDevNames and hDevMode members to handles to the DEVMODE and DEVNAMES structures that are initialized for the system default printer. Both hDevNames and hDevMode must be NULL, or PrintDlg() returns an error.

PD_RETURNIC. This flag means an information context is returned rather than a device context.

PD_SELECTION. If set, the Selection radiobutton is selected. If neither PD_PAGENUMS nor this flag are set, the All radiobutton is selected.

PD_SHOWHELP. The Print dialog box displays a Help button.

PD_USEDEVMODECOPIESANDCOLLATE. This flag specifies whether your application supports multiple copies and collation. Set this flag on input to indicate that your application does not support multiple copies and collation. In this case, the nCopies member always returns 1, and PD_COLLATE is never set in the Flags member.

The nFromPage and nToPage are the starting and ending page numbers set or selected by the user. The nMinPage and nMaxPage members are the minimum and maximum values for the page range edit controls.

The nCopies member is the number of copies to print. The hInstance member is the handle of the application and is used when you have a custom dialog box. The lCustData is 32 bits of application-defined data that can be used with the hook procedure discussed earlier. The lpfnPrintHook member is a pointer to the hook procedure, if used.

The lpfnSetupHook member is a pointer to a SetupHookProc() procedure used with the Print Setup dialog box. This member is ignored unless the PD_ENABLESE-TUPHOOK flag is set in the Flags member. The lpPrintTemplateName member is a pointer to a NULL-terminated string that names a dialog box template resource in the module identified by the hInstance member. The lpSetupTemplateName member is the name of a dialog box template resource for a custom Print Setup dialog box. The hPrintTemplate member is the handle of a memory object containing a dialog box template that replaces the default Print common dialog box. Lastly, the hSetup-Template member is like the hPrintTemplate member, except it is used with a Print Setup box.

So there you have it. Once again, a system structure is used to initialize a common dialog box when it is opened, and to store the user's selections when it is closed. Let's take a look at the main function where these are used, PrintDlg().

PrintDlg() Function

The PrintDlg() function displays the common dialog boxes for printing or to display a Print Setup box. This function should not be used with new applications. It has been superseded by the Page Setup common dialog box created by the PageSetup() function. The function is prototyped as follows:

```
BOOL PrintDlg(LPPRINTDLG lppd);
```

The parameter lppd is a pointer to a PRINTDLG structure. The return value is TRUE (nonzero) if the user clicks the OK button and FALSE (zero) if the Cancel button was clicked or if an error occurred.

This function is used when you want to initialize the Print dialog box without using the standard constructor. This makes its functionality a lot like the ChooseFont() function discussed earlier with the common Font dialog. Both result in the common Print dialog box being displayed—it just depends on what you want to do. For the most part, if you just want to print, use the constructor.

```
CPrintDialog cMyPrint;   // class constructor
cMyPrint.DoModal();      // show Print dialog, uninitialized
```

Class Methods

There are 15 class methods available for manipulating the Print dialog box. Some of these are omitted from this discussion, like DoModal(), since they are self-explanatory. The class methods provide an easy way to find, for example, the print range, or number of copies to print. If you don't see something you think you need, check the documentation. The first method is used to retrieve the number of copies the user wishes to print. The prototype is

```
int GetCopies()const;
```

The return value is the number of copies requested. Call this method after DoModal() returns with IDOK.

Next are the methods for retrieving the starting and ending page numbers for the print job. The methods are prototyped pretty much the same.

```
int GetFromPage()const;
```

and

```
int GetToPage()const;
```

The return values are the page numbers.

There are also methods for determining if the user wants to print a range or a selection. These are

```
BOOL PrintRange()const;
```

The return value is TRUE if the user specified a range of pages; otherwise, FALSE. For the text selection printing, use the following:

```
BOOL PrintSelection()const;
```

The return value is the same.

The last method is for retrieving the printer DC.

```
HDC GetPrinterDC()const;
```

If the call is successful, the return value will be the printer's device context handle; otherwise, it is NULL. If you set the bPrintSetupOnly parameter of the CPrintDialog constructor to FALSE (meaning the Print dialog box is displayed), then GetPrinterDC() returns a handle to the printer device context. It is up to you to call DeleteDC() when you're finished with it.

That's all for the class methods. As indicated, there are additional features available, so poke around in the documentation if you're curious. But for now, let's roll up our sleeves and take a look at the sample program for this chapter.

The Sample Program

The sample program for this chapter is limited in scope to the Font common dialog. The print is supported by the framework under File, and it does work. The project can be found on the companion Web site in the Example1 project. This is actually the beginning of a text editor. You've seen its features earlier in Chapters 15, "Common File Dialog," and Chapter 16, "The Find-Replace Dialog."

To see the font dialog in action, build and run the Example1 project. Open any text file to display its contents. Then, under Edit on the menubar, select Font dialog.... You can then select a new font or color and click OK. The text file will now be displayed using your properties.

How does it work? Because the example program changes what the user sees, it involves the view class. When you selected the Font dialog... option, the following message handler was called in the view class.

```
void CExample1View::OnFontDlg()
{
    // TODO: Add your command handler code here
    CFontDialog cFontDlg;
    cFontDlg.DoModal();
    LOGFONT logFont;
    cFontDlg.GetCurrentFont(&logFont);
    m_iFontSize = cFontDlg.GetSize();
    strcpy(m_lpFont,logFont.lfFaceName);
    //
    // get font color
    //
    m_RGBFontColor = cFontDlg.GetColor();
    //
    m_pFont = NULL;    // force call to GetFont()
    CExample1Doc* pDoc = GetDocument();
    pDoc->UpdateAllViews(NULL,0L,NULL);  // refresh view w/new font!
}    // end OnFontDlg()
```

The common font dialog is pretty straightforward. After the dialog box closes, a LOG-FONT structure grabs the new font. The GetColor() method is used to see if the color needs to be changed, then the view is updated. Another method, GetFont(), uses the values from the member variables to create the new font.

```
CFont * CExample1View::GetFont()
{
    if(m_pFont == NULL)
    {
        m_pFont = new CFont;
        if(m_pFont)     // CREATE THE (NEW) FONT HERE!!!!
            m_pFont->CreatePointFont(m_iFontSize,m_lpFont);
    }
    return m_pFont;
}
```

That's all it takes to use the common Font dialog. As usual, most of the work involved is with actually drawing with the right attributes. Once you have the text file open, you can print it from the menubar. If you feel stout-hearted, you might want to modify this project and implement your own custom Print dialog.

Summary

This chapter wraps up all the common dialogs. The main benefits of using these dialogs relative to enhancing your interface can be summarized as follows:

- They provide a consistent, Windows-compliant appearance.
- They make programming easier.
- They add extra features when implemented or customized.

The next chapter looks at another tool available for slicking up your interface, tabbed dialog boxes, or property sheets.

CHAPTER 18

Tabbed Dialog Boxes

A nother way to enhance your user interface is with tabbed dialog boxes. Based on class CTabCtrl, these objects are very similar to a thumb-indexed notebook. The tab control provides a quick-and-easy way to organize your dialog box by subjects. The tabs can also be owner-drawn. Figure 18.1 shown the example tabbed dialog box from the sample code for this chapter.

The tab control is used to create what are often called *property sheets*, similar to those used when activating some of the icons in the Control Panel of Windows 95/98. In effect, tab controls let you use one dialog box to do the work of several. When the user clicks the tab, the controls can be changed (remember the Visible property?) to reflect the content of the tab.

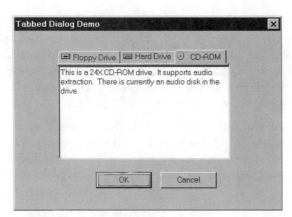

Figure 18.1   The sample tab control.

Although a tab control can give an application a facelift, use this control with discretion. First, make sure your application requires a tab control as opposed to another control that can perform the same function. Second, the number of tabs supported is limited, so the categories or subjects need to be small in number and fairly static. Tab controls are best suited for applications that share similar characteristics and data input needs. For example, use a tab control for software that tracks the spot prices of the precious metals gold, silver, and platinum, or, limited regional market locations such as north, south, east, and west. The tab control is a way to partition some aspect of the application into smaller, readily identifiable parts.

Class CTabCtrl

The CTabCtrl class contains everything you need to manipulate the tab control. If you're using App Studio, this class is available on the Controls palette. Tab controls also can be used in other windows such as MDI child windows and splitter windows. The class provides methods for setting and retrieving various properties of the control, as well as message handlers for trapping events such as a mouse click on a tab. You can also make the control owner-drawn, as demonstrated in the sample program found on the companion Web site under Example1. But the major player in the game is the TC_ITEM structure. You adjust the members of this structure and then pass them to the appropriate CTabCtrl class member to create or change a property. Here are this structure's members:

```
    typedef struct _TC_ITEM
    {
UINT mask;
UINT lpReserved1;
UINT lpReserved2;
LPSTR pszText;
int cchTextMax;
int iImage;
LPARAM lParam;
    } TC_ITEM;
```

The value of the mask member determines which of the other members are valid. For example, if you only want text to appear on the tab, set the mask member to TCIF_TEXT. If you want only an image, set it to TCIF_IMAGE. If you want both, OR these together. Another option is to set mask to TCIF_ALL to cover all the bases (for example, TCIF_TEXT, TCIF_IMAGE, and TCIF_PARAM).

The pszText member contains the text to be placed on the tab, and the cchTextMax member sets the length of this text. The iImage member is the index into the tab control's image list, or –1 if there is no image for the tab. Finally, the lParam member is application-defined data associated with the tab. For more information, consult the documentation.

Class Methods

The CTabCtrl class contains all the methods for manipulating the tab control. The most important method is the Create() function, prototyped as follows:

```
BOOL Create(DWORD dwStyle,const RECT& rect, CWnd* pParentWnd, UINT nID);
```

The rect parameter is the size and position of the tab control, the pParentWnd is the window that owns the control, and nID is the resource ID. The dwStyle parameter is the style of the tab control you create. The following styles are valid.

TCS_BUTTONS. One interesting feature of the dwStyle argument is that you can use it to make the tabs look like buttons by ORing this style with the others you assign. When used in this mode, clicking a button should execute a command instead of displaying a page.

TCS_FIXEDWIDTH. Forces all the tabs to have the same width. (By default, the tab control automatically sizes each tab to fit its icon.) You cannot use this style with the TCS_RIGHTJUSTIFY style.

TCS_FOCUSNEVER. This style prevents the control from receiving the input focus.

TCS_FOCUSONBUTTONDOWN. Indicates that a tab receives the input focus when clicked. This style is generally used only with the TCS_BUTTONS style.

TCS_FORCEICONLEFT. This style forces the icon to the left, but leaves the tab label centered. (By default, the control centers the icon and label with the icon to the left of the label.)

TCS_FORCELABELLEFT. Left-aligns both the icon and label.

TCS_MULTILINE. Causes a tab control to display multiple rows of tabs; thus, all tabs can be displayed at once. (By default, a tab control displays a single row of tabs.) Use this style if you have lots of tabs or buttons.

TCS_OWNERDRAWFIXED. Specifies that the parent window draws the tabs in the control. You can specify this style in App Studio, too.

TCS_RIGHTJUSTIFY. Right-justifies tabs. (By default, tabs are left-justified within each row.)

TCS_SHAREIMAGELISTS. This style means that a tab control's image lists are not destroyed when the control is destroyed.

TCS_TOOLTIPS. Indicates that the tab control has a tool tip control associated with it.

TCS_TABS. This causes the tabs to appear as tabs (as opposed to buttons), and a border is drawn around the display area. This style is the default.

TCS_SINGLELINE. Displays only one row of tabs. The user can scroll to see more tabs, if necessary. This is the default.

TCS_RAGGEDRIGHT. Does not stretch each row of tabs to fill the entire width of the control. This style is the default.

Besides these specific CTabCtrl styles, you can apply the following generic window styles to a tab control.

WS_CHILD. Creates a child window that represents the tab control. Cannot be used with the WS_POPUP style.

WS_VISIBLE. Creates a tab control that is initially visible.

WS_DISABLED. Creates a window that is initially disabled.

WS_GROUP. Specifies the first control in a group of controls in which the user can navigate from one control to the next with the arrow keys. All controls without this style belong to the group. The next control with the WS_GROUP style starts the next group (that is, one group ends where the next begins).

WS_TABSTOP. Specifies one of any number of controls through which the user can move by using the TAB key. The TAB key moves the user to the next control specified by the WS_TABSTOP style.

Two additional class methods that you'll use frequently are

```
BOOL GetItem( int nItem, TC_ITEM* pTabCtrlItem ) const;
BOOL SetItem( int nItem, TC_ITEM* pTabCtrlItem );
```

These work in tandem. Use the first one to read the properties of a specific tab (the nItem parameter) and the second to write the properties.

The next method is InsertItem().

```
BOOL InsertItem( int nItem, TC_ITEM* pTabCtrlItem );
```

This is an important class method, because it allows you to add tabs to the control. Fill in the TC_ITEM structure with all the properties you want, and call the class method with the tab index and TC_ITEM structure. There are also methods for determining which tab the user clicked, and for making a tab the current selection. These are

```
int GetCurSel() const;
```

This returns the zero-based index of the tab that was selected if the call was successful, or –1 if no tab was clicked. The sister to this method is

```
int SetCurSel( int nItem );
```

This is just the opposite of GetCurSel(); it sets a tab, using nItem as the zero-based index of the tab. When a tab is selected using SetCurSel(), it doesn't send a TCN_SELCHANGING or TCN_SELCHANGE notification message as expected. Instead, these are sent using WM_NOTIFY.

Another useful method, and one you'll find used in the sample program, assigns a CImageList object to the tab control.

```
CImageList * SetImageList( CImageList * pImageList );
```

The parameter pImageList is a pointer of the image list for the tab control. The return value is the handle to any previous image list, or NULL if there was no previous list.

Two other class methods that are closely related are SetItem() and GetItem().

```
BOOL SetItem(int nItem, TC_ITEM* pTabCtrlItem);
```

Call this method to set a tab controls' attributes; nItem is the index of the tab to set, and pTabCtrlItem is a pointer to a TC_ITEM structure. The return value is nonzero if the call was successful, or zero if it failed. The method for reading the attributes is

```
BOOL GetItem( int nItem, TC_ITEM* pTabCtrlItem ) const;
```

The parameters are the same as SetItem(); the return value is TRUE if the call was successful, FALSE if it failed.

CTabCtrl includes a method for finding which tab has the current focus.

```
int GetCurFocus()const;
```

The return value is the zero-based index of the tab that has the focus, or –1 if no tab has the focus. You can also delete items from the tab control using

```
BOOL DeleteItem(int nItem);
```

The parameter nItem is the index of the item to delete. The return value is nonzero if successful, or zero if it failed.

The Sample Program

The sample code is short and sweet. The menu option Tabbed Dialog under Controls on the main menubar runs the dialog box with the tab control. The dialog box was created in App Studio, and the tab control was added, too. The control is assigned the owner-drawn property and the property TCS_TOOLTIPS. The tool tips feature required that a message handler be added manually to the message map.

```
ON_NOTIFY_EX(TTN_NEEDTEXT,0,MyToolTips)
```

The real work begins when the dialog box containing the tab control is initialized. Take a look at the following method:

```
BOOL CTabDlg::OnInitDialog()
{
    CDialog::OnInitDialog();
    // TODO: Add extra initialization here
    // initialize the CTabCtrl object--then use
    // message handler to initialize for demo purposes..
    //
    TC_ITEM pTabCtrlItem;    // tab control item structure
    pTabCtrlItem.mask = TCIF_TEXT | TCIF_IMAGE;
    pTabCtrlItem.iImage = 0;
    pTabCtrlItem.pszText = "Floppy Drive";
    m_TabCtrl.InsertItem( 0, &pTabCtrlItem );    // first tab
    pTabCtrlItem.pszText = "Hard Drive";
    pTabCtrlItem.iImage = 1;
```

```
m_TabCtrl.InsertItem( 1, &pTabCtrlItem );       // second tab
pTabCtrlItem.pszText = "CD-ROM";
pTabCtrlItem.iImage = 2;
m_TabCtrl.InsertItem( 2, &pTabCtrlItem );       // third tab
//
// do image list here
//
m_ImageList.Create(IDB_IMAGEBMP, 16, 1, COLORREF(0xc0c0c0));
m_TabCtrl.SetImageList(&m_ImageList);
//
//  init the tab control & edit box
//
NMHDR nmHDR;
LRESULT pResult;
OnSelchangeTabCtrl(&nmHDR,  &pResult);       // default to floppy

return TRUE;  // return TRUE unless you set the focus to a control
              // EXCEPTION: OCX Property Pages should return FALSE
}
```

This method sets up the tabs and adds them to the tab control. Next, the image list is created and assigned to the tab control. Finally, I fake a click on the first tab to generate some visible output by calling the message handler for a tab click, OnSelchangeTab-Ctrl(). This method determines which tab was clicked. A switch statement then adds dummy text to the edit box. Although this is dummy text, this is where your application would do real work in response to a tab click.

The only other major piece of code used by this example is OnDrawItem(). Because the tab control is owner-drawn, this message handler was added in Class Wizard in response to the WM_DRAWITEM message. That handler is as follows:

```
void CTabDlg::OnDrawItem(int nIDCtl, LPDRAWITEMSTRUCT lpDrawItemStruct)
{
    if(nIDCtl == IDC_TABCTRL)
    {
        CRect rect = lpDrawItemStruct->rcItem;
        int nTabIndex = lpDrawItemStruct->itemID;
        if (nTabIndex < 0)  // nothing to do
            return;
        BOOL bTabSelected =  m_TabCtrl.GetCurSel();
        //
        char label[32];
        switch(nTabIndex) // respond to tab click, draw text & icon
        {
        default:
        case 0:
            strcpy(label,"Floppy Drive");
            break;
        case 1:
            strcpy(label,"Hard Drive");
```

```
        break;
    case 2:
        strcpy(label,"CD-ROM");
        break;
    }
    TC_ITEM tcItem;     // the TC_ITEM structure
    tcItem.mask = TCIF_TEXT | TCIF_IMAGE;
    tcItem.pszText = label;
    tcItem.cchTextMax = 32;
    tcItem.iImage = nTabIndex; // my image index...
    //
    CDC* pDC = CDC::FromHandle(lpDrawItemStruct->hDC);
    if (!pDC)
        return;
    int nOldDC = pDC->SaveDC();

    // For some reason the rcItem extends above the actual
    // drawing area. This is a workaround for this "feature".
    //
    rect.top += ::GetSystemMetrics(SM_CYEDGE);
    pDC->SetBkMode(TRANSPARENT);
    pDC->FillSolidRect(rect, ::GetSysColor(COLOR_BTNFACE));

    // Draw image
    CImageList* pImageList = m_TabCtrl.GetImageList();
    if (pImageList && tcItem.iImage >= 0)
    {
        rect.left += pDC->GetTextExtent(_T(" ")).cx;  // Margin
        IMAGEINFO info;
        pImageList->GetImageInfo(tcItem.iImage, &info);
        CRect ImageRect(info.rcImage);
        int nYpos = rect.top;
        pImageList->Draw(pDC, tcItem.iImage,
            CPoint(rect.left, nYpos
            ILD_TRANSPARENT);
        rect.left += ImageRect.Width();
    }
    if (nTabIndex)
    {
        rect.top -= ::GetSystemMetrics(SM_CYEDGE);
        pDC->DrawText(label, rect, DT_SINGLELINE | DT_VCENTER |
            DT_CENTER);
    }
    else
    {
        pDC->DrawText(label, rect, DT_SINGLELINE | DT_BOTTOM |
            DT_CENTER);
    }
    pDC->RestoreDC(nOldDC);
}
```

```
    else
        CDialog::OnDrawItem(nIDCtl, lpDrawItemStruct);
}     // end OnDrawItem()
```

Here is where all the real work gets done. This method first checks to see if the tab control needs to be drawn. This test is necessary in case you have more than one owner-drawn control on the dialog. If so, it obtains the tab clicked by the user, and (you guessed it) prepares a TC_ITEM structure to draw. Before it can be drawn, the rcItem member of the lpDrawItemStruct structure is adjusted. Left as is, the program would draw an icon in the upper-left corner of the tab, instead of centering it vertically on the left side. The line

```
    rect.top += ::GetSystemMetrics(SM_CYEDGE);
```

stretches out the bounding rectangle so that the graphics appear as desired. To see the effects of this, comment out this line in the code and run it.

You could do other things, such as changing the text color or the font, to enhance your application. To make this example more robust, I added tool tips. Here is that message handler:

```
BOOL CTabDlg::MyToolTips(UINT id, TOOLTIPTEXT * pNMHDR,
    LRESULT * pResult )
{
    TOOLTIPTEXT *pTTT = (TOOLTIPTEXT *)pNMHDR;
    UINT nID = pTTT->uFlags;
    //
    if(pTTT->hdr.idFrom == 0)
    {
        pTTT->lpszText = "Floppy drive properties";
        return TRUE;
    }
    if(pTTT->hdr.idFrom == 1)
    {
        pTTT->lpszText = "Hard drive properties";
        return TRUE;
    }
    if(pTTT->hdr.idFrom == 2)
    {
        pTTT->lpszText = "CDROM drive properties";
        return TRUE;
    }
    return FALSE;
}   // end MyToolTips()
```

Remember, this is a dummy example, so you might want to tighten up this code before using it in your applications. For example, you could #define the tab numbers instead of using the numbers 0–2 throughout the code.

```
#define FLOPPY_TAB 0
#define HARD_TAB 1
#define CDROM_TAB 2
```

Then you could replace code in the tool tip message handler with

```
if(pTTT->hdr.idFrom == FLOPPY_TAB)
{
    pTTT->lpszText = "Floppy drive properties";
    return TRUE;
}
```

This makes it easier for the user to determine the meaning of the tab(s); this is especially useful when you have more than just a few tabs as in this example.

Summary

The tab control is not appropriate for every situation. Only you can decide what applications would benefit from its use. But for those times when you can use it, it makes for an elegant addition to the user interface. I've used it in a project where I selectively hide/show controls based on the tab clicked by the user, which allows me to cram a lot of functionality into just a little space. You're sure to find uses like this, too.

The next chapter shows you how to place controls directly in your view window by using class CFormView.

CHAPTER 19

Class CFormView

This chapter deviates a bit from the beaten path and takes a look at a somewhat mysterious and often misunderstood class known as CFormView. While not every application can, or should, make use of this class, there are times when CFormView will save the day. CFormView is the base class for views in which controls are visible and accessible. CFormView is a great way to add form-based documents to an application. And because CFormView supports scrolling, your document view looks like one big sheet of paper. This eliminates the need for dialog boxes; the user simply fills in the values on the screen. If your application can fit comfortably in a window and is fairly simple, consider using class CFormView. Examples of this genre include data entry screens (literally, a form edited by the operator), process control, and security systems. Don't confuse this with applications created as CDialog objects in App Wizard, which are similar to CFormView.

Let's take a look at class CFormView and the steps you'll need to take to successfully create an application with this class. You'll find a complete CFormView project on the companion Web site in the Example4 project. This project forms the basis of the sample code discussed in this chapter.

Creating a CFormView Object

There are five basic steps you'll need to follow to create a CFormView-based application:

1. Design a dialog template.
2. Create a view class.
3. Override OnUpdate().

4. Transfer data.

5. Connect the view class.

As you read through them, notice how similar they are to the steps for creating a CDialog application.

Step 1: Design a Dialog Template

At the heart of the CFormView process is the idea of embedding controls in a view instead of in a modal dialog box. With CFormView, the application can be SDI or MDI, which avoids a separate message queue like those in a dialog box. You will still need the controls, so Step 1 is to use the dialog editor to design a dialog template. Create the dialog box and add the controls your application requires to support its design requirements. Figure 19.1 shows the example dialog box in App Studio.

Once the dialog box is configured, adjust its properties. Open the property sheet for the dialog and assign the following properties:

- In the Style box, check the Child (WS_CHILD on) box.
- In the Border box, select None (WS_BORDER off).
- Clear the Visible checkbox (WS_VISIBLE off).
- Clear the Titlebar checkbox (WS_CAPTION off).

In Figure 19.1, notice how these properties appear in the dialog template. Although the example has only a few controls, you might want more text, which eats up screen real estate. Don't worry. Because all the controls end up in your view, scrolling is supported. And the view leads us to Step 2.

Step 2: Create a View Class

The next step is to create a view class. This will lead to some work in the InitInstance() method of your application when the document template is created. While still in the dialog editor, start Class Wizard to assign your dialog template to a class. This is where you normally create a CDialog object. Instead, choose CFormView as the class type.

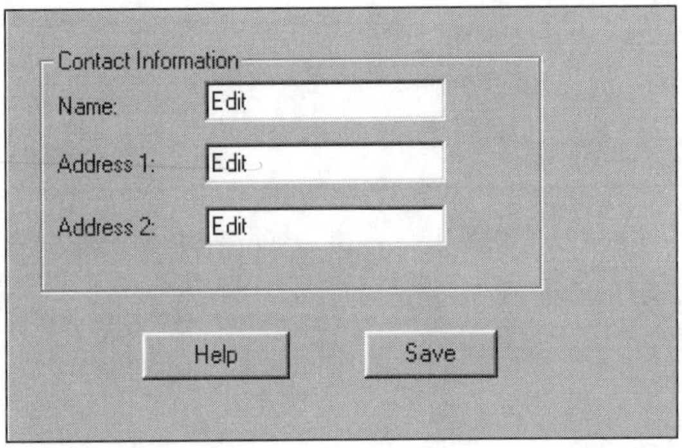

Figure 19.1 Creating a dialog resource.

Class Wizard creates a connection between this class and the dialog box. The connection is established in your class's constructor. That is, the CFormView base class constructor is called and is passed the resource ID you assigned in Step 1. For example,

```
CMyFormView::CMyFormView()
    : CFormView( CMyFormView::IDD)
{
    //{{AFX_DATA_INIT( CMyFormView )
    // NOTE: the ClassWizard will add member
    // initialization here
    //}}AFX_DATA_INIT
    // Other construction code, such as data initialization
}
```

It is the statement shown in bold that it is important—this is where your new class name (defined when you created the dialog resource) will go. If you don't use Class Wizard, you'll have to define the appropriate ID to pass to the CFormView constructor. It's quicker and easier to use the Wizard, because the Wizard declares IDD as an enum value for your class.

Although this example doesn't use them, you can use member variables with the controls. To do use member variables, use the Edit Variables button in the ClassWizard dialog box. This will give you access to the Dialog Data eXchange (DDX) mechanism and thus make it easier to read/write the controls. For your message and notification handlers, just click the Add Function button while in the Class Wizard dialog box.

We're moving along now at a pretty good clip. The next step is to make sure we can update the form's appearance.

Step 3: Override OnUpdate()

Next, override OnUpdate() in your application's view class. This member function is called to update the Form view's visual appearance. Here is where you initialize the Form view by updating any member variables from the current document. If you are using DDX, override the UpdateData() member function in CWnd and pass it a value of FALSE to update your CFormView's controls. Although this example doesn't use DDX or member variables, this override is included in the sample code as a reminder:

```
void CExample4View::OnUpdate(CView* pSender,LPARAM lHint,CObject* pHint)
{
    // TODO: Add your specialized code here and/or call the base class
}
```

The next step is to exchange data with the controls in the view.

Step 4: Transfer Data

For this step, create a member function in your new class to transfer data between the document and the view. This handler takes care of notification messages in addition to menu commands. When using DDX, call the UpdateData() member function to update the member variables in your view class. Then transfer their values to the document associated with the Form view.

If your application will support printing, also override the OnPrint() member function. The class CFormView does not support printing and print preview by default, so you'll need to set this up if desired.

Step 5: Connect the View Class

The last step is to connect your view class with a document class and a Frame-Window class using a document template. This takes place in your application's InitInstance() method. Here is a before and after look at implementing Step 5 taken from the Example4 project on the companion Web Site. When App Wizard created the Example4 project, the document creation appeared as follows:

```
CSingleDocTemplate* pDocTemplate;
pDocTemplate = new CSingleDocTemplate(
    IDR_MAINFRAME,
    RUNTIME_CLASS(CExample4Doc),
    RUNTIME_CLASS(CMainFrame),         // main SDI frame window
    RUNTIME_CLASS(CExample4View));
AddDocTemplate(pDocTemplate);
```

Now it looks like this:

```
CSingleDocTemplate* pDocTemplate;
pDocTemplate = new CSingleDocTemplate(
    IDR_MAINFRAME,
    RUNTIME_CLASS(CExample4Doc),
    RUNTIME_CLASS(CMainFrame),  // main SDI frame window
    RUNTIME_CLASS(CFmrClass));  // My CFormView here!
AddDocTemplate(pDocTemplate);
```

That's all there is to creating a CFormView-based application. There are still a few things you need to be aware of, like painting situations. Because controls are able to paint themselves, it isn't necessary to override the OnDraw() member function defined by CView. But if you plan on doing anything cool with your application, or even if you want to change the background color, you'll need to override this member function. An example of this appears in the sample program later in this chapter.

If the view becomes smaller than the dialog template, scrollbars appear automatically. Also, views derived from CFormView support only the MM_TEXT mapping mode. Remember this when you override OnDraw().

CSliderCtrl and CSpinButtonCtrl Problems

If the dialog resource used to create your CFormView object contains any slide controls or spinners, and you need to handle WM_HSCROLL or WM_VSCROLL messages, and any other messages used by these controls that will require a response by your program.

If your view contains controls that are derived from or are instances of CSliderCtrl or CSpinButtonCtrl, and you have message handlers for WM_HSCROLL and WM_VSCROLL, write code that calls the proper routines. The following example calls CWnd::OnHScroll() if a WM_HSCROLL message is sent by either a spinner or slider control.

```
void CFmrClass::OnHScroll( UINT nSBCode, UINT nPos,
    CScrollBar* pScrollBar)
{
    if ( pScrollBar->IsKindOf( RUNTIME_CLASS( CScrollBar )))
    {
        CFormView::OnHScroll( nSBCode, nPos, pScrollBar );
    }
    else if ( pScrollBar->IsKindOf( RUNTIME_CLASS( CSliderCtrl )))
    {
        CWnd::OnHScroll( nSBCode, nPos, pScrollBar );
    }
    else if ( pScrollBar->IsKindOf( RUNTIME_CLASS( CSpinButtonCtrl )))
    {
        CWnd::OnHScroll( nSBCode, nPos, pScrollBar );
    }
}
```

Notice what happens with a scrollbar message as opposed to the message sent by a slider or spinner. With a scrollbar message, you call CFormView's OnHScroll() handler. But if the message is from a slider or spinner control, you call CWnd's handler. This makes sense when you stop and think about it—controls are really nothing more than child windows, so CWnd is a perfect choice.

Class Members

There is only one class member for CFormView, and that is its constructor.

```
CFormView(LPCTSTR lpszTemplateName);
CFormView(UINT nIDTemplate);
```

The constructor is polymorphic; the first line passes the dialog box resource as a NULL-terminated string. The parameter in the second is the ID number of the resource. The CFormView window and its controls are not created until CWnd::Create() is called during the document and view creation process, which in turn is driven by the document template.

That's it for the CFormView class. Let's take a play-by-play look at the sample program from the companion Web site.

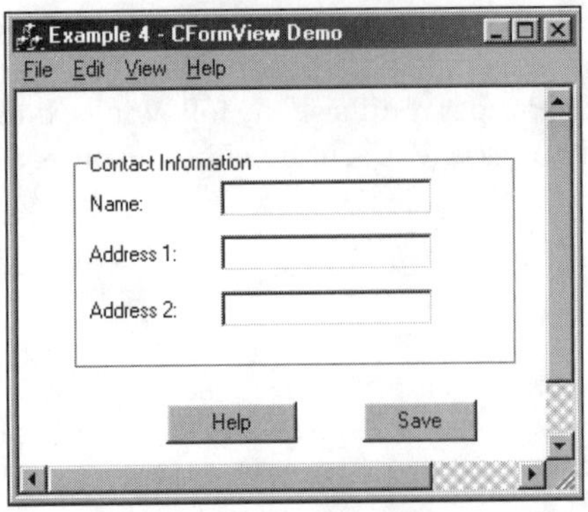

Figure 19.2 Output of Example4 project.

The Sample Program

The sample program can be found in the Example4 project on the companion Web site. This very simple example demonstrates what you can do with CFormView. The output from the program is shown in Figure 19.2.

The most obvious difference between the appearance of the dialog resource and the output is the background color of the sample program. The dialog editor automatically sets the background color to the light gray shown in Figure 19.1, while the sample program uses a white background.

You've already seen the change to the document creation process that takes place in InitInstance(), so I'll skip that and move to the drawing considerations. The following code snippets can be found in the file FmrClass.cpp. Here you'll find two global brushes used to set the background color from gray to white.

```
CBrush backBrush;    // brush of the background color
CBrush OldBrush;     // save old background color
```

When the view constructor is called, the background brush is created. In this case it is a stock white brush.

```
CFmrClass::CFmrClass()
    : CFormView(CFmrClass::IDD)
{
    //{{AFX_DATA_INIT(CFmrClass)
    // NOTE: the ClassWizard will add member initialization here
    //}}AFX_DATA_INIT
    backBrush.CreateSolidBrush(GetSysColor(COLOR_WINDOW));// new brush
}
```

Naturally, this rascal gets destroyed when the destructor is called.

```
CFmrClass::~CFmrClass()
```

```
{
    backBrush.DeleteObject();    // delete background brush
}
```

This brush is used to change the dialog box's natural color by manually adding a handler for the WM_ERASEBKGND message. To do this, edit the message map in FmrClass.cpp.

```
BEGIN_MESSAGE_MAP(CFmrClass, CFormView)
    //{{AFX_MSG_MAP(CFmrClass)
    ON_WM_CTLCOLOR()
    ON_WM_ERASEBKGND()
//}}AFX_MSG_MAP
END_MESSAGE_MAP()
```

The code for the message handler is pretty straightforward, too. It gets the window rectangle and paints it white.

```
BOOL CFmrClass::OnEraseBkgnd(CDC* pDC)
{
    // Save old brush, get white brush
    CBrush* OldBrush = pDC->SelectObject(&backBrush);
    //
    CRect rect;
    pDC->GetClipBox(&rect);   // Erase the area needed

    pDC->PatBlt(rect.left, rect.top, rect.Width(),
        rect.Height(), PATCOPY);
    pDC->SelectObject(&OldBrush); // restore old brush
    return TRUE;
}
```

There is one more thing that has to be done regarding painting. If you ran the program at this point, you'd get the output shown in Figure 19.3.

Something isn't right with this picture! The problem is, you need to handle the WM_CTLCOLOR message, too. At this point, the controls are drawing themselves, but they're using the system background color brush. To create a nice smooth color surface, trap this message and return the white brush. For example,

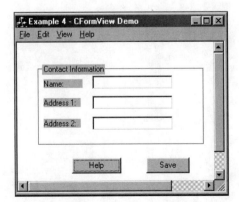

Figure 19.3 Controls not painted properly.

```
HBRUSH CFmrClass::OnCtlColor(CDC* pDC, CWnd* pWnd, UINT nCtlColor)
{
    return backBrush;  // white brush
}
```

Adding this handler produces the output shown in Figure 19.2.

Summary

This has been another one of those easy chapters—there just isn't that much you can say or do with a CFormView-based application after you've figured out how to create one. The ability to mix controls with a view can sometimes be the best solution for your application. The most likely candidates for class CFormView are those applications that convert legacy systems to Windows applications with fill-in-the-blank data-entry forms. Keep an eye out for opportunities to use this technique.

The next chapter should be a lot of fun—it's a hodgepodge of little gadgets and gimmicks that you can use to enhance your user interface. These are things that don't fit into any one category, but be sure and read through it. There's a lot of cool stuff coming up. Take a look.

CHAPTER 20

Component Gallery and Special Operations

O ne of the quickest and easiest ways to enhance the user interface is to take advantage of the Component Gallery. These are prepackaged software *widgets* that the framework will incorporate straight into your application. This chapter gives you the nickel tour of some of these components.

This chapter also is more or less a catchall for the plethora of little things that don't seem to fall into one particular classification or the other. These pertain to those elements that, when properly applied, add a nice touch to the user interface. Some of these are objects provided by the Component Gallery, such as Tip of the Day popup windows and the About box, while others are based on MFC classes such as context menus and customizing the MDI file New dialog.

Context Menus

Context menus, also known as popup or right-click menus, provide a simple yet powerful way to enhance your user interface. This section takes you through the steps for adding these to your applications, and points out a few idiosyncrasies along the way. The sample program on the companion Web site, Example1, has a context menu installed. Figure 20.1 shows a portion of the screen after a right-click in the view.

The context menu in this example doesn't do any real work, it just changes the background color of the view when you select one of the colors. However, you could adapt it to start up one of the dialog boxes from the Controls option on the main menubar. As with all the other controls and enhancements to the user interface, deciding when and where to use context menus is the real challenge.

Figure 20.1   The context menu from the sample program.

Context menus can provide specific options not found elsewhere in the application, or they can simply mirror the options found on the main menu. One of their strongest features is the fact that they're immediately available. The user doesn't have to shift his or her focus to the menubar in order to make a selection. He or she can simply right-click the mouse at the current work location on the screen. This prevents distraction and helps to keep the user on track. In addition, context menus can be used to present only those options that are most frequently used instead of a large choice of options available from toolbars and the main menubar.

Creating Context Menus

The first step in creating context menus is to decide what options are going to be on your popup menu. The nature of your choices will help you decide from where to call your menu (for example, from your document, view, or framework). For example, if a popup menu is concerned with painting the screen, add it to the view class. If a popup allows the user to open and save documents, you'd probably want to call it from your document class.

Regardless of its purpose, you need to first create the menu in App Studio. To add a context menu, open App Studio and create a new menu. This menu will only have one item on the main bar, which you can rename. This text is not displayed when the popup is drawn. It allows you to add the options under it. Figure 20.2 shows the sample menu built in App Studio.

After building the menu and deciding the class from which it will be called, use Class Wizard to override the WM_CONTEXTMENU message. The following is the handler for this message in the example.

Figure 20.2   Using App Studio to create the context menu.

```
void CExample1View::OnContextMenu(CWnd* pWnd, CPoint point)
{
    HWND hWndParent = pWnd->GetSafeHwnd();
    pWnd->GetWindowRect(&rWindow);// need window rect. for painting
    rWindow.NormalizeRect();
    //
    CMenu* pPopMain;  // the main menu bar of my popup
    CMenu* pPopup;    // the drop-down menu options part of pPopMain
    AfxGetApp()->m_pMainWnd->GetWindowRect(&rWindow);
    HINSTANCE hInstance = AfxGetInstanceHandle();
    HMENU hMenu = LoadMenu(hInstance,
        MAKEINTRESOURCE(IDR_CONTEXT_MENU));
    pPopMain = CMenu::FromHandle(hMenu);    // get main popup
    pPopup = pPopMain->GetSubMenu(0);       // get drop-down popup
    UINT iResult;                           // the user's selection
    //
    // add a title/label to the context menu
    //
    pPopup->InsertMenu(0, MF_BYPOSITION | MF_SEPARATOR, 0, "Colors");
    pPopup->InsertMenu(0, MF_BYPOSITION | MF_STRING | MF_DISABLED,
        0,"Colors");
    //
    iResult = TrackPopupMenu(pPopup->m_hMenu ,TPM_LEFTBUTTON |
        TPM_LEFTALIGN | TPM_RETURNCMD , point.x, point.y,
        0,hWndParent,NULL);
    switch(iResult)
    {
        case IDM_RED:// user clicked the "Red" option
            iColor = IDM_RED;
            AfxGetApp()->m_pMainWnd->InvalidateRect(&rWindow,FALSE);
            break;
        case IDM_GREEN:
            iColor = IDM_GREEN;
            AfxGetApp()->m_pMainWnd->InvalidateRect(&rWindow,FALSE);
            break;
        case IDM_BLUE:
            iColor = IDM_BLUE;
            AfxGetApp()->m_pMainWnd->InvalidateRect(&rWindow,FALSE);
            break;
        case IDM_YELLOW:
            iColor = IDM_YELLOW;
            AfxGetApp()->m_pMainWnd->InvalidateRect(&rWindow,FALSE);
            break;
        case IDM_WHITE:
            iColor = IDM_WHITE;
            AfxGetApp()->m_pMainWnd->InvalidateRect(&rWindow,FALSE);
            break;
        default:
            break;
    }
    DestroyMenu(hMenu);    // don't forget this!!
}        // end OnContextMenu()
```

Most of this message handler deals with painting the screen (the switch statement). The important part is the call to TrackPopupMenu(). This API does all the heavy lifting for you and is prototyped as follows:

```
BOOL TrackPopupMenu(HMENU hMenu, UINT nFlags,int x,int y,CWnd* pWnd,
    LPCRECT lpRect=NULL );
```

The return value from the CMenu class function is nonzero if the function was successful, and zero if it failed. The first parameter, hMenu, is the HMENU handle to the popup menu. The nFlags parameter is a combination of screen-positioning and mouse-button data. The screen-position flag can be one of the following:

TPM_CENTERALIGN. Centers the popup menu horizontally relative to the coordinate specified by the x parameter.

TPM_LEFTALIGN. Positions the popup menu so that its left side is aligned with the coordinate specified by x.

TPM_RIGHTALIGN. Positions the popup menu so that its right side is aligned with the coordinate specified by x. The mouse-button flag can be one of the following:

TPM_LEFTBUTTON. Causes the popup menu to track (respond to) the left mouse button.

TPM_RIGHTBUTTON. Causes the popup menu to track the right mouse button.

There are two more special flags used to determine the user's selection without having to set up a parent window for the menu.

TPM_NONOTIFY. If this flag is set, the function does not send notification messages when the user clicks a menu item.

TPM_RETURNCMD. If this flag is set, the function returns the menu item identifier of the user's selection in the return value. In this case, the return value is of type UINT, not BOOL, so be careful about data-typing your variables and testing their values.

The x parameter is the horizontal position of the popup menu in screen coordinates, and the y parameter is the vertical position of the top of the menu. The pWnd parameter is a pointer to the window that owns the popup menu. Finally, the lpRect points to RECT or CRect object containing the screen coordinates of a rectangle that defines a region within which the user can click without closing the popup menu. If this is NULL, the popup is closed when the user clicks outside the popup.

By default, context menus don't have a title, but they're easy to add. Look again at these lines:

```
pPopup->InsertMenu(0, MF_BYPOSITION | MF_SEPARATOR, 0, "Colors");
pPopup->InsertMenu(0, MF_BYPOSITION | MF_STRING | MF_DISABLED,
    0,"Colors");
```

Here is a little trick that might come in handy. To add a title, create a separator and set its text to the title you want to use (in this case, Colors). Then, insert the title making sure the MF_DISABLED flag is set but not the MF_GRAYED. This prevents the user from selecting Colors, but doesn't change its display properties.

The only thing left to do in the Example1 sample code is to paint the background. This example used Class Wizard to override the WM_ERASEBKG message. Examine the file Example1View.cpp for all the details regarding this phase of the program. But as you can see from the previous code snippet, there really isn't much to creating and using a popup menu.

A Better About Box

When you create an App Wizard-based MFC application, the framework builds an About box for you. This dialog box is frequently overlooked by developers, but can easily be modified to provide the user with more than just your product version number and address! It's easy to jazz this up with sound or an animation clip. This box can also be used to report how much disk space/memory your application consumes, and to provide a command button that launches an Internet browser that connects the user to your Web site. You can even add a command button that launches the user's email package to send you questions and comments.

The sample code for this discussion is found on the companion Web site in the Example3 project. Figure 20.3 shows the About box from the Example3 project.

Because the About box for this application has some interesting properties, I'll discuss the sample code in sections. The first section is OnInitDialog().

```
BOOL CAboutDlg::OnInitDialog()
{
    m_Email.AutoLoad(IDC_EMAIL_BTN,this); // bitmap email button
    CDialog::OnInitDialog();

    // TODO: Add extra initialization here

    return TRUE;  // return TRUE
}
```

Here, a bitmap of an envelope is added to the command button that launches the installed email program. The next important message handler is OnSetCursor(). This message is trapped in order to change the cursor to a pointing finger whenever the cursor is over the email button. Examine the following code:

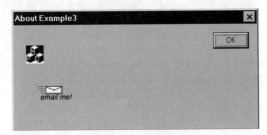

Figure 20.3 The About box from Example3.

```
BOOL CAboutDlg::OnSetCursor(CWnd* pWnd, UINT nHitTest, UINT message)
{
    // TODO: Add your message handler code here and/or call default
    //
    // if cursor is over the button, change to a pointing hand
    //
    CRect rect;
    m_Email.GetWindowRect(&rect);
    rect.NormalizeRect();
    POINT pt;
    GetCursorPos(&pt);        // where is the cursor?
    if(rect.PtInRect(pt ))   // over the email button!
    {
        CString strWndDir;
        GetWindowsDirectory(strWndDir.GetBuffer(MAX_PATH), MAX_PATH);
        strWndDir.ReleaseBuffer();
        strWndDir += _T("\\winhlp32.exe");
        // This gets cursor #106 from winhlp32.exe a hand pointer
        HMODULE hModule = LoadLibrary(strWndDir);
        if (hModule)
        {
            HCURSOR hHandCursor = ::LoadCursor(hModule,
                MAKEINTRESOURCE(106));
            if (hHandCursor)
                SetCursor(hHandCursor);
        }
        FreeLibrary(hModule);
        return TRUE;
    }    // end if cursor over email button
    return CDialog::OnSetCursor(pWnd, nHitTest, message);
}    // end OnSetCursor()
```

This code demonstrates how you can use the existing MFC cursors. Because these are discardable resources that are loaded from libraries, they are available for your use.

The following is the message handler for when the email button is clicked.

```
void CAboutDlg::OnEmailBtn()
{
    // TODO: Add your control notification handler code here
    TCHAR key[MAX_PATH + MAX_PATH];
    CString url = "mailto:kbugg@qsystems.net"; // MY EMAIL ADDRESS!!
    //
    // First try ShellExecute()
    //
    HINSTANCE result = ShellExecute(NULL,
     _T("open"), url, NULL,NULL,
        SW_NORMAL);
    //
    // If it failed, get the .htm regkey and lookup the program
    //
```

```
    if ((UINT)result <= HINSTANCE_ERROR)
    {
        if (GetRegKey(HKEY_CLASSES_ROOT, _T(".htm"),
            key) == ERROR_SUCCESS)
        {
            lstrcat(key, _T("\\shell\\open\\command"));
            if (GetRegKey(HKEY_CLASSES_ROOT,
                key,key) == ERROR_SUCCESS)
            {
                TCHAR *pos;
                pos = _tcsstr(key, _T("\"%1\""));
                if (pos == NULL)
                {                           // No quotes found
                    pos = strstr(key,_T("%1"));
                    if (pos == NULL)  // No parameter
                        pos = key+lstrlen(key)-1;
                    else
                        *pos = '\0';// Remove parm.
                }
                else
                    *pos = '\0';// Remove parm.

                lstrcat(pos, _T(" "));
                lstrcat(pos, url);
                result = (HINSTANCE) WinExec(key,SW_SHOWNORMAL);
            }
        }
    }    // end if ShellExecute() failed
}
```

The nice thing about this segment of code is it can be used to launch the installed Internet browser and take the user to a Web URL. To do this, replace the line

```
CString url = "mailto:kbugg@qsystems.net";
```

with something like the following:

```
CString url = "http://wwwdev.qsystems.net/tristar/kbugg.htm";
```

If the installed email program/Internet browser fails to run via ShellExecute(), the WinExec() tries to find the registry key to launch them. Here is that method:

```
LONG CAboutDlg::GetRegKey(HKEY key, LPCTSTR subkey, LPTSTR retdata)
{
    HKEY hkey;
    LONG retval = RegOpenKeyEx(key, subkey,
        0, KEY_QUERY_VALUE, &hkey)

    if (retval == ERROR_SUCCESS)
    {
        long datasize = MAX_PATH;
```

```
        TCHAR data[MAX_PATH];
        RegQueryValue(hkey, NULL, data, &datasize);
        lstrcpy(retdata,data);
        RegCloseKey(hkey);
    }
    return retval;
}
```

With just these few lines of code, you can greatly enhance your application's interface by providing the user with direct access to your Web site or help desk.

The component gallery also lets you include the amount of free disk space on the user's default disk. You'll find an example of this on the Web site in the Example1 project. To add this, select System Info for About Dlg in the gallery. The framework will add all the code you need except for a static text field in which to display the memory results. To add this, open your dialog box with the Dialog Editor and add two static text fields. Look for the TODO comments in your application's CAboutDlg::OnInit-Dialog() method, and uncomment them.

```
SetDlgItemText(IDC_PHYSICAL_MEM, strFreeMemory);
SetDlgItemText(IDC_DISK_SPACE, strFreeDiskSpace);
```

Figure 20.4 shows the About box for the Example1 project with these features added.

Tip of the Day Popup

The Tip of the Day feature adds the finishing touches to your application. This feature, shown in Figure 20.5, acts as a guardian angel and mini-tutorial, guiding the new user over the learning curve, and shedding new light on features sported by your application. Notice the checkbox that allows the user to turn the feature off after he or she has become familiar with the application.

Adding this feature to your application is mere child's play, because Visual C++ gives it to you for free, thanks to the power of COM. Figure 20.6 shows the Components and Controls Gallery provided by Visual C++.

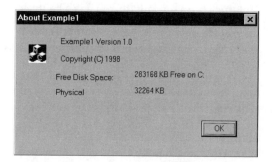

Figure 20.4   The About box for Example1.

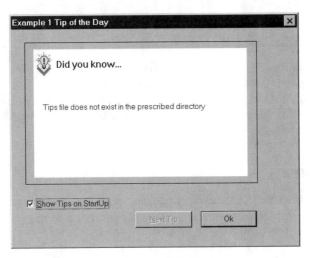

Figure 20.5 Tip of the Day dialog box.

To add the Tip of the Day dialog box, simply select it from the gallery. The framework will do all the work for you by modifying your code. All you'll need to do is create a file called Tips.txt and include it with your application. By default, this file goes in the same directory as your executable, but you can modify the code if desired. For example, you might want to specify a separate directory in your application's INI file. If you do chose to modify the code, make sure you modify your TipDlg.cpp file accordingly.

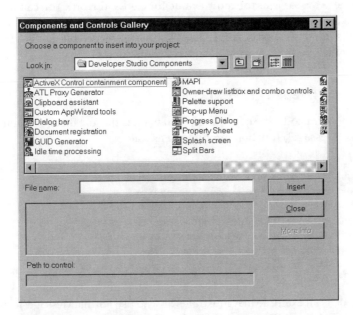

Figure 20.6 The Components and Controls Gallery.

Error Handling

Another way to enhance your application is to ensure that you've built in adequate error trapping and reporting. MFC provides you with two very useful functions, GetLastError() and FormatMessage(), for just this purpose. The GetLastError()method can be called to return an error code from some operation. The FormatMessage() method converts that code into a text message.

GetLastError() Function

Many of the Win32 API functions return a last-error code value when an error is encountered. This value can be retrieved by your application and used to display an error message. The prototype for the function is

```
DWORD GetLastError(VOID)
```

The return value is the code. You can find all these in the file WINERROR.H in your Visual C++ \INCLUDE directory. This function works on both single and multi-threaded applications. Multiple threads do not overwrite each other's last-error code, so you can always be assured your thread has the right error code.

The GetLastError() function works whenever an API uses the function to set the error condition. The function is prototyped as

```
void SetLastError(DWORD dwErrCode)
```

where dwErrCode is the same as the return value for GetLastError(). You can use these two functions to create your own custom error codes that apply to your application. The only caveat is that you must set bit 29 to 1. This is a reserved bit that is 0 for error codes defined by the operating system, which prevents conflict.

Retrieving the Error Message Text

Once you have the error code, the next thing you'll want is the text that goes along with it. Use the FormatMessage() function, prototyped as follows:

```
DWORD FormatMessage(
DWORD dwFlags, // source and processing options
LPCVOID lpSource, // pointer to message source
DWORD dwMessageId, // requested message identifier
DWORD dwLanguageId, // language identifier for message
LPTSTR lpBuffer, // pointer to message buffer
DWORD nSize, // maximum size of message buffer
va_list *Arguments // address of array of message inserts
);
```

The following code is an example that illustrates how to use FormatMessage(). First, an error code is deliberately set. Next, a call toGetLastError() is made followed by a call to FormatMessage(). The output is displayed in a TRACE message.

```
char * lpMsgBuffer;
DWORD dwErr = ERROR_FILE_NOT_FOUND;
SetLastError(dwErr);// set the error code here to file not found
dwErr = GetLastError();// now get the error code and format it
FormatMessage(
FORMAT_MESSAGE_ALLOCATE_BUFFER | FORMAT_MESSAGE_FROM_SYSTEM,
NULL,dwErr,
MAKELANGID(LANG_NEUTRAL, SUBLANG_DEFAULT),(LPTSTR) &  lpMsgBuffer,0,
NULL );
TRACE("%s\n",lpMsgBuffer);
```

When this code is executed, the message

```
The system cannot find the file specified.
```

is displayed by the TRACE statement. You also could display these error messages in an AfxMessageBox() function to the user.

Customizing MDI File New

This section shows you how to modify the default behavior when the user selects a New file in an MDI application for which more than one document class has been defined. Normally, an MDI application gives you a list of files based on the extension specified in your string table (for example, .abc). You can also define a new document type for your application and specify an additional extension such as .def. Common examples of software that support this functionality include Microsoft's Excel and Word programs. For example, in Word, you can open files having the extensions .rtf, .txt, or .doc.

To allow your application to use files with different extensions, first modify your application's InitInstance() method and specify the new document type. For example,

```
CMultiDocTemplate* pDocTemplate;
pDocTemplate = new CMultiDocTemplate(
    IDR_MYAPP_TYPE1,               // first type of file/project
    RUNTIME_CLASS(CMyAppDoc),
    RUNTIME_CLASS(CChildFrame), // custom MDI child frame
    RUNTIME_CLASS(CMyAppView));
AddDocTemplate(pDocTemplate);
//
pDocTemplate = new CMultiDocTemplate(
    IDR_MYAPP_TYPE2,               // second type of file/project
    RUNTIME_CLASS(CMyAppDoc),
    RUNTIME_CLASS(CChildFrame), // custom MDI child frame
    RUNTIME_CLASS(CMyAppView));
AddDocTemplate(pDocTemplate);
```

Next, define the additional types in your string table.

```
IDR_MYAPP_TYPE1
\nMy App-Untitled\nMy App's Project\nType 1 (*.abc) and
IDR_MYAPP_TYPE2
\nMy App-Untitled\nMy App's Project\nType 2 (*.def)
```

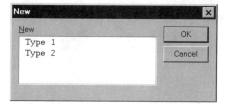

Figure 20.7 The CNewTypeDlg dialog box.

If you don't need any special processing or customization when the user specifies a new file, MFC will display a dialog box with all your document types listed in a list-box. The user simply picks one and clicks OK. You don't create this dialog box—MFC gives it to you. It is an undocumented class called CNewTypeDlg that can be found in the MFC source file docmgr.cpp. The default dialog box is shown in Figure 20.7.

If you use App Wizard to create an MDI application, the default is the dialog box shown in Figure 20.7 if you've specified additional document types in your InitIn-stance() method. Your application calls CWinApp::OnFileNew(). Look at your default message map to verify this.

Suppose you want the user to specify additional features pertinent to your application; for example, to draw in color on a black and white background (a poor example, but you get the idea). If you don't provide a custom dialog box, the user must first select a file type from the dialog shown in Figure 20.7, then your application must give the user another prompt to specify the color/black and white option. This is very messy and annoying. The solution is to override OnFileNew() and create a custom dialog box that prompts the user for all the details on one screen. You need to create this dialog box and assign it a class, and call this dialog box in your OnFileNew() method. Here is an example of this new class's OnInitDialog() method:

```
BOOL CNewDlg::OnInitDialog()
{
    CDialog::OnInitDialog();
    //
    // NOTE - "theApp" is the CWinApp object for your
    // app defined at the
    //        start of your .cpp file. E.g.:
    //     extern CMyApp theApp;
    //
    POSITION pos;  // for walking thru list of documents
    pos = theApp.GetFirstDocTemplatePosition();
    //
    CString strTypeName; // document type string
    do
    {
        pTemplate = theApp.GetNextDocTemplate(pos);
        m_templateList.AddTail(pTemplate);
        pTemplate->LoadTemplate();
        m_templateList.AddTail(pTemplate);
```

```
        //
        if (pTemplate->GetDocString(strTypeName,
            CDocTemplate::fileNewName) &&
            !strTypeName.IsEmpty())
        {
            // add it to the listbox
            m_ListBox.AddString(strTypeName);
        }
    }while(pos != NULL);

    m_ListBox.SetCurSel(0);

    return TRUE;
} // end OnInitDialog() for CNewDlg class
```

In this class's header file the following member variables are defined:

```
CPtrList m_templateList;
CDocTemplate* m_pTemplate;
```

The dialog box represented by CNewDlg must have a listbox (pointed to by m_List-Box) and the usual OK/Cancel buttons as well as any special controls you need (such as specifying color or black and white). When the OK button is clicked, you can then see what document type was selected from the listbox and the other controls.

Modifying the file New code brings up an interesting point. There's no law against using the code that comes with MFC in your own applications. The document template in this example uses code from the MFC source. Be on the lookout for opportunities like this when you develop your applications.

The Dialog Bar

Another really cool feature for some applications is the dialog bar. You can think of a dialog bar as a cross between a toolbar and a modeless dialog box. Using a dialog bar is a lot like using the CFormView class in that it uses a dialog resource and contains controls. The functionality is wrapped in the MFC class CDialogBar. Figure 20.8 is an example of a dialog bar.

In Figure 20.8, the dialog bar has been implemented in a manner similar to a docking toolbar—with one listbox control filled with items. The sample project on the companion Web site uses an owner-drawn listbox to enhance the user interface.

Although a dialog bar looks and acts like a toolbar, there are major differences between the two. A dialog bar is created from a dialog template resource in App Studio, and not a separate entity like a toolbar. Because it's a disguised dialog box, additional controls such as the animation control can be included in it. This is a great method to provide an index into a list of video clips; you could give the user a preview of a few frames in an animation control when one of the listbox items is clicked.

The modeless dialog box properties of a dialog bar are reminiscent of the Find-Replace dialog discussed in Chapter 16, "The Find-Replace Dialog." They are really extensions

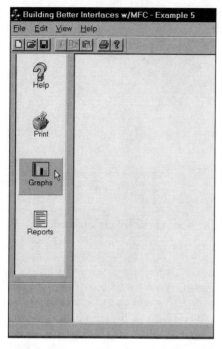

Figure 20.8 A dialog bar from the Example5 project.

to your frame window, and any CDialogBar notification messages like EN_CHANGE or BN_CLICKED are sent to the parent, your CMainFrame class.

Adding a Dialog Bar

Let's go through the steps to add a dialog bar to your application, using the Example5 project from the companion Web site as a model. With your project open, open the Component Gallery and select Dialog Bar. You'll be presented with a dialog box like the one shown in Figure 20.9.

In the example code, the name of the dialog window is changed to ContentMenu, the member variable to m_wndContentMenu, and the docking side to Left. Regardless of your implementation, close all Component Gallery windows. By default, the framework will create a dialog box for you with the resource identifier CG_IDD_CONTENTMENU. This will have one control, a static text control with the caption TODO…. Delete this and replace it with a listbox having the identifier IDC_LIST_CONTENTS. Assign this listbox the following styles:

- Owner-drawn, variable
- No Sort

Next, add the files ContentMenu.cpp and ContentMenu.h to your project. Also #include ContentMenu.h in your MainFrm.h file.

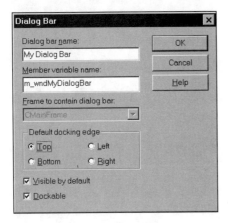

Figure 20.9   The Dialog Bar properties box.

Now define a member variable for the class CContentMenu in your MainFrm.h file.

```
CContentMenu m_ContentMenu;
```

In your OnCreate() function in MainFrm.cpp, add the following code just prior to the return 0 statement at the end of the method.

```
m_ContentMenu.SubclassDlgItem (IDC_LIST_CONTENTS, &m_wndContentMenu);
m_ContentMenu.SetItems(ContentInfo,
    sizeof(ContentInfo) / sizeof(CONTENT_ITEMS));
```

At the beginning of your MainFrm.cpp file, add a structure for storing information about the items listed in the dialog bar's listbox. This example is called ContentInfo.

```
static CONTENT_ITEMS ContentInfo[] =
{
    {IDI_HELP,   "Help"},
    {IDI_PRINT, "Print"},
    {IDI_GRAPH, "Graphs"},
    {IDI_RPTS,   "Reports"},
};
```

Next is to create a way to respond if the user clicks on one of the listbox items by adding a message handler for the LBN_SELCHANGE notification message. Modify the CMainFrame message map so that it looks like this:

```
//}}AFX_MSG_MAP
ON_LBN_SELCHANGE(IDC_LIST_CONTENTS, OnSelchangeListContents)
```

In your MainFrm.h file, add the following line to the message map:

```
afx_msg void OnSelchangeListContents();
```

All you need now is the message handler called OnSelchangeListContents(). The following was used in this example. It displays a message box that indicates what item was selected.

```
void CMainFrame::OnSelchangeListContents()
{
    switch (m_ContentMenu.GetCurSel())
    {
    case 0:
        AfxMessageBox("You have selected the Help item...");
        break;

    case 1:
        AfxMessageBox("You have selected the Print item...");
        break;

    case 2:
        AfxMessageBox("You have selected the Graphs item...");
        break;

    case 3:
        AfxMessageBox("You have selected the Report item...");
        break;
    }
}    // end OnSelchangeListContents()
```

Finally, notice that the images used are icons and not bitmaps. You can easily create these using the icon editor in App Studio.

And that, folks, is a wrap on the dialog bar. As you can imagine, creating this gadget via the Component Gallery saves you tons of time and work. Again, let me stress that you shouldn't go overboard and add things like the dialog bar just because you can—make sure your application has a need for it.

Eliminating Flicker in Controls

Here is something you'll probably want to incorporate into your applications at one time or another—eliminate the momentary flicker that can occur when a control is redrawn. Flicker occurs in the time between when a control is being erased and when the control area is refilled with text, graphics, or the background color. To eliminate flicker you need to follow three steps.

1. Override the OnEraseBkgnd() message handler for the control, as in the following example:

```
BOOL CSomeClass::OnEraseBkgnd(CDC* pDC)
{
    return FALSE;
}
```

2. Override the OnPaint() message handler for the control. The flicker is eliminated by painting the entire control into a memory device context, then copying it back into the original device context using BitBlt(). This step is made all the more easier by class CMemDC. Because the background isn't being erased anymore

(see Step 1), it is necessary to instead erase the memory device context using the control's background color. For example,

```
void CSomeClass::OnPaint()
{
    CPaintDC dc(this); // get the control's DC
    CMemDC memDC(&dc); // memroy DC
    CRect cRect;        // area rectangle
    memDC.GetClipBox(&cRect);
    memDC.FillSolidRect(cRect,GetSysColor(COLOR_WINDOW));
    DefWindowProc(WM_PAINT, (WPARAM)memDC->m_hDC,0L);
}
```

3. Override theEraseBkgnd() method of the control's parent. Actually, the control is almost flicker-free at this point. But if the user does something that causes the background of the dialog to be erased, like resizing the window, the flicker is still present. In this situation, the background of the dialog is erased first, then all the controls in the window. That makes it necessary to exclude the control's area outside of the clipping box of the control's parent. Here is an example:

```
BOOL CParentClass::OnEraseBkgnd(CDC* pDC)
{
    CRect cRect;
    m_Control.GetWindowRect(&cRect);
    ScreenToClient(&cRect);
    pDC->ExcludeClipRect(&cRect);
    //
    pDC->GetClipBox(&cRect);
    pDC->FillSolidRect(cRect,GetSysColor(COLOR_BTNFACE));
    return FALSE;
}
```

These steps will work for most controls, but some will need some extra adjustments; for example, the list control in Report mode. Here you have the column headers, and these will need to be excluded from the clip box. Here is an example:

```
void CSomeClass::OnPaint()
{
    CPaintDC dc(this);
    CRect rHeader;
    GetDlgItem(0)->GetWindowRect(&rHeader);
    ScreenToClient(&rHeader);
    dc.ExcludeClipRect(&rHeader);
    CMemDC memDC(&dc);
    //
    // additional painting code here
    //
}
```

This is a little more work, but your users will be pleased every time they use your application.

Adding a Beveled Separator

A nice touch that you can add to your dialog box is a beveled line separator. App Studio includes the frame component that is similar in function, but sometimes you just need a visual cue that distinguishes one set of controls from another. This section demonstrates how easy it is to do this by including a class from the Example1 project on the companion Web site. The files that implement this class are LineSep.cpp and LineSep.h. Figure 20.10 shows the dialog box from the sample program with the beveled line separator.

The sample program uses this technique in the dialog box that demonstrates owner-drawn command buttons. The files that have the sample code included are ButtDemo.cpp and ButtDemo.h. To use this technique in your own projects, simply add these files to your project and follow the steps.

The first thing you have to do is open your dialog box with the editor and insert a CStatic object at the location you'd like the line to appear. Change the ID from IDC_STATIC to something unique, such as IDC_LINESEP. Next, resize the object giving it the shape of a line, vertical or horizontal.

Now assign the CStatic object a member variable of type control, not value. Open the header file for the dialog box that will use the line separator and #include LineSep.h. Replace the word CStatic with CLineSep, which is the new class name. Build your project and run it.

You can look at the source code for class CLineSep and see there isn't much to it. All the work is done in the OnPaint() method.

```
void CLineSep::OnPaint()
{
    CPaintDC dc(this);  // device context for painting
    CRect r;
```

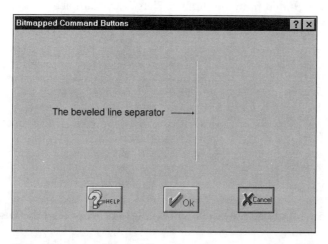

Figure 20.10   A beveled line separator to group controls.

```
      GetClientRect(&r);

      DWORD hiCol = ::GetSysColor(!m_bSunken ? COLOR_3DHIGHLIGHT :
         COLOR_3DSHADOW);
      DWORD loCol = ::GetSysColor(m_bSunken ? COLOR_3DHIGHLIGHT :
         COLOR_3DSHADOW);

      if(r.bottom > r.right) // vertical line
      {
         r.right /= 2;
         r.left = r.right - LineWid;
         r.right += LineWid;
      }
      else                    // horizonzal line
      {
         r.bottom /= 2;
         r.top = r.bottom - LineHi;
         r.bottom += LineHi;
      }
      dc.Draw3dRect(&r,hiCol,loCol);
   } // end OnPaint()
```

The member variable m_bSunken can be changed to FALSE if the line should appear raised, not lowered. You can even switch between the two at runtime by resetting m_bSunken followed by a call to CWnd::Invalidate() andCWnd::UpdateWindow().

Use the beveled line separator anywhere on any dialog box that needs some way to divide its area up into logical areas. The simple presence of this gadget gives the user some idea that each area of the screen/set of controls performs a unique task.

An Internet Browser Application

The Internet is rapidly entrenching itself in Windows applications, and this is a trend that is sure to continue and perhaps accelerate. This section provides sample code to turn your application into a Web browser. The sample code for this project can be found on the companion Web site in the Example7 project. Although this is an SDI application, the same concept applies to MDI applications. You could even turn one of the view windows in the splitter window example found in the next chapter into an Internet browser. In short, you have a lot of power at your fingertips that can be applied to make a better user interface.

Internet Explorer version 3.x comes with a Web browser ActiveX control that can be dropped into your view. In fact, IExplore.exe is just a small application that acts as a host for this control. The most important component that is used to interact with it is IWebBrowser, which is declared in Exdisp.h. This file only ships with Visual C++ version 5.0 and above, so you'll need this version to build the example. Include it in your project's Stdafx.h file. A newer IWebBrowser2 interface has a few new methods, but it is only supported by version 4.x of Internet Explorer, and its definition is not included with Visual C++ 5.0. However, you can still use Developer Studio to create a wrapper class for it.

The Visual C++ 5.0 library uuid.lib doesn't include the definition for IDD_IWeb-Browser or CSLID_WebBrowser, but these can be found in Exdisp.h or the registry. These are defined in the view class for Example7.

```
/* EAB22AC1-30C1-11CF-A7EB-0000C05BAE0B */
IID const IID_IWebBrowser={0xEAB22AC1, 0x30C1, 0x11CF, 0xA7, 0xEB,
    0x00, 0x00, 0xC0, 0x5B, 0xAE, 0x0B};

/* 8856F961-340A-11D0-A96B-00C04FD705A2 */
CLSID const CLSID_WebBrowser={0x8856F961,
    0x340A, 0x11D0, 0xA9, 0x6B,
    0x00, 0xC0, 0x4F, 0xD7, 0x05, 0xA2};
```

The ActiveX control can be added to your application by using CWnd::CreateControl() in your view's Create()method. After it is successfully created, you can use CWnd::GetControlUnknown() to find the control's IUnknown value. Then you can useQueryInterface() to get IID_IWebBrowser. After that, the rest is easy. Let's look at the code that gets this done. The following is the Create()method found in Example7View.cpp.

```
BOOL CExample7View::Create(LPCTSTR lpszClassName,

    LPCTSTR lpszWindowName,
    DWORD dwStyle, const RECT& rect, CWnd* pParentWnd, UINT nID,
    CCreateContext* pContext)
{
    // TODO: Add your specialized code here
    // and/or call the base class
    if (!CView::Create(lpszClassName, lpszWindowName, dwStyle,
        rect, pParentWnd, nID, pContext))
    {
        TRACE("Failed to create view.\n");
        return FALSE;
    }

    CRect client;
    GetClientRect(&client);
    if(!m_wndBrowser.CreateControl(CLSID_WebBrowser, lpszWindowName,
        WS_VISIBLE|WS_CHILD, rect, this, AFX_IDW_PANE_FIRST))
    {
        TRACE("Failed to create Web Browser control window.\n");
        return FALSE;
    }
    IUnknown *pUnk=m_wndBrowser.GetControlUnknown();
    ASSERT(pUnk);
    IWebBrowser *pBrowser;
    HRESULT hr=pUnk->QueryInterface(IID_IWebBrowser,
        (void **)&pBrowser);
    if (!SUCCEEDED(hr))
    {
        TRACE("WebBrowser interface not supported.\n");
        return FALSE;
    }
}
```

```
        // set to my Web page address
        CString url("http://wwwdev.qsystems.net/tristar/kbugg.htm");
        BSTR bUrl=url.AllocSysString();
        hr=pBrowser->Navigate(bUrl, &COleVariant((long)0, VT_I4),
            &COleVariant((LPCTSTR)NULL, VT_BSTR), NULL,
            &COleVariant((LPCTSTR)NULL, VT_BSTR));
        if (!SUCCEEDED(hr))
        {
            AfxMessageBox("ActiveX control could not browse!");
            return FALSE;
        }
        return TRUE;
    }
```

Your view also needs to handle changes in window size. Here is that message handler from the sample code:

```
    void CExample7View::OnSize(UINT nType, int cx, int cy)
    {
        CView::OnSize(nType, cx, cy);
        if (::IsWindow(m_wndBrowser.m_hWnd))
        {
            CRect cRect;
            GetClientRect(&cRect);
            m_wndBrowser.SetWindowPos(NULL, 0, 0,
                cRect.right, cRect.bottom,
                SWP_NOACTIVATE | SWP_NOZORDER);
        }
    }
```

The member variable m_wndBrowser is defined in the view's header file.

```
    protected:

        CWnd m_wndBrowser;      // the browser window/control
        //{{AFX_MSG(CExample7View)
        afx_msg void OnSize(UINT nType, int cx, int cy);
        //}}AFX_MSG
        DECLARE_MESSAGE_MAP()
```

That's all you need to do to add Internet browsing to your applications.

Summary

Hopefully, you've found something useful in this chapter that can be used in your projects. You've seen lots of little goodies that, when properly applied, greatly enhance the user interface. In the next chapter, I'll give you a look at another useful component of MFC, splitter windows.

CHAPTER 21

Splitter Windows

O ne of the most useful user interface enhancements provided by MFC is the splitter window. A splitter window is a window that is divided up into multiple panes, each pane containing a specialized aspect of the application. The MFC class CSplitterWnd provides this functionality. The individual panes of a splitter window are generally objects derived from CView that are geared toward delivering a dedicated service, but it can be any CWnd object. Splitter windows are in some ways a lot like class CFormView.

The Visual C++ workbench is itself a splitter window with panes for editing source files and for errors/debugging. The splitter window in the sample program for this chapter contains a TreeView control, plus an edit control view and a list control view. An illustration of the output from the sample program is shown in Figure 21.1.

Figure 21.1   Splitter window used in sample program.

Splitter windows at first can seem intimidating, but once you grasp the basics they're not that bad. Learning the terminology makes learning how to work with splitters a lot easier. The following are some common terms that will be discussed throughout this chapter.

Pane. Usually a CView object, a pane is an application-specific window managed by a parent window (the splitter window).

Splitter bar. A control placed between rows and columns of panes, used to adjust the size of the panes.

Splitter box. This applies only to dynamic splitters—it's a control placed on the top of the vertical scrollbars to the left of the horizontal scrollbars used to create new rows or columns of panes.

Splitter intersection. The intersection of a horizontal and vertical splitter bar that can be dragged to simultaneously adjust the size of a row and column of panes.

This should make it clearer to understand the components of a splitter window. Now let's get started by taking a broad look at the fundamentals and how they're tied together.

The Basics

Splitter windows come in two flavors: *static* and *dynamic*. The primary difference between the two is that the user can only change the size of the splitter window's panes and not their order or number. Hence, they tend to be simpler and easier to work with. The sample program uses a static splitter. Another difference concerns when the panes are created. In the static variety, panes are created when the splitter window is created. Dynamic panes create and destroy panes as the user splits and unsplits new views. The first pane is always created automatically when the splitter window is created. The window starts out with just a single view, and splitter boxes are provided to allow splitting. If the view is split in one direction, new view objects are dynamically created to represent the pane just created. When a dynamic window is split in two directions (as with the keyboard interface), three new views are created. When the split window has the focus, the splitter box is represented as a splitter bar positioned between the adjacent panes. These new view objects are destroyed when the split is removed, but the original view remains until the splitter window is destroyed. Common software products that use dynamic splitters include Microsoft Excel and Word.

One of the things you have to do when creating a splitter window is indicate the number of columns and rows that the splitter will supervise. For the static variety, panes need to be created that will fill all the rows and columns. The maximum number of panes is 16 rows by 16 columns. Common configurations for static splitters are

- One row, two columns, dissimilar panes
- Two rows, one column, dissimilar panes
- Two rows, two columns, similar panes

For dynamic splitters the maximum number of panes is 2 rows by 2 columns. Common configurations for dynamic splitters are

- One row, two columns; use with columnar data
- Two rows, one column; use with text or other data
- Two rows, two columns; use with matrix or table-oriented data

For the sake of simplicity, this discussion is limited to static windows. The steps to create a static splitter window are as follows:

1. Define a member variable in your CFrameWnd or CMDIChildWnd object.
2. Use Class Wizard to override OnCreateClient() for the parent frame.
3. Call CreateStatic() from inside OnCreateClient().

Step 1 is pretty easy. The following is what the MainFrm.h file in the Example6 project from the companion Web site looks like after Step 1.

```
class CMainFrame : public CFrameWnd
{
protected: // create from serialization only
    CMainFrame();
    DECLARE_DYNCREATE(CMainFrame)
// Attributes
public:
    CSplitterWnd m_wndSplitter;      // splitter window class!!
```

Notice the main frame is made *public*—now everybody can access it.

The method OnCreateClient() is where the CView object for your application is created. The prototype for this method is

```
virtual BOOL OnCreateClient(LPCREATESTRUCT lpcs,CCreateContext*
    pContext);
```

The last step is to actually create the splitter window. Although I'm going to cover CreateStatic() in more detail in a later section, here is an example taken from the sample code:

```
m_wndSplitter.CreateStatic(this, 1, 2)
```

This creates a splitter window containing one row and two columns. Figure 21.1 is in ListView mode and Figure 21.2 shows the application in SplitView mode.

There's more to this than meets the eye, but these are the fundamentals. The views for the panes have to be created, and if you use a CFormView as I do, you still have to create the dialog box template, add the controls you want, and so on. Let's look at the class methods.

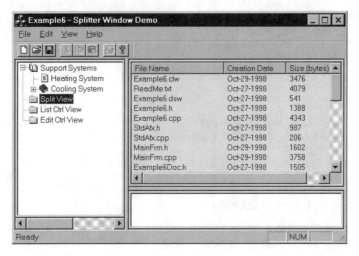

Figure 21.2 The sample splitter window with all panes visible.

Class Methods

The first method is CreateStatic(), prototyped as follows:

```
BOOL CreateStatic( CWnd* pParentWnd, int nRows, int nCols,
    DWORD dwStyle = WS_CHILD | WS_VISIBLE,
    UINT nID = AFX_IDW_PANE_FIRST);
```

This creates the static splitter and attaches it to the CSplitterWnd object. The first parameter is a pointer to the parent frame window, the second and third parameters are the number of rows and columns, respectively. The last two parameters, which default to the values shown if you don't supply them, are the style and ID. For example, the splitter shown in Figure 21.1 was created as follows:

```
if (!m_wndSplitter.CreateStatic(this, 1, 2))
{
    TRACE0("Failed to create a splitter window in
        CMainFrame::OnCreateClient()\n");
    return FALSE;
}
```

The next most important method is CreateView().

```
virtual BOOL CreateView( int row, int col, CRuntimeClass* pViewClass,
    SIZE sizeInit, CCreateContext* pContext);
```

The row parameter is the splitter window row where the new view will be placed, and col is the column. The pViewClass parameter specifies the CRuntimeClass of the new view, and sizeInit specifies its initial size. The pContext parameter is a pointer to a

creation context used to create the view. This is passed into the parent frame's On-
CreateClient(), so you'll have everything you need to create views for your panes. The
return value is nonzero if the call was successful, or zero if it failed. Here is an example
taken from the sample program:

```
if (!m_wndSplitter.CreateView(0, 0, RUNTIME_CLASS(CLeftPaneView),
    CSize(rect.Width()/3, 0), pContext))
{
    TRACE0("Failed to create left pane view in OnCreateClient\n");
    return FALSE;
}
```

To find the current row count, use GetRowCount().

```
int GetRowCount();
```

For dynamic splitters, this returns the current number of rows in the splitter. For
static types, the return value is the maximum number of rows. A related method, Get-
ColumnCount(), is available for the columns.

```
int GetColumnCount();
```

To retrieve information for a specific row, use GetRowInfo().

```
void GetRowInfo(int row, int& cyCur, int& cyMin);
```

The row parameter specifies the row about which you want to obtain information.
The cyCur parameter receives the current row height in pixels, and cyMin gets the
current minimum row height in pixels. Notice that these two parameters are passed
by reference.

The SetRowInfo()method is used to set these values. It is prototyped as follows:

```
void SetRowInfo(int row, int cyIdeal, int cyMin);
```

The row parameter is the splitter window row. The cyIdeal parameter is the ideal
height of the row in pixels, and cyMin is the minimum height. This value determines
when the row will be too small to be displayed. When the framework displays the
splitter, the panes are laid out in columns and rows according to their ideal dimensions, working from upper-left to lower-right of the splitter's client area.

Similar methods exist for working with the columns. GetColumnInfo() is prototyped
as follows:

```
void GetColumnInfo(int col, int& cxCur, int& cxMin);
```

The col parameter indicates the column that you want to obtain information. The
cxCur and cxMin parameters are the width and minimum width of the column, respectively. To set the column information, use SetColumnInfo().

```
void SetColumnInfo(int col, int cxIdeal, int cxMin);
```

The parameters are the same as for SetRowInfo(), except the first parameter specifies
the column, not the row.

A really useful class method is GetPane().

```
CWnd* GetPane(int row, int col);
```

This returns a pointer to the pane specified by the row and col parameters. This pane is usually a CView object. There is also a method for going the other way, once you have a pointer.

```
BOOL IsChildPane(CWnd* pWnd, int& row, int& col);
```

Use this method to determine if the CWnd object pointed to by the pWnd parameter is a child pane of the splitter window. The row and col parameters are references to integers that will store the row and column numbers, respectively. If pWnd is a child pane, the return value is nonzero. If not a child, the return value is zero.

To retrieve the child window ID for a pane at a given row and column, use the IdFromRowCol()method.

```
int IdFromRowCol(int row, int col);
```

The parameters specify the row and column for the pane. The return value is the child window ID for the pane. This function can be used to create a pane as a nonview and can be called for if the pane exists.

If you adjust a splitter window's row or column size, you need to call the RecalcLayout() method.

```
void RecalcLayout();
```

This is similar to redrawing a menubar after making changes to it. If you adjust the row and column sizes during creation of the splitter, it is not necessary to explicitly call this method.

To determine the shared scrollbar style for a splitter window, use GetScrollStyle().

```
DWORD GetScrollStyle() const;
```

The return value can be one of three values, which are actually window styles:

WS_HSCROLL. The splitter manages shared horizontal scrollbars.

WM_VSCROLL. The splitter manages shared vertical scrollbars.

0. The splitter does not manage any scrollbars.

That does it for the class methods, so let's move on to the sample program that puts these to work.

The Sample Program

Time once again to look at a real-world working example. The sample code can be found on the companion Web site in the Example6 project. This is an SDI application that creates a splitter window consisting of one row and two columns. The left pane contains a TreeView control that allows you to change the window by selecting the different views from this control. One pane contains a ListView control that is initialized with all the files in the current directory along with their creation dates and sizes. The other pane contains an edit control. Although this example doesn't do any real work, it does demonstrate how the splitter window can be used to provide different services to the user. For example, this could be modified so that if a file were selected in the list view, it would be opened in the edit view.

After declaring a member variable for the splitter window, the first step is to override the frame window's OnCreateClient(). Look at this method closely.

```
BOOL CMainFrame::OnCreateClient(LPCREATESTRUCT lpcs,
    CCreateContext* pContext)
{
    // TODO: Add your specialized code here and/or call the base class
    if (!m_wndSplitter.CreateStatic(this, 1, 2))
    {
        TRACE("Failed to create a
            splitter window in OnCreateClient\n");
        return FALSE;
    }
    //
    // Get the client rect & calculate the left pane size
    CRect rect;
    GetClientRect(&rect);
    //
    // create the left tree view first.
    //
    if (!m_wndSplitter.CreateView(0, 0, RUNTIME_CLASS(CLeftPaneView),
        CSize(rect.Width()/3, 0), pContext))
    {
        TRACE("Failed to create left pane view in OnCreateClient\n");
        return FALSE;
    }
    // The right pane is a frame that contains the different views.
    // The view can be set to active or non-active
    //
    if (!m_wndSplitter.CreateView(0, 1, RUNTIME_CLASS(CRightPaneFrame),
        CSize(0, 0), pContext))
    {
        TRACE("Failed to create right pane frame in OnCreateClient\n");
        return FALSE;
    }
    CLeftPaneView* pLeftPaneView = (CLeftPaneView*)
        m_wndSplitter.GetPane(0,0);
    pLeftPaneView->m_pRightPaneFrame = (CRightPaneFrame*)
        m_wndSplitter.GetPane(0,1);
    //
    // Set the left pane as the active view
```

```
    //
    SetActiveView((CView*) m_wndSplitter.GetPane(0, 0));
    return TRUE;
}    // end OnCreateClient()
```

The only complicated point here is that two new classes had to be created (and their header files included in MainFrm.cpp). These are CLeftPaneView and CRightPane-Frame. The first is derived from class CFormView and the second from CFrameWnd. Deriving CLeftPaneView from CFormView is necessary because this view contains an embedded control (the tree control).

Class CLeftPaneView includes a method that handles selections made in the tree control. Some of the tree contains dummy text just to remind you of how it can be used. The only thing that is really checked is if one of the view selection nodes was clicked.

```
void CLeftPaneView::OnSelchangedTree(NMHDR* pNMHDR, LRESULT* pResult)
{
    NM_TREEVIEW* pNMTreeView = (NM_TREEVIEW*)pNMHDR;
    // TODO: Add your control notification handler code here
    HTREEITEM hSelectedItem = m_treeCtrl.GetSelectedItem();
    //
    UINT nViewSel = 0; // item selected from tree
    //
    if (hSelectedItem == m_hSplitterView)
        nViewSel = VIEW_SPLITTER;
    else
        if (hSelectedItem == m_hListCtrlView)
            nViewSel = VIEW_LISTCTRL;
        else
            if (hSelectedItem == m_hEditView)
                nViewSel = VIEW_EDIT;
    //
    if (nViewSel)
        m_pRightPaneFrame->SwitchToView(nViewSel);
    *pResult = 0;
}
```

This code checks if the user is changing the view. If so, that view is activated. When the list view mode is selected, OnInitialUpdate() is called (remember, this is a CFormView object).

```
void CListCtrlView::OnInitialUpdate()
{
    CFormView::OnInitialUpdate();

    // TODO: Add your specialized code here and/or call the base class
    CRect rect;
    m_listCtrl.GetClientRect(&rect);
    //
```

```
    m_listCtrl.InsertColumn(0, "File Name", LVCFMT_LEFT,
        rect.Width()/2);
    m_listCtrl.InsertColumn(1, "Creation Date", LVCFMT_LEFT,
        rect.Width()/3);
    m_listCtrl.InsertColumn(2, "Size (bytes)", LVCFMT_LEFT,
        rect.Width()/3);
    //
    m_listCtrl.SetBkColor(RGB(255,255,0)); // yellow background
    m_listCtrl.SetTextBkColor(RGB(255,255,0));
    GetFiles();  // get all files in directory, put in listctrl
}   // end OnInitialUpdate()
```

The following method is responsible for setting up the columns of the ListView control. As an extra bonus, the background color is changed to yellow to demonstrate some of the things you can do. The last call in this method is to a function that gets all the files and associated data into the list control.

```
void CListCtrlView::GetFiles()
{
    CFileFind cFind;  // for finding files
    char *p;          // generic pointer to convert CStrings
    CString csTmp;
    int index = 0;    // index into list view
    int iMon,iDay,iYear;  // file creation info
    CTime timeFile; // for getting file creation date
    CString csMon[12] = {"Jan","Feb","Mar","Apr","May","Jun","Jul",
        "Aug","Sep","Oct","Nov","Dec" };
    cFind.FindFile(NULL,0); // same as "*.*"
    //
    LV_ITEM lvi;  // list view structure
    DWORD dwLen; // file length
    //
    while(1)
    {
        if(cFind.FindNextFile() == 0)
            break; // done! no more files..
        csTmp = cFind.GetFileName();
        if(csTmp == "." || csTmp == "..")
            continue;  // skip the "." and ".." entries for SFDs
        p = csTmp.GetBuffer(_MAX_PATH);
        csTmp.ReleaseBuffer();
        //
        lvi.mask = LVIF_TEXT;
        lvi.iSubItem = 0;  // first column
        lvi.iItem = index;
        lvi.pszText = p;  // name of file
        m_listCtrl.InsertItem(&lvi);  // insert into
                                      // col. 0, row = index
        //
```

```
        cFind.GetCreationTime(timeFile);  // get file creation time
        iMon = timeFile.GetMonth();
        iDay = timeFile.GetDay();
        iYear= timeFile.GetYear();
        //
        csTmp.Format("%s-%d-%d",csMon[iMon-1],iDay,iYear);
        p = csTmp.GetBuffer(_MAX_PATH);
        csTmp.ReleaseBuffer();
        //
        lvi.mask = LVIF_TEXT;
        lvi.iSubItem = 1;// second column
        lvi.iItem = index;
        lvi.pszText = p;
        m_listCtrl.SetItem(&lvi); // insert file creation date
        //
        //  now get file size
        //
        dwLen = cFind.GetLength();
        csTmp.Format("%d",dwLen);
        p = csTmp.GetBuffer(_MAX_PATH);
        csTmp.ReleaseBuffer();
        //
        lvi.mask = LVIF_TEXT;
        lvi.iSubItem = 2;   // column 3
        lvi.iItem = index;
        lvi.pszText = p;
        m_listCtrl.SetItem(&lvi); // insert size
        ++index;  // increment for next row in list ctrl
    } // end while loop thru all files in this SFD
}        // end GetFiles()
```

There are a few more functions in ListCtrlView.cpp but you've seen the bulk of this application's processing. Note that the function GetFiles()can be shortened up a bit. It isn't necessary to repeatedly adjust the following members of the list view structure.

```
lvi.mask = LVIF_TEXT;
lvi.iItem = index;
lvi.pszText = p;
```

These three members really only need to be called once at the start of the while() loop because only text is being placed in the ListView control. If you were to add icons using an image list, then the mask member would have to be changed and more code added. But you get the idea.

There are lots of additional class members, so take a look at the documentation.

Summary

The splitter window can be a mighty arrow in your quiver when it comes to delivering the right interface. They can seem a little intimidating at first, but after you've tinkered with them a while, the light comes on. The main challenge, as you've seen, comes in managing your views.

We're almost done—the next chapter takes a look at how online help can make your interface sparkle like a new penny. There's tool tips, help authoring guidelines, and a lot more, so stick around for the closing bell.

CHAPTER 22

Adding Help to the Interface

There's an old saying, "Save the best for last." The last topic is the role of help in application development, especially as it relates to the user interface. Be forewarned—I have a strong bias for the liberal use of online help, and with good reason. I've been developing (and using) software long enough to know that users never read the documentation. They like to hit the ground running. Furthermore, users have come to expect the application to provide them with meaningful help when they get stuck, and to guide them through any unfamiliar terrain or tasks.

NOTE At the time this book was written, Microsoft had recently announced a new help standard based on HTML (HyperText Markup Language) files. Previous versions of help were based on RTF (Rich Text Format) files. Microsoft has also announced that it plans to continue to support the RTF flavor of help. This chapter contains examples of both varieties. The underlying concept of incorporating help into your application is the same—the only difference is in how you create, and call, your Help file.

Role of Help

The role of help in application development and delivery is to help the user use your application. Sounds simple, but there's a lot of things to consider. Help comes in layers such as tool tips and status bar help messages. This type of help is preemptive and passive in nature; the user didn't ask for help, the application volunteered it. You should build as much of this into your application as you can. One immediate benefit of this type of help is that it keeps the user from accessing your Help file. Stop and think for a moment—if users don't know what a particular toolbar icon means because you didn't provide tool tips, how can they query your Help file to find the answer? But by providing this first layer of help, you give them a hint. Even if they don't understand the consequences of clicking the toolbar icon, they can now query the Help file to learn more.

The next layer of help is more kinetic—the user must initiate the request. An example of this is the context-sensitive help available for controls. When the control has the focus, pressing F1 pops up a help balloon similar to a tool tip that explains the purpose of the control. The question mark icon identifies context-sensitive dialog boxes on the system menubar; click this and the cursor changes to an arrow superimposed over a question mark. The user can then click a control to get more information. These visual cues are shown in Figure 22.1.

The next layers of help are more protracted. These include online tutorials, procedural-based operations, and examples. Here again, the role of the Help file is to guide users through your application so that they can successfully complete their tasks.

All three layers start with the Help file. Let's take a look at the help compiler that ships with Visual C++ and other MFC-based tools.

The Help Compiler

The help compiler, HCW.EXE, builds a Help file, using a project file that acts much like the conductor of a symphony. Your Help file contains information, organized into logical sections, that you wish to present to the user. Just as an orchestra is broken down into musical sections (for example, the reeds, brass, wind, percussion), so your Help file is broken down into topics, each of which is uniquely identified by a string name.

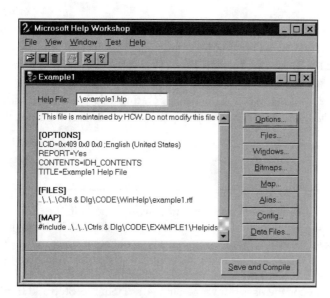

Figure 22.1 Context-sensitive cues.

These unique identifiers make it possible to jump directly to another topic; you only need to know its identifier. Strings make it possible to associate certain topics with specific points within your Windows program. For example, if an application has a dialog box with a command button labeled Help, a click of the button will open a help window containing information relevant to the context of the program (that is, the purpose of the dialog box). Thus, you can take the user directly to a specific topic, or to a table of contents. Topics, as you will see, are the atoms in the Winhelp molecule, and should be considered as the basic building blocks for your application's Help file. Topics live in one or more topic files, identified by their .RTF extension.

Topic Files

Topic files are nothing more than text files with embedded RTF formatting strings and tokens that are recognizable by the compiler. At a minimum, topic file consists of the following sections:

- RTF header (and footer)
- A font table
- A color table
- Topics

For the record, you can create RTF files using any text editor, such as Notepad. Although there are third-party tools available, you may find it easier to simply cut and paste between RTF files.

The header of every RTF file is as follows:

```
{\rtf1\ansi \deff4\deflang1033
```

The footer is simply the closing curly brace for this statement—everything else goes between these curly braces. Next up is the font table, defined as in the following example:

```
{\fonttbl
    {\f0\froman Times New Roman;}
    {\f1\ftech  Martlett;}
    {\f2\froman MS Serif;}
    {\f3\fswiss Arial;}
    {\f4\fswiss MS Sans Serif;}
    {\f5\fscript Script;}
    {\f6\fmodern Courier;}
}
```

Each of these components is nested inside the RTF header-footer curly braces. The same is true for the color table.

```
{\colortbl;
\red0\green0\blue0;
\red0\green0\blue255;
\red0\green255\blue255;
\red0\green255\blue0;
\red255\green0\blue255;
```

```
\red255\green0\blue0;
\red255\green255\blue0;
}
```

Whatever colors you need can be added to the color table. Notice that the color table is formatted much like a COLORREF object; each value of red, green, and blue can have a value in the range of 0–255. The font table is indexed starting at zero, but the color table starts at one. With these, you can now have the pieces needed to build a topic.

Topics

A topic consists of several distinct and equally important components. These can generally be recognized by the \footnote compiler token. The basic components are

- A unique topic identifier (usually has a prefix of IDH_)
- A search string
- A title
- The text of the topic

The following is an example of a topic with these elements; comments are in bold.

```
#{\footnote IDH_MYNEWPROJ_HELP}        <- the topic identifier
K{\footnote Projects, creating new}    <- the search string
${\footnote New Projects}              <- the title
{\f3\fs18 This is the text for the topic.} <- the topic text
\par                                   <- cr/lf
{\page}                                <- end of topic token
```

Every topic you create will consist of these elements. Look at the fourth line: The \f3 and \fs18 tokens specify the font and font size, respectively. You can also change the color by adding the \cf token. For example, using the color table shown earlier as an example, the following statement would display the topic using the color red.

```
{\cf6\f3\fs18 This is the text for the topic.}
```

In this example, the \cf6 token selects the sixth color from the color table, or red.

There are manyadditional tokens you can use to format your topics, such as tokens for specifying bold, italic, and underline. A complete discussion is beyond the scope of this chapter, but you'll find examples sprinkled throughout the sample program on the companion Web site in the WinHelp directory.

At this point, we have enough pieces to construct a Help file, so let's look at the next step: using the Help Compiler Workbench.

The Help Compiler Workbench

The help compiler is the application HCW.EXE that can be found in your vc\bin directory if you're running Visual C++. This tool is abbreviated to the workbench, and contains just about everything you'll need to turn out a complete Help file. Figure 22.2 shows the workbench with a project open.

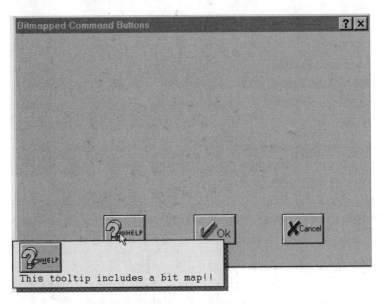

Figure 22.2   The help compiler workbench.

The workbench is user-friendly, and behaves much the way you'd expect it to; projects are created, saved, built, and so on. It follows the Visual C++ model. Before you begin, create the RTF topic file for your project using your favorite editor. Next, create a new project and include this as your topic file. Then customize other elements like the Help window's size and background color.

The single most important thing to do is create a header file that contains all your topic IDs. Give your IDs the default prefix IDH_, which prevents you from having to use aliases. An example of an entry in this header file is

```
#define IDH_CONTENTS    100
```

This technique allows all the topic identifiers to be shared between the help workbench and your native application. Not only does this reduce errors, but it makes it easier to manage your project. This header file (I usually call mine HelpIDs.h) is then added to your Windows project and to the workbench. In the later case, click the button labeled Map and browse for the header file.

Once you have a compiled Help file, you can use it to enhance your user interface in a lot of different ways. The trick to this is knowing how to use the WinHelp() API.

The WinHelp API

The workhorse for calling WINHELP.EXE is an API function called WinHelp() that is prototyped as follows:

```
BOOL WinHelp(HWND hWnd, LPCTSTR lpszHelp, UINT uCommand,DWORD dwData);
```

This function returns nonzero on success, and zero if an error occurs. The parameters are

- Handle of window issuing request
- Help filename and path
- A command used with the last parameter to specify the manner in which the Help file is opened
- 32 bits of user-defined data

Because these are so closely related, and their impact pretty powerful, here is a rundown on the possible values you can assign to the parameter typeCmd, and how each affects the dwData parameter:

HELP_CONTEXT. Assign dwData an unsigned long integer representing the context number assigned for the topic. These context numbers are assigned in the [MAP] section of your application's project file. This lets you jump directly to a specific topic. Generally, this is the flavor of the command you'll use to take the user directly to a specific command. For example, if the user clicks a command button for Help in a dialog box, you would use WinHelp() to take him or her straight to a topic that discussed the dialog box that generated the click. Here is an example:

```
WinHelp(hWnd,"DOW30.HLP",HELP_CONTEXT,DOWJONES);
```

Here, the Help file DOW30.HLP is opened to a topic identified with the unique identifier DOWJONES that has been defined in the project file as a numerical value. This process is identical to defining constants in C or C++, as in this example:

```
#define DOWJONES    0XFF
```

There is nothing to prevent you from using the numerical value directly in the API call itself. A string value (DOWJONES) is more descriptive and helpful than a numerical value (0XFF) during development and testing.

HELP_CONTENTS. Using this as the parameter for causes your Help file to open to a predefined Table of Contents. Thus, has no relevancy; it should be set to 0L. For example:

```
WinHelp(hWnd,"PAYROLL.HLP",HELP_CONTENTS,0L);
```

HELP_SETCONTENTS. This is related to HELP_CONTENTS. It lets you specify (or switch) the identifier of the Table of Contents topic. As such, dwData is the context number that is being reassigned to the topic. In other words, even your Table of Contents needs to be identified. Also, this describes which topic is displayed if the user presses the F1 key.

```
WinHelp(hWnd,"STOCKS.HLP",HELP_SETCONTENTS,AMEX);
```

Here, the Help file STOCKS.HLP is assigned the topic AMEX as its Table of Contents, or master index.

HELP_CONTEXTPOPUP. Use this value for typeCmd to force a topic to be displayed in a popup window. The topic is identified by its context number in the .HPJ file, and should be used as the value for the parameter dwData. But be careful—the topic that is displayed in the popup must not have any links to other topics; that is, no hotspots. Try building a sample program that does this and see what happens when you click the hotspot inside the popup.

HELP_KEY. This is a way to open the Help file with the Search dialog box active. When dwData contains a topic's keyword, that topic gets displayed if there is one, and only one, unique keyword found in the keyword list. If there are multiple matches, the Search dialog box is opened automatically. All matching topics are listed in the Go To list box.

HELP_PARTIALKEY. This will display a topic from the keyword list that matches a keyword supplied in the dwData parameter if there is an exact match. If there are no matches found, the Search dialog box is activated. In the case of multiple matches found, the Search dialog box is again activated, but all the matching topics are listed in the Go To list box. Again, you can use this to open your Help file with the Search dialog box active simply by using HELP_PARTIALKEY and defining dwData as a long pointer to an empty string.

HELP_MULTIKEY. Declare dwData as a long pointer to the MULTIKEYHELP structure to display a topic using a keyword from an alternate keyword table.

HELP_COMMAND. Use this to execute a Help macro by declaring dwDataas a long pointer to a string that contains the macro. In order for this command to work, Help must already be running with an open Help file. Look at the following example:

```
case HELP_MENU_OPT1:    // Assume user clicked a menu option...
                        // start Help, then jump to a topic
    WinHelp(hWnd,"HELPDEMO.HLP", HELP_CONTENTS,0L);  // run WinHelp
    retval= WinHelp(hWnd,"HELPDEMO.HLP", HELP_COMMAND,
        (LPSTR)"JumpID(\"helpdemo.hlp\",\"contxstr_1\")");
    if(retval == 0)     // *** error trap ***
        MessageBox(hWnd,"Failed to jump to
            topic having id = ontxstr_1",
            "Error",MB_OK);  //error message
    break;                   // end case statement inside switch()
```

Note the use of the backslash delimiter before the double quotes in the macro JumpID().

HELP_SETWINPOS. This typeCmd lets you specify the size and position of your Help window, both a primary and secondary window. Making dwData a long pointer to the HELPWININFO does this. Because this is a pretty important structure, lets take a quick look at its members.

```
typedef struct
{
    int  wStructSize;
    int  x;
    int  y;
    int  dx;
    int  dy;
    int  wMax;
    char rgchMember[2];
} HELPWININFO;
```

The wStructSize member is the size of the HELPWININFO structure. The x and y members are the coordinates of the upper-left corner of the window. The dx and dy members are the width and height of the window, respectively. The wMax member indicates if the window should be maximized or set to the given position and size. If this is 1, the window is maximized. If 0, the size and position are set according to the values of the x, y, dx, and dy members. The rgchMember is the name of the window.

When using HELPWININFO, don't forget that the window's size and position members are in Help units, which divides the screen into 1024×1024 units, regardless of the video resolution of the host platform. This is illustrated in the following sample code that causes the Help file MY_HELP.HLP to be displayed in a window that uses the entire left side of the video screen.

```
HANDLE hHelpWin;                // handle to Help window
LPHELPWININFO lpHelpInfo;   // pointer to HELPWININFO structure
WORD wSize;                     // size of structure
hHelpWin = GlobalAlloc(GHND, wSize); // get size
lpHelpInfo = (LPHELPWININFO)GlobalLock(hHelpWin);  // get structure
lpHelpInfo->wStructSize = wSize;      // give members new values..
lpHelpInfo->x = 0;                       // upper left corner horz.
                                           valuelpHelpInfo->y = 0;
                                         // upper left corner vert. value
lpHelpInfo->dx= 512;  // width, 1/2 screen
lpHelpInfo->dy= 1024; // height, use full leng
lpHelpInfo->wMax        = 0;             // use size & pos. values just set
WinHelp(hWnd, "my_help.hlp",HELP_SETWINPOS,lpHelpInfo); // DO IT!!
GlobalUnlock(hHelpWin);              // release memory & free it..
GlobalFree(hHelpWin);
```

HELP_FORCEFILE. This is a good safety valve, in that it is used to force any given .HLP file to be the one accessed and treated as the master file. If the correct Help file is currently being used, this WinHelp() call has no effect. But if it is not, the correct file is opened, and the topic designated as the CONTENTS in the project file is shown to the user. If no CONTENTS were defined, the first topic encountered is shown. The dwData parameter should be set to 0L when using HELP_FORCEFILE. For example,

```
WinHelp(hWnd, "my_help.hlp",HELP_FORCEFILE,0L);
```

HELP_HELPONHELP. One of the things you can do in your host software application is add a menu option under your Help entry with the title How to Use Help. When the user exercises this option, a special Help file is opened that acts like a tutorial, teaching new users how to use Help itself. Because you may want to customize this and add some flavor from your host application, use this WinHelp() call to open your own help on Help file. When using this, the dwData parameter should be set to 0L, as in this example:

```
WinHelp(hWnd, "new_help.hlp",HELP_HELPONHELP,0L);
```

Here, the file new_help.hlp is used as the Help tutorial, opened to the Contents topic (or first topic encountered).

HELP_QUIT. This call is used to notify WINHELP.EXE that the host application no longer needs the Help file. Windows will then terminate WINHELP.EXE, unless other programs are currently using Help. You should use HELP_QUIT when your user exits your Help file; this will also increase Windows' performance since it reduces the CPU overhead. Set the dwData parameter to 0L, as in this example:

```
case USER_QUIT:   // user has clicked Exit, closed window, etc.
    WinHelp(hWnd,"my_help.hlp",HELP_QUIT,0L); // close winhelp.exe
    break;         // continue with program...
```

That about does it for the WinHelp() API. Again, the best advice I can give you is to just start experimenting. Try building some simple Help files using the code from the companion Web site as a starting point, and call WinHelp() using some of these configurations. Now let's look at more easy ways to enhance your interface with help—adding tool tips and context-sensitive help.

Tool Tips

Tool tips are one of the easiest and most important ways you can build a better user interface. These are great for helping the user to learn the meaning of controls and toolbar buttons. Very little programming is required to add this feature.

Tool tips work by making use of extended notification messages. To add tool tips, you'll need to patch the message map so that the notification message TTN_NEEDTEXT is trapped, and write a message handler that does something with it. The underlying framework does the rest of the work. The sample code in the section can be found on the companion Web site in the Example1 project, in the files ButtDemo.cpp and ButtDemo.h. The following code shows the message map before and after adding the handler for the notification message.

```
BEGIN_MESSAGE_MAP(CButtDemo, CDialog)
    //{{AFX_MSG_MAP(CButtDemo)
    ON_BN_CLICKED(IDC_HELPBUTTON, OnHelpbutton)
    //}}AFX_MSG_MAP
END_MESSAGE_MAP()
```

Here is where and how you change the message map:

```
BEGIN_MESSAGE_MAP(CButtDemo, CDialog)
    //{{AFX_MSG_MAP(CButtDemo)
    ON_BN_CLICKED(IDC_HELPBUTTON, OnHelpbutton)
    //}}AFX_MSG_MAP
    ON_NOTIFY_EX(TTN_NEEDTEXT,0,DlgToolTips)
END_MESSAGE_MAP()
```

This traps the TTN_NEEDTEXT notification message and routes it to a message handler called DlgToolTips(). This needs to be declared in your header file, too.

```
// Implementation
private:
```

```
    BOOL CButtDemo::DlgToolTips(UINT id,NMHDR *pNMHDR,
        LRESULT *pResult );
```

Now for the handler itself.

```
BOOL CButtDemo::DlgToolTips(UINT id,

    NMHDR * pNMHDR, LRESULT * pResult )
{
    TOOLTIPTEXT *pTTT = (TOOLTIPTEXT *)pNMHDR;
    UINT nID = pTTT->uFlags;
    if(pTTT->uFlags & TTF_IDISHWND)
    {
        nID= ::GetDlgCtrlID((HWND)nID);
        if(!nID)
        {
            HWND hWndHelp = m_Help.GetSafeHwnd();
            HWND hWndOk = m_Ok.GetSafeHwnd();
            HWND hWndCancel = m_Cancel.GetSafeHwnd();
            //
            if((HWND)(pNMHDR->idFrom) == hWndHelp)
            {
                AfxGetApp()->WinHelp(IDH_HELP_POPUP,HELP_CONTEXTPOPUP);
                return TRUE;
            }
            //
            if((HWND)(pNMHDR->idFrom) == hWndOk)
            {
                pTTT->lpszText = "Close dialog, save changes";
                return TRUE;
            }
            //
            if((HWND)(pNMHDR->idFrom) == hWndCancel)
            {
                pTTT->lpszText = "Close dialog, ignore changes";
                return TRUE;
            }
        }
    }
    return FALSE;
}    // end DlgToolTips()
```

Stop and examine this method in closer detail. There is something special going on with the tool tip for the Help button. Instead of displaying text like the other buttons, this also displays a bitmap in the tool tip! This is handled by the line

```
AfxGetApp()->WinHelp(IDH_HELP_POPUP,HELP_CONTEXTPOPUP);
```

The topic in the Help file identified as IDH_HELP_POPUP is opened as a popup window instead of the main Help window—refer back to the WinHelp() API for more information.

HTML Help

Microsoft recently announced it is abandoning RTF-based Help files for an HTML-based version. Don't panic—Microsoft is giving away a development kit, and you can even convert your existing .HLP files to the new format. Furthermore, the RTF format will still be supported. While there is always a certain amount of anxiety that accompanies any shift in the development landscape, the move to HTML-based Help files should be fairly easy for most of us. In fact, Microsoft has quietly integrated this move for the past several years, gently moving away from InfoView and the WinHelp format. The online documentation that comes with Visual C++ (and other tools) is in fact, HTML Help. While increasing market share for its Internet products is certainly a factor, there are other compelling factors influencing the trend towards HTML help. Among these are internationalization, navigational issues, and cost reduction.

Upside-Downside

The new HTML Help system is like a stock split—you get two for one. The Help files you build using the HTML development kit can be mounted on disk, the Internet, or an intranet! Think about that for a moment—you write it once, and you can use it in a variety of places and ways. Also, the HTML Help files can support ActiveX controls, Java applets, animation, and sound. It's just too cool—and I haven't even gotten to the really exciting stuff yet (like information types—a way to tag Help topics so they can be identified as belonging to specific categories, such as context-based help, procedure-based, and so on.). The only drawbacks that I can see, and they are minor, are

- The Help author must know HTML.
- You'll have many, many .htm files instead of one (or several) .rtf files.
- Popup windows are there, but they're somewhat awkward.

Another minor annoyance is the workshop's editor, a very basic editor like Notepad. Rumor has it that a new WYSIWYG editor will be included in an upcoming new release. The fact that the Help author must know HTML shouldn't be a very big hurdle—I suspect most developers already know the basics. If you don't, don't worry. It is incredibly simple. If you have one of the later versions of Microsoft Word, you can use it to create your files and save them in HTML format. This pretty much obviates the need to even know HTML.

The last thing you need to know before jumping in is that HTML help files require Microsoft's Internet Explorer for both Web and disk-mounted applications. However, for disk-mounted systems, the toolkit includes some DLLs that allow the user to run it without having IE installed.

The Toolkit

As mentioned previously, Microsoft is giving away a development toolkit for creating HTML Help files. You can download it at

http://www.microsoft.com/workshop/author/htmlhelp/

Figure 22.3 shows the toolkit with a project open. A project has the extension .hhp and consists of the following items:

- A contents file, extension .hhc
- Topic files, extension .htm or .html
- An index file, extension .hhk

Note the tab labeled Help in the left-hand pane. The toolkit comes with a very useful Help file itself—even a quick reference for HTML tags. It also has some insightful information on planning and designing your Help system. The tool is pretty easy to use. I was able to build a little demo program right out of the box without even reading the documentation. It's a lot like the Visual C++ model—you create a project, add files, compile, and run. Now let's look at an example.

A Sample Project

Let's walk you through the steps for building an HTML Help file. This file can be found on the companion Web site in the HtmlHelp project. Although this file (called demo.chm) sticks to the basics, it has enough to get you going. This file is shown in Figure 22.4.

To begin, create a folder called Demo somewhere to contain your project. Then, start the HTML Help toolkit, and click on the New icon or menu option. You'll get a popup window that asks you what type of new file you want to create. The choices are

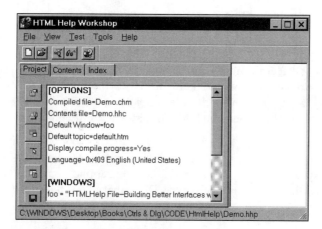

Figure 22.3   The HTMLHelp toolkit.

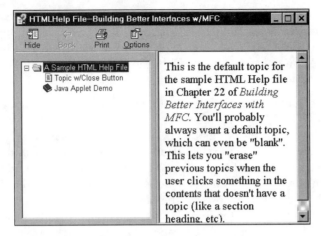

Figure 22.4 The HTMLHelp demo program.

- Project
- Text
- HTML File
- Table of Contents
- Index

Select Project and click OK. This starts up a wizard that walks you through the steps of either converting an existing WinHelp project to HTML, or a new HTML Help file. Leave the checkbox for converting unchecked and click the Next > button. This brings up the Destination window in which you give your project a name and location (it includes a Browse button). Use the Browse button to find the folder you created earlier, type in Demo in the Open box, and click OK. This returns you to the Destination window, so click Next >. The next window you'll see gives you the chance to add any existing components that you might have created to the project (for example, the table of contents, index). Leave all these checkboxes blank, and click Next >, then Finish. You have now successfully created your first HTML Help project.

The first thing you'll want to do is create a table of contents. This will go in the left pane (the navigational pane) of the Help window when it opens. The table of contents is a fancy TreeView control that expands and contracts as you click the little boxes next to the icons. To create the table of contents, click on the Contents tab. A popup dialog asks you if you'd like to create a new table of contents or use an existing one. Click the radio button for Create a new contents file (it should already be on by default), and click OK. This brings up a Save As dialog box. Give your table of contents the name Demo and click Save. The buttons on the left side of the toolkit will change to those shown in Figure 22.3, which let you add the headings and topics, and set the indentation. Insert a heading by clicking on the file folder icon. A dialog box will appear with edit boxes for the various fields. Give your heading a title (the example says "A Sample HTML

Help File") and click OK. Note that you could assign a topic to this (or any) heading by clicking the Add button and specifying an HTML topic file. Now, a default topic file must be created that will be displayed when your Help file is opened, or if the user clicks the top-level heading. Create a new HTML file and call it Default. Edit your heading and browse for this file—click OK.

The next step is to add subordinate headings, or topic pages, under the heading. You can either create a new HTML topic page now or after creating the page. Let's go ahead and get a topic file waiting in the wings by clicking New and then picking a new HTML file. The text editor opens in the right-hand pane of the toolkit with the basic HTML tags already built for you. Add some text and save the file as Topic1.html. Add a topic page by clicking on the page icon. You'll be asked if you want to insert it at the beginning of the table of contents—click No. The dialog box appears again; give it a title and click the Add button. Click the Browse button and select the file Topic1.html that you just created. Click OK to close that box, and click it again to close the topic dialog box. The left-hand pane of the toolkit now shows your top-level topic and one subordinate topic.

If you feel ambitious, you can add more topics or headings by repeating these steps. However, at this point, you have enough to build and view the project. Click the compiler icon on the toolbar (you may be prompted to save your project first—do so if you haven't already). A dialog box appears—make sure the Automatically display compiled Help file when done is *not* checked. If this is checked, the file is opened to your default topic. Instead, compile the file, then click the View compiled file icon (the eyeglasses icon). Another dialog appears—click the button labeled View and the compiled Help file shown in Figure 22.4 will appear. That's all there is to it.

Additional Features

The toolkit has lots of other features that make development easier. Under the File option there is a Preferences… command. This gives you some more flexibility over your Help projects (such as automatically loading the last project opened). You can double-click any of the listings in the Project pane to make changes. For example, you can have the compiler emit progress messages as it builds. I urge you to do this—it makes finding errors a lot easier!

The toolkit also comes with an image editor for adding graphics. As I said before, most of this stuff is pretty easy to work with right out of the box. You can also add the ActiveX control to your project, and chose to view it with a browser. Play around with these features once you've gotten a simple Help file built.

Just as you could launch WinHelp from your Visual C++ application, the new compiled HTML Help file is no exception, although you have to jump through a couple of extra hoops. In RTF-based help systems, you called WinHelp() from your application using something like the following:

```
AfxGetApp()->WinHelp(IDH_SOME_TOPIC,HELP_CONTEXT);
```

This opened your Help file to the topic identified by IDH_SOME_TOPIC. To do the same thing with HTML Help, you have to do the following:

- Link with hhctrl.lib
- Include htmlhelp.h in your project

These files are included with the development toolkit. Move them into your \lib and \include directories for future use. To open the Help file, call the HtmlHelp API, prototyped as follows:

```
HWND HtmlHelp(HWND hwndCaller,LPCSTR pszFile,
    UINT uCommand,DWORD dwData);
```

The hwndCaller parameter is the handle of the window making the call. When the Help window exits, the focus returns to this window unless it's the desktop window. In this case, the focus is set by the operating system. Also, if the Help window returns any messages, they'll go to this window. The pszFile parameter is the name of your compiled Help file. It could also be a URL, or a window definition (which must be preceded by the > character, just like with secondary windows in the old WinHelp system). This parameter can be NULL if the command being used (the uCommand parameter) does not need a file or URL. The uCommand parameter specifies the action to be performed. Valid values are

- HH_DISPLAY_TOPIC
- HH_HELP_CONTEXT
- HH_DISPLAY_TEXT_POPUP
- HH_SET_WIN_TYPE
- HH_GET_WIN_TYPE
- HH_GET_WIN_HANDLE
- HH_TP_HELP_CONTEXTMENU
- HH_TP_HELP_WM_HELP

The first two are used the most when invoking Help from an application. The last parameter, dwData, specifies any additional data needed, and depends on the value of the uCommand.

Let's look at a quick example. Suppose you want to open your HTML Help file to a certain topic when the user starts your application. In your project's InitInstance() method, you would do something like this:

```
HWND hwndCaller= AfxGetApp()->
    m_pMainWnd->GetSafeHwnd();// app. handle
HtmlHelp(hwndCaller,"demo.chm",HH_HELP_CONTEXT,IDH_SOME_TOPIC);
return TRUE;
```

Here, the compiled HTML Help file called demo.chm is opened to the topic identified by the topic ID IDH_SOME_TOPIC. This just opens the file to the topic—you don't see the navigation pane. On the other hand, if you wanted to open both panes, you would do something like this:

```
HWND hwnd= AfxGetApp()->
    m_pMainWnd->GetSafeHwnd();// handle to app window
ShellExecute(hwnd,"open", "demo.chm",NULL,NULL,SW_SHOWNORMAL);
```

The call to ShellExecute() requires that you link with kernel32.lib (don't forget that if you cut and paste this code into your own examples).

Another important point to make concerns the dwData parameter. I strongly suggest that when you first create your Visual C++ application you add a special header file devoted strictly to defining your topic IDs. I usually call mine HelpIDs.h, and include it in the CWinApp header file for the project—that way, it is in scope for all modules. You can then include this header file in your HTML Help project to keep everything in synch. As you add new help buttons or menu options to your VC++ project, you can quickly and easily add them to the HelpIDs.h file. This allows you to build at the very least the skeleton of your Help file topics—you can always go back later and add the actual flesh of the topics.

Adding Context Help

As desktop applications become more powerful, and widespread, so grows their complexity. Let's face it, no one uses the user manual if he or she can help it. Users have come to expect the application to contain enough embedded help that they feel they shouldn't have to look it up. The use of training cards is a classic example—if you get stuck, you simply pause and run a procedural- or contextual-based tutorial. That last phrase was deliberate, as it points out one of the things you can do with the new HTML Help system: group topics into categories of *information types,* and provide links to them. But another, more humble technique involves something that has been around in VC++ for some time: context help.

Context help can be recognized by the arrow cursor with a question mark. Dialog boxes supporting this can be recognized by the ? icon in the upper right-hand corner of the box. If the user doesn't understand the function of some control, all he or she needs to do is click the icon, move the cursor into the control of question, and left-click the mouse. For controls that can have the input focus without generating a command message (like edit boxes), simply pressing the F1 key has the same effect. A popup window appears containing help text that you embed in your application. Adding context help using the HTML popup window is incredibly easy, and you can even customize (standardize) its properties. The basic steps are as follows:

1. Enable context help for the dialog box in App Studio.
2. Assign help text to the controls in your string table.
3. Trap the WM_HELP message in the dialog box class.
4. If the handler gets called, make a call to the HtmlHelp() API.

You won't find HtmlHelp() in Class Wizard—it's called WM_HELPINFO instead. The message handler for this is where the rubber meets the road, but as you'll see, it isn't rocket science. You'll find the first item in the Extended Styles tab of the dialog box property page; it's a checkbox labeled Context help. Item 2, adding strings, can be done from App Studio by clicking New String under Insert on the menubar. A popup appears, and you can select the resource ID from the combo box and enter your help text in the Caption section. All that's left to do is add a message handler to respond to the user's request for context help. For this, select the WM_HELPINFO message for the dialog box in Class Wizard, and add code. The following is the message handler from the sample program on the companion Web site.

```
BOOL CDemoDlg::OnHelpInfo(HELPINFO* pHelpInfo)
{
    CPoint pt;
    GetCursorPos(&pt);
    // trap cursor position, show help if necessary
    //
    //    This method does all the work
    //
    ShowContextHelp (CWnd::FromHandle(
        (HWND)pHelpInfo->hItemHandle),pt);
    return(TRUE);              // tell app we processed the msg.
}
```

As noted in the comments, the method ShowContextHelp() is where all the heavy lifting is done. This method takes two parameters: a pointer to the window, and the CPoint object where the help request occurred. It's a pretty short method.

```
void CDemoDlg::ShowContextHelp(CWnd *pWnd, CPoint point)
{
    // Try to load a string corresponding to the control ID
    CString strTextPopup;
    int iCtrlID= -1;
    iCtrlID = pWnd->GetDlgCtrlID();
    // ID of control init. help request
    if (strTextPopup.LoadString(iCtrlID))
    // load help text from table
    {
        HH_POPUP hPop;     // HTML Help popup structure
        memset(&hPop,0,sizeof(hPop));
        // init. help struct to NULLs
        hPop.cbStruct = sizeof(hPop);     // set size of structure
        hPop.clrBackground = RGB(255,255,208);
        // yellow bkg. color
        hPop.clrForeground = -1;
    // default font color
        hPop.rcMargins.left = -1;
        // use default margins
        hPop.rcMargins.top = -1;
```

```
        hPop.rcMargins.bottom = -1;
        hPop.rcMargins.right = -1;
        hPop.pt = point;
        hPop.pszText = strTextPopup;        // msg. from string table
        hPop.pszFont = NULL;                // use default font
        HtmlHelp(NULL,NULL,HH_DISPLAY_TEXT_POPUP,(DWORD)&hPop);
    } // end if found a help string for this request
}       // end ShowContextHelp()
```

The HH_POPUP structure is used to display the context help in a popup window. The structure has members for setting the foreground/background colors, for adjusting where the popup will be displayed, and for selecting the font to use. The actual text displayed can reside in a resource file (as in the sample program), or in a text string. The HTMLHelp toolkit documentation says you can also put it in a text file, but this is not true for version 1.

Summary

The Help file is often the forgotten stepchild of application development, but it can serve you very well when properly designed and implemented. Furthermore, it can act as a living document during the design cycle, serving as a repository for design features, properties, and goals. Regardless, you should plan to include tool tips and context-sensitive help for all your toolbars and dialog box controls. This will greatly enhance the user's experience of using your application by reducing the learning curve and getting up to speed in terms of navigating through your application.

What's on the Web Site

The Web site contains all the sample code from the book, plus links to the free toolkits needed to build the projects. They are packaged as zip files, so you will need WinZip to download and open them. The contents are as follows:

- **Example1** This is the largest and most detailed project. It contains examples of most of the controls: Buttons, Edit Boxes, Combo Boxes, and so on. It also includes the "Tip of the Day" feature, and the CFont and Find-Replace common dialog boxes.

- **Example2** This project covers the File Open/Save and Common Color dialog boxes. Also included is a multimedia Help file.

- **Example3** This project demonstrates multimedia features, the new extended common controls (for example, the Date-Time Picker), and the Spin Control.

- **Example4** This is a "blank" project provided for your convenience—use it to experiment with features from the other projects.

- **Example5** This project demonstrates how to add a dialog bar (for example, CDialogBar object) to your application.

- **Example6** This project demonstrates the splitter window from Chapter 21.

- **Example7** This project illustrates how to add the Internet browser control to your applications.

- **WinHelp** This project contains the code that demonstrates the RTF-based Help file features.

- **HtmlHelp** This project contains the code that demonstrates the HTML-based Help file features.

What is Freeware/Shareware?

The Web site contains links to two freeware products, HTML Help toolkit and the VidEdit utility, both available from Microsoft. Both are required if you wish to build your own HTML-based Help files or multimedia animation clips (AVI files).

Installing the Software

To download and build Example1–Example7, follow these steps:

1. Create a project directory on your hard drive (that is, Example1).
2. Create a \res directory inside inside the project directory.
3. Download the project into the project directory.
4. Unzip the file.
5. Copy the res.zip file into the \res directory, and unzip it.
6. Start Visual C++ and open the project workspace.
7. Build and run the project.

To install the WinHelp project, follow these steps:

1. Create a project directory on your hard drive.
2. Download the WinHelp project into the project directory.
3. Unzip the file.
4. Start the WinHelp compiler located in the \vc\bin directory of your Visual C++ installation.
5. Build the project (that is, Example1.hpj).

To install the HTML Help project, follow these steps:

1. Download and install the HTML Help toolkit from the Web site.
2. Create a project directory.
3. Download and install the HTML Help project from the Web site into this directory.
4. Start the HTML Help toolkit, then open and build the sample project (for example, Demo.hhp).

User Assistance and Information

The software accompanying this book is provided without a warranty or support of any kind. If you require basic installation assistance, or if your media is defective, please call our product support number at (212) 850-6194 weekdays between 9 A.M. and 4 P.M. Eastern Standard Time. You can also reach us via email at:*wprtusw@wiley.com*.

To place additional orders or to request information about other Wiley products, please call (800) 879-4539.